From Reconstruction to Integration:
Britain and Europe since 1945

From Reconstruction to Integration: Britain and Europe since 1945

Edited by

Brian Brivati and Harriet Jones

Leicester University Press
Leicester, London and New York

Distributed exclusively in the USA and Canada by St. Martin's Press

Leicester University Press
(a division of Pinter Publishers Ltd)
25 Floral Street, Covent Garden, London, WC2E 9DS

First published in Great Britain 1993

© Editors and contributors 1993 except Chapter 16 © Lord Donoughue of Ashton 1993

British Library Cataloguing in Publication Data

A CIP catalogue record for this book is available from the British Library

ISBN 0 7185 1482 3

Library of Congress Cataloging-in-Publication Data

From reconstruction to integration: Britain and Europe since 1945 /
    edited by Brian Brivati and Harriet Jones.
        p.   cm.
    Selected papers from the final three days of the Institute of
Contemporary British History Summer School, 1992, organized jointly
by the ICBH and the Departments of Government and International
History of the London School of Economics.
    Includes bibliographical references and index.
    ISBN 0-7185-1482-3
    1. Europe–Relations–Great Britain–Congresses. 2. Great
Britain–Relations–Europe–Congresses. 3. European Economic
Community–Congresses. I. Brivati, Brian. II. Jones, Harriet.
D1065.G7F76 1993
303.48'24104–dc20   93-1074
                                                           CIP

Typeset by Florencetype Ltd, Kewstoke, Avon
Printed and bound in Great Britain by Biddles Ltd of Guildford and King's Lynn

Contents

List of Contributors

Dr Brian Brivati is Deputy Director of the Institute of Contemporay British History, and teaches in the History departments of Birkbeck College and the University of Westminster. His publications include *What Difference did the War Make?* (Leicester University Press 1993) edited with Harriet Jones. He is currently writing a bibliography of Hugh Gaitskell.

Dr Lawrence J. Butler lectures in the Department of History, Queen and Mary and Westfield College, the Department of History at the University of Westminster and is a fellow of the Institute of Contemporary British History. His publications include 'The Ambiguities of British colonial development 1938 to 1948' in Gorst, Johnman and Lucas (eds), *Contemporary British History 1931–1961* (Pinter Publishers 1991) and *British History 1900–1964: A Documentary Reader*, (forthcoming).

Dr Miriam Camps served during and after the war in the US State Department before moving to a distinguished career in journalism and academics. She was the author of the first major study of Britain and the EC: *Britain and the European Community 1955 to 1963* (1964). Her other publications include, *The Free Trade Area Negotiations* (1959).

Dr Anne Deighton is a fellow of St Anthony's College Oxford. Her publications include, (ed), *Britain and the Cold War* (1989), and *The Impossible Peace: Britain, the Division of Germany and the Cold War* (1991).

Dr Stefano Dejak lectures in politics at the State University of Milan. He writes regularly for Italian journals on British history and politics.

Bernard Donoughue was created a life peer as Lord Donoughue of Aston in 1985. He was Senior Policy Adviser to the Prime Minister 1974 to 1979. His publications include *Wage policies in the Public Sector* (1962), *The People into Parliament* (1966), with George Jones, *Herbert Morrison: Portrait of a Politician* (1973) and *Prime Minister* (1987).

Dr Stephen George lectures in the Department of Politics, University of Sheffield. His extensive publications on Britain and the Community include, *An*

Awkward Partner: Britain in the European Community (1990) and *Britain and European Integration since 1945* (1992).

Dr Sean Greenwood lectures in the Department of History, Canterbury Christ Church College. His recent publications include 'Bevin, the Ruhr and the Division of Germany, August 1945 to December 1946', *Historical Journal*, Volume 26, 1986, and 'Ernest Bevin, France and "Western Union", August 1945 to February 1946', *European History Quarterly*, Volume 14, 1984.

Ros Herman lectures in the Communication of Science in the Department of Science and Technology Studies at Imperial College London. Her publications include *The European Scientific Community* (1986).

Reginald Hibbert was knighted in 1982. He is a retired member of HM Diplomatic Service. He entered the Foreign Service in 1946 and served in Bucharest, Vienna, Guatemala, Ankara, Brussels, Singapore and Bonn. He was Ambassador to France between 1979 and 1982. He wrote *Albania's National Liberation Struggle: The Bitter Victory* (Pinter Publishers 1991).

Douglas Jay was created a life peer in 1987 as Lord Jay of Battersea in Greater London. He was Labour MP for Battersea constituencies from 1945 until 1983. He chaired the Common Market's Safe Guards Committee between 1970 and 1977. His publications include, *After the Common Market* (1968), *Sterling a Plea for Moderation* (1985) and *Change and Fortune* (Memoirs, 1980).

Wolfram Kaiser is a Research Student at the Europa Institute of the University of Edinburgh.

Professor Brigid Laffan is Jean Monnet Professor in the Department of Politics, University College Dublin. Her publications include, *Integration and Cooperation in Europe* (1992).

Dr Klaus Larres, Department of History, University of Ulster at Belfast. He completed his PhD thesis at the University of Cologne on 'Grossbritannien und die Gipfeldiplomatie, Churchill, Eisenhower, der Kalte Krieg und die Westintergration der Bundesrepublik 1945–1955', in 1992.

Dr Richard Mayne was a professional associate, friend and translator for the memoirs of Jean Monnet, he is a writer and broadcaster. His publications include, *The Community of Europe* (1962), *The Recovery of Europe* (1973), *Postwar: the dawn of today's Europe* (1983) and *Federal Union: the Pioneers* (1990).

Dr Eva A. Mayring is a Fellow of the German Historical Institute in London.

Professor Kenneth Owen Morgan is Principal of University College of Wales at Aberystwyth and Pro-Vice Chancellor and Professor in the University of Wales. Among his many publications are *Rebirth of a Nation: Wales 1880–1980* (1982),

Labour People (1987), *The Red Dragon and the Red Flag* (1989) and *The People's Peace: British History 1945–1989*, (1991).

Athena Syriatou is a research student in the Department of History of University College London.

Helen Thompson is a research student in the Department of Government at the London School of Economics.

Daniel Wincott is Jean Monnet Lecturer in Law and Politics of European Integration at the University of Warwick. His publications include 'After Maastricht: British Party Politics and European Union', *Leicester University Discussion Papers in Politics*, 91/2 and 'The Conservatives and Europe', *Politics Review*, Volume 1, Number 4, April 1992.

Professor John W. Young is head of Politics at the University of Leicester. His publications include (ed) *The Foreign Policy of Churchill's Peacetime Administration* (1988), with Michael Dockrill, *British Security Policy 1945–1956* (1988) and *France, The Cold War and the Western Alliance* (1990).

Preface

This volume is the fourth in a series drawn from the Institute of Contemporary British History Summer Schools, organised jointly by the ICBH and the London School of Economics Departments of Government and International History. Given the historical significance of 1992, it seemed appropriate to focus on the theme of Britain and Europe at the Summer School of that year. The papers included here are drawn from the final three days of the conference, and cover the period since the Second World War. A separate volume covering the inter-war period, *Britain and the Threat to Stability in Europe*, edited by Peter Catterall and C.J. Morris, will be published by Leicester University Press later this year.

We would like to thank the Presidency Unit of the Foreign and Commonwealth Office for sponsoring the conference, which was an official event in Britain's six month Presidency of the European Community. This support allowed us to invite speakers from Italy, Germany and Eire. BAT industries also sponsored the conference and we would like to express our thanks for their generous donation. Professor Peter Hennessy, Professor John Young and Professor William Paterson acted as day chairmen for the final three days. Their help was invaluable in ensuring the success and smooth running of the conference. At the LSE John Barnes, of the Government Department, and Professor Paul Preston, of the International History Department, provided much help and advice. The final session of the School, sadly not included in this volume because of lack of space, was an Audit on British Membership of the EC. We would particularly like to thank Dr Simon Bulmer, Dr Andrew Scott, Sir Russell Johnston and Dr Martin Holmes, for making this session such a success. The ICBH is also particularly grateful to Professor Paterson for bringing down from the Europa Institute of the University of Edinburgh, his unrivalled knowledge of the community, and for chairing the final day with such style, wit and insight.

The work of the ICBH depends on the effort and enthusiasm not only of its staff but also of those volunteers who give their time and effort to the promotion of the study of Contemporary British History. We would like to pay tribute here to Virginia Preston, Kate Huddie, Simon Down, Dr Peter Catterall, Anthony Gorst and Daniel Wincott.

This book is dedicated to the memory of Lorenzo Alfonso Brivati.

Brian Brivati
Harriet Jones
ICBH, December 1992

Introduction

Brian Brivati and Harriet Jones

And what is the plight to which Europe has been reduced? . . . over wide areas a vast quivering mass of tormented, hungry, care-worn, and bewildered human beings gape at the ruins of their cities and homes, and scan the dark horizons for the approach of some new peril, tyranny or terror . . . Yet all the while there is a remedy which, if it were generally and spontaneously adopted, would as if by a miracle transform the whole scene, and would in a few years make all Europe, or the greater part of it, as free and happy as Switzerland is today. What is this sovereign remedy? It is to recreate the European family, or as much of it as we can, and provide it with a structure under which it can dwell in peace, in safety and in freedom. We must build a kind of United States of Europe.

Winston Churchill, Zurich, September 1946.

Winston Churchill's words in 1946 raised expectations amongst European federalists that Britain might take the lead in transforming the vision of a United States of Europe into practical reality. But British interests, as Churchill himself would stress in the following year, lay at the heart of three interlinking circles: Europe, the Commonwealth, and the Atlantic Alliance. This position has complicated the British relationship with Europe throughout the post-war period. The chapters included here explore Britain's participation in the process of European integration and examine its reputation as the Communities' 'awkward partner'.

This volume is divided into three chronological sections: I 'The New Jerusalem, 1947–56'; II 'Britain in Search of a Role 1957–73'; and III 'Britain in the Community, 1973–92'. Each section in turn is introduced by a general overview, followed by accounts from witnesses to key events, and concludes with papers from academic specialists.

These years saw both the birth and rapid rise of the European Economic Community and a series of profound challenges to Britain's traditional role as a major international power. Thus it is not surprising that in each of these three periods contradictory signals were sent from different places within the British foreign policy-making community. The ambiguity evident in official circles has been evident as well in the cultural and political responses of the British to the question of European integration.

In her introduction to 'The New Jerusalem', Dr Anne Deighton stresses the link between Britain's cold war and European policy, a link which is often missing in analysis of this period. She concludes that, for these early years, it was the need to cement American participation in the security of Western Europe which determined Britain's European policy. This point is reinforced by Dr Klaus Larres who argues that Britain's support for Western European defence arrangements was based on ensuring a US commitment to European collective security. In contrast, Dr Sean Greenwood examines the brief attempt by Ernest Bevin to establish a British-led 'Third Force' in Europe to rival the two superpowers. However, there were those in Britain whose belief in a European ideal went beyond considerations of *realpolitik*. Dr Stefano Dejak reminds us of the advocates of Western Union who campaigned on the left of the Labour Party in this early period. Nor was Britain's involvement in Europe merely based on schemes for future organisations. As one of the occupying powers, Britain had an important role to play in the reconstruction process. Dr Eva Mayring considers the ways in which British democratic socialism was reflected in its policies towards occupied Germany.

The price of victory for Britain was a misleading sense of satisfaction with existing institutions and a certain complacency about Britain's continued position as one of the leading world powers. This has had two extremely significant repercussions. First, the fact of victory has become a powerful icon in post-war British society. Professor Kenneth Morgan explores the continuing cultural significance of victory on the British people. Second, victory separated Britain from the rest of Western Europe, and prevented it from throwing in its lot with the defeated countries of Continental Europe. This was a source of particular frustration for Anglophiles among the founders of the European Community. Chief among them, of course, was Jean Monnet. Richard Mayne, a long time professional associate and personal friend of Monnet's, recalls his often overlooked association with this country in a fascinating witness account.

In his introduction to the second section, Professor John Young describes the background to Britain's gradual acceptance of the need to join the European club, in the face of its inability to sustain a world role independently. For a section of the policy-making élite, the decision to apply for membership of the Community reflected a genuine change of heart. For others, it reinforced long-standing scepticism about Britain's place in the European experiment. These differences are illustrated in the witness accounts of the diplomat, Sir Reginald Hibbert, and the dedicated anti-marketeer, Lord Jay.

The motives behind Britain's first bid are the subject of a developing historiographical debate, centered on Macmillan's intentions. Dr Miriam Camps, the author of the first major study of this subject, argues here that the Prime Minister was genuinely anxious to succeed in his initial bid. Wolfram Kaiser, however, describes Macmillan's policy as one based, not on the importance of joining the EC, but on appeasing both the young President Kennedy and the pro-European forces within the Conservative Party.

One of the major constraints on Macmillan's freedom of action, of course, was Britain's interest in maintaining its links with the Commonwealth. Dr Lawrence Butler describes how the process of decolonisation began to shift this concern as a priority of British foreign policy. But the relationship between Britain and Europe is not only about high politics. Athena Syriatou examines the way in which European history has been taught in British secondary schools between 1945 and 1975, and concludes that while the British may have a rather superior attitude regarding the relative stability of their history compared to that of the Continent, the history of Britain is nevertheless depicted as inextricably tied to that of Northwestern Europe.

The third section is introduced by Dr Stephen George, who considers the range of problems associated with Britain's awkward partnership in the EC, and the challenges and possibilities which underly Britain's future in the Community. Both political parties have experienced division and discord over the European question since 1973. For Harold Wilson's Labour Government of 1974–76, this provided the context for the renegotiation of Britain's original terms of entry into the Community. Lord Donoughue was a member of Wilson's political team at that time, and he recalls here the months in which both renegotiation and the referendum took place. For the Conservative Party, Europe has been the source of problems of a similar magnitude. Daniel Wincott assesses the particular problems which the social chapter of the Maastricht Treaty have raised for the New Right. Helen Thomson traces the story of Britain's relationship with the European Monetary System, and considers the decision to enter the Exchange Rate Mechanism, a subject of particular interest in light of the developments of the autumn of 1992. The differences in policy priorities between British and European governments is illustrated by Ros Herman's paper on science policy. British reluctance to commit state funding for research and development contrasts sharply with the Continental bias towards more interventionist policies.

These essays all confirm the well-known tendency for Britain to favour an intergovernmental approach to European co-operation, instead of supranational models which involve some loss of national sovereignty. Thus both NATO and the Council of Europe, in which representatives from European countries met to discuss how to co-operate to achieve specific goals, originated with British policy-makers at the outset of the cold war. The supranational structures of later institutions were inspired on the other side of the Channel.

For the British, the need for closer co-operation in Europe was at first a practical affair, part of a wider strategy to prevent a future European war and to unify the states of Western Europe in the face of the emerging threat from the East after 1945. When those initial aims had been achieved, the British saw no need for participation in a more elaborate form of integration in Europe. In May 1950 the Attlee Government supported the Schuman plan for a European Coal and Steel Community because it was designed to tie the economies of France and Germany together, thus preventing any future European war. But Attlee would not allow Britain to take part largely because the Labour Government had just nationalised coal and was in the process of nationalising steel – British foreign policy interests in Europe at that time still permitted domestic political considerations to take priority in a decision of this magnitude.

It seemed timely to us a year ago to plan a conference considering the historical background to the events of 1992. We could hardly have guessed the way in which the events of this year would propel the country into an unprecedented debate over its relationship with the Community. Without an understanding of how we arrived at the current situation it is impossible for policy makers, students of Europe and the general public to make informed decisions. We hope this collection of essays on the subject of Britain's road from the Schuman plan to the Maastricht Treaty will make a useful contribution to academic debate.

I
The New Jerusalem, 1945–55

1

Britain and the cold war 1945–55: an overview

Anne Deighton

Introduction

In the second half of 1992, Britain held the Presidency of the Council of Ministers of the European Community (EC). This was during a critical and particularly difficult period of the Community's development, as the Maastricht Treaty, signed but not yet ratified by the EC countries, received an increasingly hostile reception throughout Western Europe. Furthermore, the war in the former Yugoslavia presented the EC and her strongest supporter, the US, with new and potentially dangerous policies that demanded decisions on difficult defence and security principles for the West. Moreover, the hopes of a developing European coherence within the framework of the EC, which had been reinforced by the Single European Act of 1987, also appeared to be slipping away. Since 1989, it had widely been expected that the collapse of the Soviet imperium in eastern Europe would bring rapid political and economic changes there. But, by 1992, it became clear that a process of unravelling was also taking place in the Western international system.

Britain, traditionally sceptical about the wilder claims of the European integrationists, with both major political parties as divided about 'Europe' as ever, and without clear signposts or European consensus, has found itself in the unenviable position of trying to manage change on a large scale. It is hard to avoid the conclusion that the structural system that helped to lay the basis for the shape of Europe as represented by the EC (and NATO) has its heart deep inside the international system created by the cold war, and that Britain's cold war and European policies in the decade following World War II are therefore central to an understanding of the last forty-five years. Thus Western perceptions of what the Soviet Union might try to achieve in Europe after the war, and the way in which the British sought to deal with this issue, cannot be ignored in any study of the development of Britain's European policy during these years.

The cold war partly determined the physical shape and agenda of the Community, as well as its often complicated relationship with the chief supporter and paymaster of Western Europe, the US. Britain was a major world and

European player in the cold war years under consideration. Although bankrupt after the Second World War, she retained an extensive Empire/Commonwealth, and a role as one of the four occupying powers in the defeated Germany. She was to have a permanent seat on the United Nations Security Council and retained a determination that she had both powers and obligations to fulfil. She took an important part in the international cold war diplomacy of the 1940s and 1950s, and a keen interest in the future direction of Western Europe.

It is a curious phenomenon that the historiography of the cold war has diverged, until quite recently, from the historiography of European integration. But at the time, the relationship between the cold war and European integration seemed very close. Jean Monnet (1978), who played a key part in the creation of the European Coal and Steel Community (ECSC) and the European Economic Community (EEC) stated boldly that in 1950, he was thinking that '[mens'] minds are becoming focused on an object at once simple and dangerous – the cold war', and thought it was hard, in the 1970s, to recall the atmosphere of fear in 1950, and the precariousness of the post-war settlement. Walter Hallstein (1972), first President of the EEC Commission, warned of expansionist forces from the East that were sustained by a quasi-religious fervour and missionary zeal. Altiero Spinelli, Italian thinker and also one-time President of the EEC Commission, talked frequently of the communist threat to post-war Western Europe, and Robert Marjolin, first Secretary-General of the Organisation for European Economic Cooperation (OEEC) and then a Commission Vice-President stressed the importance of the perceived Soviet threat for the success of the OEEC.

Subsequent scholarship on integration became more concerned with the internal dynamics of West European integration – with the development on social science-based theories of neo-functionalism – and with teleological, federalist aspirations; while cold war scholarship sought to deal with the broader issues of superpower politics, particularly Soviet-American relations, and tended to ignore the role of the West European players. Recent work, by Alan Milward (1984) and Michael Hogan (1989), among others, take some fresh approaches to the themes of integration and the cold war.

Post-war; cold war

After 1945, British policy was primarily driven by a desire to achieve a satisfactory European and global balance of power. It is untrue to argue that fears of a Soviet threat did not emerge until 1947, as, very soon after the war, fear of Soviet power was high in the minds of British, some American, and indeed some French policy makers (for example Foreign Minister Georges Bidault, who privately expressed fears of cossacks on the Place de la Concorde). Prime Minister Clement Attlee once argued that Britain was up against a world power, and had to have another world power to act as a balance. This meant that any satisfactory balance in the post-war world had to include the US, and that Britain's European policies would have to be conceived within the framework of a global strategic policy.

Neither in Britain, nor in the United States, was there a monolithic view of what a 'cold war' meant in 1945. Daniel Yergin's pioneering study (1977), reveals two strands of American thinking, which he called the Riga (hard-line) and Yalta (more moderate) axioms. Within the British Foreign Office, there were those, like

Frank Roberts, *chargé d'affaires* in Moscow, who argued that the Soviet Union was not going to act like a normal country with whom British relations would be easy. The

long term aim of the Russian leaders is to consolidate around her boundaries a belt of states subservient to Russia so that she may build up strength without fear of attack. It is considered . . . that such an aim implies the gradual but continual broadening of the belt . . . such expansion will be sought by all means short of war until she has enough strength to embark on agressive[sic] action.[1]

However, as he later remarked in an interview (Zametica, 1990, p.90), he thought that 'these people were hostile, but if you handle them the right way you can live with them'. This view corresponds closely to the 'Chatham House view' of the cold war as 'all mischief short of war': ideological, potentially disruptive, but admitting of diplomatic management. The Soviets were cautious, they understood strength and the increasing cohesion of the West, but would continue to seek for diplomatic and psychological gaps in the Western armoury. In one sense, this view implicitly distinguishes between the short-term need for co-existence between great powers, while not ignoring the long-term roots of Soviet policy, whose origins were deemed to lie in a blend of traditional Russian expansionism and Marxist-Leninist beliefs on the inevitable collapse of capitalism.

A harder line was taken by the Chiefs of Staff, supported by some in the Northern Department of the Foreign Office (Smith, 1990). The military planners saw a continuum between cold war and hot war, a view that was increasingly expressed after the Soviets acquired the nuclear bomb. By 1950, as the Americans also were defining the cold war in terms of their own messianic role in the world, particularly in NSC 68 of June 1950, the British Global Strategy paper argued that 'Allied defence policy had been confused by the lack of a clear definition of what we are fighting for and by a failure to recognise that our aim in this struggle in its present cold war phase as well as in a possible total war phase'.[2]

But British perceptions of cold war cannot be understood in a vacuum, and have to be seen in light of a number of other characteristics of British thinking. First, there remained through these years an overriding concern with sustaining British power and keeping a global role for Britain, despite her bankruptcy by the end of the war. As Ernest Bevin remarked, Britain was a world power or was nothing (Holland, 1991; Reynolds, 1991). These assumptions of greatness lay behind the rapid, and hardly discussed decision that Britain should develop its own nuclear bomb at a time when only the Americans had this technology. In opposition, Winston Churchill (1950), summed up British élite attitudes to their role in the world in a speech made to the Conservative Party conference in October 1948, when he publicly elaborated on the theme of the three circles: Empire/ Commonwealth; United States; Europe; and the unique place that Britain had straddling all three. 'As I look out upon the future of our country', he said,

. . . in the changing scene of human destiny I feel the existence of three great circles among the free nations and democracies . . . These three majestic circles are co-existent, and if they are linked together there is no force or combination which could overthrow them, or even challenge them effectively. Now if you think of the three interlinked circles you will see that we are the only country which has a great part in every one of them. We stand in fact at the very point of junction, and here in this island at the centre of the seaways and perhaps of the airways also, we have the opportunity of joining them all together. If we rise to the occasion in the years to come we may well once again hold the key to opening a safe and happy future in humanity and gaining for ourselves gratitude and fame . . . Over and above all special questions there rises before us the dread and solemn issue of the survival of Great Britain and her Empire as a united power in the first rank among nations.

The Empire/Commonwealth had an importance it is sometimes hard to fathom now. The informal but powerful links of common language, family connections and of traditions of overseas service were compounded by a realisation that the Empire/Commonwealth rested at the heart of Britain's own greatness and world role, as Churchill explained.

But it was the American link that came to be encapsulated in the phrase 'Special Relationship', and became the central focus for British policy in our period. But this is not to say that the British simply ran for cover under the financial and military protection of the United States after 1945. The relationship was far more complex, and there still existed a sense of being able to steer the US, that great 'unwieldy barge', and to use manipulation and influence over the American foreign policy machine. Disappointment when the Americans refused to see the world through British eyes – over the loan negotiations in 1945, for example, or during the 1950s – was always acute.

Second, British élite perception of the post-war world was deeply influenced by the experience of the history of the twentieth century. Bevin and his generation had their most scarring experiences in the First World War. By the 1940s they were confronted with the effects of the inter-war appeasement of Nazism and fascism. These two factors account for a great deal of the fear of the horrors of war, and also, ironically, the other danger of not 'standing up' to those who threatened Europe. This influence was both informal and was also specifically taken into account by planners. For example, the Global Strategy Paper of 1950 referred to above, also argues that the 'war of nerves by Hitler from 1933 to 1939 was in many ways similar to the present cold war and the history of that period is eloquent proof of what happens if foreign policy and military preparedness do not march hand in hand'.[3] France's weakness in the inter-war years was used as an example to show that countries had also to be domestically strong, as well as militarily prepared, to be able to face up to external threats. Democratic states, which, without vigilance could be prone to communist penetration, and in which movements (e.g. for disarmament) could grow, seemed more vulnerable than communist ones, in which the government could act untrammelled by public opinion.

Britain, the cold war and the problem of Germany

Underpinning Britain's cold war and post-war European policy lay, perhaps inevitably, the problem of Germany. What seemed to be needed was a policy of double containment – primarily of Soviet power, as has been shown, but also of German power in the longer term. This latter took two forms in the period 1945–55.

The first form was what to do with Germany? Though defeated, Germany was of immense geostrategic importance to those countries who were her neighbours, as well as those further afield. Furthermore, the memories of the failure of the settlement after the First World War lingered in the minds of decision-makers. During the years 1945–47, Britain was to play her fairly meagre diplomatic hand with considerable skill. In these years, she took a powerful part in securing a Germany that remained, at least in the short term, divided along the zonal borders fixed as the war was ending. At the Councils of Foreign Ministers, Britain helped to ensure that the priorities of German reconstruction prevailed over reparations, that those of creating a democratic system in the Western zones prevailed over any desire for unification (Deighton, 1990). Moreover, British diplomats drew the US, relatively unsure of her own future role at first, further and further into the post-war European web. They drove ahead with a policy that overturned French wishes – particularly the dismemberment of Germany, until, by spring 1948, the French were faced with an Anglo–Saxon *fait accompli* over the future of the Western zones.

At the heart of this policy by Britain lay a determination, increasingly shared by many American decision-makers, that the root of recovery was German recovery. For western Germany's recovery was essential to Western Europe's economic recovery and an economic cesspool in the middle of Europe, breeding uncertainty and discontent, would have wrecked chances of a post-war economic revival. Therefore, by 1947, decisions about how to use the Marshall Aid funds included the provision of funds for the three western German zones, although the political consequences of this in terms of excluding the fourth Soviet zone from the scheme (unless the Russians capitulated and agreed to play by Western rules) were well appreciated. As Bevin whispered to his PPS, Pierson Dixon at the July Paris meeting (called to decide on a response to Marshall's offer) as the Russians prepared to leave – 'we are witnessing the birth of the Western bloc' (quoted in Deighton, 1990, p. 187). So the first dimension of the German problem, what to do with Germany, was partially resolved by the decision to develop those zones over which the British, Americans and French did have control, to allow the western German economy to recover, and political institutions to develop.

The second dimension of the German problem for Britain, which became acute in the 1950s, was what would Germany do, and how would she perform in the new emerging bipolar structure? The overriding issue of this decade was the way in which the newly created Federal Republic of Germany would integrate herself into Western Europe. In particular, the central issue was, what would be the military role of Germany herself, acting for her own defence and the defence of the West. The British knew that a divided Germany was a high risk strategy. It meant that German demands for unification would always be left on the table. It also left Germany as something of a prize for the West and the Soviet Union alike. To rearm Germany against a Soviet threat meant that Germany herself would become a key player, with all the uncertainties about the future of German policy that this implied.

In part because of these concerns, the 1950s became the years when cold war politics and the politics of supranational European integration became more closely intertwined than ever, as the European Coal and Steel Community (ECSC), Western European Union (WEU) and the EC were created. Indeed, it is arguable that the integration process of the 1950s was possible because Germany was now divided and contained. These were also the years when the West Germans began to flex their own muscles, when, for example German Chancellor Konrad Adenauer (as worried as anyone about German domestic opinion), could play a brilliant hand to secure the establishment of the Federal Republic in the West while first following the French line on ECSC and the European Defence Community proposal, and then finding a role for Germany in NATO and WEU.

Britain's western strategies, 1945–55

The key to understanding the thrust of British policy during the years 1945–55 can be summed up in one phrase: the West. The West meant capitalism as opposed to communism and Western style democratic institutions as opposed to 'peoples' democracies. It also implied the involvement of the US in the international politics of the post-war world. According to Alan Bullock (1983), Ernest Bevin's policy reached its greatest creative moment in 1949, with the creation of NATO, which he had always wanted, which fits well with Attlee's sentiments about a new, global balance of power. It is, however, more accurate to say that there was no straight line between the realisation that the global balance of power required US intervention, and the emergence of NATO in the form it took by 1949. It is indeed further possible to argue that the high point of British cold war/European policy was in fact 1954, when she brokered WEU, which also enabled West Germany to join NATO in 1955.

There was no inevitability about the creation of NATO in its 1949 form. After 1947, there was a great deal of debate about the construction of a Third Force. Early in 1948, in the Western Union debates, there emerged the idea that the British, with the French and their colonies/Commonwealth, could occupy the 'middle of the planet', and create a bloc that would be able to say 'no' to both the Soviets and the Americans. The effect of this would, of course, also be to enhance British power and influence. There has been some interesting and provocative work on this theme, including that by Sean Greenwood (Chapter 5 in this volume), which was a more ambitious concept than other socialist thinking about a third, socialist, European force (Young and Kent, 1992. See also Shlaim, 1978). But several notes of caution need to be raised about the Third Force idea.

The first moments of serious discussion with the French took place at the end of 1947, and the beginning of 1948. But, during these months, the British were all too aware that the French were in a diplomatic panic about Germany; communists; strikes; too much American influence; too little American money; as well as France's own domestic political instability. Indeed, when British talks took place on military questions with the Americans, the French were left out, because the government was considered unreliable. Much of what passed between the two governments during the frantic months in the autumn of 1947 was said to try to reassure the French, while securing their support for Anglo-Saxon policies in Germany. (Deighton, 1990; Young, 1991). Second, however much Bevin liked the idea of being beholden to no one, and of straddling the middle of the planet, the British themselves were not prepared to put military backing behind the idea of a Third Force, and indeed, in 1948, did not want even to funnel troops into the defence of Europe, which was considered largely undefendable. This put the British in a delicate position for, as British Ambassador to Washington,

Inverchapel admitted. For, without 'assurance of security, which can only be given with some degree of American participation, the British Government are unlikely to be successful in making the Western Union a going concern . . .'[4] What was created was the Five-Power intergovernmental Brussels Treaty Organisation of 1948, which later had significance in an unexpected way in 1954.

Last, and probably most important, is that the idea of the Third Force that could say no to the other superpowers was a very long term and indeed vague notion. The Third Force would be a Western force – spiritual, ideological, economic as well as military, and the Western Union debates in the British Cabinet in January 1948 strongly reinforce this idea, as Greenwood shows. In that context, the US was the only possible paymaster and the natural ally. So while it is possible to draw on American sources to show that they too were briefly attracted to the Third Force idea, the whole concept became overwhelmed by both practical developments. The financial and military weakness of the two major European protagonists, France and Britain; the Czech coup; and the obvious intense involvement that the Americans now had with Germany revealed by their military efforts throughout the Berlin Blockade all point to this. As Bevin said in 1950, 'On which basis are we going to build? In our opinion the answer was Atlantic . . . I had reached this conclusion not because I was anti-European, but because I did not believe Europe alone could ever be strong enough to defend itself. It was a practical, not a sentimental question'.[5]

By 1950, the British had given up this notion for the wider concept of the Atlantic Community. It was not possible to match the strength of the Soviet Union and her satellites with the Empire/Commonwealth and Western Europe without the full support of North America. Indeed as Bevin reflected, the Atlantic Community would make it easier for Britain to operate, as it would draw together the three main pillars of her policy – the Commonwealth, Western Europe and the US. The drive for the 'Pax Atlantica' reached its height in early 1950. By then, the British military had decided that they were too overstretched to sustain a strategy of defence of the Middle East, and the Global Strategy Paper reveals a new, primary commitment to the defence of Europe. With this came a British acceptance that the new Federal Republic, created in August 1949, would somehow have to be brought into the Western system.

The documents for early 1950, which have been painstakingly edited in the 'Documents on British Policy Overseas' volumes (DBPO, 1987) reveal a sense that British planners thought they had now found a way forward that would both present a strong front against Soviet Union and would also protect British interests. The security of NATO, though still a 'paper treaty', would be supplemented by British support for intergovernmental organisations like the Brussels Treaty Organisation and the OEEC. There was no longer any sense in thinking in terms of British strategy, or even of a Western European strategy. What was needed was collaboration with the US in both policy and method. But there was also a determination to try to stop the Americans from thinking of Europe as a separate unit, and to develop the Atlanticism that appeared now to be feasible, for the Atlantic Community would avoid Britain being led, so far as Europe was concerned, either to sacrifice the UK's national sovereignty in vital matters of defence or finance, or to be put in the position of appearing to be the one obstacle in the way of the idea of closer European co-operation.

At this point the rumbling disagreements between the UK and her continental partners about Western European integration came out again into the open, and the last six months of 1950 witnessed rude shocks for British policy makers as the hopeful idea that an Atlantic Community led in Europe by the British, and supported by a web of loose, inter-governmental European organisations, was shattered. In June 1950, the first clear parting of the ways emerged when the British declined to participate in the Schuman Plan to establish a Coal and Steel Community (ECSC). In London, it was argued that Britain would have far more to give up in any abrogation of her sovereignty, than did the continental Europeans, who still suffered from a 'well-known shakiness of morale'. This was to be most clearly expressed on the conclusion of a fact-finding exercise conducted during 1951, into the character and direction of the continental integration movement. The Permanent Under-Secretary's Committee concluded thus:

The United Kingdom cannot seriously contemplate joining in European integration. Apart from geographical and strategic considerations, Commonwealth ties and the special position of the United Kingdom as the centre of the sterling area, we cannot consider submitting our political and economic system to supra-national institutions. Moreover, if these institutions did not prove workable, their dissolution would not be serious for the individual European countries which would go their separate ways again; it would be another matter for the United Kingdom which would have had to break its Commonwealth and sterling area connexions to join them. Nor is there, in fact, any evidence that there is real support in this country for any institutional connexion with the continent. (DBPO, 1986)

The Empire/Commonwealth connection, seen as a source of strength in the 1940s, was beginning to force British policy away from developments on the continent. This was exacerbated by the attachment, revealed in the above quotation, to the notion of British parliamentary sovereignty, which precluded anything more than intergovernmental cooperation, and which remained, and remains, a ground for clarion calls against integration.

The ECSC marked a breakthrough both for Franco-German relations and the awareness that the US was anxious to support rapprochement between the two countries, and it was also the decisive moment at which the differences between Britain and her continental partners seemed to become more obvious than their similarities. The ECSC model – a political commitment to integration by the Six, followed by the specific abrogation of national sovereignty in specific areas of policy, was to be built upon by the Rome Treaty of 1957, which established the EEC, and from which the British also excluded themselves.

But it was not just in the area of civilian integration that the British hopes of early 1950 were later disrupted. By the summer of that year, the Korean War had broken out, and with it came strong American demands that the Federal Republic of Germany would have to be further integrated into the West, this time in the area of defence. This exposed the weak underbelly of Western policy towards the FRG to that date. For residual fears about German military power could not now be ignored. In Britain, there was a gradual realisation that the incorporation of the FRG into NATO was inevitable, and was the best way of tying the Germans down in a Western defence structure.

The Americans suggested an integrated European defence force with an

American military presence and Supreme Commander and with the inclusion of West Germany under the NATO Commander. The British agreed to the package as it would have meant a further American military commitment to Europe, although Ernest Bevin would have preferred a German federal police force in the short term. The French, however, were most alarmed, and proposed the creation of a European Army which would contribute to the defence of the European NATO area. This army would contain a German military contribution, but the Germans alone would have no defence command, or additional, separate national army. The French proposals, when they emerged as the Pleven Plan, met with a frosty reception initially, the British always declining participation in this 'sludgy amalgam'.

In December 1950 the Western powers decided upon a twin track approach by discussing both the French and the NATO proposal, but by 1951 it seemed as though the French plan would provide the route forward, as the Americans had swung round to this idea, and the British had little option but to follow, although they reiterated that they would not participate in the European Army. By May 1952, the European Defence Community (EDC) treaty was signed, but doubts about the EDC grew to a crescendo over the next two years, and the French Parliament finally rejected ratification. The British had sought to allay French fears through these years, first by a technical association, then by offering guarantees if any country unilaterally seceded from EDC, and finally by a military guarantee. But Winston Churchill's personal initiatives from May 1953 towards the Soviets also unsettled the already nervous French and possibly contributed to the final collapse of the project.

So in August 1954, the French finally killed off their own idea. But for the British, the defeat of the EDC was to enable them to come forward with a proposal that the Brussels Treaty Organisation of 1948 should be transformed into Western European Union, that they would agree to station army divisions and a tactical air force in Germany, and that Germany should, after further changes in the contractual agreements, join NATO (Dockrill, 1991). By 1955, West Germany was a member of NATO and the intense period of alliance building and military preparation for a war across the sensitive heartland of Europe could begin. The London Conference of 1954 was thus arguably the high point of British influence in Europe in the 1950s.

Conclusion

There is a sense in which Britain's most solid contribution to the creation of the cold war and the West was completed by 1955. She had played an important role in creating a Western system that gave a strongly favourable balance of power to its members. Britain's European vision remained of an Atlantic Community in which the US played an active role in Europe both to balance Soviet power, and also to sustain the uneasy division of Europe which a divided Germany symbolised. As in 1950, the British failed to participate actively in the French-led diplomacy that led to the creation of the EEC and Euratom after 1955. For this, there has been much criticism, both on the grounds that there was a lack of imagination at the highest levels, and also that the British had become completely boxed in by the Empire/Commonwealth, with the 'Special Relationship' that seemed to preclude active

involvement on the continent and with their preoccupation with national sovereignty. As Helmut Schmidt once put it, the problem with the British was that they
had never been able to rid themselves of the illusion that they had emerged
victorious from the war (quoted by Holland, 1991, p.346). Noel Annan, (Annan,
1991) has likewise reflected that the British were haunted by the ghosts of their
irresolution and fell victims of their own rhetoric as a world power. Furthermore,
by 1955, the British no longer had the kind of influence that they had been able to
exercise immediately after the war. Between 1945 and 1947, they had been key
players in the early cold war, ensuring that the Americans would participate fully in
West Europe and in Germany. The way in which Marshall Aid was administered
owed much to Britain's role, and the creation of NATO was similarly strongly
influenced by British diplomacy. This had been seen as essential to secure a
favourable balance of power in the cold war world, and to maintain a distinct role
for the British themselves. But, as American policy became clearer, as the
demands of the Korean War determined policy, as the French became more
confident and the West German state was established, Britain's own place became
less clear. In 1954, the British were able to resolve the desperate security dilemma
for the West that the French had created by proposing a European Army, and then
rejecting it. WEU was an astute compromise that fulfilled many of the long-term
interests of the British themselves, while also ensuring that continental integration
would be largely confined to civil policies for the next thirty years, enabling the Six
to relaunch European integration with the EEC and Euratom, without the UK, but
with NATO providing Europe's defence umbrella. After Britain's 1954 swansong,
the next decade of European politics was to be dominated by France.

Notes

1. PRO FO 371 56831, 20 March 1946, Roberts to FO.
2. 'Defence Policy and Global Strategy', reproduced in *Documents on British Policy Overseas*,
   1991, ser.II, vol.IV, London, HMSO.
3. Ibid.
4. Foreign Relations of the United States, 1948, vol.III, US Government Printing Office,
   Washington, p.19, 6 February.
5. *Documents on British Policy Overseas*, 1989, ser.II, vol.III, no.114, London, HMSO.

References

Annan, Noel (1991), *Our Age*, London, Fontana.
Bullock, Alan (1983), *Ernest Bevin: Foreign Secretary, 1945–1951*, London, Heinemann.
Churchill, W.S. (1950), *Europe Unites: Speeches, 1947 and 1948*, London, Cassell.
Deighton, Anne (1990), *The Impossible Peace: Britain, the Division of Germany and the Origins
   of the Cold War, 1945–1947*, Oxford, Clarendon Press.
Dockrill, Saki (1991), *Britain's Policy for West German Rearmament, 1950–1955*, Cambridge,
   Cambridge University Press.
Documents on British Policy Overseas, 1986, ser.II, vol.I, no.414, London, HMSO.
Documents on British Policy Overseas (1987), ser.II, vol.II, London, HMSO.
Documents on British Policy Overseas 1991, ser.II, vol.IV, London, HMSO.
Foreign Relations of the United States, 1948 (1973), vol.11, Washington, United States
   Government Printing Office.

Hallstein, Walter (1972), *Europe in the Making*, London, George Allen & Unwin.

Hogan, Michael (1987), *The Marshall Plan: America, Britain and the Reconstruction of Western Europe, 1947–52*, Cambridge, Cambridge University Press.

Holland, Robert (1991), *Pursuit of Greatness: Britain and the World Role, 1900–1970*, London, Fontana.

Marjolin, Robert (1989), *Memoirs, 1911–1986*, trans. William Hall, London, Weidenfeld & Nicolson.

Milward, Alan (1984), *The Reconstruction of Western Europe*, London, Methuen.

Monnet, Jean (1978), *Memoirs*, trans. Richard Mayne, London, Collins.

Reynolds, David (1991), *Britannia Overruled: British Policy and World Power in the 20th Century*, London, Longman.

Shlaim, Avi (1978), *Britain and the Origins of European Unity, 1940–1951*, Reading, Graduate School of Contemporary European Studies.

Smith, Raymond (1990), 'A climate of opinion: British officials and the development of British Soviet policy, 1945–47', in Anne Deighton, (ed.), *Britain and the First Cold War*, London, Macmillan.

Yergin, Daniel (1977), *Shattered Peace*, Boston, Houghton Mifflin.

Young, John (1991), *France, the Cold War and the Western Alliance, 1944–1949*, Leicester, Leicester University Press.

Young, John, and John Kent (1992), 'British Policy Overseas: The "Third Force" and the Origins of NATO – In search of a new perspective', in Beatrice Heuser and Robert O'Neill, (eds.), *Securing Peace in Europe, 1945–1962*, London, Macmillan.

Zametica, John, (ed.) (1990), *British Officials and British Foreign Policy, 1945–50*, Leicester, Leicester University Press.

2

Jean Monnet, Europe and the British: a witness account

Richard Mayne

Many people nowadays regard Monnet as a federalist. I think this is an exaggeration, because he was never very systematic in his political thinking. He had certain basic principles: he believed, for example, that men died and traditions only lived on through institutions. He believed that equality was a necessary condition of proper relations between states. He believed that the lack of international law and order in the world had been a major catastrophe and that one needed to work towards some sort of system among countries such as exists within countries, i.e. democratic rules and institutions which people obey.

He was not a systematic thinker. He just groped his way forwards from one perception to the next; and when one's talking about the goals of Europe, Monnet was never a great one for formulating very precise, long-term goals. But he was very good at trying to define the next practical step, which would bring one closer to what was a generally but rather vaguely defined goal.

So Monnet doesn't have to be regarded as on one side or the other in the row about subsidiarity or federalism. He's not M. Delors, he's not Mr Heseltine, he's not Margaret Thatcher, and therefore in that sense he's unique.

Monnet's relations with Britain began in 1904 at the age of sixteen, when he was sent to London by his father to learn English and live with a wine merchant in the city. That is a very long time ago, and it was a very different London, a very different Britain, from the Britain we have now. It was a Britain of horse-drawn omnibuses, of very early motor cars: a Britain where people wore top hats quite frequently, certainly wore bowler hats, and where young men wore grey spats. It was the world of early P.G. Wodehouse. It was almost the world of Dornford Yeats's early stories. The Britain that Monnet encountered was an Imperial power; London was the financial capital of the world. Britain was self-confident, and hadn't yet realised that the Victorian age, which had just ended, meant the end of a long, long period of prosperity, based on investment and being first in the Industrial Revolution. It was a Britain, in other words, where one could very easily be over-impressed; and Monnet was very deeply impressed. He always regarded the British as very good at running institutions. He thought that when they joined the Community they would bring to it an institutional experience and *savoir-faire* which some of the other countries lacked. He was convinced that the British kept their word. He was very impressed that in the City you didn't have to write an agreement down and sign it with witnesses; you just said it and shook hands and that was a deal.

That old-fashioned Britain – a very respectable and likeable Britain in many ways – was the Britain that Monnet kept in his head from the start. He had immense respect for the British and a lot of affection for them. He had many very influential British friends; and although he spent much of his time later in America, and of course lived in France a great deal, nevertheless, Britain was his second home. It was the place that he had gone to when he first went abroad, and we all know that the country you first go to when you first go abroad has a special place in your feelings. He was very concerned that this priority of the British in his own mind should not be misunderstood by the British. He feared that he would be regarded as, somehow, anti-British because he had started the European Coal and Steel Community without them and he'd imposed various conditions on the negotiations – asking them to accept, for example, the supranational High Authority, in 1950. He was most concerned that it shouldn't be regarded as somehow his wish to exclude the British from the Community: so much so that when he was preparing to write his memoirs, one of the jobs he asked me to do was to go through all his archives and write a long (and exceedingly boring) memorandum based on his everyday contact with the British from as far back as the records went. The records didn't go back very far because they had been destroyed by his family during the war when France was occupied, for fear of reprisals by the Germans, so that pre-war records were very scanty; but Monnet's long relationship with the British was fairly well documented and still is.

After he'd been in Britain for two years learning English, he was sent at the age of eighteen to sell brandy in the United States and Canada, because his father ran the brandy firm, J.G. Monnet and Co., which still exists although the shares now belong to the Germans. It was on the way back from his exploits in North America that Monnet passed through London in 1914 to see people at the Hudson's Bay headquarters in London. There he discovered that, although war had just broken out, the British and the French were not coordinating their supply arrangements. He came back to Cognac where his family lived – he'd been excused military service because he had nephritis, a kidney disease. When he got home he said to his father: 'Look, this is terrible. I've got to see the Prime Minister'.

'What!', said his father, 'You can't possibly. You're only a very young man.' Monnet was twenty-six at this time. 'It's ridiculous. You've got all these ideas, it sounds wonderful, but what do you know about it? The Prime Minister has plenty of other fish to fry. He won't see you.'

Monnet was very, very persistent, even in those days, and he persuaded his father to see a local lawyer, who had been at law school with the Prime Minister, Rene Viviani, and after much badgering the lawyer was persuaded to take Monnet up to Paris from Cognac to see Viviani. It happened that that very morning Viviani had had news from the Western Front that his two sons had been killed in action; and here comes this short, stocky, cocky little man of twenty-six, who proceeds to lecture him about the way in which France and Britain are running their supply lines. To everybody's amazement, except Monnet's maybe, Viviani was very impressed, and said: 'Right, you've defined a real problem. Go ahead and deal with it.' So Monnet was given the job, in a fairly subordinate capacity to begin with, of trying to co-ordinate British and French supplies. It took him about three years before anything serious happened, but he shuttled between London and Paris. He worked with Arthur Salter, later Lord Salter; and out of that experience, I think, came first, a friendship with Salter which was very, very close, and secondly, some ideas about what should happen after the First World War. Arthur Salter wrote a book, now neglected and forgotten, called *The United States of Europe*, (Salter, 1933) just after the war and this must have been the fruit of the kind of discussions he had with Monnet during the war. It was a kind of blueprint for the League of Nations, but on a European basis. Well, when the League of Nations was finally set up after the Peace Conference, Monnet was invited to become Deputy Secretary General to Drummond who was the Secretary General, and there he worked on a number of projects: he rescued various countries and solved their financial problems and so on. He stayed for quite a long time, and his methods of work were described in a very interesting book by Louise Weiss, called *Memoires d'une Europeenne*, (Weiss, 1978) as being extremely informal, as they remained in fact to the end of his days. He never seemed to be in the office at the right time; dossiers would pile up on one end of his desk and, instead of reading through them as a good, conscientious civil servant might be expected to do, he would call in the author, and say 'Tell me, what is in this document? What are the salient points?', and then he would argue and discuss. It was all done *viva voce* rather than by pouring over the print, and this disconcerted some people, but it was obviously more creative than just plodding, in a bureaucratic way, through the mass of paper, which finally drowns people. Anyway, Monnet was there for quite a while, and then two things happened which caused him to leave. One was that he had a disagreement with Raymond Poincaré about the imposition of sanctions and repressive measures against Germany. But more particularly, the family firm, the cognac firm, was getting into great difficulties, and Monnet came back to try to put it on its feet. He realised, for example, that they had to sell cheaper cognac, as well as top-range cognac; that they had great difficulty fighting the established brandy firms, like Hennessy. So Monnet dealt with the family firm, and then he went into international banking; he made a fortune on Wall Street and lost most of it in the 1929 crash. He went off to China to help the Chinese reorganise their railroads, and he spent a lot of time with American bankers, notably with Blair and Co.; and it was during this period that he got to know a lot of people in the United States, with whom he made very good, very influential friendships. So during this period, the inter-war period, after the initial British experience, he had the American experience. In his memoirs he talks quite eloquently about the way in which, to a Frenchman, America seemed a place of unlimited possibilities, a place of great energy, of expansion, of enormous freedom and goodwill. He told the story of one particular event, when he was earlier trying to sell brandy, and he arrived in some hick town and was looking for a livery stable to find a horse to ride off into the wilderness with his brandy samples. He met a man outside the saloon and he explained his problem, and the man said 'Well, that's all right, you can take my horse.' Monnet thanked him, but asked: 'What do I do when I've finished with it?' 'Oh, just hitch it up outside the saloon.'

This was amazing to a Frenchman brought up on protocol and suspicion of strangers and concern to get it in writing before you did anything. That sort of liberality, that feeling of openness, which he felt in America, was very important to him. He tried to introduce it into every aspect of his own work. Anyway, there he was, working with the Americans, and the War was clearly on its way. Hitler had unbounded ambitions, and Monnet knew that people with unbounded ambitions were extremely dangerous. During this time he was used by the French Government to try to organise US aircraft supplies for the French Air Force. He went to America and he negotiated with the aircraft suppliers, and he was even, with his technical colleagues, shown some prototypes that were not supposed to be shown to anyone but Americans at the time. There was a small scandal about that. But he did, in fact, place a lot of aircraft orders and these orders were in process when the War began. They were still in process by the time France fell in June 1940, and the aircraft orders were then signed over to the British for the symbolic sum of one dollar. So in a sense Monnet's work for the French was transferred to the British, and helped them win the second Battle of Britain, the bomber battle. I remember going to one of Monnet's birthday parties, at which a colleague, Etienne Hirsch, raised his glass to Monnet and said 'Without your efforts, many of us would not be alive', meaning that the War would have taken longer. As John Maynard Keynes said Monnet had abridged the War by about a year – but also that these American aircraft were a very important munition for the British at a time when they were alone fighting the Nazis.

Anyway, Monnet did this job for the French Government. Then came September 1939 and war, and not waiting for any prompting, Monnet wrote immediately to Edouard Daladier, who was then the French Prime Minister, suggesting that he do the same job in World War Two as he'd done in World War One, that is co-ordinate French and British supplies. The need for this was very clear. In one of the official histories of British war supplies there is an account of the French and the British bidding against each other to buy Australian tallow, and this in full wartime. Why were they bidding against each other? Even worse was the fact that, when they discovered what was actually happening, it was also found that the French were bidding for themselves, and the British were bidding on behalf of the French Ministry of Food. So it wasn't even the French bidding against the British; it was the French bidding against themselves. Now this kind of confusion does take place, but it was the sort of thing that Monnet abominated and did his best to root out. This time, unlike World War One when it had taken three years, it only took him about three months to deal with the problem and set up the requisite joint supply arrangements.

Then, of course, came the catastrophic news of the invasion of the Netherlands and Belgium by the Germans, and the push towards France and the flanking of the Maginot line and the sudden turning of the phony war into a real war.

Monnet had three roles at this point. One, which he was very concerned with, was to draw up a balance-sheet of German, British and French capabilities. He tried to find out from his colleagues in London and Paris, what potential the Germans had in the way of how many guns, how many planes, how many troops, how many aircraft, how many tanks could they produce, and so on and so forth. Nobody seemed to know completely, and even stranger, nobody seemed to know what the resources and future capabilities of the French and the British were, so they could not draw up a balance-sheet of who had the bigger arsenal. This again seemed absurd to Monnet, so he set civil servants to work, trying to draw up this balance-sheet, and it of course showed that in certain sectors there was a very severe allied deficit.

Balance-sheets were always very important to Monnet, in that he always thought that the truth emerged in the bottom line, that – as when he had had to look at the affairs of his own father's company – you really had to read a balance sheet carefully and see whether you were losing or making money. He was very, very concerned to get that sort of thing right, however much trouble it took: he had an almost spinsterly insistence on getting the figures right. He was not a great mathematician, he certainly was not a trained economist or anything like that, but he really believed, as I say, in this rather frugal peasant way that you must get the columns in the balance sheet balanced.

That was the first thing he was doing in the early months of 1940. The second thing, when the battle of France was on and before Dunkirk, was that he tried to persuade Churchill to throw the Royal Air Force into the Battle of France. Churchill stubbornly refused to commit the whole of the Royal Air Force to fighting on foreign soil. Monnet later admitted that Churchill had been right and that he had been wrong, because the whole of the requisite part of Fighter Command might well have been destroyed in France, before it had a chance to defend Britain later on. But anyway, that was an abortive attempt.

Then, of course, came an even more dramatic moment when France itself was in the process of falling; and Monnet in fact begins his own memoirs with his proposal at that point for Franco-British union – one government, one parliament, one navy, one airforce, one army. Some people have thought, in retrospect, that this was just an attempt to keep the French fleet in the War; but from Monnet's point of view it was a very, very serious effort, not only at fighting a joint war effort in a very systematic and politically-based way, but also a possible vision of an embryo of some kind of future Europe. If you could actually get the British and the French to unite politically then you would have a very strong base for creating something more.

Well, as we all know, the plan failed, but it didn't fail for want of trying or for want of support from not only Churchill, of all people – the great old Imperialist – but also General de Gaulle. De Gaulle was willing to accept this and he was going to go across to France to sell this plan to the then tottering government of Paul Renault. But then came the news that Renault was suing for peace and that there was nothing doing, and so de Gaulle did not go, and nor did Churchill. But Monnet said 'Let us make one last effort', and he went. He flew to Bordeaux – where the government had taken refuge – in a Sunderland flying boat called the *Claire*, a big, old, fat-bellied aircraft that could land on water. The reason he took the flying boat was that he hoped to bring back the whole French Government. But he had a very miserable time in Bordeaux; the place was crowded, there were no hotels, no restaurants. He and his assistant, Rene Pleven – later Prime Minister of France – sat in the Allee de Tourny in Bordeaux, eating their sandwiches on some of the stone benches there, and he went round to all the various dignitaries in the place, trying to persuade them to join him, but the Government would not do it; it was too late. Even old Edouard Herriot would not do it and finally Monnet came back disappointed, with refugees in the flying boat.

So that attempt failed. Monnet always admitted his failures. When he was preparing to write his memoirs he looked at de Gaulle's memoirs and said 'You know, the funny thing about de Gaulle's memoirs is that he was always right.' He determined that he would *not* be always right himself. Unfortunately he did not actually pen the memoirs in person; they were ghosted for him by a colleague who is, in fact, a very well-known novelist now, Francois Fontaine; and Fontaine is a great admirer of Monnet. And therefore the element of self-criticism, which one might have otherwise found in the memoirs, is a little diminished by the fact that a third party has written them, and a third party who greatly admired the supposed author. Anyway, returning to 1940, Monnet was now in London, a strange figure, much distrusted by some people. Sir Oliver Harvey described him in his diary as 'a mixture of gangster and conspirator'. There is a story that at one point MI5, the security service, put a tail on Monnet because they regarded him as a very dangerous alien who was floating around London. At that time he did have a slightly raffish air; he had, after all, been the hero of a runaway marriage, which he had to celebrate in Moscow because the woman with whom he had run away was already married to a Catholic in Italy, and they had had to circumvent the ban on divorce by getting married in Moscow. In his earlier years he used to wear a long, rather saturnine, moustache which made him look like a villain in some farce, but he was distrusted to some extent, by the British. I remember talking to one very senior British civil servant and I said something about Monnet. He said 'Oh, Monnet's just an adventurer'. There was that feeling about Monnet that he was not quite an ordinary, respectable citizen, politician, civil servant. Nobody could quite grasp what he was, and therefore he was regarded with a certain suspicion by the stuffier elements in the British establishment, though he had many friends, among the bankers particularly.

So there he was in London and the problem was, for Monnet, how to pursue the War. De Gaulle was there and had come to see Monnet at his flat in London; and as usual Monnet had not been on time, he had been working in the office very late. De Gaulle arrived with Geoffroi de Courcel, his *aide de camp*, and Madame Monnet received them. Madame Monnet was sitting on one side of the fireplace and Courcelle was sitting on the other, and there was de Gaulle, standing in the middle, with his hands behind his back, as he frequently did. Madame Monnet politely said to him 'Are you here on a mission, *mon General*?' De Gaulle drew himself up and said 'Je ne suis pas en mission, Madame. Je suis venu pour sauver l'honneur de la France.'

'Oh really', said Madame Monnet, 'how do you plan to go about it?'

De Gaulle drew from his pocket the draft of the speech he was going to make on the BBC on 18 June. But instead of handing it to Madame Monnet, on one side of the fireplace, he handed it to De Courcel on the other side, and De Courcel had to get up and walk round him and hand it to Madame Monnet. It was a gesture worthy of a head of state, which later on, of course, de Gaulle became, showing that there was a certain self-importance in the man. Anyway, Monnet arrived late, as I say, and when he arrived, there was his chauffeur capering in front of the mirror, trying on de Gaulle's kepi and waving his baton which he had left in the hall. That added a little bit to the comedy of the occasion. Monnet then went in to dinner with de Gaulle, Madame Monnet and a few other people and they discussed the situation, and later told me, though I am not sure that it was not, perhaps, embellished by memory, that at that meeting he had the impression that de Gaulle was less concerned with winning the War, than with securing

France's position after the War as an equal member of the alliance. There may have been hindsight in this – I do not know – but if he saw it then that was very acute because I am sure that it was true. After all, de Gaulle had no troops; he had a few volunteers, he had a few people who had come out of France and went back again as part of his own little espionage and sabotage service – the RF section of SOE – but basically – to quote W.H. Auden, 'All I have is a voice to undo the folded lie' – all de Gaulle had was a voice which he used with immense effect over BBC radio, rather as the Ayatollah Khomeini used his cassettes when he distributed them from France prior to the Iranian Revolution. He was a voice, and Monnet wanted to persuade de Gaulle to take the voice, take himself, to North Africa and rally the troops, because there were still armies in North Africa: Peyrouton and others were there, and Monnet's idea was that de Gaulle should go to North Africa and put himself at the head of these armies who were still not certain in their allegiance to marshal Petain and Vichy. De Gaulle disagreed entirely. So that would not work. Monnet was not too happy to work in London with de Gaulle because there was nothing much for him to do there. But he was invited by the British to become the deputy-head of the British Supply Council in Washington, whose job was to secure from America as much as possible in the way of munitions and armaments, rather as he had done the same job for the French earlier on.

At that point there was a parting of the ways between de Gaulle and Monnet. De Gaulle actually wrote him rather a nice letter at the time saying something like 'We see things differently, but I am sure that in the long run we are all on the same side' – something of that sort. They were clearly not on bad terms, although they disagreed. But Monnet became, for a while, a British Civil Servant. He had already been awarded, in World War One or after it, an honorary KBE, which would have made him Sir Jean Monnet, if he had been allowed to use it – rather like Bob Geldof who is not called Sir Bob, I think, because it is only an honorary distinction since neither Geldof nor Monnet is or was British. Anyway, Monnet went off to the United States with his own French passport, countersigned by Winston Churchill – which greatly puzzled the American immigration authorities when he arrived on the other side. He had become, as I say, a British civil servant, having been an allied civil servant – as *The Times* called him – in the early months of World War Two.

He stayed in America for quite a while. The head of the British Supply Council was in fact killed in a terrible plane accident in Scotland in 1941. During this time, Monnet had many conversations with his various friends in Washington, including, notably, Felix Frankfurter, the Supreme Court Judge; and it was in 1943 that he finally was asked by President Franklin D. Roosevelt to go to North Africa to sort out the problems that had been created by the escape of General Giraud, aided by the Americans, from a German prison, in order to head the Free French in North Africa. Remember that de Gaulle was in London. North Africa had been liberated by Operation Torch in late 1942 and there was still quite a strong Vichy element among the North African troops there and Giraud himself was, in fact, an extremely reactionary figure; rather anti-semitic and certainly not the inspiring leader that de Gaulle was and would later become.

There was great danger, in fact, that the French could be divided into two parties – the Giraudists and the Gaullists – and when de Gaulle finally arrived in

North Africa, after he had managed to consolidate the French Resistance behind him thanks to the work of Jean Moulin, there were these two leaders in the provisional Government of France sitting in the same room together: de Gaulle highly intelligent, de Gaulle who had become, in a way, the symbol of resistance, with the Resistance at his back; Giraud, the puppet of the Americans, rather stupid, rather reactionary. Monnet's job was to reconcile them, but he very soon came to the conclusion that what would really have to happen was that de Gaulle would have to rule the roost, and finally that is indeed the way it worked out. But I think it would have happened anyway, whether Monnet had been there or not, because de Gaulle could outsmart anyone in that room.

One link that Monnet made at that time, in North Africa in 1943, was with Harold Macmillan, who was also there as British Resident in Algiers, and Macmillan records, in his autobiography, long conversations that he had with Monnet at the Roman ruins at Tipasa, outside Algiers, with the smell of the wild thyme and these old rocks and going bathing together and talking about the future, and I think that maybe one of the reasons why Macmillan, of all the British politicians, was one of the first to try to bring Britain into the Community.

Monnet, at that time as always, was thinking about the future. He gave, around this time, an interview to John Davenport of *Life* magazine, in which he talked about the future, or the successor, of the League of Nations, and he said 'Well, it is only going to be a switchboard through which nations communicate with each other. It will not be a body with real power and something else will be needed to create the sort of international institutions and rules that we really seek'. In fact, he wrote a number of memoranda, at that time, together with Rene Mayer, who was later another French Premier and also Monnet's successor as President of the High Authority of the Coal and Steel Community. He was thinking, in other words, about the future of Europe and about the way in which one could deal with the German problem and the British problem and make something out of these disparate warring nations, which were in deep civil war. He was sent off by the French Provisional Government to make some more deals in the United States to raise money and get help for the reconstruction of France, and it happened – I think it was at Washington airport – that he talked with de Gaulle about post-war reconstruction. It was then that he proposed to de Gaulle the Modernisation Plan, the Modernisation Plan with which he was chiefly associated with people's minds immediately after the war. The Plan was not a prescriptive plan; it was indicative planning. It was an attempt to bring together, in a way that the NEDC later tried to do in Britain, three groups of people, who did not normally talk on a regular basis: i) the employers, ii) the trade unions and iii) the Government, or the Civil Service; to bring them together to try to agree on targets for production in France after the War. Monnet said to de Gaulle: 'You're always talking about grandeur, but there's no grandeur, no greatness, without sufficient resources. In the past France has been a country of Malthusianism, a country with a restrictive, unimaginative, protected economy; and we have to make it expand. We have to make it modernise itself; we have to bring it into the twentieth century'. That was what the Modernisation Plan was intended to do.

Monnet set it up with a very small staff in the Rue Martignac, where it still is, in just an ordinary, rather large private house. It was extremely effective in those days: it braced the French to face the future. It also made Monnet even more aware that you could not build a future for France alone; you had to deal with the economic future of Europe. How otherwise would you deal with German competition? How otherwise would you have a big enough home market on which to base industries of world size? I think that the experience of the Plan was one of the reasons that led Monnet to go further in his thoughts about economic unity among more than two European countries.

In 1949, in what looks, in a way, like a replay of his attempt to unite the British and the French politically, he had the idea that the British and the French should make joint planning arrangements. He was the head of the French Plan; the British had a planning authority under Sir Stafford Cripps, which was headed by Edwin Plowden, now Lord Plowden, and Monnet proposed, through Petsche, the Finance Minister, to Stafford Cripps that there should be a joint planning set-up. The two systems of planning were not really compatible but it would have made a lot of sense for the British and the French to put their ideas together. Well, three people came out to see Monnet at his house in Houjarray, about forty minutes drive, outside Paris – an old farmhouse looking over the fields towards Rambouillet. The three people were Plowden himself, Robert Hall and Hitchman. Monnet had with him Etienne Hirsch, who was his deputy at the Plan, and Pierre Uri, who was Monnet's chief economic guru. They sat down together to discuss the idea which Stafford Cripps had very enthusiastically endorsed, in fact – this joint planning idea. But the discussions were extremely nugatory – even Plowden admits as much in his memoirs – and they were nugatory because there was a typical clash of a French view of things, which was a view of structures and objectives, and a British view of things, which was about facts and immediate needs. The British thought that Monnet was proposing that British coal should be swapped for French meat, and the Monnet side, Hirsch, Uri and Monnet himself, thought the British were not interested in any long-term arrangement but only in some sort of *ad hoc* thing. During the conversation, Uri raised the point: 'What do you propose to do about Germany? How do you propose to face the competition from Germany?' and the British did not really have an answer to that because – I think – they did not yet regard the Germans as a serious economic rival.

So that attempt to do something with the British immediately after the War in 1949 fell to the ground, as the 1940 attempt had fallen to the ground. This time, probably, it was the fault of the British, whereas previously it had been the fault of the French; and some people believe – I am not sure I do – that this was the point at which Monnet thought 'Well, we can't do anything with the British; we'll have to do something with the Germans themselves. We'll have to start making Europe with Germany, rather than making it with the apparently easier neighbour, Britain'.

Germany had always been a subject of discussion in the Monnet family. Monnet's father was afraid of Germany; he was almost anti-German, and that was quite natural after three wars had divided the Germans and the French. Monnet, on the other hand, was very conscious of Germany; very conscious that the only way to deal with Germany was by, as it were, taming her. The Nazi regime had been destroyed; there was still a lot of anti-French feeling in Germany, which, for example, Robert Schuman experienced when he went there on his first post-war trip as Foreign Minister – a very chilly reception from the press – and the French, of course, were sick of the sight of field-grey uniforms, Nazi helmets and SS flashes, and they had seen quite enough of the occupying power in their own streets. So it was still a very difficult time: it was only five years after the end of the war; and the idea of doing something immediately with the Germans, on a basis of equality rather than repression, was quite novel.

Monnet had the idea of taking two particular industries, coal and steel, where the French and the German resources matched each other, and where you could build something together in a concrete way as a basis for further developments. This really was the genesis of the Schuman plan. It could have been the Bidault plan, because Monnet first of all tried to get George Bidault, the Prime Minister, to accept it, but Bidault, unfortunately, put it in a drawer or left it on the end of his desk without reading it. Monnet was getting a little impatient about this and so he talked with Bernard Clappier, later Governor of the Bank of France, who was at the time the *chef de cabinet* to the Foreign Minister, Robert Schuman. Clappier was very impressed by the idea of a coal and steel pool, and he said 'I'll take it to Schuman. He's going off to his country house at Sey-Chazelles this weekend, but if he reads it over the weekend we'll see what can be done.' And he did. When Schuman came back on Monday morning, Clappier met him at the station, and Schuman said something like: 'I agree, I'll make it my business to do it. That's all right. Tell Monnet.' Cleppier came to tell Monnet, and Monnet was of course delighted. But then Bidault heard about this and was very cross. 'Why have you been doing something with my Foreign Minister when you haven't mentioned it to me?' 'But I have mentioned it to you,' said Monnet, 'you have the paper and there it is.' And so it became the Schuman Plan. Schuman added a little preamble to it, and on the 9 May 1950 at the Quai D'Orsay in the Salon de l'Horloge, Schuman made the proposal public to the press, at about four o'clock in the afternoon, in time for the morning papers, and there was great surprise everywhere. There was no surprise in Germany because Adenauer had been tipped off by a special emissary, whose role was only very recently brought to light; but there was great surprise in Britain because the British Foreign Secretary, Ernest Bevin, had not heard about this, although Dean Acheson, the American Secretary of State, passing through Paris by chance on his way to London to a four-power conference, had heard about it because he had been told by Monnet. When Acheson arrived in London, there was Bevin saying 'What's all this in the papers about this coal and steel thing? You know, this Franco-German proposal. Do you know anything about it?' and Acheson did not dare say that he had heard about it. This is all in Acheson's two separate volumes of memoirs, described more eloquently in the first and less formal volume. But Bevin was quite cross about that; he thought he had been outwitted; he thought the Americans were in the plot and so on. It wasn't true – but that may just possibly have been one of the contributory factors in the British not joining the Coal and Steel Community.

However, one of Monnet's first stops, after the acceptance of the Schuman plan, was to London to try to sell it to the British. The British once again, as with Plowden and the economic planning discussions, wanted to know the answers to a whole series of very specific questions which Monnet was naturally unable to answer. He could only talk about the general principles. But one principle on which he insisted was that the British should agree that there should be a supranational element in this new Community, called the High Authority, which had been proposed in the Schuman declaration; that it should be above

Governments, that it should, essentially, be rather like the International Ruhr Authority, but on a bigger scale.

The British did not like that proposal at all and a long succession of telegrams was exchanged between London and Paris, in which the French, i.e. Monnet, tried hard to explain that you did not necessarily have to accept this definitively: all you had to do was accept it as a basis for negotiation, and then if the resultant treaty were not to your liking you did not have to sign it. This was a point that the Dutch had already accepted because they too had some suspicion of this unknown, strange body, the High Authority. But again, the British would not buy that, and although some people, such as Kenneth Younger and Edward Heath and one or two others in Britain were willing to go further, the British did not join the Coal and Steel Community at the outset. Monnet, once again, tried hard to have very close relations with the British on the Coal and Steel Community. He was appointed President of the High Authority, and the first people to accredit a delegation to the Coal and Steel Community were, in fact, the British, followed on the second day by the Americans. The British also made an association agreement with the Community in 1954, but Monnet saw this agreement as the first step towards membership. It was not: in fact, the British did something very soon after the ratification of the association agreement which was actually against the agreement, without consulting the High Authority. Nevertheless, there they were associated with the community, and Sir Cecil Weir, who was the Head of the British Delegation in Luxemburg got on very well with Monnet. Weir was a Scottish industrialist, and some time later on Monnet went to stay with Weir in his Scottish estate, and noted in a diary, which he very, very seldom kept, 'I nearly caught a salmon'. So there was a friendly relationship between Monnet and the delegation, and, in fact, one of its most intelligent members, Derek Ezra, later head of the Coal Board and now Lord Ezra, had immense affection, admiration and liking for Monnet. So again, on a personal level, relations with the British were very good.

Monnet wanted the British to join the Common Market when that was set up. He was disappointed that they had not joined the European Defence Community, which he proposed, and many people, including the Belgian Statesman Paul-Henri Spaak, believed that the absence of the British from the EDC was one of the reasons why it failed. I am not sure that is true myself; Monnet himself believed that it failed because he did not pay enough attention to it and he left it all to the French Foreign Office and Herve Alphand to negotiate, and that if he had really put his back behind it, it could have succeeded. But when it failed in the French Assembly in 1954, Monnet was quite discouraged. He was never totally disappointed in anything, but he had not been very well that summer and he decided that he had better resign from the High Authority in order to devote his efforts to corraling the French back into a European frame of mind, and pursuing further efforts towards European integration. I remember seeing the people in Luxemburg shortly after the EDC failure and they were like the advance guard of an army that had been defeated in the rear; there they were stuck out on a limb and very much afraid that their pioneering efforts were just going to go by the board, especially when Monnet decided to resign. However, Monnet resigned and he spent a lot of time travelling around, talking to various people, and he actually proposed – many people think it was a Benelux proposal, it wasn't: it was a Monnet proposal – the Common Market. When Spaak produced the Benelux paper which led to the Messina meeting, he sent a copy of it to Monnet with a note saying, 'Voici votre bebe'. In other words it was Monnet's baby, even if the actual midwifery had taken place up in Brussels and the Hague.

Anyway, Monnet was very pleased about this, and when the Messina meeting produced its agreement on negotiating for a Common Market in Euratom, he even tried to retract his resignation from the Coal and Steel Community, but he did not succeed, and he passed on and cast about as to what he should do. Somebody suggested that he should sit for the French Parliament, but that was not a very good idea. (That was actually suggested by a colleague of mine, Francois Duchene, a fellow Englishman who was working with Monnet). But Monnet finally set up his action committee for the United States of Europe, which was a kind of official pressure group, composed of all the non-communist and non-Gaullist political parties and trade unions of the original Community six. This continually pressed for British membership of the Community. Monnet was always keen to have the British in and he was even fairly enthusiastic – at first – about the British proposal of a free trade area around the Community, although he did not see it as anything but a step towards membership. When the British finally did propose membership in 1961, Monnet worked consistently behind the scenes to try to solve problems; and when de Gaulle finally broke off negotiations because they had gone on too long and he had freed his hands in Algeria, and was therefore free to concentrate once again on Europe, Monnet was very unhappy about that.

In the first week after this he came over to Brussels, and we were talking together – and I said 'C'est deprimant'. And he said 'Non, C'est attristant'. Then he went on to see what could be done next.

He even proposed, with Ted Heath, the idea that there should be some deal on the British and French nuclear forces. He was quite close to Ted Heath; he liked Ted Heath very much and Ted, I know, admired him. But that plan did not work. It obviously would not have washed with de Gaulle anyway, even if the British had been able to get it through Parliament, and so came this long ten-year period when the British were out. But when the new negotiations began, again Monnet was very assiduous in trying to solve difficulties and make friends with people. He was very close to the chief Commission negotiator, Jean-Francois Deniau, who is an old friend of mine, and there is no doubt at all that until the British joined Monnet was very, very intent on bringing them.

Now whether he would have been disappointed by the British apparent lack of enthusiasm for Europe I think is a very moot point. He was very pleased with the result of the 1975 referendum. After that had happened, he and I had a celebratory lunch together at Prunier, in Paris, and a long talk about things. He was very pleased that the British had finally cast their lot in fully with the Community and had shown it by a majority of seventy per cent or more, in the referendum. We discussed various things: he talked about his memoirs, he talked about the early days when there was so much discussion of supranationality and the High Authority; and he said one thing that was quite striking. 'We were wrong in those early days to talk about a power above nations, the High Authority, as a supranational power. What eventually emerged, even in the Coal and Steel Community days, was a dialogue between the independent body, which was the High Authority, and the Ministers representing the Nation States.' It was that dialogue that Monnet believed to be the motor of integration, and he said that we were wrong in those early days because we had a very simplistic view of the way things would work. I personally think it was a military view. We had been used, in the War, to command structures rather than democratic structures; we had been used to solving problems in post-war Europe through UNRRA and things like that – you know, men in khaki shirts and epaulets, supplying food and fitting stand-pipes for the populace in the ruined cities. And when Monnet made the original Schuman plan, he was reacting against the impotence of the Council of Europe, and the veto, and the weakness of OEEC. The Council of Europe, which had been a real disappointment to anyone who seriously wanted a politically united Europe – was little more than a talking shop and the OEEC, with its committee of ministers – had spent some of the time dragging its feet and indeed later, under British guidance, trying even to stop the Common Market coming about. So the original Schuman proposal did not include either an Assembly or a Council of Ministers; it proposed only the High Authority and some system of arbitration, i.e. the European Court. It was the Dutch who produced the Assembly; they said 'We've got to have a democratic system'; and it was everybody, all the Ministers, who said that there must be a Council of Ministers. But in the Schuman treaty it was described as the *Special* Council of Ministers and its duty was to coordinate National Policy with the policies of the High Authority. A very strange model: that already assumed that there was something called the High Authority which had policies and that somehow the member states had got to coordinate their policies with a preexisting supranational one.

Well that was wrong, obviously wrong, and Monnet recognised that, and I think it is a measure of his pragmatism that he was prepared to say that quite happily, even after the British had triumphantly won their referendum.

Everybody always asks: 'What would Monnet do now? What would he propose now?' and I have ventured into print sometimes on this subject. I think it is very hard to tell; I think he would be quite pleased that John Major has decided to be at the centre of Europe and, while having to face a lot of Euro-scepticism, has decided to stay in the ERM. I think he would be quite pleased that Mrs Thatcher's view of Europe has been largely discredited, even among some of her supporters. But one can only speculate about what Monnet might say. The nearest I can get to evidence on the subject is a conversation I had with him for the BBC, and therefore in English, on one occasion after de Gaulle had died. I said to him 'Do you think de Gaulle helped matters, or hindered matters?'. There was a terribly long pause – about thirty seconds, which is a very long time when you've got a tape running – and then he said: 'I think both. Some people may think he delayed matters – maybe he did – but at the same time, because he was a great speaker, he was able to convince people that Europe was important, and it takes time to make people aware and he helped in that'.

Well, you might say the same, perhaps, about Mrs Thatcher, but I don't know whether Monnet would say it. Monnet was, in a sense, ambivalent about de Gaulle. I remember once going into his room in Houjarrey when de Gaulle had just been making some really rather extreme speech, and Monnet said 'Il est fou. Il est fou.' But when de Gaulle died, it happened that it was on November which was actually Monnet's birthday, and I said 'What a wonderful birthday present!' and Monnet looked absolutely furious, his face contorted with pain and rage, and it was clear he regarded this as a remark in the worst possible taste – as it was. Another coincidence, though, about Monnet's birthday is that it was also the day when the Berlin Wall fell, so 9 November is a day I think we ought to celebrate, perhaps even more than 9 May: the birthday of Monnet, the death of de Gaulle, the end of the Berlin Wall – I don't know when Mrs Thatcher left office, the eleventh or nineteenth? Anyway, November seems an important month for Europe.

Monnet's view of Europe was not *L'Europe des etats*, as de Gaulle envisaged it. A Europe of the states would not have institutions or common rules; and Monnet always insisted that it is necessary to have institutions and rules in order to ensure that the present temporary situation – the good guys you have around the table now – continues, even when you have lukewarm successors. Because human experience lasts only as long as the human being, unless it is embodied in traditions, institutions, laws and so on. I think that the same would apply, to some extent, to the idea of a looser, broader community. To have a looser community around the community makes sense, but to think that you can somehow enlarge the community almost *ad infinitum*, maybe to twenty-four members, without its being changed thereby, I think is an error. You know, two's company, three's a crowd. Twenty-four is a mob and it takes too long to take decisions. You have got to do something else. Monnet's objectives in the Community – I have always thought – could be summed up under four headings:

i) (Which we have achieved) Franco-German reconciliation. Peace in Western Europe.
ii) The prevention of trade war or destructive economic rivalry and protectionism. (Which we have more or less got rid of, though it is a continual struggle to keep the markets open and so on).
iii) (Is, and remains) The creation of an entity in Europe which is as powerful as the United States but friendly to it, unlike the former Soviet Union.
iv) The introduction into international affairs of some modicum of law and order. (Which the United Nations still seems largely incapable of doing).

Now we are not very far along that road, but at least we have transformed relations between the members of the European Community. The Community has not been able to produce a peacekeeping force, although we see immense challenges on our borders and in the Middle East, which an agile united Europe could do much more to meet. Unfortunately we have not got the structure yet to do that, and it would take a long time a) to create the structure and b) to get the structure to operate, because it would have to be with the agreement of a lot of individual states and so on. It is very, very difficult to deal with big political masses when you are a sort of half-built house, and Europe is still only a half-built house.

But I think that Monnet would be very much concerned that Europe should act as a pacifier in Yugoslavia and that Europe should hasten its own development in order to be able to take on gradually the other countries of Western Europe – mostly the EFTA countries – and finally those countries of Eastern Europe that feel that they can face the competition. But, if you are going to do that, you are going to get a big community and then you have got to find procedures of decision-making which are more rapid than the ones we have now, which are very slow even in economic matters, let alone when you try and decide whether you are going to recognise Croatia or put a force into Sarajevo or whatever. I do not think Monnet would fully endorse the simplistic line that the more there are the worse it will be and therefore the tighter the institutions have got to be. We have got to be more imaginative than simply saying: 'All right, give the power to the Commission' or 'Have more majority voting'. It is not just that; you have got to find procedures whereby you maybe have some countries doing certain things and some not, because if we have a Defence Community again, the Irish will be very doubtful about being members of it. So will, if they join, the Swedes and the Swiss, so one may have to indulge in variable geometry, although that, to Brussels purists, of whom Walter Hallstein was one, looks like the dissolution or disintegration of the Community. I am not sure that it is; I think that it may be the only way forward. Even if all the member states at length come into line, there is variable geometry on a chronological basis. And of course there are association agreements. Turkey is an associate member. Greece was for a long time. We have association agreements with others. We have a special preference agreement with Romania. There are a number of formulae; it does not have to be neat, and that is why I started by saying that Monnet was never a great systematiser, he believed in solving practical problems, but with always a little push, a little opening towards the future. He saw the Community as a process, not as a product, not as something which is finite, which you make and that is it. Whereas the Council of Europe, the OECD as it now is, these are things that were made and they stay largely the way they are. The Community is always evolving, and that is why the Euro-sceptics are so scared, because they do not like being on a moving platform. It is like the departure hall at Dulles airport, Washington; you get into what appears to be a room and then it suddenly starts moving across the ground and it is, in fact, a kind of trolley, a transit system. The whole Community is a transit system. The destination we do not know. Nobody has ever defined it. It is not for us to do it, after all it is for our children and their children. You cannot lay down rules for the future. All you can do is solve the problems of the present in a way that does not preclude anything in the future. Andrew Shonfield said it all when he gave the Reith lectures way back: he called the series 'journey to an unknown destination'. And that, of course, perfectly describes the human condition.

References

Salter James Arthur, (1933), *United States of Europe and other Papers*, edited with notes by W. Arnold-Forster, London Allen & Unwin.

Weiss Louise (1978), *Memoires d'une Europeenne*, edition definitive, Paris, Albin Michel.

3

The Second World War and British culture

Kenneth O. Morgan

The main problem of the history of Britain since 1945 is that it is generally seen as post-war history. The images of the wartime experience of 1939–45 remain powerful in the national psyche down to the 1990s, and in a way and to a degree that is characteristic of no other country. In the recent past, a series of episodes have reinforced the point. There has been the intense attention focusing on successive volumes of Martin Gilbert's official biography of Winston Churchill. There was the publishing explosion in 1989 to commemorate the fiftieth anniversary of the outbreak of war. In a late flurry in the summer of 1992, there was fierce controversy over the Queen Mother's unveiling a statue in London to Air Chief Marshal 'Bomber' Harris, the head of Bomber Command and architect of the notorious bombing onslaught on Dresden.

None of this need arouse surprise or cynicism. It is not surprising that the success of British arms during the war years, with episodes like the Battle of Britain, the battle of El Alamein, the storming of the Normandy beaches or the marches of the 'Chindits' in Burma should be a source of intense national fascination and pride. To the overwhelming majority of the British people, the war against Nazism and fascism was a good war, fought to defend democratic values against the menace of totalitarianism (Watt, 1989, p.623). The fact that war casualties, although totalling over 360,000 killed in all (including civilian victims of bombing raids), fell far short of the 750,000 in 1914–18 added to national satisfaction.

What is, however, more surprising, and certainly worthy of historical examination, is that memories of the war should linger so long in the national consciousness. Of the other victorious Allies, the United States has long relegated the Second World War to a remote place in the national pantheon, years before Korea and more especially Vietnam. Franklin D. Roosevelt is recalled for the New Deal, not as a war leader. France also appears largely to have relinquished moral and emotional contact with the same ambiguous victory in 1945 (after all, there was always Vichy to recall, too), at least since the departure of de Gaulle in 1969. In any case, the de Gaulle of the sixties was identified primarily with the modernization and social advance of the post-war period, whereas the Churchill myth in Britain symbolized ancient memories of imperial greatness. The so-called 'British disease' of which much used to be heard, has been linked with a variety of themes from public-school homosexuality to compulsory Latin. But one component, it may be argued, has been a continuing obsession with the increasingly distant events of 1939–45, an emotional obstacle which in many ways has been damaging to the attempts of an ageing post-imperial nation to adjust to the challenges of the contemporary world.

The contrast with the Great War of 1914–18 could not be more marked. That tragic experience also lasted long in the public memory. For instance, the idea of the 'missing generation' of young men, lost on the fields of Flanders or in the mud of the trenches, cast its shadow over the subsequent generation. It played some part in shaping the 'appeasement' of Hitler and Mussolini in the 1930s. The critics of the war and 'the system of Versailles' that followed it, encouraged a belief that there should henceforth be peace at all costs. That old dissenter, A.J.P. Taylor, famously and controversially pronounced that Munich in 1938 was a 'triumph for all that was best and most enlightened in British life' (Taylor, 1964, p.235).

But this underlines the essential feature of popular recollection of the First World War – that by the 1930s it was widely regarded with distaste, even abhorrence. The religiosity surrounding the erection of Lutyens' cenotaph in Whitehall was not robust in quality. The war poets and pacifist writers like Wilfred Owen and Siegfried Sassoon built up an image of meaningless violence which had sacrificed in vain the lives of an entire generation across Europe. Generals like French and Haig were popular whipping-boys years before Joan Littlewood's 'Oh! What a Lovely War' derided them anew in the 1960s. John Maynard Keynes, in perhaps the most influential anti-war tract of the century, *The Economic Consequences of the Peace* (1919), depicted the war as marked by lust for revenge and a Carthaginian peace. It was the origin of a punitive and utterly impractical economic settlement, based on reparations, which created mass unemployment, monetary instability and industrial stagnation (Skidelsky, 1983, pp.384–400).

Similarly, the First World War leaders of 1914–18 were derided and disregarded. Lloyd George, 'the man who won the war' in 1918 and leader of the post-war coalition for four years thereafter, was perhaps the supreme casualty. He paid for his war glory with twenty years in the political wilderness, waiting for a call that never came. False hopes kindled in 1918 of 'a land fit for heroes' were set against the actual record of class conflict, economic decline and diminished national self-esteem (K.O. Morgan, 1979, pp.7–9). Keynes attacked him as the major architect of a disastrous reparations settlement. Winston Churchill too, until his unexpected rehabilitation from 1938, was also something of a suspect figure for much of the inter-war years, tarred with memories of the failure at the Dardanelles. The mighty Kitchener became 'the magnificent poster' of Lloyd George's satire. The new heroes after 1918 were men like Ramsay MacDonald, critics of the government during the war, and the very embodiment of 'brave new world' utopianism and the dream of a new international order. Academics like Sir Alfred Zimmern, holder of the Woodrow Wilson Chair of International Politics at Aberystwyth, and Gilbert Murray at Oxford – both of them apostles of the civic imperatives of the Greek Commonwealth – became fashionable exponents of the ideals of the League of Nations Union, the politically correct cult of the post-war world.

The second world war, however, has been quite different over the past forty-eight years. There was no 'goodbye to all that' this time around. To almost the entire population it has been an immediately accessible source of national pride. The images conjured up by the Battle of Britain pilots or the 'desert rats' of the Eighth Army are very different from those of the trenches on the western front. No 'Old Bill' emerged this time, to advise his equally stoical companion that if he knew of 'a better 'ole' he should go to it. Alexander or Mountbatten were never controversial in the manner of Haig or Jellicoe. Montgomery, undoubtedly a figure who aroused political and personal controversy, was nevertheless hailed as the nation's most authentic military genius since the Duke of Wellington. While there was, of course, anti-war writing of an identifiable kind during the war years, notably in Cyril Connolly's brilliantly iconoclastic magazine *Horizon*, there was no significant school of war poets this time, and certainly no sustained literary critique of the war or its purported objectives (Fussell, 1989, pp.209–22). Eliot's final 'Quartets' use the war to celebrate historic Englishness. Even some deliberately reactionary wartime writing has served to confirm the popular image of the war years as a period of egalitarianism and solidarity. It is instructive that perhaps the most notable wartime novel is Evelyn Waugh's upper-class 'fantasy of not-war', *Brideshead Revisited* (Fussell, 1989, p.223).

During the war years, British artists were in the main associated with promoting images of social patriotism and civic virtue: Kenneth Clark's War Artists' Advisory Committee was particularly active in this respect. Thus Henry Moore's remarkable sketches of London life during the blitz conveyed the idea of human solidarity and communal sharing. John Piper's sketches and watercolours celebrated the ageless charm of the British landscape, churches and country houses. Music, too, was in general enlisted to promote the patriotic cause, from Dame Myra Hess's famous recitals in the National Gallery to the schmalz of Vera Lynn's ballad of the White Cliffs of Dover. John Barbirolli returned from the United States at the height of the war in 1943 to conduct the Halle, while William Walton wrote patriotic music for the Ministry of Information and film themes along the lines of the 'first of the few'. Much more unusual was the pacifism of two composers, Benjamin Britten and Michael Tippett. The latter served three months in prison as a conscientious objector; his emotions were movingly expressed in 'A Child of our Time'. In general, though, artists conveyed an uncomplicated sense of national celebration, with cultural no less than political implications, and with few dissenters at any point along the political spectrum. There was simply no 1939 equivalent of the dissenting pressure-group, the Union of Democratic Control, or the Bloomsbury intellectuals, calling for an alternative foreign policy and a negotiated peace.

Even in the 1990s, there was credit to be derived from a distant association with the Second World War. The BBC still preserved, notably in its world service, something of the cachet derived from its being a unique source of free information during the war. In the shaky ranks of the royal family, the Queen Mother retained a unique affection as a long-time heroine of the London blitz, who had suffered amongst her people during the war, even if it partly took the form of eating spam from a gold plate. The 'heritage' industry in the 1980s was quick to recapture images and themes from the war years (Biggin Hill airfield, for example) as part of Britain's seamless tradition of greatness.

In the 1990s, indeed, the war lingers on in many aspects of national culture.

This is, however, largely an English phenomenon. The Scots have not evoked the memory of the war in their literary or artistic traditions; Edwin Muir's 'Scotland 1941' ignored the war completely. The Welsh exemplify this in equal measure. A rare exception was the distinguished Bangor poet, Alun Llewelyn-Williams. He was himself seriously injured during war service; he later observed that the war gave him 'a direct experience of human folly of which I had previously been a passive observer' (Evans, 1991, p.38). His volumes of poetry, *Cerddi*, laid emphasis on the part played by the war in heightening his literary sensibility. But, in general, the war passed most Welsh poets and prose writers by. Perhaps the more nationalist of them were embarrassed by the controversial neutrality of Saunders Lewis, president of Plaid Cymru, during the war years, in which his writings were accused of showing some evidence of anti-semitism and social corporatist forms of fascism (Davies, 1983, pp.236–7).

Amongst the British in general, the cinema was a unique form of war celebration. Angus Calder has shown how the Blitz, for example, became a source of much cinematic innovation at the time (Calder, 1991, pp.228–50). From the 1950s onwards, notable war themes formed the substance of films like *Bridge over the River Kwai*, the *Dambusters* and the *Wooden Horse*. Subsequently given frequent showings on television (where they proved to be particularly popular at holiday seasons such as Christmas) they prolonged the mystique of clean-cut, upper-class Battle of Britain pilots as played by English actors like Kenneth More or Anthony Steel, or cheerful, tolerant and vaguely classless servicemen in the North African desert, the merchant navy or the airborne landings at Arnhem. The fact that Spitfire pilots, for instance, included many Australians, Czechs or Poles was ignored. They also played their part in spreading a pervasive stereotype of the German as the obvious national enemy, an aspect taken up with enthusiasm by 'skinhead' football supporters and other harbingers of casual violence. A different aspect of wartime was the theme of separation and personal dislocation picked up in *Brief Encounter*, another immensely successful picture, frequently re-shown. In some sense, this kind of patriotic offering could be linked with the imperial nostalgia which animated films like *Zulu* or *Lawrence of Arabia* in the 1950s and 1960s. But the latter clearly related to a lost, fantasy world, whereas the war films embodied political and emotional realities easily identified by the average patriotic middle- or working-class filmgoer.

In the 1970s and 1980s, television, particularly the BBC, added powerfully to the mystique of the war. Sometimes the message was dramatic (as in *Tenko*, a saga of Changi prison camp in Singapore), sometimes humorous. But they all added to the pervasive nostalgic mood. In which other country in modern times, one wonders, would programmes such as *Dad's Army* and, far more egregious, *'Allo, 'Allo*, with its ageless stereotypes of humourless Germans and foolish French, be so popular? The image was perpetuated of continentals as unreliable or simply comic. Again, the Germans emerged as the natural enemies. Sport, ever a source of nationalist hysteria, added to the impact. The most famous football match in English history, the world cup victory in London in 1966, had an extra savour because it was the (West) Germans, once again, who were defeated, and in extra time, to add to the impact. Terrace hooligans in subsequent international matches would chant nationalist slogans proclaiming victories in 'two world wars and one world cup'. These war images, moreover, were both durable and usable. The cultural protest of the so-called 'angry young men' of the 1950s, the doctrine of sexual and personal 'permissiveness' in the 1960s were in their different ways transient or negative. Each left a powerful public reaction in their wake. By contrast, the war legacy conveyed a solid and permanent image of what it meant to be British, or rather English, in terms of an enduring and ageless national pride.

To what degree has this continuing impact of the Second World War impinged on public policy in Britain over the past forty-odd years? In terms of domestic policy, the impact appears to have been relatively transient at first glance. The mood of wartime collectivism and social citizenship, hailed in the *Daily Mirror* and J. B. Priestley's broadcasts and endorsed by the voters massively in 1945, did not last long. It was much weakened by the economic and financial crisis of 1947 which undermined confidence in the imperatives of wartime physical planning. (Cairncross, 1985, pp.121–64). It was already in retreat in the last phase of the Attlee government with its policy of 'decontrol'; it largely disappeared with the Conservative election victory in 1951 with its emphasis on 'setting the people free'. It was noticeable that J.B. Priestley, so powerful an advocate of a folksy socialist/ populism in 1945 was much less effective in the election of 1950. *Picture Post*, another powerful voice for wartime planning, was by this time losing its *élan* as its proprietor, Edward Hulton, drifted to the right; later in the 1950s it went out of business altogether. A literature of protest against immediate post-war assumptions and the doctrines of controls and austerity began to emerge, for instance in the writing of Angus Wilson.

Yet the social landmarks of the war years continued to be revered decades after their passage. This especially applied to the 1942 Beveridge Report, which continued to serve as the intellectual foundation of welfare policy until its insurance provisions were substantially modified by Barbara Castle's scheme of 1976 which introduced the new principle of an earnings-related pension for some twelve million people (Castle, 1980, pp.751–52). The 1944 White Paper on Employment, perhaps less deservedly so, given its hesitant introduction, also enjoyed continued reverence as the epitome of applied Keynesianism and the basis of the post-war corporate partnership between unions and government (Middlemas, 1986, pp.68–70).

A major point here is that there appeared to be continuity between wartime Britain and the policies of the Attlee Labour government that followed on from 1945. This gave the impact of the war years much more strength and solidity across the political spectrum. There is a profound contrast, again, between the effect of the first and the second world wars upon the British psyche. After 1918 the Lloyd George government was widely identified with betraying wartime pledges about creating a land fit for heroes and a better and more durable international order. The years following the armistice in November 1918 were linked in popular memory with mass unemployment, severe deflation and the Geddes Axe. Conversely, the years after May 1945 were identified with a contractual form of social reconstruction that endured for at least a quarter of a century. Full employment, economic growth and 'cradle to the grave' forms of welfare provision were the fruits of wartime innovation. Long after VE Day in 1945, the legends of social solidarity and common citizenship were linked variously with the

Blitz and wartime ideas of planning, even if writers like Angus Calder (Calder, 1991) and Geoffrey Pearson (Pearson, 1983, p.241) have taught us that the reality was somewhat different.

The continuity with wartime change was, naturally, most strongly evident in the policies of the Attlee government from 1945–51. After all, apart from ideological considerations, Attlee, Bevin, Morrison, Dalton and others had been significant ministers on the home front during the so-called 'People's War'. But the return of the Conservatives in 1951 brought no obvious change of mood or direction. Of course, Tory Prime Ministers down to October 1963, Churchill, Eden and Macmillan, were all strongly identified with central features of wartime policy and strategy. Churchill until 1955 showed himself anxious to retain his wartime reputation as a national figure devoted to social peace, a reputation powerful during the halcyon Liberal era of social reform before 1914, but long since muffled by memories (or myths) of Tonypandy and the general strike (Seldon, 1981, pp.29–30).

Sympathy with wartime social and economic policies was even more entrenched amongst civil service policy-makers in Whitehall. The years between 1939 and 1945 had become a hallowed period, unique in British history, for the public servant. Ideas of indicative planning, Keynesian demand management industrial regeneration and relocation and social welfare had been in the ascendant. After 1945, powerful administrative figures like Edwin Plowden, 'Otto' Clarke, Robert Hall and Alec Cairncross were on hand to take the message further. The course of policy took a variety of forms in the 1950s and 1960s, and was much buffeted by economic and foreign policy setbacks; but the gospel of wartime planning remained vigorously alive until at least the mid-1970s. It was in the late 1970s, in the aftermath of the IMF crisis of late 1976, that old Keynesians like Sir Bryan Hopkin and Sir Douglas Wass felt that the intellectual tide was beginning to turn against them (Hopkin, 1981, p.47). But not until the Thatcher years from 1979 was an open attack mounted on the legacy of 1945, somewhat erratically down to 1983, but with full rigour thereafter. One much-noted feature then was the revival of the ideas and reputation of the veteran Austrian economist and philosopher, Hayek, whose theories had been rebuffed by the Labour planners of the Gaitskell/ Jay/Durbin school in 1945 and whose name had featured in the 1945 election only as Attlee's scapegoat in response to Churchill's bogey figure of Harold Laski (H. Young, 1989, p.405). By the 1980s, Conservatives of Thatcherite persuasion identified the war, as Keith Joseph had boldly proclaimed in the early 1970s, with the encroachment of the state in economic management, with a stifling corporatism in labour relations, and with debilitating and culturally dependent welfare programmes which had given neo-socialists their opportunity during three decades of national decline.

In terms of narrow party politics, Conservatives to some degree continued to treasure the memories of the war years. Churchill's wartime legacy was still to some degree a usable one for the Tories after 1951. When the legacy seemed to be briefly threatened in 1952 with Butler's ROBOT scheme to float the pound, Eden and Cherwell evoked wartime memories of social cohesion to demonstrate to the Cabinet the dangers that deflation and rising unemployment would pose to social harmony. In the choice of a Prime Minister in January 1957, a factor of some import in determining the views of key Conservatives was that Butler was thought to have been equally unreliable over Suez and over appeasement of the dictators during his time at the Foreign Office in 1938–40. Macmillan, on the other hand, as Minister-Resident in North Africa was widely believed to have had a good war (the revelations of Count Nikolai Tolstoy still lay far in the future!). As Prime Minister, Macmillan made some effort to trade on his wartime relationship with Eisenhower in North Africa, though with no great success. In October 1963, another period of extreme uncertainty in the Conservative leadership, the same doubts continued to be harboured over Butler, whereas in the case of Lord Home (who as Lord Dunglass had actually been Chamberlain's PPS at the time of Munich) his background apparently counted for less.

But the real citadel of wartime memories at home was not the Conservative Party, despite Churchill's long post-war eminence, nor the Liberals (despite memories of Beveridge and Keynes) but the Labour Party. More than any other party, Labour promoted the image of social patriotism of 'the people's war'. It was a victory won as much by Bevin, Morrison, Dalton and Attlee on the home front, as by Churchill in directing war strategy. This was the thrust of much Labour propaganda in the 1945 general election and was ratified by mass popular approval. This legacy straddled the Labour movement in general, from Shinwell on the left to Morrison on the right. It was particularly influential among trade unionists who took pride in their success in maintaining wartime production and public services. The message continued to retain its appeal amongst those of the wartime generation. It is perhaps best captured in the powerful, if sentimental, concluding sentences of *English History 1914–1945* by the Oxford historian, A.J.P. Taylor, following the mode of Priestley or Orwell. 'England had risen all the same' (Taylor, 1965, p.600).

Throughout the decades, Labour leaders continually turned to the memories of 1939–45 for their inspiration. In the mid-1950s, Gaitskell, Attlee's successor as party leader, along with Douglas Jay, who had served with him in the administrative policy machine during the war, looked back to the indicative planning of the kind carried on by the Board of Trade under Hugh Dalton (Jay, 1980, pp.113–22). This especially applied to the handling of the relocation of industry with much use of physical controls and industrial licences. Labour's Bad Godesburg-style revisionist programme of 1959 was really a fleshing out of the wartime emphasis on fiscal policy, controls and investment policies, given a new coherence by Tony Crosland's powerful work, *The Future of Socialism* (Brooke, 1992, pp.258–62). Nationalization, by contrast, was in visible retreat.

When Gaitskell unexpectedly died in January 1963, his successor Harold Wilson looked back with equal fervour to his own wartime experience – in this case, work for Beveridge on industrial and welfare policy in 1942–45. Wilson's emphasis on 'science', modernization and Labour's capturing the initiative during the 'white heat' of a new industrial revolution, was based above all on his own recollections of the application of science to the machinery of government during the war. He enlisted former wartime scientific aides such as Professor Patrick Blackett to give these notions more substance. Time and again, the wartime legacy was the basis for Labour's vision of social change at this time. Richard Crossman, a former Oxford Greats don, unexpectedly made shadow Minister of Science by Wilson, a political ally, frequently evoked memories of wartime. He told a Fabian gathering in November 1963 that between 1940 and 1945 Britain had been the best-governed country in the world, a claim by no means demonstrably untrue (A. Morgan, 1992, p.249).

An increasingly powerful Labour figure from 1964 onwards was James Callaghan. In April 1976 he was to succeed Wilson as Labour's Prime Minister. First elected to parliament in 1945, Callaghan drew special inspiration from the memories of social partnership during the war, together with the particular impact of naval experience in the Far East, in his own case. His messages to the public during his remarkably successful conduct of economic and social policy in 1977–78 were flavoured with the rhetoric of wartime of the 'Let's all pull through together' variety. Earlier, when accused of racial prejudice during his handling of immigration issues while Home Secretary in 1967–70, Callaghan was quick to respond with references to wartime naval service with black seamen. More than most Labour leaders, memories of the Second World War was an abiding point of reference for him.

Even in the 1980s, when the Conservatives were busy trampling on the legacy of 1945 during the heyday of Thatcherism, Labour continued to replay some of the old tunes. In the savage deputy-leadership contest of 1981, Denis Healey and Tony Benn, who agreed on little else, were as one in hailing anew the liberating social effects of the Second World War and the 'peaceful revolution' of 1945. After all, both of them had fought in that war themselves. Michael Foot, Labour's leader in 1980–83, was perhaps even more influenced by recollections of the social potential of the war years, along the lines of George Orwell's *Lion and the Unicorn* (1941). He flavoured speeches in the 1983 election with references to the war years; one, delivered in Oxford Town Hall which included a vigorous attack on Lord Hailsham, long ago the victor of the Oxford by-election in 1938, seemed to go down particularly well with historically-minded undergraduates, though other voters in 1983 were evidently less impressed.

Labour's love affair with the war appeared finally to come to its pre-destined end in October 1983 with the election as leader of Neil Kinnock, who had been a mere three years old when the war ended. Kinnock struck a bold note of modernization and revisionism which came fairly close to achieving electoral victory in the 1992 general election. Yet even the youthful Kinnock remained partly seduced by wartime and post-war memories. Labour and its leader were still most comfortable on decades-old (though still highly pertinent) themes such as the National Health Service, full employment, housing and education, and less at home when outlining economic and environmental fiscal proposals for the future.

The impact of the war, however, has been most continuous and powerful on the conduct of British overseas policy since 1945. The abiding impression of the war on the British people was that Britain remained still a major international power, one of the 'big three' at Potsdam whose forces had been heavily engaged from the Malayan jungle to the deserts of Africa. It exerted a particularly important influence in the Middle East after 1945, but remained significant also in the Far East and most of Africa, while for a time it appeared to be the supreme power in western Europe as well. Its world-wide role was reinforced by leadership of the sterling area and headship of a global multi-racial Commonwealth. This image of great power status survived for at least two decades after 1945.

The end of empire did not generate the kind of overwhelming strains in Great

Britain visible in France in the retreat from Indo-China or Algeria – nor, indeed, apparent in somewhat more subtle ways in the United States after failure in Vietnam. The withdrawal from India and Pakistan in 1947 produced little domestic strain in Britain; neither did the withdrawal from the Suez Canal base in 1954 (the calamitous Suez venture of 1956 notwithstanding). The disengagement from imperial rule in central Africa between the dissolution of the Central African Federation in early 1963 and the granting of independence for Rhodesia/Zimbabwe in 1979 was equally far from traumatic, and the withdrawal from Hong Kong in 1997 seems very likely to be the same. Apart from the aged Lord Beaverbrook and a small group of 'Suez rebels' in 1956–57, the *colon* mentality in Britain was not widespread. The civilized way in which the world-wide empire was dissolved relatively peaceably between 1945 and 1979 provoked national satisfaction and international congratulation.

What caused much more difficulty was the mystique of great power status which the war years inevitably reinforced. This was very slow to evaporate. The Attlee government after 1945 was deeply permeated by the sense of wartime partnership with the United States above all. This broad identity of outlook was axiomatic with Bevin at the War Office, through the formation of 'Bizonia' in western Germany in 1947 and the Berlin airlift to the founding of NATO in 1949. It reached its apogee with the ambassadorship of Sir Oliver Franks in Washington in 1948–52, when the essential need to prove that Britain was 'first in the queue' among the European powers led him to argue powerfully for British military involvement in Korea (K. O. Morgan, 1984, p.423). Franks's strong personal influence with both Attlee and Bevin (and his intellectual prestige in Washington) made him a unique voice for renewing the wartime Anglo-American alliance.

This broad policy of continuing the wartime alliance with the United States was the pivot of policy for all British governments down to that of Mrs Thatcher. One partial exception was that of Edward Heath in 1970–74 who was less instinctively sympathetic to the United States. Interestingly, he would invoke wartime memories of a different kind, such as Churchill's appeal to France for a confederal relationship in June 1940. For the rest, British administrations, Labour and Conservative, devoted their efforts to trying to underpin American attempts at 'summit diplomacy' down to the atomic test ban treaty of 1963 when Britain's presence at the conference was more obviously ceremonial. Wartime and post-war links with the United States were drawn on very heavily by the Labour governments of 1964–70 and 1974–79. This applied especially to the international outlook of James Callaghan, foreign secretary in 1974–76, whose essentially transatlantic viewpoint was founded on a close personal relationship with Henry Kissinger, the US Secretary of State. After his retirement as leader in 1980, Callaghan built up a warm friendship with ex-President Gerald Ford. In the 1980s, Mrs Thatcher, for all her proud statements of national sovereignty, also made much of the Anglo-American relationship in her close involvement with President Reagan. As noted, memories of 'Winston' were often enlisted.

Naturally the presumed 'special relationship' between Britain and the United States found its antecedents far beyond the outbreak of the Second World War and indeed were rooted in the very origins of the American colonies. But the memories of 1941–45 gave the relationship a substance it had previously lacked. For Britain, the war was seen as conferring anew a geopolitical eminence. It had also created the basis for a continuing financial and monetary eminence, associated with Keynes's role at Bretton Woods in 1944 and the protected role of sterling as a reserve currency. Bretton Woods was the monetary embodiment of the wartime Anglo-American partnership (Gardner, 1975, pp.202–29). Even after the ending of the Bretton Woods preconditions in the 1970s the wartime legacy continued to haunt many British politicians, especially on the Labour side. For instance, it led to some confusion for the Callaghan government, notably in discussions of the need to fund the sterling balances and to gain US assistance in this, at the time of the IMF loan discussions in the autumn of 1976 (Burk and Cairncross, 1991, pp.111–26).

Defence policy was also much shaped by Britain's vision of post-war eminence. In the period immediately after 1945, Britain appeared to be for a time the main instrument of western responses to presumed Soviet aggression, in the Iran crisis of 1945–46 and in a succession of instances in western Europe. As a result, the decision to proceed with an independent British atomic weapons programme in February 1947 was governed by the need to protect Britain's wartime great-power status (Hennessy, 1986, pp.131–3). Prestige as much as security considerations predominated, for instance in discussions over British defence needs at Bermuda in 1957 and in exchanges between Kennedy and Macmillan at Nassau in December 1962, following much British *angst* at the American failure to promote the Skybolt missile programme (K.O. Morgan, 1992, pp.216–17).

Wartime experience continued to promote an inflated view of British international significance and the military role that this dictated. The decision to withdraw from British military commitments east of Suez, long anticipated from the time of the Duncan Sandys defence white paper of 1957, did not finally take effect until 1969–71, while the subsequent decision to proceed with the enormously expensive Chevaline warhead in the 1970s and to renew the Trident programme in 1978–80 reflected the same misplaced sense of British international significance. Accelerating and inflated defence expenditure, for all the various crises of the British economy, were the response of successive British governments to a presumed wide-ranging international role founded on the wartime alliance with the United States.

Dissenting movements such as the Campaign for Nuclear Disarmament (CND) had to battle against this orthodoxy. Interestingly enough, CND did so by promoting a rival version of British post-war influence, an emphasis on moral and ideological leadership for non-aligned humanity. This was the outlook of the Nye Bevan of 1944–45 rather than the more bellicose Bevan of 1957 urging that Britain should remain in the nuclear alliance and not be left naked in the conference chamber, undefended and alone. In their totally opposite ways, Duncan Sandys and Bertrand Russell, the Ministry of Defence and the anti-nuclear dissenters, both took their stand on inflated views of British international authority.

But the most striking, and arguably the most damaging, of the post-1945 images related to British policy towards Europe. Of course, British fears of continental entanglements went back many centuries, with a variety of political, geographical and cultural elements intertwined. Famous dates in British history – 1588, 1688 and 1815 – reinforced the same message. But it can hardly be disputed that the triumphant record of the Second World War strengthened amongst the British people a powerful sense of detachment from continental Europe. Dunkirk, the Battle of Britain, the image of 'standing alone' and subsequently saving a stricken continent from itself went deep into British folk memories. It was widely assumed that the wartime experience had impelled Britain in a totally different direction from the defeated continental nations between 1940 and 1945. Historians might recall also that Lloyd George's attempts to involve Britain in continental Europe at the Cannes and Genoa conferences in 1922 had led directly to his subsequent downfall at the time of Chanak. Bonar Law had then powerfully argued against Britain's being 'the policeman of the world' and the message struck home (K.O. Morgan, 1979, p.329).

As a result, a pervasive view amongst politicians and foreign office advisers that the alliance with the Americans, the existence of the Commonwealth, and the detachment borne of wartime experience impelled Britain in a quite distinctive direction governed attitudes towards any form of European unity for decades to come. The Attlee government in 1950–51 was strongly opposed to involvement in the Schuman plan for coal and steel; only a few minor ministers such as Kenneth Younger took a dissenting view and they were easily overridden. (Young, 1984, pp.150–7). Bevin insisted that there was a world of difference between the functional view of 'Western Union' Britain had championed in the Brussels defence treaty of 1948 and over economic collaboration in OEEC, and the integration of 'Unity' – as, indeed, there was (Bullock, 1983, pp.615–17). After 1951, Churchill blankly refused to make anything of his opposition pledges on the need for a closer relationship with continental Europe. In 1953–55 he was far more active in breathing new warmth into his old wartime relationship with President Eisenhower. His successor, Eden, was if anything even more resistant to political involvement with Europe.

In 1955–57 there was immense Foreign Office scepticism of the Messina conference and the subsequent Treaty of Rome. Much of this was explicitly founded on recollections of the Second World War. It was argued that the war years confirmed the age-old animosity of Teuton and Frank, the political unreliability of Italy, the semi-fascism of the Flemish in Belgium and the marginality of the Dutch. At times, it seemed as if the Foreign Office believed that firm support for European integration was rooted only in the miniscule duchy of Luxemburg (K.O. Morgan, 1992, pp.135–6). The contempt of the diplomats and envoys was matched by that of the great British public. Changes in post-war mores in cuisine, clothing, entertainment, or design, the growing popularity of holidays in countries such as Spain, served only to make the gulf between the British and the continentals ever wider.

The tension over Europe, as is familiar to any student of British history over the past 30 years, lingered on powerfully. Macmillan himself was by no means as committed a European as later legend would have it. Half-American himself, his instincts were mid-Atlantic. Negotiations were forced upon his government through economic weakness and political isolation in 1961 and they failed, through de Gaulle's veto. Much the same was true of Wilson's negotiations with the EEC in 1967 where again the British were wary and anxious to stress their multiplicity of roles and loyalties. Labour, even more than the Conservatives, contained a large element of sceptics or opponents of European involvement. Douglas Jay, on the right of the party, placed some emphasis on the wartime record in denouncing any move to join the EEC – for instance through reference to Commonwealth support for a beleaguered Britain in 1940 (Jay, 1968, p.99).

Edward Heath, of course, took a totally different line and achieved the goal of British membership of the EEC on 1 January 1973. Even so, and despite the endorsement of membership in the referendum of May 1975, Britain remained a semi-detached member of the European Community through the 1970s and 1980s, down to the Maastricht treaty of December 1991, on a variety of political, economic and emotional grounds. In each instance, rooted historical or geographical objections were given new force by wartime memories. When Mrs Thatcher, herself a ferocious Euro-sceptic, denounced the centralizing tendencies of Jacques Delors and others as in her 1989 Bruges speech attacking European federalism, it was natural that she should refer to how the 'chimes of Big Ben' symbolized the essence of freedom for continentals during the war (Thatcher, 1988). As arguments intensified over membership of the European Regulatory Mechanism (to which Mrs Thatcher had been persuaded to agree), opposition to 'Europe' sometimes adopted a frankly anti-German tone, notably in opposition to the controlling power of the German Bundesbank and its interest-rate policy over the sovereignty of sterling. Some anti-German rhetoric by Nicholas Ridley, the Trade and Industry minister, in a magazine interview which included free reference to Hitler, led to the minister's resignation in July 1990.

In 1992 it was clear that the arguments over the appropriate British relationship with Europe were gaining in intensity. Europe had cost Mrs Thatcher five leading Cabinet ministers between 1986 and 1991 – Michael Heseltine and Leon Brittan (over Westland helicopters), Nicholas Ridley, Nigel Lawson and finally Geoffrey Howe. Heseltine and the last two were prime movers in her fall from power. Different postures over Maastricht posed a serious threat to Tory unity even after John Major's electoral victory in April 1992. This reached a dramatic climax in September 1992 when a sterling crisis saw Britain leave the ERM and, in effect, devalue the pound. A flood of anti-Bundesbank or simply anti-German rhetoric followed in Tory ranks, with free reference to Germany's long-term hostility to Britain throughout the century. Meanwhile Labour's defeat and the subsequent retirement of Neil Kinnock as party leader led to some sign of coolness in Labour's enthusiasm for Maastricht and European economic integration.

In 1992, therefore, as continuously since 1945, confused views over Britain's appropriate international role and the right way of conveying Britain's wartime eminence in contemporary terms, frustrated a positive and coherent British policy towards Europe. No one would dispute that the arguments for and against closer European integration are weighty and very far from simple. Equally, they were seldom considered in their own right, free from historic associations. This applied with most force in the late 1940s and early 1950s, when Britain could easily have provided a clear leadership for Europe which could mould the new organization in terms of British needs. When Britain finally entered the EEC in 1973 it did so as an unsuccessful supplicant. Dunkirk has much to answer for.

On balance, the impact of the Second World War upon British culture and public policy has been unfortunate. It has led the United Kingdom into a half-world of illusion in contemplating its past and its present. At home, while it promoted positive values of social citizenship and national cohesion, it also helped to encourage immobilism. This occurred partly through the generating of myths (as over an exaggerated view of wartime egalitarianism) and by preventing wider reform. One clear instance is constitutional reform (a bill of rights, for instance) which has repeatedly been frustrated by national conservatism, founded in some measure in the 'Big Ben' image of the Houses of Parliament as the custodian of national liberties rooted in memories of 1940.

Externally, the war has encouraged an over-extension of national resources, financial and military, an ill-founded view of British economic and strategic importance, and a fifty-year inflation of the national ego. Post-war foreign policy has had an enduring Dunkirk fixation. Many societies in the modern world have been harmfully influenced for decades by memories of military defeat. The American South is a continuing example; inter-war Germany perhaps the most alarming one. Great Britain, almost uniquely in the contemporary world, has remained cribbed, cabined and confined by recollections of victory.

References

Brooke, S. (1992), *Labour's War: The Labour Party During the Second World War*, Oxford, Clarendon Press.

Bullock, A. (1983), *Ernest Bevin: Foreign Secretary*, London, Heinemann.

Burk, K. and Cairncross, A. (1991), *Goodbye, Great Britain: The 1976 IMF Crisis*. Newhaven and London, Yale University Press.

Cairncross, A. (1985), *Years of Recovery: British Economic Policy, 1945–52*, London, Methuen.

Calder, A. (1971), *The People's War*, London, Pan Books.

Calder, A. (1991), *The Myth of the Blitz*, London, Jonathan Cape.

Castle, B. (1980), *The Castle Diaries, 1974–1976*, London, Weidenfeld & Nicolson.

Davies, D.H. (1983), *The Welsh Nationalist Party, 1925–45*, University of Wales Press, Cardiff.

Evans, E. (1991), *Alun Llywelyn-Williams*, Cardiff, University of Wales Press.

Fussell, P. (1975), *The Great War and Modern Memory*, Oxford, Oxford University Press.

Fussell, P. (1989), *Wartime, Understanding and Behaviour in the Second World War*, Oxford, Oxford University Press.

Gardner, R.N. (1975), 'Bretton Woods' in M. Keynes (ed.), *Essays on John Maynard Keynes*, Cambridge, Cambridge University Press.

Hennessy, P. (1986), *Cabinet*, Oxford, Blackwell.

Hopkin, B. (1981), 'The development of demand management' in F. Cairncross (ed.), *Changing Perceptions of Economic Policy*, London, Methuen.

Jay, D. (1968), *After the Common Market*, Harmondsworth, Penguin.

Jay, D. (1980), *Change and Fortune: A Political Record*, London, Hutchinson.

Keynes, J.M. (1919), *The Economic Consequences of the Peace*, London, Macmillan.

Middlemas, K. (1986), *Power, Competition and the State*, vol. I, London, Macmillan.

Morgan, A. (1992), *Harold Wilson*, London, Pluto Press.

Morgan, K.O. (1979), *Consensus and Disunity: The Lloyd George Coalition of 1918–22*, London, Clarendon Press.

Morgan, K.O. (1984), *Labour in Power, 1945–1951*, Oxford, Oxford University Press.

Morgan, K.O. (1992), *The People's Peace: British History, 1945–1990*, Oxford, Oxford University Press.

Orwell, G. (1941), 'Lion and the Unicorn', in Orwell, S. and Angus, I., *The Collected Essays, Journalism and letters of George Orwell*, vol. II, *My Country Right or Left*, Harmondsworth, Penguin edition, 1970.

Pearson, G. (1983), *Hooligan: A History of Respectable Fears*, London, Macmillan.

Seldon, A. (1981), *Churchill's Indian Summer: The Conservative Government, 1951–55*, London, Hodder and Stoughton.

Skidelsky, R. (1983), *John Maynard Keynes: Hopes Betrayed*, London, Macmillan.

Skidelsky, R. (1992), *John Maynard Keynes: The Economist as Saviour, 1921–1937*, London, Macmillan.

The Spectator, 12 July 1990.

Taylor, A.J.P. (1964), *The Origins of the Second World War*. 2nd edn, Harmondsworth, Penguin.

Taylor, A.J.P. (1965), *English History, 1914–1945*, Oxford, Clarendon Press.

Thatcher, M., 1988, *Britain and Europe*, London, Conservative Political Centre.

Watt, D. Cameron, (1989), *How War Came*, London, Heinemann.

Young, H. (1989), *One of Us*, London Macmillan.

Young, J.W. (1984), *Britain, France and the Unity of Europe, 1945–51*, Leicester, Leicester University Press.

4

Labour and Europe during the Attlee Governments: the image in the mirror of R.W.C. Mackay's 'Europe Group', 1945–50

Stefano Dejak

Developments in British and European societies over the last few years make the promotion of British history absolutely necessary. If we are to believe what David Cannadine wrote a few years ago in *Past and Present*, (Cannadine, 1987, p.169), that Britain has a 'weaker sense of nationl identity than at any time this century', there must be a new awareness among historians of the field that their work might be needed today even more than it was in the past. Today, Britain is much more of a European country than in the last two centuries, and is currently taking her part in the creation of a European Union. That is precisely where British history may add to the development of a growing consciousness of European history.

It is particularly important to open up the European public to a wider knowledge of British contemporary history. The lack of such knowledge has in fact affected the chances of a better appreciation of the peculiarities of both British history and people and, hence, has allowed Britain to be perceived much too often as sometimes hopelessly detached from her European dimension. I have witnessed this in my own country, where British history (and especially contemporary British history) continues to be almost completely neglected even at university level.

There is also a case in favour of drawing in the points of view of historians other than British who work in this field. This is because of the vital importance of the British experience for European history, but also as the late Rosa rio Romeo once remarked (Romeo, 1990, p.453–55), British historians might find it valuable to compare their experiences with the points of view held by historians who are not British.

There is more than a link between these views and my studies of the experiences of the British Labour Party in European matters after 1945. The double enthusiasm of victory in war and victory for the first majority Labour Government in British history laid emphasis on the chance for Britain to continue as a great power, which indeed was what was meant by being a full member of that most exclusive club, the 'Big Three'. The whole evolution of the Attlee Governments' foreign policy could never have reconsidered this deeply ingrained conviction, the much more so as Ernest Bevin plunged undauntedly into the parallel projects of setting up a Western Alliance aimed at stemming the Soviet expansion, and of giving birth to a new, juster, Commonwealth intended to provide Britain with the strength it needed in order to sustain her continued role as a great power. In May 1952, the Italian review *Il Ponte*, edited by one of the outstanding political personalities of the time, Piero Calamandrei, devoted a whole issue to the 'Socialist Experience in Britain'.[1] In that issue, it was remarked that the Labour Governments found themselves facing the conflicting alternatives of either implementing its domestic programme, or following a wholly independent and socialist foreign policy. By setting the foundations of the Welfare State in Britain, the Labour Governments had clearly opted for the first alternative, although Bevin at the Foreign Office managed to stamp his impressive mark on foreign policy which, in Alan Bullock's words, had, for the first time since Britain began to play a leading part in world affairs in the eighteenth century, to account for the lack of the economic and financial power with which to sustain Britain's leading role in the world (Bullock, 1983, p.49). Unfortunately, a certain number of the 1945 intake of Labour MPs found themselves consistently out of tune with the Labour Government's foreign policy, much more so as Bevin had to run against time in order to turn the British withdrawal from unsustainable engagements abroad to the American direct involvement in Europe, so departing from the idea of a *socialist foreign policy*, which had been longed for by many Labour Party activists.

This is a point which was made clear to me by Lord Bruce of Donington, Private Parliamentary Secretary to Aneurin Bevan at the time, and a prominent critic of Ernest Bevin's foreign policy from the 'Keep Left' group, when he said: 'Although we understood what was happening, I don't think we realized the extent to which British foreign policy had to take into account the economic power of the United States as against the economic weakness of the United Kingdom'; Lord Bruce went in fact as far as declaring that 'looking back at it now, I wonder myself whether had I been in office at the time, whether I could have, even if I had wanted to, carried out the policies that we in the 'Keep Left' group were advocating'.[2]

The Labour Party at large, in fact, forgot in a matter of months after July 1945 the spirit of unity that prevailed during the war: both the left and the governing right wing of the Party resumed the attitudes to one another which caused so many bitter clashes in the 1930s. This was particularly relevant to foreign policy, as Bevin held in particular disdain those 'intellectuals' on the left who started very early to question his line.

Bevin responded by providing them with a complete lack of information about what was *really* going on in the international arena. This is a crucial point if we want to take a closer look at the Labour Party divisions over Europe in those years. The issue of European integration, in fact, became embroiled in the clash between Bevin and his critics, and went down as one of those issues where the hopeful declarations of policy elaborated before the war could not be translated into actual policies.

It was no one less than Clement Attlee who had declared to the Parliamentary Labour Party in November 1939 'that there must be recognition of an international authority superior to the individual states and endowed not only with rights over them but with power to make them effective, operating not only in the political but in the economic sphere: Europe must federate or perish'.

The same sort of ideas seemed to rally the Fabian Society in 1943, when the *Fabian Research Paper* 'Labour and Europe' stated that:

. . . we cannot win the war, nor can we establish an international authority, unless we can create new political loyalties in Europe. . . . we cannot, at this stage in the war, construct a hard and fast form for the future European organisation, but whatever it is to be, we must be prepared to use the power which we shall have to aid the democratic and Socialist forces to establish themselves in a framework in which they will have a chance of surviving, and we must make it clear that we shall break with all pro Facist elements. . . . But, although we cannot now say that we shall or must set up any rigid form of political institution, it seems obvious that the form most suited to a high degree of economic control at the centre, with room for 1*o* cal control of regional affairs, is that of a federation, in which the constituent members would conserve some independence, and would be subject, so far as defence and economics were concerned, to the decisions of the Central Government. (Lipgens, 1986, pp.243–44)

This same feeling was still popular both with the Party and with the Labour Left in April 1944, when Aneurin Bevan wrote more or less on the same lines in an article in *Tribune*:

The unification of Europe must be the independent act of Europe itself, and the aim of British Labour should be to enable her to do it as easily and peacefully as possible. . . . as a first stage – an organic confederation of the Western European nations, like France, Holland, Belgium, Italy, Spain, the Scandinavian nations along with a sane Germany and Austria, and a progressive Britain, is the only solution likely to lay the foundation for peace and prosperity in Europe. It is this solution that Russia, because of her fears, cannot initiate, and that America and Britain, with their present policy of reaction, will be unable to bring about. It remains, therefore, for British Labour to show the way. To do otherwise is for us to admit that the end of the war finds us with no policy to avoid a recurrence of the present insanity. (Lipgens, 1986, ed, pp.258–59)

In the wake of the great war effort, many creative political ideas were forged in Britain just as much as in the other European countries; and the one concerning European integration followed in the steps of the inter-war initiatives. Britain had her part in these initiatives, especially during the war, starting with the formation (in November 1938) of the Federal Union. On the other hand, the advocation of a 'United Socialist States of Europe' was particularly popular among the ranks of the Independent Labour Party, and was translated into a resolution carried by the Labour Party Conference of Blackpool in May 1945. This second group in particular argued the case of forming a third bloc in Western Europe on the basis of democratic socialism as against both the totalitarian Soviet Union on the one hand, and the capitalist United States of America on the other. The Federal Union had a less socialist, but more European and pacifist, stance. In order to peer briefly into the history of this movement, we need to trace its roots.

In the period between Munich and the fall of France, there was, in Britain, intense discussion of the causes of failure of the League of Nations, and of the need to establish a system for a just and durable peace. It was precisely the outbreak of the Second World War that ignited this debate. A way out of that situation which caused the war was to be found in the discussion of federal ideas and, especially, those aimed at the shaping of a European Federation. These were quite popular at that time, when Wilson Harris, editor of *The Spectator* wrote, in March 1940: 'There is no question about the hold the idea of federal union has taken on certain sections of opinion in this country, particularly that all-important section, youth'. Federalism, and especially European federation, had by then turned into the most common of all proposals for establishing a lasting peace when the war was over. Its advocates were to be found in almost every part of the political spectrum, and their ideas were translated into many books and pamphlets. The heart of this movement was a body called Federal Union, together with the Federal Union Research Institute (whose head was Sir William Beveridge).

Federal Union was founded late in 1938 by Derek Rawnsley, Charles Kimber, and Patrick Ransome, and could rely on a panel of advisers including such personalities as Lord Lothian, Wickham Steed, Barbara Wootton. It was in 1940–41 that this organization reached the height of its effectiveness, having grown with astonishing speed. During the first phase of the movement, the main theme was that the cause of war was essentially the state of anarchy created by nation states. Hence, the only real chance to prevent a repeat of anarchy and new wars, lay in the establishment of a federal government which could manage common affairs between nations. To advocate such a solution, a first 'Statement of Aims' was formulated in the spring of 1939, soon to be further analysed by the Federal Union Research Institute which suggested that a post-war federation should initially comprise Britain, France, Germany, and the smaller European democracies. A flow of publications expounded on this issue. Among personalities such as Ivor Jennings and William Beveridge, we may remember a book called *Federal Europe*, by an author whom we are to discuss shortly: R.W.G. Mackay.

The Federal Union kept on pressing for European Federation through all of the war years. Notwithstanding its apparent strength, though, as soon as the war ended and the cold war took its place, the whole issue of a European Federation as part of a wider world federation looked a less and less likely prospect. Most of the supporters of Federal Union, gave up their hopes of an effective world peace: the movement declined accordingly.

Nevertheless, the Federal Union was still influential enough, during the summer of 1945, to ask every candidate in the election the following questions:

1. Are you in favour of a United States of Europe?
2. If elected, are you prepared to advocate the establishment of a democratic federation of Europe, including this country, as part of the new world order?

The results were quite disappointing, as only five members of the organization sat as 'federalist MPs' in the newly elected House of Commons: Boyd Orr, Gruffydd, Horrabin, Mackay, Parker. Only one of them worked effectively for the cause of a European Federation: that Australian-born barrister, whom Stafford Cripps had persuaded in 1934 to follow a political career in the Labour Party ranks, Ronald William Gordon Mackay.

An excellent political organiser, Mackay had left the Labour Party in 1940 to help build the Common Wealth Party, of which he became President in 1941, before re-joining the Labour Party in January 1945, and managing to be elected in July for the Hull North West constituency. Mackay had developed throughout the war years, his ideas about a European Federation, and became Chairman of the Executive Committee of the Federal Union in 1940–41.

In 1940, he published his book *Federal Europe*, which was the first in a series of books devoted to the cause of European federalism. In his first book, Mackay went as far as to put forward a draft constitution for a Federation in Western Europe, trying to be more realistic than most of the pacifists in the Federal Union. Peace was surely to be the main aim of the project; but any serious proposals for Federation should meet the claims of the three major West European countries: security for France, justice and democracy for Germany and a new place in a European and world order for Britain. As he wrote in his book:

The policies of the three countries obviously are bound together. France wants security, which she cannot get without a permanent and adequate guarantee from Britain. Britain will not give such a guarantee, unless justice is being done to the German people. How, except through a Federation can any of these three points of view be reconciled? A Federation gives security to France, and justice to Germany, and brings Great Britain into a European order, in a way in which she has never entered one before. A common government of the three countries removes the causes of conflict between them. (Lipgens, 1986, p.69–71)

Being a socialist himself, Mackay could not fail to pay attention to what seemed to be the main cause that could rally socialists in the Labour Party to his point of view. He did so by quoting the concluding lines of *Equality* Professor R.H. Tawney:

What confronts us today is not merely the old story of the rivalries of ambitious nations, or the too familiar struggles of discordant economic interests. It is the collapse of two great structures of thought and government, which for long held men's allegiance, but which now have broken down. The first is the system of independent national States, each claiming full sovereignty as against every other. The second is an economic system which takes as its premise that every group and individual shall be free to grab what they can get, and hold what they can grab. (Lipgens, 1986, p.141)

Mackay commented on these words by pointing out that:

The solution of the problem of national States must take priority over the solution of any other political question. It is a condition precedent to the solution of any other question. No other political problem can have prior attention until this one has been dealt with. The system of national States has collapsed, and we must substitute for the collapsed system a European Federation, or all that we value may perish in the collapse. (Lipgens, 1986, p.141)

And, as far as the actual socialist issue was concerned, he added:

If a Socialist in Great Britain will consider the problem of European Federation impartially, he will appreciate how necessary it is that some form of common government such as a Federation provides must be established. . . . A majority Labour Government in this country would have power to pass such legislation as may be necessary to establish a Socialist State in England. It could do this, because there are no limitations on the power of the parliament of Great Britain. Thus it is necessary that there should be no limitations of an effective character on the powers of a European Federation. If the Parliament of the Federation were to be as limited in its powers as the Parliaments of United States or the

Commonwealth of Australia, then, however strong the Socialist Government in the Federation might be, it would never have sufficient power to convert the capitalist economic system of Europe into Socialism. The division of powers between the Federation and the States must be such that the Federal Parliament will be able to deal with all the major problems of the industrial and economic system of Europe, in the same way as the Parliament of Great Britain can do at the present time. (Lipgens, 1986, p.142)

These ideas were to be persistently propagated by Mackay throughout the years to come, and, from July 1945, as a Labour MP in the House of Commons. It was at that time, for instance, that he declared his commitment to the establishment of 'a real federation of Europe on a democratic base' which could also serve the purpose of a 'third force' in the new international situation. In October 1945 he wrote:

A Federation of Europe is the first step towards the political stability of the world, . . . and a significant step towards removing war and securing law and order in Europe by uniting itself: the Federation of Europe is priority number one in foreign affairs. (Lipgens, 1987, p.137)

Notwithstanding this personal determination the mood concerning Europe in the Labour Party and more generally in Britain, was changing at the same time as Mackay was writing down the basic tenets of his European creed. François Bondy, a French socialist and federalist, remarked on the change during the same year, when he noticed: .

. . . that many British personalities, including well known economists, who in 1940 had supported the idea of European Federation and encouraged our enthusiasm by their writings, have since lost their whole interest and their whole belief in this solution, and the majority of those who favour a common solution of common European problems, reject political solutions and urge 'functional' ones. (Lipgens, 1986, p.161)

Clearly enough, the one field where Mackay could possibly generate some interest for his European plans was the one interlinked with the debate on the 'third force' option in the Labour Party, and the feasability of a 'socialist foreign policy'. That was in fact the field where 'Kim' Mackay decided to work, by becoming a founding member and a prominent organiser of the Keep Left group, formed by, among others, Richard Crossman, Michael Foot, and Ian Mikardo. As a matter of fact, Mackay was really the mind behind those parts on the unification of Europe which appeared in the 'Keep Left' manifesto, published as a pamphlet in May 1947 as a formalization of the group which coagulated after the letter to Attlee on foreign policy of October 1946, and following the 'rebellion' of Crossman's amendment to the King's speech which had carried the names of 42 Labour MPs in November of the same year.

The 'Keep Left' manifesto argued, against Bevin's line as Foreign Secretary, that the anti-British policy of the Soviet Government had been a 'disastrous mistake' but that, by relying on American support to counter it, Britain had endangered its relations with democratic forces, allowing them to be squeezed out by the division of every country into communist and anti-communist. The recent signature of the alliance with France was seen as a welcome sign that the Government might now be trying to redress the balance and, as the French were bound to the Soviet Union as closely as Britain to the United States, Keep Left argued that France and Britain could determine whether Europe would be divided into two parts or united through the Anglo-French alliance as the keystone of world peace. The British, it continued, had now to become Europeans whose prosperity and security was at one with the rest of the continent. As the manifesto itself described the point further:

Working together, we are still strong enough to hold the balance of world power, to halt the division into a Western and Eastern bloc, and so to make the United Nations a reality. But if we permit ourselves to be separated from France, and so from the rest of Europe, and if we take cover under the mantle of America, we shall not only destroy our own and Europe's chances of recovery, but also make a third world war inevitable . . .

A Socialist Britain cannot prosper so long as Europe is divided. The goal we should work for is a federation which binds together the nations now under Eastern domination with the peoples of Western Europe. But this is a long way off. For the present it would be wise to concentrate on less spectacular forms of European collaboration designed gradually to remove the Iron Curtain. (Keep Left, 1947, p.38)

Unfortunately, the activities of the Keep Left group were driven to a sudden halt just after the publication of its manifesto. During the same year, the Labour Party published a pamphlet called *Feet on the Ground*, written by Denis Healey, Secretary of the Party International Department in October 1948, which laid the ground for Ernest Bevin's famous speech at the Party Conference of Margate, in May 1947, where he accused the 'rebels' of Keep Left of 'having stabbed him in the back' on the day of Crossman's amendment. After such a powerful act of censorship from the Party, the group found itself virtually isolated, and scaled down most of its activities, at least until January 1950, when its second manifesto 'Keeping Left' prepared the ground for the Bevanite rebellion which was to follow soon afterwards.

Undaunted by the evident failure of the 'third force' line in the Party (further reinforced by the fear which spread among Labour MPs with marginal seats, like most of the group, as the Tories gained popularity during the fuel crisis of that winter), Mackay set himself on a brand new project: a Europe Group of the Parliamentary Labour Party which could advocate more efficiently the cause of European unification. That was established in December 1947, and gathered the support of 36 Labour MPs. Mackay himself became Chairman of the group, and Christopher Shawcross was appointed its Secretary.

The immediate aims of this group were to establish contacts with other European minded socialists on the continent, and to prepare for the debate on foreign affairs at the House of Commons due for the following January. A few meetings took place in the following weeks with Belgian and French socialists in London, and a few members of the group flew to some of the main European capitals (Amsterdam, Rome, Paris, Brussels, Oslo) in order to establish contacts with like-minded organizations across Europe. But the crucial events for the Europe Group were going to take place in Britain and, more specifically, in the Labour Party. The first, and worst, blow to any hope of carrying some support for a federal Europe in the Labour Party came with Winston Churchill's moves to seize the European issue with the unparalleled powers of his fame across Europe:

from his rather vague speech in Zurich (September 1946), to his launching of the 'Movement for European Unity' in London (June 1947).

As Mackay published, in January 1948, in his book *Britain in Wonderland*, dedicated 'to Attlee, Bevin, Bevan, Cripps, Dalton, and Morrison on whom the destiny of the peoples of Europe depends', the Labour party was quickly moving against the prospective Congress for European Unity to take place in The Hague in May.

At the time of the Conference of Selsdon Park, the Labour Party had put forward its view that socialist parties had better not participate in the forthcoming The Hague Congress, by stating that:

The survival of democratic socialism as a separate political form is closely bound up with the survival of Western Europe as a spiritual union. This in itself imposes an obligation on Socialist Parties to work for a closer association of the free countries of Western Europe. And the obligation is greatly strengthened by the danger that the concept of European Unity may be corrupted in the hands of reaction. Socialists everywhere must guard against the prostitution of this great constructive ideal into the vulgar instrument of anti Soviet propaganda, by discredited politicians who hope to rebuild their shattered fortunes under the protection of its popular appeal. This is not to say that socialists alone are capable of disinterested passion for European Unity. But the danger exists, and it can best be reduced if socialists themselves take the initiative in promoting the ideal on the plane of constructive realism. (Newman, 1983, p.128)

A memorandum of the International Department of the Party written for the National Executive Committee meeting of 20 April 1948, described further and more privately the reasons behind such a stand:

a) The achievement of general economic stability in Western Europe must precede any political union. (Socialists particularly must insist on this order of priority, since at the moment the economic stability of the various countries in Western Europe is almost directly proportional to the degree in which Socialists control their governments. So, for example, the Scandinavian socialist democracies are unwilling to jeopardise their own economic well-being by committing themselves politically to permanent union with countries like France and Italy, whose economic and social policies at the moment are *laissez-faire*, and whose administrative apparatus is too corrupt and inefficient to take the strain of a state planned economy.

b) Economic stability in Western Europe depends on efficient national economies and on a vast extension of mutual co-operation in which the main instrument should be the continuing organisation set up under the European Recovery programme. The decisions of this continuing organisation should depend on mutual agreement for the time being, since any attempt to give it supranational powers would prevent many countries from participating at all. (Newman, 1983, pp.128–29)

The crucial shift in the Executive of the Labour Party took, the shape of a letter which the Secretary, Morgan Phillips, sent to all Labour MPs, forbidding anyone in the Parliamentary Labour Party to attend the Congress in The Hague. This was the real turning point for Mackay's Europe Group; by shifting the European issue to a matter of obedience to the National Executive Committee of the Party. The group never really recovered from that stark choice which drew it to a sudden halt.

Nevertheless, on 1 April 1948 a resolution was moved in the House of Commons in favour of 'A European Union', stating that 'the long-term policy should be to create a democratic federation of Europe, with a constitution based on the principles of common citizenship, political freedom, and representative government, including a charter of human rights' which 'defined powers with respect to such matters as external affairs, defence, currency, customs, and the planning of production, trade and power and transport'. However, the mentioning of a 'trading area large enough, with the Colonial Territories, to enable its component parts to achieve economic recovery and stability', pointed to a short-term policy which seemed to resemble more and more a mild 'functional' approach, very far indeed from the aims of Mackay. The resolution, furthermore, was tabled by an 'all-party group', and never received the honour of a debate, or of a vote, mainly because of Government opposition.

The following May, in Scarborough, the Labour Party put the seal on the Party line on European integration with the words of Hugh Dalton, who accused Mackay of being a 'doctrinaire' devoted to an idea of federalism which consisted of nothing else but 'conclaves of chatterboxes'.

To leave neither doubts nor expectations behind his words, Dalton concluded his speech at the Conference:

We in Britain have fought through long years to win power for Socialism, and as a result today we have full employment which we would not have except for the Socialist Government . . . and we are not going to throw it away . . . to have majorities of reactionaries who might be thrown up from any part of Western Europe having the power to decree that we in Britain shall go back to the inter-war years of trade depression and all the rest of it. (Labour Party Annual Conference Reports, 1950, p.179)

Was it not strange, then, this being the official Party line on the issue, it was precisely Hugh Dalton who was later appointed to lead the British delegation to the Council of Europe?

The final word about European integration was written by Denis Healey, the author of *Feet on the Ground*:

It is possible that a growth of mutual confidence due to successful co-operation on all the major issues may persuade the countries to submit to such a (supranational) authority. But it is certain that few, if any, would wish to do so. Any attempt to limit national sovereignty would quickly disintegrate what common organization does exist. (Healey, 1948, p.23)

After the choice forced on the members of the Europe Group by the National Executive Committee, it was now the turn of Mackay himself to decide whether he was meant to wait in the dark for the forthcoming triumph of socialism in Europe, hoping that one day those socialist governments might eventually agree to create a United Socialist States of Europe, or if he was, instead, to press on his advocation of European unity notwithstanding its political characterization.

By June 1948, only a month after Scarborough, Mackay had made up his mind for the second option, and went to meet Attlee and Bevin on behalf of the 'British

Section of the International Committee of Movements for European Unity' whose leader was Winston Churchill.

Mackay still tried at the Labour Party in 1950, with his book *Heads in the Sand*, aimed at criticising the Party line; but he could not restrain himself from accusing the Labour Party of refusing to look beyond Britain, by pointing out that 'if the Labour Party, like Mr Churchill, does not want Britain to join in any effective political organization in Europe, it should at least say so in specific terms. That would be better than remaining in the Council of Europe while trying to sabotage its development and growth'. (Mackay, 1950, p.VIII). That was, quite clearly, the path Dalton was following at the Council of Europe. And it was Dalton again who reiterated his case at the Margate Conference of 1950: 'we are determined not to put our gains in peril through allowing vital decisions on great issues of national economic policy to be transferred from the British Parliament at Westminster to some supra-national European assembly . . . we intend to hold what we have gained here in this island' (Labour Party Annual Conference Reports, 1950, p.179).

Drawing from his experience as Chancellor of the Exchequer and as a University professor, Dalton expressed in July the ideas which had led him throughout those years and were to lead him further when he wrote:

I am quite sure . . . we must think first of all of our own Commonwealth and of the development of its boundless resources . . . The Labour Party and the Labour Government . . . are determined that our ties with our kinsmen in other parts of the Commonwealth shall be strengthened and not weakened in the years to come. (Newman, 1983, p.137)

It goes without saying that Dalton was not talking too much to his fellows at the Fabian Colonial Bureau, who could have told him some hard truths about the issue of developing colonial resources as well as about the worsening relationship of Britain with 'their kinsmen' around the globe.

There was, in fact, something at the same time deeper and simpler to Dalton's stark rejection of any plan for European integration. It was more of a psychological belief he was putting forward, when he wrote to Bevin, in August 1950, these very telling lines:

No doubt . . . the experiences of war, including the experience of being occupied by the enemy has broken the back of nationalist pride in many of these countries and this helps to popularise the federalist myth. (Newman, 1983 p.239)

Besides the harsh realities of power and, indeed, the achievements of the Attlee Governments, a deeply ingrained belief in the continued greatness of Britain as a world power, and a definite pride in the success of British Socialism, along with Churchill's 'great fraud' in advocating a European unity he later proved unwilling to implement, led the Labour Party to cast aside any move towards the goal of European integration. But it was the same deep scepticism, if not aversion, of the British people at large that was really at the root of the whole issue; so much so, that the supposed internationalism of the Labour Party could not possibly manage to step into line with its European variety.

In the words of a well known (although still unpublished) study by Richard Rose:

European Union was an issue in which a strong British lead might well have produced significant results. The lead was not given although statements by leaders of the Labour movement created hopes that it would be given. For more than 30 years British Socialists had urged a supra-national authority to control the vested interests of the capitalist nation states. When the Labour Government came into office, it found that British workers, as well as capitalists, had a vested interest in national sovereignty. The electoral plea, 'Put the Nation first', had an unintended double meaning. (Rose, 1959, p.280)

The reasons behind the stands which were taken by the Labour Party in those fateful years cannot, then, be detached from a whole set of beliefs which marked British society in every one of its shades. I would like to pay a tribute to the work of Peter Calvocoressi by quoting his unparalleled words in describing the cornerstone of that set of beliefs

England has been a very great power and a world power. In 1945 it was no longer, but what people chose to believe was less apocalyptic. They concluded that England, having been a world power grade one, had become a world power grade two. But there is no such thing as a world power grade two. This error, venial but costly, delayed for a generation the British withdrawal from distant theatres, the abnegation of the role of international financier and adjustment to the realities of what was, within limits, still a powerful position. Calvocoressi, 1979, p.199)

What had happened to Mackay in his party, then, was nothing but a tiny mirror, where the wider image of Britain's self-consciousness as a great power was reflected: an image, perhaps, too rooted into a past which eventually proved itself to be far more distant than politicians and historians at the time could possibly have realized.

Notes

1. *Il Ponte*, 1952, VIII, pp.5–6
2. Interview with author

References

Bullock, A. (1983), *Ernest Bevin Foreign Secretary*, London, Heinemann.
Calvocoressi, P. (1979), *The British Experience 1945–1975*, Harmondsworth, Pelican.
Cannadine, D. (1987), 'British History: past, present and future', *Past and Present*, vol. 116, p.169.
Denis Healey, (1948), *Feet on the Ground*, London, Labour Party.
Keep Left, (1947), London, New Statesman Publications.
Labour Party Annual Conference Reports, 1948, London, Labour Party.
Labour Party Annual Conference Reports, 1950, London, Labour Party.
Lipgens, W. (1982), *A History of European Integration*, Oxford, Clarendon Press.
Lipgens, W. (1986), (ed.), *Documents on the History of European Integration*, Berlin, Walter de Gruyter.
Mackay, R.W.G. (1948), *Britain in Wonderland*, London, Victor Gollancz.

Mackay, R.W.G. (1950), *Heads in the Sand*, London, Basil Blackwell.

Newman, M. (1983), *Socialism and European Unity*, London, Junction Books.

Romeo, R. (1990), *Scritti Storicic 1951–1987*, Milan, Il Saggiatore.

Rose, R. (1959), 'The relationship between Socialist principles and British Labour Foreign Policy, 1945–1951', unpublished PhD, thesis, Oxford.

5

The Third Force in the late 1940s

Sean Greenwood

The roots of the British 'Third Force' policy which flickered – but did not, in the end, flame – in the last years of the 1940s go back to discussions in the Foreign Office during 1944. At the heart of these discussions were uncertainties amongst British officials about the post-war intentions of the Soviet Union.

Mounting evidence that the Soviets intended to spread their influence in Eastern Europe did not produce any consistent vision of an inevitable clash between East and West. It was not fears of innate Soviet hostility which alarmed officials. What worried them was the absence of any power structure in Western Europe to balance that which was emerging in the East under Russian influence. A deepening concern was that such a Western vacuum might result in the lesser powers of Western Europe being drawn willy-nilly into the Soviet orbit.

A rash of discussion papers sympathetic to the idea of what came to be termed a Western bloc now followed. This was not viewed in the Foreign Office as an anti-Soviet instrument. The hope was that, whilst increasing stability in Western Europe by diminishing the political attractions of the Soviet Union, the Western bloc would, at the same time and by placing more controls upon a defeated Germany, enhance the prospects of continued Anglo-Russian co-operation. A renaissance of German power rather than existing Soviet strength continued to be viewed as the real threat to the peace of post-war Europe.

An added attraction of such an anti-German bloc, was that it might provide a specific solution to the unresolved problem of American reliability. Fears that the pull of isolationist opinion in the USA would prove irresistible refused to subside. If these fears were realised and if a proposed World Organisation proved to be still-born then Britain might be faced with the impossible onus of containing Germany in the West alone. A regional military and defensive arrangement on the lines of the suggested Western bloc would, it was believed, provide some insurance against this. Nevertheless the bloc was not intended as an alternative to the World Organisation which, it was insisted, should still be tested. Indeed it was argued that the construction of a Western bloc would help convince the USA, the USSR and the Dominions that the United Kingdom would not only be willing but able to play an effective part in peacekeeping. The bloc would demonstrate to all three that Britain was a worthwhile partner which would not necessarily have to call upon their assistance in cases where, in collaboration with her European neighbours, she could preserve order herself. This argument was clearly not far removed from the contention that the Foreign Office, by promoting the Western bloc, were intent upon achieving a political prominence more equal to that of the Russians and the Americans. This consideration, though, did not play a critical part in the original deliberations on the Western bloc. Nevertheless, as enthusiasm for the scheme spread the feeling did take hold that the bloc 'might serve to refute suggestions made in the USA and USSR casting doubt upon the will and capacity of the UK to play its part adequately and make an effective contribution equal to that of the other two World Powers'.[1]

By the beginning of 1945 the whole question of a Western bloc had come to rest upon a projected Anglo-French treaty. 'The more one examines the matter', Gladwyn Jebb of the Reconstruction Department minuted on 12 January 'the greater the impression that a firm alliance with France, which could embody provision for West European defence machinery, under the general aegis of a World Organisation should be one of the chief objectives of our foreign policy'.[2] Henceforward the Anglo-French alliance was viewed by the Foreign Office as the indispensable platform upon which the Western bloc might be constructed. The search for an Anglo-French alliance and the desire to develop a security system in Western Europe became, for a time, parallel and hardly distinguishable objectives.

The most immediate obstacle to Foreign Office policy towards Western Europe was the Prime Minister. Apart from being fiercely opposed to the whole concept of a Western bloc, Churchill was also unwilling to initiate any treaty discussions with France, the country which the Foreign Office saw lying at the heart of the entire structure. To Churchill a Western European Security Group would involve Britain in ruinous expenditure in order to maintain a large army to defend the hopelessly weak nations of Western Europe when air and naval power would be sufficient for the purposes of Britain's own self-protection. Added to this Churchill was of the opinion that France was untrustworthy. In particular, he suspected that de Gaulle might opt to work with the Russians and, in order to achieve this objective, would kindle Soviet suspicions of a Western bloc as a way of undermining close Anglo-Russian relations. On the other hand, enthusiasm within the Foreign Office could not alter the fact that the Western Security bloc remained a flimsily thought-out affair. Implicit within the bloc proposal was that a choice might eventually have to be made between Western Europe on the one hand and Britain's more mighty Allies on the other. It was always clear that if it came to this the Europeans would come off second best. The Foreign Office, naturally enough, preferred to keep their options open.

But the French proved unexpectedly difficult. De Gaulle's flirtations with Moscow at the end of 1944 were worrying enough. Yet there were other indications too that the General was about to embark upon policies contrary to British interests. De Gaulle had already made it clear that he expected the settlement with Germany to include the permanent control of the Rhineland and the establishment of an independent state in Rheno-Westphalia. French influence in these regions would clearly be preponderant if these objectives were achieved. What was more, if de Gaulle managed to construct a French alliance system in Western Europe, as he demonstrated an inclination to do, the influence of France would become hazardously unbalanced – the more dangerously so if France continued to lean towards the Soviet Union. The adopted solution was for Britain to resist

French demands over Germany whilst, at the same time, pushing ahead with an Anglo-French treaty which would serve as the basis for a Western bloc constructed principally on British initiatives.

This was the state of play by the summer of 1945. Although it appears that Ernest Bevin entered the Foreign Office in July 1945 with no fixed ideas on British relations with France or with Western Europe as a whole, within the short space of a month this had changed and the new Foreign Secretary was energetically proposing a scheme for Western European co-operation with Anglo-French collaboration at its core. Immediately upon his return from the Potsdam Conference Bevin was presented with a memorandum outlining the Western bloc policy and presenting the difficulties which the Foreign Office had encountered in attempting to fulfil it. Bevin was left in no doubt that the Foreign Office enthusiasm for a bloc was as strong as ever and that its implementation was deemed a matter of some urgency. He now made it clear to his officials that

. . . in reference to the personal antagonism of de Gaulle and Winston he had no *amour propre* and had no feelings of that kind at all, but he wished to get better relations with France. . . . He wished particularly to build up our trade with France and to develop a kind of vested interest in good relations with the different French Ministers. He wished to strengthen them as against the personal policy of de Gaulle.[3]

At the same time Bevin revealed his wider objective of using Anglo-French co-operation as a springboard for more general European collaboration. He pointed out that

. . . his long-term policy was to establish close relations between this country and the countries on the Mediterranean and Atlantic fringes of Europe – e.g. more especially Greece, Italy, France, Belgium, the Netherlands and Scandinavia. He wanted to see close association between the United Kingdom and these countries – as much in commercial and economic matters as in political questions. It was necessary to make a start with France. . . .[4]

Bevin also saw Dalton, Chancellor of the Exchequer, and Cripps, President of the Board of Trade, spelling out his European objectives in somewhat more detail. In particular he drew attention to future relations with Greece, Italy, Poland and France stating that he wished to

push on with the outstanding problems in these countries simultaneously with the end in view of establishing, as far as possible, workable understandings with a group of friendly countries around Germany.

He was careful to stress that

. . . he did not wish to talk in terms of a Western Bloc, which would upset the Russians, but he wanted to settle outstanding points and establish closer relationships with the countries he had mentioned.[5]

The purpose of the meeting was to discover whether the Treasury and Board of Trade could provide commercial inducements which might ease political discussions with the countries Bevin had in mind. The response was not encouraging. Both Treasury and Board of Trade were anxious not to ruffle relations with the Americans and were wary of getting into difficulties over Article VII of the Lend-Lease Agreement which committed both governments to the reduction of tariffs and trade barriers. Dalton and Cripps wished to await a review of Britain's financial, economic and commercial relations with the Americans before pressing forward with European arrangements. Bevin saw the situation differently. In common with his two Cabinet colleagues he hoped for a continuation of close Anglo-American co-operation but he seemed less convinced than they that this would be attainable. Because of this uncertainty, the very roots of his European plans were based upon a specific desire to achieve economic independence of the United States. One adviser noted that in putting forward his views on European co-operation Bevin was

. . . much concerned with the danger of unemployment after the war and wished by closening relations with France and Italy to improve the balance between industry and agriculture in our own country. He evidently fears America will fall into a panic and put up tariffs and we must be able to stand more on our own.[5]

Bevin's distrust of the Americans proved slow to recede and, indeed, was to be reinforced by events over the next few months.

In the meantime he continued to press and to develop his European policy. He met Dalton and his officials again in August in order to restate his case. By then another element had been added to his scheme. For some time Bevin had shown interest in the idea of cutting the Ruhr away from the rest of Germany as a means of depriving her of the economic potential for aggression. Now he took up the idea of an internationalised Ruhr made to serve the European economy which had first been suggested by the French. In discussions with the Western Department of the Foreign Office he told officials that 'he had an open mind about the French Rhineland plan and was ready to study it; he rather favoured, in fact, a separate republic for the Ruhr.'[7]

Henceforth, the idea of an internationalised Ruhr rested at the heart of Bevin's European objectives. He told Dalton that

his view was that whatever the ultimate disposal of the territory the Ruhr industries (in particular steel and chemicals) ought to be publicly owned and an international body set up to run them in order to ensure a regulated output to fit in with the economy of other countries.

The record of the meeting added:

Top Secret: The Secretary of State's long-term objective was to make the Ruhr industries a central pivot in the economy of an eventual 'Western Union'. In this way the industries (steel and chemicals) would be merged into the trade of the 'Western Union'.[8]

Bevin's energetic and imaginative approach seemed to bring a breath of fresh air into the Foreign Office and to provide hope that the drift and delay on European policy which had existed under Churchill and Eden would now be transformed into positive action. This was, however, premature. Bevin's initial demonstration of vigour was deceptive. His enthusiasm did not eliminate caution. Even as he elaborated his wider European designs Bevin also warned that 'he did not wish to take any active steps towards the conclusion of a Franco-British alliance or the formation of a Western group until he had more time to consider possible Russian reactions'.[9]

This reluctance to feed Soviet suspicions was, and continued to be, a strong brake upon any moves in the direction of European co-operation. Nevertheless even had Bevin decided to lay his cards on the table and frankly state his policy to the Soviets the problem remained, as one official commented, that 'the whole idea of a Western group is still so nebulous that there is nothing concrete we can tell them'.[10] In fact Bevin's stance on Western Europe was hardly a policy at all but a series of thoughts and aspirations improvised during his first weeks in office. His private secretary noted that Bevin had taken up his new post 'bursting with ideas' (Dixon, 1968) but what they amounted to in real terms was far from clear.

This apart, Bevin's intended approach to Western Europe duplicated the stated policy of the Coalition Government to pursue, above all else, the continuation of collaboration between the wartime Allies. What Bevin brought to the policy however, was a more distinct assertion of British independence, a vision that by means of collaboration with the Western European nations Britain's voice might more nearly match those of her mightier partners. His desire to reduce Britain's economic dependence upon the United States while re-assuring the Soviet Union that he had no antagonism towards them indicates the central position which he envisaged Britain taking up between the two Powers.

Temperamentally opposed to spheres of influence and blocs which represented, to him, the old, power-political diplomacy, Bevin favoured a more indirect approach which would provide for European reconstruction and the necessary security against Germany without arousing other inter-Allied antagonisms. He was, he told the French Socialist leader Léon Blum, 'aiming at increasing economic and cultural co-operation in the hope that out of such co-operation should arise a common outlook in defence matters'.[11] Akin to the idea of a 'Third Force' its edges were more blurred and less provocatively focused in a way which might smack of any political entity. This reflected not only his own predilections but also an acute aversion to alarming the Soviet Union. Whether the latter would make the same fine distinctions remained in doubt.

The lack of precision which characterised Bevin's approach to European collaboration was never satisfactorily tackled and seriously impaired its implementation. Enthusiasm alone could not diminish the real impediments strewn across the route. The reactions of the Americans, as well as the Russians, remained, at best uncertain and on past form were likely to be unhelpful. More immediately, with an uncooperative Government in power in France, the key to British European policy might not turn in the lock.

Given Bevin's trade union past and his thwarted ambition to be Chancellor of the Exchequer rather than Foreign Secretary in the Labour Government, the economic emphasis which he brought to the Western bloc idea is not surprising. Clearly what he was doing was tapping a reservoir of thoughts on the connection between peace and economic prosperity and the necessity for regional economic groupings which he had championed in the 1920s and 1930s. This sets him in the context of a widespread resurgence of enthusiasm for a new European order which existed both in Britain and on the Continent.

Several influential British voices called for an imaginative policy towards Europe and especially for leadership of a European 'middle way' between Soviet communism and American capitalism. These included men of the political right such as Robert Boothby, R.A. Butler and Duff Cooper though the most vocal champions of the notion of a 'Third Force' were on the left wing of the Labour Party. Bevin's objectives, indeed, had rather more in common with the views of his colleagues on the left than is sometimes recognized. The hope, for instance, of Richard Crossman, that Britain might 'form with the peoples of Europe a common market big enough . . . to stand up to . . . American business' (Bartlett, 1977) was quite at one with what Bevin had in mind. Apart from the fact that Bevin had not got on well with the American leaders while at Potsdam, he sensed an American proclivity to fall back upon economic nationalism in times of recession. Britain needed, therefore, to be able to stand more on her own. As for the Soviets, he intended to convince Moscow that the European group which he aimed to construct was not an anti-Soviet instrument and to make no concrete steps forward until this had been done.

But working with the Soviet Union was to prove more difficult than Bevin assumed, and the breakdown in relations between the wartime allies was, in the long term, to swamp his cooperative plans for Europe. More immediately, though, the difficulties he had begun to experience with both his allies strengthened his desire to find a 'middle way' between them. At the end of 1945, some months after he had outlined the essence of 'Western Union' to his advisers, Bevin was speaking of his perception of a world which was dividing into 'Three Monroes', a reference to the century-old declaration of a United States sphere of interest in the Americas. A Soviet 'Monroe', he said, was now emerging from the Baltic to the Pacific. Bevin's third 'Monroe', he told his officials, should be based on 'our right to maintain the security of the British Commonwealth on the same terms as other countries are maintaining theirs, and to develop, within the conception of the United Nations, good relations with our near neighbours in the same way as the United States have developed their relations on the continent of America'.[12] The attractions of this possibility were to persist. Early in 1946, Bevin spoke to the French Foreign Minister, Georges Bidault, of the possibility of Britain and France leading a Western European group which would have at its disposal a vast array of colonial possessions, suggesting that 'if our two empires were coordinated we had together the greatest mass of manpower in the world' (Rothwell, 1982). A year on from this, in September 1947, he repeated the same view to the French Prime Minister, Paul Ramadier, suggesting that this would allow Western Europe to be an equal to the Superpowers. Bevin perceived a world divided into three spheres of influence – the Western hemisphere, the Soviet sphere and what he termed 'the middle of the planet' where Western European influence and control would be paramount.[13]

Clearly, during the first two years after the war Bevin's thoughts were developing in quite significant directions. By contrast, attempts actually to initiate a new European system were sporadic. It was not until a year after his ideas had first been spelled out in the Foreign Office that Bevin pressed his officials, in August 1946, to prepare a Cabinet Paper on a proposed Western European customs union. Not until January 1947 did this paper finally come before Cabinet. This stressed the need to develop even closer economic ties with France as an overture to tighter economic and political bonds with Western Europe as a whole. It never happened. Though Bevin's European objectives were yet to have their final flowering a year later, in his famous 'Western Union' speech of January 1948, nothing much was done, in the meantime, to provide closer economic bonds with France. Moreover, approaches from the Belgians and Dutch for a more integrated approach were politely, but firmly, rebuffed.[14]

It was the impact of a series of interlocking difficulties, rather than a failure of will, which really hampered Bevin's progress. These were threefold: firstly, Britain's difficult relations with her allies at a time when the wartime partnership was beginning to dissolve; secondly, problems with France, which at times during 1946 and 1947 seemed perilously near to succumbing to communism; and thirdly, the fundamental problem of Britain's economic weakness. Each presented Bevin with a tangle of overlapping problems which worked against any easy implementation of his European projects

In the long run, it was Britain's economic decline which, more than any other factor, induced that severe reassessment of her world role that was eventually to edge Britain into Europe. On every occasion when Bevin actively tried to get the customs union rolling, the economic departments kicked it into touch. Their objections were that the Americans, who were opposed to regional economic arrangements would be offended, that trade with the Commonwealth might be injured and that, anyway, economic integration with the dislocated French economy held no advantage. These were to become familiar arguments and were a source of frustration to those who shared something like Bevin's vision. As Duff Cooper, British Ambassador in Paris at this time and a convinced integrationist, put it, 'the mere words "customs union" produce a shudder in the Treasury and nausea in the Board of Trade'.[15] Certainly, the views of the economic experts appear pedestrian and cautious alongside Bevin's vision. Having said this, Bevin does seem to have been slow to grasp the depth of Britain's economic problems, which he initially viewed as merely short term. Eventually he was disabused of this, and Britain's lack of economic muscle was to provide a major and irritating obstacle to his European schemes. In the end, it was to be views akin to those of the economic departments which were to dominate British attitudes towards Europe for the next two decades and it was Bevin's vision which was to succumb to more pressing concerns.

Just how far-reaching his objectives had become by the end of 1947 emerges from a conversation between Bevin and the French Prime Minister, Paul Ramadier, which took place in Paris on 22 September. Here, Bevin told the French premier that Britain and France 'with their populations of 47 million and 40 million respectively and with their vast colonial possessions . . . could, if they acted together, be as powerful as either the Soviet Union or the United States'. The rich source of raw materials in their colonies meant that 'if it were possible to achieve a real common front, the two countries in unison could almost immediately occupy in the world a place equivalent to that of Russia and of the United States'. Some days later, he informed his Foreign Office advisers that he and Ramadier had 'the impression that the division of Europe into Eastern and

Western Groups was now inevitable and it therefore became necessary to attempt to organise the Western States into a coherent unity. The Marshall Plan offered an opportunity of making the first step in this direction by endeavouring to form a customs union.'[16] In October 1947 officials from several government departments were told that Bevin's aim was to create 'a stable group between the United States and Soviet Russia' to include, alongside Britain and France, Portugal, Italy, Eire and the Benelux countries (Warner, 1984).

Bevin's first statements on 'Western Union' in August 1945 had not mentioned colonial cooperation. The extension of his earlier ideas specifically to embrace European colonial possessions, and the emergence of what have been termed Bevin's 'world third force' objectives occurred in 1947 as a response to changed circumstances. It was in that year that Bevin had to concede that the economic fragility of Western Europe would not permit the development of a 'Western Union' if this were to be attempted on the basis of the Western European economies alone. Britain's economic difficulties, judged at the end of the war to be only temporary, were understood by early 1947 to be too profound to be solved by a European customs union. The loan from the United States which had been negotiated in 1945 was running out faster than anticipated and was likely to bring British dollar requirements, vital for recovery, to crisis point. When the pound was made freely convertible against the dollar in July 1947, as the terms of the loan had stipulated, a potentially disastrous run on the pound ensued. As if all this were not bad enough, the British economy had been thrown into disarray at the start of the year by the most bitter winter weather of the century.

We need to see Marshall Aid in this setting, and note that while Bevin eagerly accepted American financial help, he also remained determined to preserve Britain's political independence from the United States. The solution still seemed to lie in cooperation with Europe and, especially, between the European colonial systems. More precisely, the key increasingly appeared to be Africa. Here British and French possessions provided huge potential in terms of markets and resources and might therefore be a base for European recovery. Moreover, as recent government reports showed, Britain's colonies in Africa were sources of crucial strategic raw materials in which the United States was not self-sufficient. As Britain began to abandon her commitments in Asia and the Near East throughout 1947 – in India, Palestine, Turkey and Greece – Bevin increasingly focused on Black Africa. Not the least of its attractions as a foundation for European cooperation was that the American presence there was minimal. 'African colonial resources', as a study of this question states, 'would enable Britain to give the economic lead to Europe' which the Marshall Plan was threatening to prevent; they could provide an opportunity to create what Bevin had earlier termed 'the vested interests' which would encourage a union of Western European states' (Kent 1989).

The culmination came in a speech to the House of Commons on 22 January 1948 which brought into public view the whole notion of the 'world third force' which had been gestating for almost a year. His starting point was the Soviet threat to Western Europe which, he asserted meant that 'the time is ripe for consolidation.' This should be done, he suggested, by extending the existing Anglo-French Treaty to include the Benelux states. But this was just the start. He emphasized that his vision involved

. . . the closest possible collaboration with the Commonwealth and with overseas territories, not only with British but French, Dutch, Belgian and Portuguese. These overseas territories are large primary producers . . . and their standard of life is capable of great development. They have raw materials, food and resources which can be turned to very great common advantage, both to the peoples of the territories themselves, to Europe and to the world as a whole. (Bullock, A. 1983)

He christened this proposed edifice 'Western Union', the first time the term had seen the light of day since he had used it to describe his intentions in August 1945.

Although negotiations which had already begun between the British, the French, the Dutch and the Belgians resulted in the military/defensive Brussels Treaty (including Luxembourg) on 17 March rather than the broader collaboration presaged in the Western Union speech, it should not be assumed that the former was Bevin's intention all along. Indeed, the stress which the Foreign Secretary continued to give throughout February 1948 – in Cabinet, to European officials and amongst his advisers – to the more radical economic cooperation which would underpin defence arrangements suggests otherwise. Nor was the Brussels Pact merely a device to draw the Americans into a larger system for the protection of Western Europe. Washington was kept closely informed, but Bevin's intention was that 'we should use US aid to gain time, but our ultimate aim should be to attain a position in which the countries of Western Europe would be independent both of the US and the Soviet Union'. (Kent, 1989) It was the Soviet-backed communist coup in Czechoslovakia early in March which galvanized the negotiators and coloured the treaty in practical, defensive drab. Even so, the military clauses remained imprecise and in many ways the main purpose of Brussels was to stiffen anti-Communist forces in the West rather than provide practical support.

The Brussels Treaty did contain references to economic collaboration but it was the swan song of Bevin's 'Third Force' objectives. From here on his principal success lay in the creation of a security system which set Britain and her European neighbours firmly in the American camp. Thus, the signing of the North Atlantic Treaty in April 1949, while a considerable achievement, was not the outcome of impressive foresight and dogged determination but, to an extent, an admission of failure. Bevin had never wanted a purely military system, nor had he wanted a defensive organization which made Britain dependent on the United States. Given the deepening world crisis, he had to take what he could get. NATO, of course, would sit reasonably neatly alongside the other organs of European cooperation, like the Council of Europe and the Coal and Steel Community, which were beginning to emerge on the Continent. But it was not looking down the same road to the future as they.

As for Bevin, his close association with the founding of NATO, and his scepticism towards the Schuman Plan have earned him an unjustified reputation as an enemy of European cooperation. Yet the clear threads between the first revelation of the 'Grand Design' (1945), thoughts on the 'Three Monroes' (1945), pressure for a European customs union (1946–47) and Bevin's thinking on a 'world third force' based upon European colonial territories (1947–48) indicate rather more than a veneer of interest in collaboration. The ideas of Monnet and Schuman were objectionable to him because of their supranationality and because they seemed to move too far too quickly. Acceptance of the Schuman Plan would also, of course, imply a transfer of initiative from London to Paris and Bevin had always viewed the British at the centre of cooperative developments. This is what separated him from Churchill who saw Britain as the distant sponsor of integration rather than an active participant. Interestingly too, as late as February 1947 Bevin condemned Churchill's United States of Europe Movement as inherently anti-Soviet and expressed alarm at the 'mischief' it might cause amongst the wartime allies.[17]

Some of the most relentless opponents of Bevin's ideas and a significant cause of his failure to implement them were ministers and officials in the Board of Trade and the Treasury. From mid-1945 through to 1948, whenever Bevin raised the issue of a customs union he was blocked at Cabinet level by the Chancellor of the Exchequer, Hugh Dalton, the President of the Board of Trade, Sir Stafford Cripps, and his successor Harold Wilson. The danger, as these ministries saw it, was that close economic cooperation with Europe would mean the end of British economic independence, would antagonize the Commonwealth and irritate the United States. When the Marshall Plan negotiations destroyed the validity of the latter argument the Board of Trade and Treasury concentrated on the others. Once Bevin had turned his attention to European colonial cooperation, Cripps (who by this time had replaced Dalton as Chancellor) had become an ally, but he now faced stiff opposition from the Colonial Office, which criticized his African schemes as exploitative.

By the summer of 1948 Bevin had been worn down by this resistance. His hope of organizing what he called the 'middle of the planet' – stretching from northern Europe to southern Africa – had been a response to the assertion that a European customs union could not alone solve British economic difficulties. Now the cumulative advice of the Colonial Office and other government departments suggested that the African colonies, because of their own economic and technological backwardness, would not do the trick either. Although in October Bevin still seemed hopeful that if Britain 'only pushed on and developed Africa, we could have US dependent on us, and eating out of our hand, in four or five years', this was, by this time, no more than wishful thinking for Bevin was setting up his own barriers to European cooperation (Kent, 1989).

In June 1948 the Soviet blockade of Berlin and the consequent Western airlift had begun. Lack of firm leadership in Western Europe in the face of this new crisis depressed Bevin and reinforced his growing belief that Britain's future lay, after all, in cooperating with America and the Commonwealth. Faith in a 'spiritual federation' now went into sharp decline. As the new year opened, Bevin was arguing that economic collaboration with Europe was not only undesirable but dangerous, a view reinforced in April 1949 by another sterling crisis from which only the United States could provide relief. The notion of colonial cooperation was formally abandoned.

Bevin's European ideas are open to criticism on the grounds that, at root, they were based on old-fashioned British nationalism rather than a response to the new post-war age and that his 'interest in Europe had been related neither to functionalism, federalism nor socialism, but to economic self-interest linked to the creation of an imperial grouping able to achieve independence from the Americans' (Kent, 1989). Given that most forms of European-mindedness spring from such national self-interest, it may be, nevertheless, that there was an inevitability about Bevin's final acceptance of the views of the economic departments and that, notwithstanding his vision, the more obvious alternatives of sterling bloc and Commonwealth as bases for British economic strength were likely to prove persuasive in the end. His ideas on Euro-African cooperation were also founded, it might be argued, on outmoded notions of imperialist exploitation which flew in the face of a process of decolonization soon to begin. Yet this is asking Bevin to have foreseen the unpredictable; and, as one authority points out, 'for the British government to have embarked upon a policy of precipitate withdrawal in the later 1940s would have been widely regarded as defeatist and as a premature act of abdication entailing prospective material as well as immediate political loss' (Bartlett, 1989). This was just what Bevin's European schemes were intended to prevent. Oddly enough, perhaps, for a man of such vigour, his actions proved fatally hesitant. Fearful, ever since he had entered the Foreign Office, of Soviet antagonism and American displeasure, he had delayed to the point where opportunities for British initiatives on European cooperation had become fatally limited. In the end, it was his misfortune that the Cold War intensified before any of the major obstacles to his European policies could be overcome and in the face of the apparent threat from the East, military rather than economic consolidation came to dominate his policy and Britain was forced into the slipstream of the United States in the bi-polar world which had now emerged.

Notes

1. PRO FO 371 U5419/445/70.
2. PRO FO 371 U167/1/70.
3. Oliver Harvey Papers, diary entry for 13 August, 1945.
4. PRO FO 371 Z9595/13/17.
5. PRO FO 371 UE3683/53.
6. Oliver Harvey Papers, diary entry for 13 August, 1945.
7. ibid.
8. PRO FO 371 UE3683/3683/53: meeting bewteen Bevin and Dalton 17 August, 1945.
9. PRO FO 371 Z9595/13/17.
10. PRO FO 371 U7042/445/70: minute by Ward, 19 September, 1945.
11. PRO FO 371 11077/13/17: Bevin to Blum, 19 September, 1945.
12. PRO FO 800, Bevin Papers, 478/MIS/45/14.
13. PRO FO 371 Z9053/25/17: conversation between Bevin and Ramadier, 22 September, 1947.
14. PRO FO 371 Z7116/65/17; CAB 128/9, CM (47) 13.
15. PRO FO 371 Z10270/17: Duff Cooper to Bevin, 16 October, 1947.
16. PRO FO 371 Z9053/25/17.
17. PRO FO 371 UN876/842/78: Bevin to Duff Cooper, 3 February, 1947.

References

Bartlett, C.J. (1977), *A History of Postwar Britain*, London, Longman, p.19.
Bartlett, C.J. (1989), *British Foreign Policy in the Twentieth Century*, London, Macmillan, p.73.
Bullock, A. (1983), *Ernest Bevin: Foreign Secretary*, London, Heinemann, p.520.
Dixon P. (1968), *Double diploma: the Life of Sir Pierson Dixon*, London, Hutchinson, p.178.

Greenwood, S. (1984), 'Ernest Bevin and "western union" August 1945-February 1946, *European History Quarterly*, vol.14 no.3, pp.319–37.

Kent, J. (1989), 'Bevin's Imperialism and the Idea of Euro-Africa 1945–1949', in Dockrill, M. and Young, J.W. (eds), *British Foreign Policy 1945–1956*, London, Macmillan, pp.52–55 and p.62.

Rothwell, V. (1982), *Britain and the Cold War 1941–47*, London, Cape, p.442.

Warner, G. (1984), 'The Labour Government and the Unity of Western Europe', in Ovendale, R., *The Foreign Policy of the British Labour Government 1945–1951*, Leicester, Leicester University Press, pp.61–82.

6

A search for order: Britain and the origins of a Western European Union, 1944–55

Klaus Larres

During the post-war era the UK has been the country which identified itself most clearly with the NATO alliance and an Atlantic security conception. Britain has therefore been extremely resistant to an independent European security arrangement. Particularly the Western European Union (WEU) has never been regarded as anything other than a not very important bridge between the North Atlantic alliance and the European Community. Any attempt by the WEU to assume a more active role in the formulation of a common European security policy has met with strong opposition in British governmental circles. Thus, Britain has always had a very complicated relationship with the Western European Union concept and the very idea of an independent European security and foreign policy role in international affairs. Surprisingly, it was a British Labour government which first took the initiative to create the Brussels Treaty Organisation (BTO) in 1948 which was reorganized and turned into the WEU in 1954 by a Conservative government. However, for Britain both the BTO and the WEU were merely a means to an end: to realize the creation of NATO and to succeed in facilitating the rearmament of West Germany which then could become a member of NATO. The ultimate aim of the two major parties in Britain was the creation and then the maintenance of an Atlantic connection. Anything like a 'Western European Union' was merely regarded as a suborganisation for some more valuable alliance with the United States.

However, in the years before 1948 this had not always appeared to be the case. Occasionally, during post-war planning exercises in 1944 and in the immediate post-war era Britain seemed to be more interested in entering into economic and military agreements with France and using the concept of a 'Western Union' as the means to build up a British led 'third force' in world affairs. After all, Britain could never be sure that there would be an active and benevolent American involvement in the affairs of Western Europe. Thus contingency planning was necessary and indeed vital if the continent was to survive both economically and militarily. This, in fact, represented Britain's search for order in an anarchic post-war world where the position of the UK as a great power was seriously threatened. Without Allies – either the US, the preferred option, or France and a western European association, the compromise solution – the British could not hope to impose at least some degree of discipline on international affairs which, it was hoped, would be strongly tilted in their favour.

The following overview attempts to clarify the development of the British attitude towards American involvement and 'Western Union' from 1944, the year serious discussions about the issue were first held in the Foreign Office (FO), to 1955 when for the first time in history a Western European Union (WEU) was founded. First of all the origins of the Western Union concept during the Second World War will be analysed. Subsequently Foreign Secretary Bevin's ambiguous attitude to the creation of a Western Union will be considered. In fact Bevin attempted to bring about an American commitment to Europe from the very beginning of the formation of the Labour Government in July 1945. Therefore, Bevin's hesitation to draw too close to the French and to commit himself too firmly to the attempt to turn Western Europe into a 'third force' in world affairs and give it an independent role between the two superpowers will be analysed. The third part of the chapter will deal with the Dunkirk Treaty of March 1947. This Treaty which is usually regarded as an isolated and rather old-fashioned and backward looking agreement, was embarked upon as a means to provide some alternative in case the US were serious about their withdrawal into isolation. Bevin hoped to use the Treaty as the core for some future European economic and possibly military bloc. The Dunkirk Treaty was in fact the apex of Britain's search for a Western European Union. Soon afterwards the UK's interest in such an association declined rapidly as the Truman Doctrine and the Marshall Plan spelled out the responsibility the United States felt towards the devastated continent. Thus, lastly, the decline of the idea of creating a genuine Western European bloc will be looked into. Since the formation of NATO in 1949 Britain has been firmly committed to the Atlantic connection and was not interested anymore in building up Europe as a third and independent power in world affairs. The creation of the WEU in 1954 was just a means to obtain French agreement to German rearmament. The WEU was never given a sovereign and independent voice in international affairs. Partly thanks to the efforts of the British Government this has hardly changed since the WEU was revived in 1984.

The origins of the Western Union concept

On 8 January, 1948 British Foreign Secretary Ernest Bevin submitted a Cabinet paper entitled 'The First Aim of British Foreign Policy'. He wrote:

The Soviet Government has formed a solid political and economic block. There is no prospect in the immediate future that we shall be able to re-establish and maintain normal relations with European countries behind their line . . . Indeed we shall be hard put to it to stem the further encroachment of the Soviet tide . . . This in my view can only be done by creating some form of union in Western Europe, whether of a formal or informal character . . . the moment is ripe for a consolidation of Western Europe. This need not take the shape of a formal alliance . . . It does, however, mean close consultation with each of the Western European countries, beginning with economic questions. (Bullock, 1983, pp.516–7)

Contrary to conventional thought even as late as 1948 Bevin's Western Union plan was still based on the idea of an economic and commercial grouping of the European democracies. He did not regard it principally as a defensive organisation although this soon dominated the internal FO and Cabinet deliberations and the public discussions which followed his 'Western Union' speech in the House of Commons on 22 January 1948.[1] Bevin at first – in 1945 and 1946 – considered the Western Union scheme as a possibility to establish a 'third force' in world politics which would enable Britain, France and other European nations to play an independent role between the two superpowers (Greenwood, 1984, p.318).

Thus, for once the Foreign Secretary of Prime Minister Attlee's new Labour government had a similar attitude as the left wing of the party. Shortly after the Second World War most politicians in the Labour party held the conviction, as Michael Foot expressed it, that Great Britain now stood at the summit of her power and glory because the country, as a capitalist society run by a socialist government, could offer a middle way between Communism and Capitalism to the world. If Britain combined the Soviet Union's 'economic democracy' with the western world's 'political democracy', Foot believed, Britain would be able to form a 'third force' and claim global moral leadership.[2] In March 1946 Richard Crossman followed this idea up by suggesting a Western Union Treaty. The Western European states and Britain and her Commonwealth should conclude such a treaty and sign a solemn declaration that they would remain neutral in a war between the superpowers. (Cook and Sked, 1984, p.50) Crossman was by no means the first one to suggest the formation of a Western Union. By 1946 Bevin had already considered Britain's long-term strategy towards Western Europe without, however, having made any decisions about the formation of a Western European bloc. In a discussion at the Foreign Office on 13 August 1945 on his return from the Potsdam Conference, Bevin proclaimed that he first wished to obtain a clearer picture of Soviet intentions before taking any decisons on Britain's policy towards an association of the countries of western Europe. (Woodward, 1976, p.198).

Consideration of a Western Union was not a novel idea. Occasionally it had played a prominent role in post-war planning discussions in London. As far back as the autumn of 1942 Foreign Office advisers had spoken of the need for a Western European security group. Trygve Lie, the future UN Secretary General, proposed some kind of Atlantic pact as early as December 1940 in his capacity as the foreign minister of the Norwegian government in exile in London (Baylis, 1984, p.616). Within the French government in exile in Algiers serious discussions about Western European co-operation began in September 1943. These deliberations were strongly influenced by considerations of the role of post-war Germany and by ideas of an economic federation between France, Belgium, Holland and 'Rhenania' – the German Rhineland and Ruhrgebiet which the French wished to separate from Germany. An accession of Italy and Spain to the envisaged federation was also held possible. In late 1943, Jean Monnet, economic adviser to de Gaulle's government in Algiers, was already prepared to accept a loss of French sovereignty in return for the establishment of close European economic co-operation (Young, 1990, p.11).

This was, however, not the way de Gaulle viewed the post-war world. Although the General regarded European economic collaboration as vital both for the future containment of Germany and for France's well-being after the war, he did not hesitate to add the security aspect to the ideas voiced by his advisers. He believed that future security requirements in Europe would not only make the economic but also the military co-operation of France with the Benelux countries and possibly Britain absolutely necessary. By early 1944, particularly the Dutch had come round to a similar point of view. They conceded that a Western European bloc seemed to be required to control Germany militarily and to make sure that German economic resources would be available for the reconstruction of Europe. However, despite the general concern about the future security of the European continent, even de Gaulle viewed European co-operation principally as economic collaboration in the form of a customs union which would benefit European security requirements only indirectly. In a speech to the Consultative Assembly in Algiers, de Gaulle announced in March 1944:

. . . that a kind of western group . . . principally formed on an economic base . . . could offer great advantages . . . [and] would seem to constitute a central pillar in a world organisation of production, trade and security. (Young, 1990, p.13)

Immediately the Soviet Union complained about not having been consulted in respect to a Western European bloc led by France. Moscow suspected that the underlying aim of such a grouping was the isolation of the USSR from Western Europe. Moreover, the Belgian and Dutch representatives did not seem too keen anymore on the French proposal. They now appeared to prefer close economic collaboration with Britain rather than France and they expressed the hope, as did René Massigli, the French Commissioner for Foreign Affairs, that London would feel obliged to take over the leadership of Western Europe. They professed to have learnt a lesson in 1940. Thus, on 23 March 1944, Paul Spaak, the Belgian Foreign Minister, asked Eden whether the British Government objected to the extension of the envisaged customs union between Belgium, the Netherlands and Luxembourg to France. He added that the Belgian and Dutch governments were also very interested in concluding military agreements with other European countries including Britain after the end of the war (Woodward, 1976, pp.181–82).

In response to Spaak's initiative which the Belgian politician had followed up by sending Eden a lengthy memorandum on his ideas, FO official Gladwyn Jebb, the Head of the FO's Economic and Reconstruction Department, was asked to draw up an internal memorandum. The final version of this paper dated 9 May 1944 was entitled 'Western Europe'. In the same month Jebb wrote a second memorandum on 'British policy toward Europe'. Both papers were subsequently submitted to Eden as a 'combined memorandum' with the title 'Western Europe' on 20 June 1944.

Jebb was in favour of working toward some form of a regional European system, particularly one encompassing security matters. The memorandum took Spaak's view into consideration that such a grouping should not divide Europe into two blocs (a Russian and a British sphere of influence) but be part of a general European security system which in turn should be embedded within the envisaged world order. The first aim of such a world organisation had to be the prevention of renewed German aggression in the post-war world. While it was necessary that Britain had to shoulder a heavier defence burden in the beginning, the British government should assist the rapid economic recovery of France and the smaller European nations to enable them to take part in this plan. Jebb's memorandum expressed the opinion that within a 'United Nations Commission for Europe' Britain should work for the organisation of a scheme of mutual defence agreements between London and Paris in the first place. He hoped that it would also be possible to conclude such pacts with the Benelux countries, Norway, Sweden and maybe even Spain, Portugal and Italy (Woodward, 1976, pp.183–87; Baylis, 1984, p.616). A similar case for close British military association with the Western European states was made by Deputy Prime Minister Attlee in late July 1944 (Dilks, 1985, pp.28–29). Jebb was careful to point out that his envisaged scheme would not encompass any continental commitment for Britain but merely the standardisation of equipment, the maintenance of a considerable amount of armament in Britain and France, and the planning of common defence schemes. He was optimistic enough to believe that Moscow would not object to his plan if the Soviet Union could be convinced that such a Western European defence scheme was not a bloc directed against the USSR but against Germany. Jebb was in favour of giving Stalin a free hand to develop a similar defence scheme for Eastern Europe. He explained that his plan had the advantage of providing a line of defence against Germany and also against the Soviet Union should this prove necessary.

Jebb's papers were given considerable attention within the FO. Above all, officials were concerned with the important question whether the linkage of Britain to a Western European bloc would strengthen the UK by providing a defence in depth or whether it would weaken the country by committing Britain to the defence of the European continent at the expense of its overseas commitments. Britain might soon find itself dependent on the land armies of the weak continental nations. However, it did not yet seem possible to give conclusive answers to these considerations (Woodward, 1976, pp.186–89).

In view of Churchill's general lack of interest in post-war planning, and his well known hostility to talks about the formation of a Western European bloc, Eden asked the Chiefs of Staff to comment on the 'combined memorandum'. Because of the Normandy landing and other military problems at this time they were only able to do so at the end of July 1944. Even then the COS were too pressed to be able to analyse the document properly and add new insights. However, the COS spelled out that in the long run not so much renewed German aggression but the UK's relationship with the Soviet Union would be crucial. Unless a world organisation could be successfully organized to balance the interests of the great powers, they expected a clash of interests between the UK and Russia in which the potential of Germany would play an important role. The COS were also doubtful whether it would be possible to set up a Western European bloc without, sooner or later, including all or at least some parts of Germany (Woodward, 1976, pp.189–90).

A similar opinion was held by Duff Cooper, the British Representative to the French Committee of National Liberation in Algiers. The Francophile Cooper was sceptical about the prospects of a world organisation. He advocated a military alliance of the western democracies as a precautionary measure against the domination of the Continent by Moscow. However, this was rejected by Eden on 25 July 1944 during a meeting of the War Cabinet. Eden and Churchill agreed that any leakage of the intention to divide the world into blocs would antagonize

Stalin. This in turn would endanger the chance of Anglo-Soviet collaboration and European recovery in the post-war world. It could also be expected that American President Roosevelt would only be prepared to accept some commitments in regard to Europe on the basis of a world organisation. The creation of a Western European Union would only convince Washington that its help was not really needed anymore. As a consequence the US would be even more inclined to withdraw into isolation. Already in mid-July 1944 Eden had told other European governments that at present he was not prepared to enter into any detailed considerations of a Western European pact (Charmley, 1985, pp.55–57; Woodward, 1976, pp.190–91).

In early October 1944, Spaak took the intiative once again and on 20 October another meeting was held in the FO to discuss the Western bloc idea. It was agreed that initially France and the Benelux countries and as soon as possible Denmark and Norway should begin discussing military and technical arrangements for a Western European association aimed at security against Germany. However, no immediate conclusion of a formal agreement should yet be attempted. While the COS accepted this in principle on 8 November, Churchill objected and instructed Eden not to open discussions with the Western Countries. He was still convinced that France and the Benelux countries were so weak that an agreement to defend them would not be in Britain's interest. When Spaak visited London in early November discussions were confined to a general exchange of views. Churchill and Eden were also vague about the formation of a Western European bloc during their visit to France in November 1944: They told Bidault, the President of the Conseil National de la Résistance, that the British Government had not yet come round to consider Spaak's memorandum which he had submitted during his visit in November (Woodward, 1976, p.197).

In the same month, the interdepartmental Post-Hostilities Planning Staff (PHPS) in London produced a memorandum entitled 'Security in Western Europe and the North Atlantic'. The conclusion was similar to the one produced by Jebb five earlier. As the developments in air power and long range missiles dramatically changed Britain's strategic situation, the PHPS advised that it was vital for British security to form and be part of a West European security group consisting of France, the Benelux and the Scandinavian countries and one day maybe even Germany. Furthermore, it recommended that this organisation should co-operate closely with both the Commonwealth and the United States in order to eventually create something like a North Atlantic organisation which seemed to be necessary to avoid a Soviet domination of Western Europe (Baylis, 1984, p.617; Zeeman, 1986, pp.350–51).

However, Churchill and to some extent also Eden were still very sceptical whether the European nations would have the necessary resources to participate in such an alliance. Both politicians were also still worried about antagonizing the Soviet Union. The best policy seemed to be to build up the European nations 'one by one' starting with France and continuing with the smaller European nations. These countries and Britain could then attempt to draw up a common plan for their mutual defence. Gradually the British Government was warming up to the idea of some kind of defensive agreement with Western Europe which would make some British military commitment to the continent obligatory. Eden concluded at the time:

I think we should have to reconcile ourselves to making a rather larger land contribution than the famous two divisions which was all we had to offer last time [in 1939]. (Barker, 1971, pp.20–21)

Bevin and Western Union

By mid-1945, however, no progress had been made towards the construction of a Western European security group. Despite the various wartime analyses and an increasingly clear picture of Soviet expansionist intentions in Eastern Europe no long-term strategy decisions in regard to Britain's Western European policy had been taken. To no small degree this was due to Churchill's lack of interest in a Western European bloc which did not include the US. But above all progress towards a Western Union was prevented by an increasingly tense relationship between Britain and France. Churchill and an influential section of the FO were hostile to a closer alliance with the apparently arrogant and self-righteous de Gaulle. The initiative should at least come from the French they insisted. De Gaulle in turn demanded a solution of the serious Anglo-French disagreements about Allied policies towards both the Levant and the problem of the Ruhr before he was prepared to enter into any alliance negotiations (Greenwood, 1984, pp.320–21; Rothwell, 1982, p.414; Young, 1990, pp.14ff.).

Ernest Bevin, the new Foreign Secretary, shared these views.[3] However, he regarded a solid partnership with France of prime importance to establish close commercial, economic and political relations with the countries of Europe. Between 10 and 17 August 1945 Bevin held several meetings with FO officials and cabinet colleagues primarily to discuss Anglo-French relations. On 10 August, in conversation with Hugh Dalton and Stafford Cripps, the Chancellor and the President of the Board of Trade respectively, Bevin expressed his strong belief in the continuation of the Anglo-American 'special relationship'. He had, however, strong doubts whether anything like that would find American support and feared the US would retreat into an economic 'fortress America' with high tariffs and a consequent dire economic situation all over Europe including high levels of sustained unemployment. Therefore it seemed necessary to him to achieve some degree of economic independence from Washington and embark upon serious European co-operation. During a meeting with officials of the FO's Western Department on 13 August, the Foreign Secretary supported the concept of a Western Union based on close Anglo-French collaboration and even extended it to such countries as Greece, Italy and the Scandinavian nations. Four days later, in yet another meeting with Dalton and some of his advisers, Bevin even supported the French scheme of dismembering Germany by setting up a separate 'Rhenanian' republic. This would put the Ruhr industries under international control thus checking Germany's future military potential. Britain's backing of such a plan seemed to have the advantage of bringing about European reconstruction by facilitating the creation of an economic union with France in the short run and with the smaller European nations in the long run (Greenwood, 1984, pp.322–24).

Thus, due to the 'financial Dunkirk' which Britain faced, Bevin began to turn away from the plans drawn up during the war which had been increasingly preoccupied with military co-operation in post-war Europe. He had also asked his advisers to draw up contingency plans in case the US lost all interest in Europe and decided to cut its losses by withdrawing into isolationism. Therefore, Bevin had started to give more attention to possible European economic collaboration and was soon moving closer to the idea of Western Europe as an independent 'third force' between the superpowers. In September 1945 he told the French socialist Léon Blum that he was 'aiming at increasing economic and cultural co-operation in the hope that out of such co-operation should arise a common outlook in defence matters' (Greenwood, 1984, p.325). Like de Gaulle in 1944, Bevin viewed military co-operation in Western Europe merely as an indirect result of the apparently more important economic partnership. The FO, however, was still convinced that a defence alliance of the European countries was necessary to contain both a possible Soviet bloc in the East and renewed German aggression in the West. It also seemed to be helpful in order to counterbalance the expected withdrawal of the US into isolationism. FO officials were aware that such a military alliance would arouse the suspicions of the US and the USSR who were both opposed to any 'sphere of influence' solutions which had thus to be approached in a cautious way. (Baylis, 1984, pp.617–18)

Gradually Bevin came round to incorporating the FO view of Western Union into his own ideas about Europe's potential as a 'third force' in world affairs. The London Council of Foreign Ministers' Meeting in September and early October 1945 was particularly decisive for Bevin's realization of the incompatibility of the Western and Soviet approach to post-war politics. This meeting with its fierce clashes between the Western allies and Soviet Foreign Minister Molotov over Romania, Bulgaria and Tripolitania proved highly symbolic for future East-West relations. However, Bevin fell out also with the impulsive James Byrnes, his American counterpart. The British felt pushed aside as a mere junior partner by both the Soviet and American delegations which in turn made Bevin increasingly interested in pursuing the re-creation of a close relationship with the French. (Kessel, 1989, pp.33–38; Deighton, 1990, pp.37–46)

On the 3 October 1945, the very first day after the end of the London conference, Bevin approached French Foreign Minister Georges Bidault about the opening of early negotiations on an Anglo-French treaty. He had already asked his officials to draw up a draft treaty (Greenwood, 1984, p.327, 330; Bullock, 1983, pp.147–48). The British Foreign Secretary clearly had in mind to lay the foundations for a European 'third force' between the superpowers. Therefore he did not hesitate to explain during a debate in the House of Commons on 22 November 1945 that he could not agree to the notion, 'that all my policy and the policy of His Majesty's Government must be based entirely on the "Big Three" '.[4] However, as Sean Greenwood has contended, it would be 'rash to suggest that by the end of 1945 Bevin had decisively determined upon any rigidly defined centre path for Britain between her two partners in the Big Three'. As Bevin was principally still interested in maintaining the unity of the great powers, his foreign policy was merely 'pragmatically picking its way through the snares of an emerging new international order'. His remark to Byrnes at the Moscow Conference of Foreign Ministers in November and December 1945 that there soon might be 'three Monroes' backed by the US, the USSR and Britain respectively seems to support this view (Greenwood, 1984, pp.328–29).

Bevin's plan to begin some form of Western Union as a 'third force' in international affairs by first creating a close Anglo-French 'special relationship' was not based on any preconceived attitudes based on ideological illusions as was the case with Michael Foot and Richard Crossman. Rather it represented Bevin's desperate search for order in a world where Britain seemed to be losing out. It was similar to the situation in 1940, when Churchill offered common citizenship and an Anglo-French union when the collapse of France before Hitler's forces seemed to be inevitable, (Barker, 1971, pp.18–19) something new and unique had to be attempted. At the end of 1945 only close Anglo-French relations leading to an independent Western European bloc in the long run seemed to be able to prevent a potentially disastrous situation developing into utter chaos.

However, in the course of 1946 no such alliance emerged. Despite the sudden resignation of General de Gaulle on 20 January 1946, due to problems over the Levant and disagreements about the export of Ruhr coal and the dangers of the industrial revival of Germany, co-operation started only slowly (Baylis, 1984, pp.617–18; Young, 1990, p.121; Rioux, 1987, pp.97ff.). Moreover, the apparently increasingly unstable political situation in France contributed to British unwilling-ness to construct a Western Union on the basis of close collaboration with France. The general elections of October 1945 made the Communists the largest party in France. This combined with the deteriorating food situation which developed from January and February 1946 (Rioux, 1987, pp.54ff., pp.122ff.) led British politicians and officials to believe that disturbances and riots could occur at any time. At one point Bevin was so full of despair that he seriously expected that the Sovietization of France was about to occur. Although the situation soon improved and the British foreign policy élite became less panicky and more rational again, confidence in the French political system had been seriously eroded (Greenwood, 1984, pp.330–34).

Occasionally there was further talk of the need for an Anglo-French alliance, but British enthusiasm for such co-operation had been undermined – though in theory it was still regarded as sensible. Above all Bevin was now interested in realizing a European customs union in order to create a market which could compete with the American one and provide a better export outlet for British goods. In September the British Chancellor of the Exchequer, the French Finance Minister, Hugh Dalton and Robert Schuman respectively, held full discussions on economic problems and an Anglo-French Economic Committee was set up to meet on a regular basis. It was more or less an extension of a similar committee founded by France and the Benelux countries. Although an agreement to remove destructive competition between the two countries was signed and some debt matters resolved at the meeting in September 1946, the discussions did not come close to approaching anything like economic integration between the two countries. Some rapprochement in the economic field had been made but dis-agreements on other issues continued, particularly about the German question (Young, 1990, pp.121–22; Kessel, 1989, pp.126ff., 161ff.). The British vision that a close Anglo-French partnership could be the cornerstone of a Western European Union was not revived. Despite some improvement in recent Anglo-French relations, this idea seemed to have suffered a death blow in early 1946 (Greenwood, 1984, pp.330–34; Young, 1990, pp.121–22).

The Treaty of Dunkirk

However, by the end of 1946, ideas about close Anglo-French co-operation were once again at the forefront of political opinion in Britain. Bevin was still interested in making sure that Europe would reorganize and rebuild itself as a sizeable force in world affairs. American support for Western Europe did not seem to be forthcoming. In order to ensure British leadership in Europe, close Anglo-French collaboration was indispensable. However, the French, not the British, took the initiative to embark on another attempt at improving Anglo-French relations. The new and very shortlived minority government of the anglophile socialist Léon Blum, which came to power in mid-December 1946, expressed an interest in further economic co-operation with Britain. French Ambassador Massigli however was told by the British that his government's ideas about economic co-operation should not be discussed at governmental level for the time being but in the Anglo-French economic committee. London was still very concerned about the apparently highly unstable internal situation in France (Young, 1990, p.131; Morgan, 1984, p.267).

Surprisingly, at first sight, not so much economic co-operation but renewed concentration on military collaboration with France was soon adopted. This was the result of an initiative taken by Ambassador Duff Cooper in Paris. Without having received authorization to do so on Boxing Day 1946 Cooper told the French Prime Minister who also acted as his own Foreign Minister that he should use his probably short period in office to achieve the conclusion of an Anglo-French treaty of alliance (Charmley, 1985, p.60; Young, 1990, p.131; Cooper, 1953, p.369).

Encouraged by Cooper and by Pierre-Olivier Lapie, the Under-Secretary for Foreign Affairs at the Quai d'Orsay, Blum attempted to exploit his close links to the British Labour Party by writing to Prime Minister Attlee on 1 January 1947. As a matter of urgency Blum asked for increased coal supplies from Britain and in addition he suggested to conclude an Anglo-French alliance 'with no prior solution of outstanding problems'. Blum also expressed the wish to visit London to discuss these matters with Attlee and his Foreign Secretary (Bullock, 1983, p.357, Baylis, 1984, p.618; Young, 1990, p.132).

Much to the surprise of most FO officials Bevin strongly endorsed the conclusion of an agreement with the French during a cabinet meeting on 6 January 1947. Only in December, when the FO had finally concluded it was worth risking American and Soviet displeasure for moving towards a European association as the basis of achieving equality with the superpowers, Bevin had been in favour of not reacting too quickly. Now, however, the Foreign Secretary wished to include a passage on a new Anglo-French entente in the final communiqué reporting on Blum's visit to London from 13–16 January 1947. However, once again, the emphasis on military co-operation was only meant to serve wider aims. Military co-operation was merely regarded as the means to lay the foundation for close Anglo-French relations generally. A military alliance, ostensibly targeted at Germany, had the advantage of lessening Soviet suspicions that an Anglo-French alliance was primarily directed against Moscow. It would also soothe American antagonism about an alliance of the world's two predominant imperialist powers (Morgan, 1984, pp.267–68). Bevin was primarily interested in continuing his old

policy of creating an Anglo-French 'special relationship' which had been temporarily upset by the internal events in France in early 1946. As far as the Dunkirk
Treaty was concerned, Bevin's biographer, Lord Bullock, states rightly:

Nothing was said of a threat from any other direction than the Germans but Bevin hoped
that a specific British guarantee would help to reduce the greatest obstacle to closer
collaboration between the two countries, their disagreement over the treatment of
Germany. (Bullock, 1983, p.359)

Bevin now even revived the idea of an Anglo-French customs union and
suggested to his officials to look into other forms of economic co-operation with
France and the other Western European countries – not least in order to strengthen the anti-communist forces in France and elsewhere. Bevin was seriously
thinking along the lines of 'creating a community of commercial interests' (Bullock, 1983, p.358; Greenwood, 1984, p.334; Charmley, 1985, pp.60–61) – or, as
one could have put it, a Western European bloc based on economic collaboration
but aiming at co-operation in other fields as well.

Blum's highly successful visit in mid-January, 1947, which committed France
publicly to negotiate a new Anglo-French alliance, created the impression, as
Young contends, as if 'in the atmosphere of Socialist brotherhood, all the old
Anglo-French differences suddenly seemed unimportant' (Young, 1990, p.132).
While the FO with regard to possible Soviet and American suspicions preferred to
move in a rather cautious way and to limit the text of the Treaty to vague
statements of future co-operation, Duff Cooper, and to some extent also Blum and
Massigli (Young, 1990, p.136) had grander things in mind. There is, however, no
evidence that Bevin was thinking along similar lines though it would not have been
unlikely. Ambassador Cooper believed that Anglo-French collaboration on the
basis of the envisaged Treaty would ensure that Western Europe, and of course
Britain, would remain part of the Big Three. Embarking on a 'third course' in
world politics did not seem to be impossible after all:

. . . the time has arrived for a most momentous decision in British foreign policy. If we now
succeed in identifying our interests with those of France, we shall with our two vast empires,
be able to remain not only one, but possibly not the least important, of the Big Three.
(Charmley, 1985, p.61)

In mid-February 1947 draft agreements were exchanged between the two
countries. Both sides intended to base their fifty years alliance on their respective
treaties with the Soviet Union. However, the British made sure that a French
clause with reference to 'any new menace' from Germany was not incorporated as
it did not occur in the Anglo-Soviet Treaty of 1942 and seemed moreover to be
too vague and far-reaching. The American Congress felt sufficiently encouraged
to argue that a US commitment to Europe was now no longer necessary. 'Too
great independence of the United States would be a dangerous luxury' a FO paper
of early 1947 explained with some understatement (Adamthwaite, 1985, p.227).
An all-embracing Soviet-British-French anti-German system therefore did not

seem to be advisable (Young, 1990, pp.135–36). But Britain did promise that if there were hostilities with Germany, it would come to the help of France with 'all the military and other support and assistance' possible. The Treaty also committed the two parties to constant consultation as far as their mutual economies were concerned (Bullock, 1983, p.359). On 4 March, 1947 the Anglo-French Treaty of alliance was signed in Dunkirk.[5]

Partly because of the symbolism embraced by signing the Anglo-French Treaty in Dunkirk, at first sight the new alliance merely seemed to complete the 'triangular mutual defence system' against Germany which had begun with the 1942 Anglo-Soviet Treaty and the Franco-Soviet pact of 1944 (Fremaux and Martel, 1985, p.93). Britain appeared to have eventually accepted her interests in the security of the European continent. However, it was abundantly clear, that the Treaty's reference to Germany was only a pretext for calming French fears about renewed German aggression (Deighton, 1990, p.38–39) in order to enable the two parties to embark on close Anglo-French relations in the economic and security field. After all, on 11 March 1946, almost exactly a year before, Churchill had delivered his so-called 'iron curtain speech' in Fulton, Missouri. With the knowledge and tacit approval of the British Labour government he had used strong language to warn about the imminent danger of Soviet encroachment on Western Europe (Larres, 1992, pp.50–54, Harbutt, 1986, pp.183ff.; Ryan, 1979, pp.895ff.). A year after Churchill's speech and only a week after the Dunkirk Treaty had been signed, Britain seemed to have succeeded in persuading the US to take over the responsibility for enabling Greece, Turkey and Iran to stay in the western camp. Although the Truman Doctrine, announced on 11 March 1947, was more far-reaching and sounded more belligerent than the British Government would have liked, there can, however, be no doubt that it had been Bevin's policy all along to commit the US to a loose defensive system against Stalin's Soviet Union on a global scale and particularly as far as Europe was concerned. Although throughout 1946 and early 1947 Bevin did try to prevent an East-West split, ever since the Conference of Foreign Ministers in Moscow in April 1947 he had no illusions about the real danger threatening Europe (Deighton, 1990, pp.135ff.). With the notable exception of a considerable number of French politicians very few statesmen in the West were deceived about the realities of the post-war world.

Contrary to the conventional view, the Treaty of Dunkirk was more than just an old-fashioned bilateral treaty directed against renewed German aggression. As the British government could not yet be sure of a lasting American commitment to Europe, the Treaty's overriding purpose was to bring France into close co-operation with Britain which might be the basis for wider West European collaboration both in the economic and in the security field. The East-West conflict and increasing economic problems made sure that Britain no longer regarded the containment of Germany as absolute. Instead, Britain became more and more interested in enabling Germany to improve her industrial capacity and standard of living in order to reduce the responsibility of the occupying powers and decrease the danger that communist ideas would spread in Germany (Dilks, 1985, p.44).

Rather than representing a traditional view of the world, the Treaty of Dunkirk symbolizes that British foreign policy was in the process of transformation. Britain had indeed seen the need to accept a certain commitment to ensure European security – but the country was also aware of the realities of the post-war world.

These realities made it necessary that Britain took the lead in bringing together a Western European Union on the basis of Anglo-French co-operation to ensure that the Europeans would have a degree of influence on their future fate. In the absence of the US, the Treaty of Dunkirk was yet another attempt by Britain to impose some order on the chaos of the post-war world in Europe while at the same time making sure that the British government would be in control of the situation. French Ambassador Rene Massigli commented that 'between the American giant and the Russian colossus, England is taking notice of its European interests . . .' and General de Gaulle was even more visionary by assuming that the Dunkirk Treaty would tie France indirectly to an alliance with the United States (Young, 1990, p.136). Both were correct. The Dunkirk Treaty was an alliance which had the purpose of enabling Britain to survive even without an American commitment to the continent. At the same time the British government wanted to ensure that the US government did not receive the impression that American support was not necessary anymore. The Dunkirk Treaty would allow Britain to either take the road to reliance on a Western European Union or to opt for pursuing the path of an Atlantic alliance.

Thus, with the conclusion of the Dunkirk Treaty the British Government attempted to keep all options open. Kenneth O. Morgan's contention that the treaty was 'a finite, self-contained episode, with no wider implications' is therefore entirely beside the point (Morgan, 1984, p.268). After all, soon after the Anglo-French entente had been signed, the Belgian and Dutch governments voiced their conviction that the Dunkirk Treaty could provide the model for the conclusion of further bilateral treaties with France and Britain. Bevin agreed principally, and in early May 1947 he suggested a similar idea in an internal Foreign Office memorandum (Baylis, 1984, p.618). In his memoirs Bidault claimed that when he put his signature under the Treaty of Dunkirk he already had in mind that the Treaty could 'provide an essential basis for other agreements' if it seemed necessary to organize a defensive system against the Soviet Union (Bidault, 1967, p.142; Young, 1990, p.138). Indeed already in February 1947 French Prime Minister Paul Ramadier had said in an interview with an American newspaper that France was interested in concluding an alliance with the United States (Young, 1990, p.139). Thus, despite all its vagueness and alleged lack of content and clear purpose, the Dunkirk Treaty did provide the core for future Anglo-French, if not European military co-operation against the USSR should this prove necessary as seemed more and more likely. But most important, the Dunkirk Treaty left the door open to military and economic co-operation with the United States.

The decline of the idea of a Western European bloc

The United States did indeed soon feel obliged to become involved in safeguarding the future of Europe. The difficult food and coal situation in Europe and the impending economic collapse of most Western European countries including Britain propelled the Truman Administration into action. On 5 June 1947 Secretary of State George Marshall delivered a speech at Harvard University which soon became known as the Marshall Plan. Bevin immediately took the initiative. He regarded Marshall's offer 'like a life-line to sinking men' to avert 'the looming shadow of catastrophe' on Western Europe (Baylis, 1984, p.619).

Consequently, on 27 July 1947 Bevin chaired a conference of fourteen nations in Paris to consider the implications of American willingness to provide economic assistance on a huge scale to participating countries as outlined in Marshall's speech. The conference led to the formation of a Committee of European Economic Co-operation and to decisive American economic and political involvement in Western Europe's future role in world affairs. Soon the OEEC in Paris, a new European Payments Union and the European Recovery Programme was set up. Britain and the western zones of Germany were the main beneficiaries of American financial and economic aid (Milward, 1984, pp.56ff.)

In autumn 1947 there were talks about even closer Anglo-French economic co-operation although Bevin was not interested in economic integration, an idea both the French and the Americans attempted to popularize. Soon Bevin, like before him the Canadian Foreign Minister St.Laurent, began talking about the necessity of a new political and security organisation in Western Europe. In October 1947 the British Foreign Secretary expressed the belief that the Europeans should think about creating a western alliance with the Benelux countries, Portugal and even Italy on the basis of the Anglo-French Dunkirk Treaty. The breakdown of the last Conference of Foreign Ministers in New York in December 1947 gave even more credence to this idea. Shortly after the collapse of the Foreign Ministers' conference, Bevin explained his idea of a Western Union to Marshall and Bidault who both heartily endorsed a new political and defensive agreement between Britain, France and the Benelux countries. Bevin insisted, however, on the need for American assistance and participation in a loose and flexible 'spiritual federation of the West' (Baylis, 1984, p.620; Bullock, 1983, p.537; Morgan, 1984, p.273).

Unlike a year earlier, this time Bevin did not hesitate to clarify in a speech to the House of Commons on 22 January 1948 that such a treaty would be directed against the threat posed to Western Europe by the Soviet Union. The impact of the coup in the CSSR in February and rising Soviet intransigence over Berlin gave even more credit to Bevin's pronouncements. On 17 March 1948 a Western European Treaty for economic, political, cultural and military co-operation with a duration of fifty years was signed in Brussels. Although not all historians agree (Warner, 1980, p.316) it is, however, fair to state as John Baylis does: 'For Bevin, the Brussels Pact was not enough' (Baylis, 1984, p.627). After all, the United States had not yet been fully persuaded to accept a European commitment (Bullock, 1983, p.537).

Almost immediately after the Treaty had been signed the Brussels Treaty powers and the United States and Canada entered into top secret exploratory discussions about setting up a North Atlantic Treaty Organisation (Wiebes and Zeeman, 1983, pp.351ff.) The Brussels Treaty had indeed been the precondition for such talks. The United States had hinted that the European powers should first of all show their willingness to take the initiative to provide some degree of European security co-operation before the US was prepared to become involved. After the Brussels Treaty Organisation (BTO) had been founded the American Government showed much less hesitation to embark upon discussions with Britain and other European countries on a military asssociation. The NATO Treaty was signed in Washington on 4 April 1949 (Ireland, 1981, pp.82ff.)

Formally the BTO continued to exist until it was officially incorporated into

NATO on 20 December 1950 (Zeeman, 1989, p.400). In reality its functions had already been submerged with the NATO alliance.

In September–October 1954, after the rejection of the proposal of a European Defence Community (EDC) by the French parliament on 30 August, the British FO suddenly remembered the existence of the Brussels Treaty. The BTO was renamed Western European Union (WEU) and exploited to override French objections to Germany's and Italy's entry into NATO. As the NATO alliance did not allow its participants a veto over the rearmament of their fellow member states, Germany and Italy were invited to become members of the WEU where such veto rights existed. Moreover, the imposition of extensive arms production controls on West Germany and Italy was feasible within the framework of the WEU. Thus, in the autumn of 1954 the Western European Union was created to allow for West Germany's and Italy's admittance to NATO. Both countries became a member of WEU and NATO in May 1955 (Larres, 1992, pp.600–02; Dockrill, 1991, p.139ff.). The WEU did not have an existence in its own right. It was clearly subordinated to NATO. Basically it only existed for a few months after its creation in October 1954 to ensure Germany's integration with the West by being able to soothe French objections to German rearmament. Small wonder that until 1984 when an attempt at resuscitation was made, the WEU did not play any active role in international affairs at all (Cahen, 1989, pp.8ff.).

As soon as the United States became involved in providing for the security of Western Europe, Bevin's enthusiasm for setting up a genuine Western European bloc faded quickly. The desire of the British Government for a Western European Union as a means to ensure that Britain would be able to play the role of a 'third force' in world affairs had always been regarded as a compromise solution, as a mere alternative to an American commitment to Europe. It represented Britain's attempt to create some sort of order in an anarchic post-war world which was threatening Britain's position as a great power. An Anglo-French entente, a customs union with other European nations, a so-called Western European Union or bloc had, however, never been much more than a contingency plan to face the problems of the post-war world without being able to rely on Washington. As soon as the US announced the Marshall Plan and it became clear that American political and military involvement might be forthcoming as well, Bevin started working on bringing this about.

His initiative as far as the BTO was concerned was not so much dictated by his desire for a Western European defence organisation but by his overriding interest in making sure that in the long run the United States would feel obliged to commit itself to a certain amount of responsibility for European security matters. Therefore, not so much the Brussels Treaty but the Treaty of Dunkirk epitomizes the point when Britain was seriously considering dropping the hope of American involvement and turning towards the European option. Early in 1947, before the announcement of the Truman Doctrine, Bevin could not expect that Washington would be willing to once again help out the Europeans. In December 1947, after the breakdown of the last Foreign Ministers' Conference, when he first seriously discussed his 'vision' of a Western Union Treaty, American involvement could be expected although some degree of insecurity remained. Thus, the Dunkirk Treaty can be regarded as the decisive junction. Without the announcement of an American commitment to Europe by means of, above all, the Marshall Plan Britain might well have pursued a different approach to the cold war. Britain's and Europe's incapability to remain part of the Big Three and form a 'third force' would, however, have hardly been overcome by this.

Notes

1. HC Deb., 5th ser., 1947–48, vol.446, 383–409.
2. See also Bevin's statements in Parliament, e.g. HC Deb., 5th ser., 1945–46, vol.415, 7 November 1945, 1334, 1340.
3. See Wuerzler, 1989, pp.141ff. for an excellent account of the role of Western Europe in British defence policy from 1945–55. See also the review article Reynolds, 1985, pp.497ff.
4. HC Deb., 5th ser., 1945–46, vol.416, 762.
5. Various differing interpretations of the purpose and motivations behind the Dunkirk Treaty are discussed in Zeeman, 1986, pp.349ff. See Kent and Young, 1992, pp.166ff., for an interesting overview of the relationship between the Western Union idea and developments in British defence strategy.

References

Adamthwaite, Anthony (1985), 'Britain and the world, 1945–49: the view from the Foreign Office', *International Affairs*, 61, pp.223–35.
Barker, Elisabeth (1971), *Britain in a divided Europe, 1945–1970*, London, Weidenfeld & Nicolson.
Baylis, John (1982), 'Britain and the Dunkirk Treaty: the origins of NATO', *Journal of Strategic Studies*, 5, pp.236–47.
Baylis, John (1984), 'Britain, the Brussels Pact and the continental commitment', *International Affairs*, 60, pp.615–29.
Bidault, Georges, 1967, *Resistance: the Political autobiography of Georges Bidault*, London, Weidenfeld & Nicolson.
Bullock, Alan (1983), *Ernest Bevin: Foreign Secretary, 1945–1951*, London, Heinemann.
Cahen, Alfred (1989), *The Western European Union and NATO: building a European Defence Identity Within the Context of Atlantic Solidarity*, London, Brassey's.
Charmley, John (1985), 'Duff Cooper and Western European union, 1944–47', *Review of International Studies*, 11, pp.53–64.
Cook, Chris and Sked, Alan (1984), *Post-war Britain: a political history*, Harmondsworth, Penguin.
Cooper, Alfred Duff (1953), *Old Men Forget: the Autobiography of Duff Cooper*, London, Hart-Davis.
Deighton, Anne (1990), *The Impossible Peace: Britain, the Division of Germany and the Origins of the Cold War*, Oxford, Clarendon Press.
Dilks, David (1985), 'The British view of security: Europe and a wider world, 1945–1948', in: Olav Riste (ed.). *Western Security: The Formative Years: European and Atlantic Defence, 1947–1953*, Oslo, Norwegian University Press, pp.25–59.
Dockrill, S. (1991), *Britain's Policy for West German Rearmament, 1950–55*, Cambridge, Cambridge University Press.
Frémaux, J. and Martel, A. (1985), 'French defence policy, 1947–1949', in: Olay Riste (ed.), *Western Security: The Formative Years. European and Atlantic Defence, 1947–1953*, Oslo, Norwegian University Press, pp.92–103.
Greenwood, Sean (1983), 'Return to Dunkirk: the origins of the Anglo-French Treaty of March 1947', *Journal of Strategic Studies*, 4, pp.49–65.

Greenwood, Sean (1984), 'Ernest Bevin, France and Western Union': August 1945-February 1946', *European History Quarterly*, 14, pp.319–38.

Harbutt, Fraser, J. (1986), *The Iron Curtain: Churchill, America, and the Origins of the Cold War*, New York/Oxford, Oxford University Press.

Ireland, Timothy P. (1981), *Creating the Entangling Alliance. The Origins of the North Atlantic Treaty Organization*, London, Aldwych Press.

Kent, John and Young, John W. (1992), 'The Western Union concept and British defence policy, 1947–48', in: Richard J. Aldrich (ed.), *British Intelligence, Strategy and the Cold War, 1945–51*, London and New York, Routledge, pp.166–92.

Kessel, Martina (1989), *Westeuropa und die deutsch Teilung: Englische und franzoesische Deutschlandpolitik auf den Außenministerkonferenzen von 1945 bis 1947*, Munich, Oldenbourg Verlag.

Larres, Klaus, W. (1992), *Grossbritannien und die Gipfeldiplomatik: Churchill, Eisenhower, der Kalte Krieg und die Westintegration der Bundesrepublik 1945–1955*, PhD thesis, Cologne, Cologne University.

Milward, Alan S. (1984), *The Reconstruction of Western Europe, 1945–51*, London, Methuen & Co. Ltd.

Morgan, Kenneth, O. (1984), *Labour in Power, 1945–1951*, Oxford, Clarendon Press.

Petersen, Nikolai (1982), 'Who pulled whom and how much? Britain, the United States and the making of the North Atlantic Treaty', *Millenium*, 11, pp.93–114.

Reynolds, David (1985), 'The Origins of the Cold War: The European Dimension, 1944–1951', *Historical Journal*, 28, pp.497–515.

Rioux, Jean-Pierre (1987), *The Fourth Republic, 1944–1958*, Cambridge, Cambridge University Press.

Rothwell, Victor (1982), *Britain and the Cold War, 1941–1947*, London, Cape.

Ryan, Henry, B. (1979), 'A New Look at Churchill's "Iron Curtain" Speech', *Historical Journal*, 22, pp.895–920.

Warner, Geoffrey (1980), 'Die britische Labour-Regierung und die Einheit Westeuropas 1949–1951', *Vierteljahrshefte für Zeitgeschichte*, 28, pp.310–30.

Wiebes, Cess and Zeeman, Bert (1983), 'The Pentagon negotiations March 1948: the launching of the North Atlantic Treaty', *International Affairs*, 59, pp.351–63.

Woodward, Llewellyn Sir (1976), *British Foreign Policy in the Second World War*, vol.V, London, HMSO.

Wuerzler, Heinz-Werner (1989), 'Westeuropa im Kalkül britischer Sicherheits- und Verteidigungspolitik (1945–1954/55)', in Gustav Schmidt (ed.), *Großritannien und Europa*, Bochum, pp.141–67.

Young, John W. (1990), *France, the Cold War and the Western Alliance, 1944–49: French foreign policy and post-war Europe*, Leicester University Press, Leicester and London.

Zeeman, Bert (1986), 'Britain and the cold war: an alternative approach; the treaty of Dunkirk example', *European History Quarterly*, 16, pp.343–67.

Zeeman, Bert (1990), 'Der Bruesseler Pakt und die Diskussion um einen westdeutschen Militaerbeitrag', in Ludulf Herbst, et al. (eds), *Vom Marshallplan zur EWG. Die Eingliederung der Bundesrepublick Deutschland in die westliche Welt*, Munich, Oldenbourg Verlag, pp.399–425.

7

British policy in occupied Germany: democratisation and social democracy

Eva A. Mayring

'The purpose of democracy is to enlarge the number of those who share in the benefits of available welfare by enlarging the number of those to whom the rulers of a society are responsible . . . A democratic society is rational, constitutional, pushed by its inner logic, to set freedom in the context of equality'. (Laski, 1943, p.253). When the leading Labour politician Harold Laski wrote these sentences in 1943 he was thinking of Germany as much as Britain. He was reflecting on how a post-war Germany could be reformed and how the danger of reverting to a totalitarian dictatorship could be avoided in the future. He believed that this could be achieved only by changing social and economic structures (ibid., pp.95–127, pp.130–32, pp. 138–39). One of the main demands of German politicians and heads of administration after the Second World War was for social democracy. 'Social democracy' in this context refers not to the political party, the Sozialdemokratische Partei Deutschlands (SPD), but describes a specific form of democracy with political, economic and social dimensions. Social democracy in this sense goes beyond the fundamentals of representative democracy – the constitution and limitation of political power – aiming to fulfil demands for autonomy, participation and co-determination, and to put into practice ideas of social equality (Niclauß, 1974, pp.29–35; Vilmar, 1985, pp.144–45). There was a general consensus, cutting across all party political divisions, that a future Germany should be restructured and reformed along the lines of social democracy. Britain could have provided a model for this concept.

Since the 1940s Britain itself had been developing into a modern welfare state, giving life to the 'New Jerusalem'. Comprehensive social reforms were introduced after the Labour Party's victory at the polls in 1945. But how does this relate to policy in occupied Germany? Could such ideals of social democracy be realised in post-war Germany? Were they of any relevance to British occupation policy? To understand the range of democratisation policy and the chances for its implementation, the constraints under which it had to operate, and the intentions of its authors, we must take into consideration the wider circumstances in which the British policy for democratising Germany after 1945 was formulated, and the place of this policy within the whole range of British policy for Germany.

Democratisation was one of the central goals of British occupation policy in Germany. It was also one of the main aims of the Allied powers in rebuilding and restructuring Germany after 1945. The Potsdam Conference of July/August 1945 specified denazification, decentralisation, demilitarisation and democratisation – the so-called 'four big Ds' – as guide-lines for Allied German policy. These were the few points concerning German policy on which the Allies could agree. On other questions, such as the level of reparations or German central adminis- trations, there were difficulties from the start.

Democratisation and occupation would appear to be mutually exclusive. The restoration of democratic conditions on the orders of an occupying power – 'decreed democracy' – could be called a contradiction in terms. However, the democratisation programme contained an important argument justifying and legi- timising the occupation (Niclauß, 1974, pp. 18–19). This was of particular relevance to Britain's occupation policy, which was governed by a 'constructive pragmatism' (Schneider, 1985, p.49). Thus British Military Government stressed economic reconstruction in Germany earlier than, for example, its US counter- part, which followed the restrictive Directive JCS 1067 for longer. In Britain's view democratisation was the only constructive and positive reform programme in the context of such 'negative' measures as disarmament, demilitarisation, denazifi- cation and reparations.[1] Thus democratisation was referred to in all areas of planned reform: politics, the economy, and German society after 1945. Democratisation was the buzz word of British occupation policy.

However, it should be pointed out that democratisation and democratisation policy were subject to certain constraints. It must be seen in the context of British foreign policy, and within an international framework. This placed certain limits on the development of Britain's ideas for democratising Germany. Under the terms of the Potsdam Agreement, the Allied powers were obliged to co-operate in Germany, as they were exercising supreme authority 'each in his zone of occu- pation and jointly in matters affecting Germany as a whole'.[2] Thus British occupation policy – including democratisation – depended on relations between the Allies. But inter-Allied relations were not dictated solely by developments in Germany. They were also influenced by events elsewhere, in the Middle and Far East for instance; relations with the USA, the USSR and France in these places had a direct impact on policy in occupied Germany. Britain's German policy was thus closely related to the general international climate. The development of the Cold War, in which Britain played an important part (Deighton, 1990), meant that democratisation policy in Germany was brought into line with a policy motivated by national interest, ideology, and anti-Communist and anti-Soviet attitudes. Further democratisation came into conflict with other aims of occupation policy, dictated by Britain's need for security against both Germany and the Soviet Union. The ultimate aim of British policy was for Germany to become a member of a community of civilized, peaceful and democratic nations and be accepted into a Western orientated international community.

In addition, developments at home in Britain influenced the direction of occupation policy, and thus also the course of democratisation. The economic and financial crisis Britain was experiencing was exacerbated by the cost of occupying, administering and supplying Germany. In terms of population the British Zone was the largest of the four occupation zones with a constant and growing influx of

refugees. As the British Zone was a highly industrialised region and not agricultur-
ally self-sufficient as was the Soviet Zone, it was desperately in need of food
imports. To cover all these demands Britain was forced, in 1946, to introduce
bread rationing at home. The British Zone also harboured the most serious
political problems of restructuring: the regional re-organisation based on the
dissolution of Prussia (a protracted process which continued until the autumn of
1946), the decision concerning the future of the Ruhr and the control of
Germany's heavy industries. The last two aspects were vital not only to the future
development of Germany, but also to the economic reconstruction of Europe.
Britain in particular found itself in a dilemma. How could it encourage industrial
reconstruction in Germany and at the same time dismantle industries and fulfil
reparations demands? The British Zone was not capable of supporting itself, but it
also had obligations to export coal to the other occupation zones, and to neigh-
bouring European countries. The financial burden of occupation was undoubtedly
greater for Britain than for any of the other occupying powers. This was not only
because war damage and consequently the task of reconstruction and its costs were
enormous. The British occupation authorities also maintained a large administration in Germany. The Military Government administration in the British Zone
was the largest and most expensive of all to run. In 1946 more than 26,000 British
officers were employed by Military Government (plus 30,584 German staff) as
compared with only 6,000 US Military Government officers (Carden, 1979,
pp.537–38).[3] This huge administrative body was often criticised by the British
press and MPs as a 'gargantuan family' and another 'Poona' (ibid., p.551).[4] The
work and the priorities of the British occupation authorities in Germany came
under general attack: 'The ordinary people (in Germany) look to their standard of
life, of employment, of food and clothing . . . If we (the British) cannot see that the
people have these needs satisfied, a lot of talk about democracy, a new intellectual
outlook, and re-education and all the rest of it seems to be rather hypocritical and
rather false.'[5] The cost of running the British Zone, the immense size of British
war debts and the financial crisis at home could only be met by raising loans from
the USA. This financial dependence on the USA had a strong impact on British
occupation policy.

    Given all these overriding problems, it seems highly doubtful that the new social
course upon which Britain embarked after Labour's election victory in 1945
fundamentally changed the direction of British foreign and occupation policy.
There had been a lengthy debate about whether Labour's foreign policy should
concentrate solely on national interests, or adhere to socialist principles. At its
conferences and in its manifestos of 1945, Labour had committed itself to
pursuing a socialist foreign policy. But with the outbreak of the Cold War the
Labour Party soon adopted the foreign policy of Churchill's government. Ernest
Bevin, former trade unionist and Foreign Secretary from 1945, became one of the
most vehement opponents of the Soviet Foreign Minister, Molotov. There was
also a high degree of personal continuity within the British Foreign Office, which
exerted a great deal of influence over government policy.

    The impetus and activity of the Labour Party focused on domestic policy in
Britain rather than on social reform in Germany. Labour's interest in developments in Germany was also limited because after two world wars and the horrors
of National Socialism, relations between the Labour Party and its political partner

in Germany, the SPD, were at an all-time low. Thus the European Group of the Labour Party established contact with the French, rather than German, socialists (May and Paterson, 1977, pp.77–92).

But what about the Military Government personnel in Germany? Were they likely to formulate or implement a reform programme? This is difficult to assess as there are few sources providing details of the personal and professional background of Military Government officers on the ground (see also Reusch, 1980; Reusch, 1992). Nor is there much information on the recruiting policy followed. One of the most competent and efficient groups was the Political Division and the Manpower Division of the British Control Commission, which consisted of officials from the Foreign Office ranks or from the Ministry of Labour. Other Military Government staff had been recruited from colonial posts. At a time of demobilisation in Britain, Military Government employment in Germany attracted many people.

From the start, therefore, Britain's policy of democratising Germany was subordinate to other policy interests, be they international or domestic. None the less, 'democratisation' remained the slogan of British occupation policy. But what exactly did the British mean by democratisation? How was it to be implemented and what was the main area of concern – politics and/or the economy? What inconsistencies became apparent and how did the British react to German ideas and demands?

If we analyse the actual policy of democratisation it becomes apparent that Military Government officials used two different lines of argument – one in communications with the Germans and another when dealing with British authorities in London responsible for German policy. On 19 November 1945, at a meeting with the newly installed German *Oberpräsidenten* and *Landespräsidenten* (heads of provinces and heads of *Länder*) in the town hall in Detmold, General Templer, Deputy Chief-of-Staff of the British Military Government declared:

You are to be quite clear that one of our major objects in this country is to develop democracy having due regard to the German character, history and present political development. You are also to be quite clear in your minds that we have no intention of imposing a purely British conception of democracy on Germany.[6]

The frequently cited principle of 'not to impose', however, did not mean that British ideas of democracy were not introduced at all.

A more ideological concept was developed by the Deputy Military Governor, Brian Robertson, at a meeting with the House of Commons Select Committee on Estimates July 1946, in which he justified the occupation authorities' application for money:

Finally in a few words, I would like to tell you now what we are trying to do with the £80 millions that we are asking for . . . The first thing I claim that we are trying to do is that we are trying to ensure that the settlement of the German problem shall be influenced by British policy . . . Secondly, we are trying to penetrate the iron curtain. I do not mean by just walking across the border of the Russian Zone, but we are trying to get along with these Russians. We are trying to show them that it is possible for the two of us to work together and reach an agreement. Thirdly, we are trying to put across on the Germans our own ideas of democracy – democracy as we understand it, democracy as our Government understands it. The form in which we are putting it across is the form of a socialised democracy.[7]

Reading this, we must remember that Robertson needed the Labour Government to approve his budget. He went on to explain how the Military Government intended to implement its policy of democratisation, pointing to institutions such as political parties, trade unions, and the churches in Germany.

Since the beginning of the occupation the British authorities had been emphasising an understanding of democracy which was defined by the provision of democratic institutions. The phrase 'developing genuine democratic institutions' recurs frequently in British instructions. The aim was to create the framework for institutions which could provide the basis for a democratic order. This was to be achieved by licensing political parties and trade unions, setting up local and regional administrations, and preparing local elections. The British concept of democratisation was based on the Westminister model of a liberal, parliamentary representative democracy. One of the few existing quotations on the British understanding of democracy, found in the Military Government papers, simply cites Abraham Lincoln's Gettysburg Address of 1863: 'Government of the people, by the people, for the people'.[8]

Apart from these vague statements, few direct statements are documented about what exactly either the British Military Government in Germany, or the British ministries and authorities in London responsible for German policy, meant when they spoke of democracy and democratisation. In 1945, democracy was first seen simply as an antithesis to totalitarian dictatorship and National Socialism. Initially the point of reference for the re-organisation and reconstruction was Germany's first democracy, the Weimar Republic. However, this was clearly regarded in a negative light because it had exhibited too many weaknesses. In the British view it had been unable to resist totalitarian dictatorship.

British democracy and political traditions provided the model. Thus British democracy was described in British instructions as 'the most robust in the world. It is on British soil that it flourished best but we do export it and, tended carefully, it grows and flourishes in diverse lands, even if it takes a long time to acclimatize itself'.[9] In the name of British democratisation policy many more political than social and economic reforming initiatives were undertaken. This can be illustrated by reference to a number of examples.

Political parties were regarded as an important democratic institution and the mainstay of democratic reconstruction in Germany after 1945. Although the British Military Government claimed to be neutral in party political terms and in its relations with German political parties, its specific licensing practice ultimately created a system primarily based on two mass parties (see also Marshall, 1989, pp.208–214). Completely new party-political movements were at a disadvantage here compared with other parties which, like the SPD, could revive structures of communication and organisation from pre-Nazi days. The forming and licensing of political parties was permitted again from September 1945 in the British Zone.[10] It had begun as early as June 1945 in the Soviet Zone, which set a precedent.[11] In granting licenses, the British Military Government was concerned to prevent the formation of splinter parties, the proliferation of which was seen as one of the main weaknesses of the Weimar Republic, and one of the reasons for its failure.

Licensing policy followed the overall principle that democratisation was a gradual process and that 'German political life should be an organic growth from the bottom upwards, rather than something artificially imposed from above.'[12] Thus political parties were first established at local level, that is, in parishes, towns and *Kreise* (districts). Anyone applying for a licence had to give the local Military Government details of party programme, committee members, sources of finance, and membership fees. The Military Government examined these applications and approved or rejected them.

From October 1945 onwards the formation of the SPD, CDU and KPD was facilitated and accelerated because these three parties did not have to go through the same licensing procedure as other political parties, which held up some applications for several months.[13] Two months later branches of the SPD, CDU and KPD were organised and established at local level all over the British Zone. Because they were so widely dispersed, the Military Government granted them permission to form central party committees in the British Zone on 3 December 1945. The licensing of other political parties was still confined to the local level and as soon as they could demonstrate sufficiently strong local support Military Government considered licensing them at regional and zonal level.[14] This gave parties which could revive communication structures from before the war a definite advantage. Also crucial was another Military Government instruction which brought to a standstill the registration of small and any new parties during the campaign for the first local elections in the British Zone, that is, from June until September/October 1946.[15] This licensing policy gave particularly the SPD, CDU and KPD such a large organisational and political head-start, that the other parties were never able to catch up.

On the question of which electoral system should be introduced in Germany after 1945, the British authorities at first insisted on the introduction of majority voting, and rejected the proportional voting system which had been in use in Germany before 1933 (Lange, 1975),[16] and which was reintroduced after 1945 in the American, Soviet and French Zones. From the British point of view, majority voting was intended to help instil in the Germans a 'new conception of party politics' (Rudzio, 1969, pp.220–21). In general, it was believed that majority voting was the more democratic system. As a British memorandum explained: 'One of the main arguments in favour of this system is that it provides strong government and tends towards simple two-party politics, thereby avoiding splinter parties and political bargaining'.[17] But the British view in this matter was not unanimous. The Political Division of the British Control Commission in particular was not averse to proportional representation, whereas the Foreign Office and, most of all, the Home Office in London strongly supported the introduction of the majority vote in the British Zone. Ultimately, however, a mixed system of majority and pro-portional voting was introduced in 1946, taking account of German attitudes and proposals in this matter, and above all, the preference of the political parties for proportional representation. The German Minister, John B. Hynd, explained this position to the Home Secretary in February:

What I of course want to avoid if at all possible is thrusting on the Germans in the name of democracy an alien system which is not acceptable to the German political parties. I think I should have great difficulty in defending such a policy to the House of Commons.[18]

Trade unions were another mainstay of democratic reconstruction emphasised by the British. From August 1945 the Military Government permitted the creation of the first workers' committees on the condition that they were limited to individual firms. However, the British pursued a very restrictive policy towards the rebuilding of trade unions, slowing down the process of establishing a trade union organisation in the British Zone. They feared the possibility that trade unions might become a politically powerful instrument, and in particular, Communist influence. The British saw these fears confirmed by the creation of the central trade union organisation in the Soviet Zone, the *Freier Deutscher Gewerkschaftsbund*, which was regarded as a Russian-organised body (Steininger, 1978, p.66). Two factors influenced the development of trade unions after 1945. First, the actual setting up of a trade union organisation was impeded by a complicated, three-stage licensing procedure. Secondly, the Military Government insisted on the British system of individual unions for each individual professional group or trade. Given the negative experience during the Weimar Republic with trade unions attached to political camps (*Richtungsgewerkschaften*) which also caused social tensions, most German trade unionists in 1945 advocated a single, centralised union (*Einheitsgewerkschaft*), which would embrace workers, white-collar employees and civil servants (Plum, 1976, pp.93–94; Steininger, 1978, p.64; Hubsch, 1989, p.73). The crucial step in deciding the future shape of German trade unions was taken in the North Rhine province, the most industrialised region in the British Zone. On 23 November 1945 the British Military Government's Manpower Division organised a meeting in Düsseldorf between German trade unionists and a delegation from the British Trade Union Congress during its visit to the British Zone. On this occasion the British trade unionists rejected German proposals for a trade union organisation as over-centralised (Hubsch, 1989, p.273). After a second meeting with German trade unionists in Berlin the TUC delegates in a letter to Hans Böckler, the German union leader, advised him in favour of the Military Government's idea of forming individual and independent unions. On 7 December 1945, trade unionists from the North Rhine province decided to follow this advice and organise in industrial unions in order to get some sort of organisation and work started (Steininger, 1978, pp.82–83). This set the course for the development of unions in the whole of the British Zone. In the autumn of 1946 the Military Government relaxed its regulations concerning the establishment of unions provided that the real independence of individual member unions was not diminished. However, British policy on trade unions in Germany had long kept the unions fragmented, and thus weakened their political power and ability to influence such issues as co-determination. On the other hand, it could be argued that this policy was in line with the concept of decentralisation. In April 1947 the central organisation of German trade unions, the *Deutsche Gewerkschaftsbund (Britische Zone)* was founded.

Administrative reform is another example illustrating the political and institutional democratisation of Germany. No large-scale administrative reform took place in Germany after 1945. The structure of the *Reich* administration was retained in principle and the many specialised agencies (*Sonderverwaltungen*) which were set up during the Third Reich were not immediately dissolved. Administrative reform was limited to personnel. In this context democratisation was reduced to denazification and decentralisation. Any wide-ranging structural reform would have brought the danger of administrative collapse. Thus any idea of structural reform was abandoned for pragmatic reasons. All efforts were concentrated on local government. This is a striking example of how British conceptions and traditions were transferred to Germany.

Local government in the British Zone was modelled on the British system. Under the split system of local government an honorary *Bürgermeister* was installed, just like an English mayor, while a *Gemeinde-/Stadtdirektor* assumed the functions of a town clerk in England. Thus a strict separation was introduced between political, executive and administrative functions (Rudzio, 1968; Rudzio, 1969, p.221).[19] In addition, local self-government was strengthened on the English model. The 'Military Government Directive on Administration, Local and Regional Government and the Public Services' of September 1945 justified this by reference to the English system:

In England national government is entirely distinct from local government. In Germany on the other hand, There was at every level a 'balance of power' between state government and self-government. Throughout state and self-government were in part running parallel and in part interlocked . . . This antithesis was made more complicated by the existence of state functions which were 'delegated' to local authorities. This dual system will be broken down. The regional administration will not therefore be an organ of state government . . . As many functions as possible will be decentralised to *Kreis* and *Gemeinde* level.[20]

The German reaction to this reform of local government was negative. At their first meeting in Hamburg on 29 October 1945 the heads of provinces and *Länder*, pointing to long-standing German democratic traditions, rejected the British model as imposed from above.[21] However, the British authorities prevailed. They introduced a system of local government whose basic features have been retained in northern Germany to the present day.

These examples demonstrate how the British policy of democratising German political life was influenced and guided by British political traditions and historical experiences. In order to gain an overall picture of British democratisation policy, its impact on economic structures in Germany after 1945 must be assessed. Because of the problems encountered in this area during the Weimar Republic, advocates of social democracy aimed to sweep away the contradiction between a democratic constitution and the influence of industrial pressure groups (Niclauß, 1974, p.29). Three basic demands stand out as central to social democracy: the demand for a planned economy, co-determination, and the nationalisation (socialisation) of certain industries (ibid., pp.30–32).

Until 1947 the British Military Government's economic policy aimed to create a planned economy, attempting to direct industrial production centrally and comprehensively. The so-called Sparta Plans, introduced by the Military Government from 1946, provided for the distribution of raw materials (especially coal and steel) to specific industries. These plans favoured primary industry and the capital goods industries (*Grundstoff und Investitionsgüterindustrie*), while the production of consumer goods was reduced to a minimum (Drexler, Krumbein and Stratmann, 1985, pp.245–63). 'Given that money and the market were almost totally excluded as regulators, and that the aim of the British was to direct the economy almost completely by granting permits for production, controlling distribution, and so on', this can be seen as the beginning of a planned economy (ibid., p.261). The Sparta Plans, however, were limited to specific industrial sectors. It is doubtful whether this planned economy was an ideologically motivated, socialist system of planning and control. If this were the case, corresponding measures such as democratising the economic administration would also have been introduced (see also Petzina and Euchner, 1984). British economic policy needed to transform a wartime, command economy into a self-sufficient peace-time economy. Given the material war damage suffered by Germany, the ailing currency, and the constraints under which Allied economic policy operated, the consequences of the war could not be overcome without direct control of production and distribution (Plumpe, 1987, p.335). On the other hand, however, the Military Government gave German politicians, administrators and industrialists a certain amount of latitude, within which alternative models of economic planning could be developed. Whether or not they were put into practice is not the main concern of this discussion. On 21–22 June 1946 a conference of experts on economic planning and control was held in Hamburg. This conference, approved by the British Military Government, provided a forum in which ideas for Germany's future and social order could be discussed (Abelshauser, 1976, pp.415–49).

Many discussions were held on the issue of co-determination. The Allied Works' Council Law of 10 April 1946 (ACC Law No 22) provided an important foundation for the right of codetermination. This law represented a mixture of Weimar legacy and Anglo-Saxon legal traditions. While it provided the legal basis for worker representation on company boards, it did not define their scope of action. The rights, duties and responsibilities of workers' representatives were essentially left to be negotiated between employers and works' councils (Muller, 1987, p.49). The issue of what specific works agreements were reached gained special significance. On 15–16 February 1947 the Zonal Secretariat of the *Deutscher Gewerkschaftsbund (DGB)* produced a model agreement which contained a number of minimum rights of participation for workers' representatives (ibid., p.149). The Military Government, however, did not permit this model agreement to be used in any of the companies under its direct control (ibid., pp.151–52). On the other hand a specific form of co-determination was agreed upon for the iron and steel industry in the British Zone in January 1947. This provided a model for other regulations and laws after 1949. When the iron and steel industry was decartelised, management structures were also reorganised.

Representatives of workers and trade unions were appointed to the supervisory boards of the independent firms which were being formed. A labour director sat on the management board with the other two directors, and enjoyed equal status with them. The labour director was responsible for financial and technical matters, personnel and social policy (Hubsch, 1989, pp.286–87). All attempts to expand works' councils rights further were rejected by the Military Government and the Foreign Office, who opposed the ideas and demands of the *DGB* (see also Roseman, 1992).

The nationalisation of industries – not only in Britain – was a political issue of some importance to the British Labour Government. For some time it was also a major aim of British occupation policy. Since the summer of 1945 government committees in London had discussed 'socialising' industries in the British Zone. However, it was felt that direct British intervention in German economic structures of ownership was undesirable, as was any move which pre-empted the Germans' freedom of decision. In response to miners' demands, however, the

British government later indicated that it would introduce 'a system of ownership which will be consistent with democratic principles' (Lademacher, 1985, p.105; see also Steininger, 1985, pp.135–50). In December 1945 the first confiscations took place in Germany – the Ruhr coal mines were placed under British control. The final Cabinet decision was made on 21 October 1946, and on the following day in the House of Commons Ernest Bevin announced the 'socialisation' of key industries in the British Zone. International involvement complicated and delayed the process; France and the Benelux countries demanded that their financial claims should be met if German industries were socialised (ibid., p.109). In 1947 the USA rejected socialisation in principle. The Washington Coal Conference in August-September 1947 actually forced a postponement of British socialisation plans by referring to Britain's financial dependence on the USA. From that time on socialisation was practically put on ice. The *New Statesman* reported that Britain was caught between American dollars and socialist principles (Carden, 1979, p.550). The socialisation of German industries was frequently mentioned during House of Commons debates; MPs repeatedly stressed the importance of the socialisation policy, thus also justifying and defending the policy of nationalising British industries.

In 1948 the British Military Government, after having first encouraged plans for socialisation in the individual *Länder* of the British Zone, finally vetoed the socialisation bills put forward in North Rhine-Westphalia and Schleswig-Holstein. US influence on decisions such as this is only one side of the story. Opposition to the socialisation of industries was also growing among the Germans. Only a small majority supported the bills in North Rhine-Westphalia and Schleswig-Holstein. Thus in May 1948 the British authorities referred to the decision of the London Foreign Ministers' meeting of November-December 1947 that socialisation should go through only with the consent of the German people. On 21 May 1948 the Foreign Office announced that 'until a properly representative German body has been constituted this decision cannot be taken' (Rudzio, 1981, p.347).

From 1948 the main concern of the Military Government was not to pre-empt decisions about Germany's social and economic system, but to leave such decisions to a future West German government. It is often pointed out that from 1948 British policy followed US policy on Germany; but at the same time German opposition to 'socialist' planning was growing. A new model of a social market economy was developed (see also Ambrosius, 1977; Ambrosius, 1979, pp.74–110). However, the Basic Law of 1949 did not explicitly define the structures of the Federal Republic of Germany's social and economic system. Political parties discussed alternatives – such as a planned or a market economy – and issues such as this provided the focus of the election campaign in 1949.

In this respect it could be argued that British democratisation policy achieved its aims. But it must be admitted that this policy was not entirely consistent. In some areas of political reform purely British conceptions were introduced, in other areas they were not. The same applies to economic reform. But was it possible to implement a consistent policy? Several factors influenced the formation of British policy in Germany and its democratisation policy. In the international context, American policy, Anglo-American co-operation and anti-Communist attitudes had a strong impact. But even more important and chacteristic for the British approach was the high degree of communication and co-operation between British officials and German politicians, heads of administration, and trade unionists, and a willingness on the British side to take German concepts into consideration.

Notes

1. PRO FO 371/55611, Address by the Deputy Military Governor to the Zonal Advisory Council, 6 March 1946. Research for this article is based on the reading of archival sources in the PRO Kew/London, primarily the files of the Control Commission for Germany (British Element), and literature referred to in the attached bibliography.
2. PRO CAB 99/38, 'Terminal' Record of the Proceedings of the Berlin Conference 17th July to 1st August, 1945, III. Protocol, p.276.
3. Parliamentary Papers, Reports from Committees, 1945/46, vol.VII, House of Commons Select Committee on Estimates, 2nd Report, 'The Control Office for Germany and Austria (Expenditure in Germany)', pp.15–16; see also one year later the 8th Report from the House of Commons Select Committee on Estimates, 'British Expenditure in Germany', ibid., Reports from Committees, 1946/47, vol.VIII.
4. 27 November 1946, Hansard, 5th ser., 430:1700; 5 February 1947, Hansard, 5th ser., 432:1830, 1788; 28 February 1947, Hansard, 5th ser., 433.
5. 4 August 1947, Hansard, 5th ser., 441:1004.
6. PRO FO 1050/149.
7. Parliamentary Papers, Reports from Committees, 1945/1946, Vol.VII, House of Commons Select Committee on Estimates, Minutes of Evidence, 2 July 1946, p.491.
8. PRO FO 1060/1151, Military Government Directive on Administration, Local and Regional Government and the Public Service, Part I, 2nd edition, revised, 1 February 1946; PRO FO 1049/432, W.R. Hinde, BTB Berlin, 12 August 1946.
9. PRO FO 1060/1151, Military Government Directive on Administration, Local and Regional Government and the Public Service, Part I; see also: PRO FO 1050/432.
10. PRO FO 1030/423, Military Government Ordinance no.12, 15 September 1945.
11. SMAD Order no.2, 10 June 1945.
12. PRO FO 1050/150, Heymann, 28 September 1945.
13. PRO FO 1049/142, ALG Bünde, 3 October 1945; ibid., Political Division, Lübecke, 9 October 1945.
14. PRO FO 1030/423, Zonal Policy Instruction no.19, 3 December 1945.
15. PRO FO 1050/19, ALG Bünde, 12 June 1946.
16. PRO FO 1049/239, Zonal Policy Instruction no.9, 30 November 1945; see also PRO FO 1050/140, discussion between H. Ingrams and E. Holderness at the Home Office, 23–26 October 1945.
17. PRO HO 45/25173, memorandum for the German Working Party on Electoral Procedure, 13 February 1946.
18. PRO HO 45/25173, John B. Hynd to Chuter Ede, 11 February 1946.
19. PRO FO 1050/432 and FO 1060/1152, Military Government Directive on Administration, Local and Regional Government and the Public Services, Part I, 2nd edition, revised, 1 February 1946.
20. ibid.
21. PRO FO 1050/149.

References

Abelshauser, W. (1976), 'Freiheitlicher Sozialismus oder soziale Marktwirtschaft? Die Gutachtertagung über Grundfragen der Wirtschaftsplanung und Wirtschaftslenkung am 21. und 22. Juni 1946', *Vierteljahrshefte für Zeitgeschichte*, 24 (4): pp.415–49.

Ambrosius, G. (1977), *Die Durchsetzung der sozialen Marktwirtschaft in Westdeutschland 1945–1949* (Studien zur Zeitgeschichte, 10; Beiträge zur Wirtschafts- und Sozialpolitik in Deutschland nach 1945, I), Stuttgart Deutsche Verlags-Anstalt.

Ambrosius, G. (1979) 'Marktwirtschaft oder Planwirtschaft? Planwirtschaftliche Ansätze der bizonalen deutschen Selbstverwaltung 1946–1949', *Vierteljahrschrift fur Sozial- und Wirtschaftgeschichte*, 66 (1): pp.74–110.

Carden, R.W. (1979), 'Before Bizonia: Britain's economic dilemma in Germany, 1945–46', *Journal of Contemporary History*, 14, (3): pp.535–55.

Deighton, A. (1990), *The Impossible Peace: Britain, the Division of Germany and the Origins of the Cold War*, Oxford, Clarendon Press.

Drexler, A., Krumbein, W., and Stratmann, F. (1985), 'Die britischen "Sparta-Pläne" 1946', in: Foschepoth, J. and Steininger, R., eds, *Die britische Deutschland- und Besatzungspolitik 1945–1949* (Sammlung Schöningh zur Geschichte und Gegenwart), Paderborn Ferdinand Schöningh, pp.245–63.

Hubsch, P.(1989), 'DGB economic policy with particular reference to the British Zone', in: Turner, I.D., (ed.), *Reconstruction in Post-War Germany: British Occupation Policy and the Western Zones 1945–1955*, Oxford, Berg, pp.271–300.

Lademacher, H. (1985), 'Die britische Sozialisierungspolitik im Rhein-Ruhr-Raum', in: Foschepoth, J. and Steininger, R., eds, *Die britische Deutschland- und Besatzungspolitik 1945–1949*, Paderborn, Ferdinand Schöningh: pp.101–117.

Lange, E.H.M. (1975), *Wahlrecht und Innenpolitik. Entstehungsgeschichte und Analyse der Wahlgesetzgebung und Wahlrechtsdiskussion im westlichen Nachkriegsdeutschland 1945–1956* (Marburger Abhandlungen zur Politischen Wissenschaft, 26), Meisenheim am Glan, Verlag Anton Hain.

Laski, H.J. (1943), *Reflections on Revolutions of Our Time*, London, George Allen & Unwin Ltd.

Marshall, B. (1989), 'British democratisation policy in Germany', in: Turner, I.D., (ed.), *Reconstruction in Post-War Germany: British Occupation Policy and the Western Zones 1945–1955*, Oxford, Berg, pp.189–214.

May, J.P. and Paterson, W.E. (1977), 'Die Deutschlandkonzeption der Britischen Labour Party 1945–1949', *Politische und ökonomische Stabilisierung Westdeutschlands 1945–1949. Fünf Beiträge zur Deutschlandpolitik der westlichen Alliierten* (Veröffentlichungen des Instituts für Europäische Geschichte Mainz, Abteilung Universalgeschichte, Beiheft 4), Wiesbaden, Franz Steiner Verlag GmbH: pp.77–92.

Müller, G. (1987), *Mitbestimmung in der Nachkriegszeit. Britische Besatzungsmacht – Unternehmer – Gewerkschaften* (Düsseldorfer Schriften zur Neueren Landesgeschichte und zur Geschichte Nordrhein-Westfalens, 21), Düsseldorf, Schwann.

Niclauß, K. (1974), *Demokratiegründung in Westdeutschland. Die Entstehung der Bundesrepublik von 1945–1949* (Texte und Studien zur Politologie, Piper Sozialwissenschaft, 23), Munich, R. Piper & Co. Verlag.

Petzina, D. and Euchner, W. (eds), 1984, *Wirtschaftspolitik im britischen Besatzungsgebiet 1945–1949* (Düsseldorfer Schriften zur Neueren Landesgeschichte und zur Geschichte Nordrhein Westfalens, 12), Düsseldorf, Schwann.

Plum, G. (1976), 'Versuche gesellschaftspolitischer Neuordnung – Ihr Scheitern im Kräftefeld deutscher und alliierter Politik', *Westdeutschlands Weg zur Bundesrepublik 1945–1949*, Beiträge von Mitarbeitern des Instituts für Zeitgeschichte (Beck'sche Schwarze Reihe, 137), Munich, Verlag C.H. Beck: pp.90–117.

Plumpe, W. (1987), *Vom Plan zum Markt. Wirtschaftsverwaltung und Unternehmerverbände in der britischen Zone* (Düsseldorfer Schriften zur Neueren Landesgeschichte und zur Geschichte Nordrhein-Westfalens, 22), Düsseldorf, Schwann.

Reusch, U. (1980), 'Die Londoner Institutionen der britischen Deutschlandpolitik 1943–1948. Eine behördengeschichtliche Untersuchung', *Historisches Jahrbuch*, 100: pp.318–

443.

Reusch, U. (1992), 'Der Verwaltungsaufbau der britischen Kontrollbehörden in London und der Militärregierung in der britischen Besatzungszone', in: Birke, A.M. and Mayring, E.A., (eds), *Britische Besatzung in Deutschland. Aktenerschließ und Forschungsfelder*, London: pp.35–59.

Roseman, M. (1992), *Recasting the Ruhr, 1945–1958. Manpower, Economic Recovery and Labour Relations*, Oxford, Berg.

Rudzio, W., 1968, *Die Neuordnung des Kommunalwesens in der Britischen Zone. Zur Demokratisierung und Dezentralisierung der politischen Struktur: eine britische Reform und ihr Ausgang* (Quellen und Darstellungen zur Zeitgeschichte, 17), Stuttgart, Deutsche Verlags-Anstalt.

Rudzio, W., 1969, 'Export englischer Demokratie? Zur Konzeption der britischen Besatzungspolitik in Deutschland. Dokumentation' *Vierteljahrshefte für Zeitgeschichte*, 17 (2): p.219–36.

Rudzio, W. (1981), 'Großbritannien als sozialistische Besatzungsmacht in Deutschland – Aspekte des deutsch-britischen Verhältnisses 1945–1948', in: Kettenacker, L., Schlenke, M. and Seier, H., eds, *Studien zur Geschichte Englands und der deutsch-britischen Beziehungen*. Festschrift für Paul Kluke, Munich, Wilhelm Fink Verlag: pp.341–52.

Schneider, U. (1985), 'Nach dem Sieg. Besatzungspolitik und Militärregierung', in: Foschepoth, J. and Steininger, R., eds, *Die britische Deutschland- und Besatzungspolitik 1945–1949*, Paderborn, Ferdinand Schöningh: pp.47–64.

Steininger, R. (1978), 'England und die deutsche Gewerkschaftsbewegung 1945/46', *Archiv für Sozialgeschichte*, 18 (1): pp.41–118.

Steininger, R. (1985), 'Die Sozialisierung fand nicht statt', in: Foschepoth, J. and Steininger, R., eds, *Die britische Deutschland- und Besatzungspolitik 1945–1949*, Paderborn, Ferdinand Schöningh: pp.87–98.

Vilmar, F. (1985), 'Demokratisierung', in: Nohlen, D., Schultze, R.-O. (eds), *Pipers Wörterbuch zur Politik, Bd.1, Politikwissenschaft, Theorien, Methoden, Begriffe, T.1*, Munich, R. Piper & Co. Verlag: pp.144–45.

II
Britain in Search of a role? 1956–73

8

Britain and the EEC, 1956–73: an overview

John W. Young

The Suez Crisis of 1956 not only highlighted Britain's inability to dictate world events, it also presented an opportunity to reconsider the country's international role, and in early January 1957 the Foreign Secretary, Selwyn Lloyd, proposed to the Cabinet that Britain should seek a European future. In the dying days of Anthony Eden's premiership, Lloyd argued that Britain should co-operate with the West European nations particularly in the area of nuclear energy, and should create a third power able to match the US and USSR. However other Cabinet ministers, stunned by the rift with Washington during the Suez Crisis, were firmly opposed to such an option[1] and, in the early months of his premiership, Harold Macmillan concentrated on restoring the 'special relationship' with America. Thus in March 1957 Macmillan met President Eisenhower in Bermuda, while that same month the French – alienated by the British 'betrayal' over Suez – joined West Germany, Italy, Belgium, Holland and Luxembourg in signing the Treaties of Rome, creating a European Economic Community (EEC) and an atomic energy authority (Euratom). At the outset Britain failed to join the EEC, which soon became a powerful trading bloc, benefiting from high growth rates among its members. Relations with this new force in world affairs soon became important to British politicians and the public, as Britain's own standing continued to decline. In 1961, with the days of Empire numbered and the US showing strong support for European integration, Macmillan was to seek common market membership. Yet it took another twelve years to achieve the aim.

The free trade area proposal, 1956–59

The potential economic strength *and* political significance of the Common Market was already of concern to British policy makers when the Six EEC powers began their negotiations in 1955–56. In November 1956 Britain announced its desire to form a 'free trade area' (FTA) between the Six and other European powers, using as a base the Organisation of European Economic Co-operation (formed in 1948). There were several differences between the British FTA and the EEC. Most importantly the FTA would involve no 'pooling of sovereignty' among members, it would allow countries to follow their own trade policy towards the rest of the world, and it would only involve industrial products, since a common policy on agriculture was likely to demand a 'closed' market with high prices to protect European farmers. In other words, the FTA was designed to preserve Britain's independence, its world trade role and its advantages as an industrial power. At this time Britain was still the strongest West European economy and the Six proved ready to consider the FTA proposal. However, they were already suspicious that Britain aimed to 'sabotage' the EEC, they were determined (despite some differences among themselves) to safeguard the hard-won Treaties of Rome, and they did not feel that the FTA offered them many advantages (Camps, 1964). As one Foreign Office official acknowledged, the Commonwealth (with trade preferences in Britain) 'could expose European goods coming into Britain to competition which British goods entering the Common Market would not suffer'. Another official, the Ambassador to Paris, Gladwyn Jebb, did not believe the FTA would solve Britain's European dilemma anyway since, even if the FTA succeeded, it would not prevent the EEC becoming a powerful political-economic group (Gore-Booth, 1974, p.247; Jebb, 1972, pp.292–99). Britain's freedom of manoeuvre seemed strictly limited. Any wholehearted attempt to destroy the EEC was out of the question since it could well fail, would alienate the Six, and would be opposed by the Americans, who saw the EEC as a way both to tie West Germany to other liberal democracies and to create a thriving, anti-communist bloc in Europe. On the other hand, there was little enthusiasm among British political leaders to pool sovereignty with the EEC, the public were as yet hardly aware of the Treaties of Rome, and 43 per cent of British trade was with the Commonwealth. Indeed, at the 1957 Commonwealth conference, Canadian premier John Diefenbaker proposed a rejuvenated Commonwealth trade system.

The FTA never made swift progress and was eventually killed off by the French. There was an initial delay because the Six insisted on ratifying the Treaties of Rome *before* discussing the FTA. This itself put Macmillan's chief negotiator, Reginald Maudling, in a weak position *vis-à-vis* the Six. Talks got underway in the OEEC in October 1957, but they were highly technical and could not overcome the basic problem: why should the Six allow FTA members access to the Common Market without accepting all the obligations of the Treaty of Rome, such as common institutions and a commitment to common agricultural policies? Then, in May 1958, came the demise of the Fourth Republic and the coming to power of Charles de Gaulle. Although no economic expert, and despite his initial pre-occupation with the colonial war in Algeria, he was determined to defend French interests and could see little to gain from the FTA. His negotiators took a tough approach to the talks before, in November, making it clear that the FTA was only possible if it became a virtual carbon copy of the EEC, which was out of the question for Britain and other countries. This could be seen as de Gaulle's first 'non' to a British attempt to come to terms with the Common Market. However, there had been plenty of problems *before* de Gaulle came to power.

A commercial division of Western Europe was avoided on 1 January 1959, because the Six agreed to extend the tariff cuts, due among themselves on that date, to the other OEEC States. Many OEEC members were none the less extremely concerned about the first steps towards a common market, especially countries like Denmark, Austria and Switzerland, which depended on West German markets. It was partly in order to reassure these countries, that in May

1959 the British government decided to pursue a limited free trade agreement with Sweden, Norway, Denmark, Austria, Switzerland and Portugal. The agreement to create a European Free Trade Association (EFTA) was signed in November in Stockholm, where the Swedish government had been enthusiastic about the proposal. However, in itself EFTA was only part of the solution to Britain's problems. Maudling's memoirs are clear that 'the purpose of EFTA . . . was that it should form a basis for negotiating a comprehensive European settlement' (Maudling, 1978, p.78). British businessmen only saw the seven-power EFTA as useful if it led to a deal with the Six, whose markets must be kept open to British goods on the basis of equal trade. Macmillan himself, despite winning the October general election, was as worried about the EEC as ever, telling Selwyn Lloyd, 'For the first time since the Napoleonic era the continental powers are united in a positive economic grouping, with considerable political aspects, which . . . may [exclude] us from . . . European policy' (Macmillan, 1972, pp.54–56). By now de Gaulle had established good relations with Germany's Konrad Adenauer, while Eisenhower met Nikita Khrushchev in late 1959 at the first US-Soviet summit. Excluded from the superpower relationship and the Franco-German relationship, with the African colonies set for independence and with no signs that de Gaulle wanted an EEC-EFTA deal, it is not surprising that Macmillan began to consider Common Market membership for Britain.

Macmillan's bid to 'enter Europe', 1960–63

In early 1960 officials working in the Economic Steering (Europe) Committee, under Sir Frank Lee, became more sympathetic to an application for EEC membership. At the same time the Americans made clear their dislike of an EFTA-EEC trade arrangement because this would harm US exports without bringing the potential benefits of the Treaty of Rome. The public were still poorly informed about the EEC, but by the middle of the year some newspapers too were in favour of EEC entry, and at the same time considerable debate began about Britain's economic under-performance, its declining power and its social divisions. Never the less, when the EEC problem was discussed by the Cabinet in mid-1960 Macmillan refused to press the issue too quickly. The Cabinet decided simply to draw closer to the EEC in some indeterminate way.[2] This showed a recognition of the power of the Six and acknowledged that Britain's three circles' policy, of maintaining links to America and the Commonwealth, as well as Europe, was no longer sufficient. But Macmillan needed to tackle a number of problems before he decided whether actually to apply for Community membership. One early move was to appoint 'pro-European' ministers to the Cabinet, notably Edward Heath, who was given special responsibility for European affairs. Then, in August, Macmillan visited Germany's Chancellor Konrad Adenauer in Bonn, where they reached agreement on official talks between their two countries on linking Britain to the EEC. There was an exchange of views with Commonwealth representatives in September 1960 and in November the Federation of British Industry declared its support for membership of the EEC. Macmillan was also keen to win the support of the new Kennedy administration in America for British membership and, over Christmas, drew up a long memorandum which set out a 'Grand Design' for reconciling British, American and European needs. Macmillan always recognised, however, that the key to a successful application would be de Gaulle's attitude. All the other Community members were likely to favour British entry, but if de Gaulle was opposed there was no point trying. Macmillan could be satisfied therefore that, when he visited the French President in January 1961, it was agreed to begin Franco-British talks about the EEC, similar to those with Germany. De Gaulle may have agreed to this because of Macmillan's positive view of ideas for French-British nuclear co-operation. For de Gaulle was determined to increase France's standing in the world but, whilst she had exploded an atomic bomb in 1960, she lacked a missile system to deliver it.

During early 1961 British statements showed that they still felt in a strong negotiating position. Heath made it plain that special arrangements would be needed for the Commonwealth and EFTA before Britain joined the EEC, and that there could be no Community interference in foreign and defence policy (such as was currently being discussed by the Six). Ideally Britain would have preferred to know what conditions she could obtain *before* submitting a formal application. The nationalist wing of the Conservative party, pro-Commonwealth politicians (in both main parties) and the farming lobby were still anti-Common Market. But the pressures to submit an application continued to mount. The Six felt this the best way forward, public expectations had now been raised and President Kennedy strongly favoured such a move. Also, the quicker Britain entered, the sooner she could influence EEC developments and prevent a tariff 'wall' between herself and the continent. In July the Cabinet finally agreed to apply for EEC membership, and Macmillan subsequently told the Commons that this move would pay economic dividends, would strengthen Britain's international role and need not infringe sovereignty too much. Yet he always acknowledged that the Commonwealth, EFTA and agricultural problems would cause problems for the application. These issues all figured highly in Heath's opening statement to EEC ministers when negotiations began in October 1961.

In November, when experts of Britain and the Six began to look in detail at the application, de Gaulle visited Macmillan and showed continuing doubts about British membership. In particular, the General believed Britain's links to America and the Commonwealth would upset the balance of the EEC in which France was currently the leading power. In January 1962 furthermore, the application was complicated when the Six agreed on the first moves towards a Common Agricultural Policy (CAP) which guaranteed high incomes for farmers, but did so by pushing up food prices and restricting agricultural imports – neither very appealing for Britain, which was allowed no influence on the CAP talks. Genuine negotiations on EEC entry only got underway in May, when the experts' studies were completed, setting out the main areas of disagreement. In June Macmillan had a more hopeful meeting with de Gaulle, at the Chateau de Champs, when the General seemed genuinely to favour British membership, but French officials adopted a tough line over the following months in talks on access for Commonwealth produce to the EEC. Meanwhile Macmillan's government was heading towards a crisis for other reasons: in July, in the 'Night of the Long Knives' he sacked a number of leading ministers. In September the Commonwealth Prime Ministers' conference was openly divided on the Common Market and the Labour leader, Hugh Gaitskell, decided to exploit the situation by attacking EEC membership. And, as problems mounted at home and in the

Commonwealth for Macmillan, so de Gaulle's position was strengthening. In 1962 the long war in Algeria came to an end, and in November his supporters easily won a general election.

It is difficult to say when de Gaulle decided to veto Britain's first EEC application. Pierson Dixon, the Ambassador to Paris, had long expected that de Gaulle would await the French elections and then end the British bid; but Macmillan considered Dixon's view as 'unbelievable' (Roth, 1972, p.162; Dixon, 1968, pp.282–3) and in mid-1962 at least de Gaulle seemed positive about the application. The event which finally pushed him into using his veto was the Nassau Agreement between Macmillan and Kennedy in December, by which Britain purchased American 'Polaris' missiles in order to launch its nuclear weapons. Although a similar deal was offered to France, de Gaulle's determination to stand independent of America was well known and he was angry at the new Anglo-American link. In January 1963 he not only vetoed Britain's application, claiming Britain was not 'European' enough, but reforged his links to Adenauer with a Franco-German Treaty on co-operation. (Adenauer was determined to end the centuries-old enmity with France.) The veto upset the rest of the EEC and the Americans, and led Macmillan to claim that de Gaulle wanted 'a Napoleonic or Louis XIV hegemony' in Europe (Macmillan, 1973, p.366). Yet no other power was willing to enrage de Gaulle for Britain's sake, and it was Macmillan who paid the price for the veto. By October 1963, when he was forced to resign as Prime Minister through ill-health, Macmillan's political position was already weak, thanks partly to his EEC failure. Despite his reputation as a 'pro-European' minister he did not press EEC membership with much vigour during 1960–63, and would have preferred an FTA-type deal. He ultimately put the US alliance at the forefront of his concerns (as he had in March 1957).

The Wilson Government, 1964–70

When Harold Wilson defeated Alec Douglas-Home to become premier in October 1964 another application to 'enter Europe' seemed unlikely. The new government had a narrow majority; the previous Labour leader, Hugh Gaitskell, had declared that EEC membership would 'betray a thousand years of British history' (Williams, 1979, Chapter 18); and many Labour leaders continued to put great faith in the Commonwealth and in the American alliance. But Britain's poor economic performance in 1964–66 continued to contrast with growth rates in the EEC, and the five Community members other than France still wanted Britain to join. In early 1965 a new attempt to link EEC and EFTA countries together in a trade arrangement came to nothing, and meanwhile the Common Market continued to develop, notably with agreements on the protectionist Common Agriculture Policy (CAP). In spring 1965 support for Community membership strengthened in two key ministries: the Department of Economic Affairs, a new ministry designed to direct national economic policy, under Labour's controversial deputy leader George Brown, a firm 'pro-European', who believed membership would improve British competitiveness and provide a stronger base for British political influence in the world; and the Foreign Office, under Michael Stewart, where the leading advocate of a new application to join was Sir Con O'Neill, who had been Ambassador to the EEC in 1963–65. In December 1965 Brown and

Stewart tried to circulate a Cabinet paper urging EEC entry, but this was scotched by Wilson (Crossman, 1975, entries of 31 January and 2 February 1966). Many ministers, especially left-wingers, but also moderates like trade minister Douglas Jay, argued that the EEC would undermine Britain's independence and world role, and increase food costs, thus worsening the balance of payments. Wilson could not afford to let the issue divide the party before he had secured a comfortable Commons majority, as he did in the March 1966 general election.

Once the election was won, however, Wilson moved fairly quickly towards an EEC application. A manipulative individual, determined to prove his party's ability to govern, and lacking any genuine idealism about European unity, Wilson may only have been motivated by party-political considerations. Public opinion polls were favourable to the EEC in 1965–67, businessmen were pressing for membership, and the new Conservative leader, Edward Heath, was firmly pro-Europe. But Wilson may also have been influenced by a desire to strengthen British industry – and especially by the potential for European technological co-operation – and by the failure of the US alliance and Commonwealth to bolster British power. Wilson's relations with America's President Johnson were poor and the Commonwealth was divided over Rhodesia. Wilson also seems to have been impressed by General de Gaulle's refusal to surrender French sovereignty to the EEC. In 1966 de Gaulle secured the 'Luxembourg Compromise' allowing EEC members to veto policies which threatened vital national interests. In contrast to the Foreign Office, where Con O'Neill was critical of de Gaulle's disruptive policies, Wilson evidently believed he could co-operate with the French President to minimise any loss of national sovereignty in the EEC. Wilson was probably moving towards the idea of an application before the 1966 election, because immediately afterwards he gave Brown authority to concentrate his energies on the EEC. And, although the Labour manifesto said that Britain would only join the EEC 'provided essential . . . interests are safeguarded', Wilson soon interpreted this as meaning that the *principle* of *trying* to secure favourable entry terms was decided.

A Cabinet Committee on Europe, chaired by Wilson, began meeting in May and identified two problems with an EEC application. First, de Gaulle was still 'probably hostile'. Second, the British economy was in a weak state, (as confirmed in the July 1966 sterling crisis) and Brown believed a devaluation would be necessary to prepare the country for European competition (Crossman, 1975, entry of 9 May 1966). Wilson did not want to make Labour 'the party of devaluation' but he was ready to try to win the French round to another British application. In talks with France's prime Minister, Georges Pompidou, in July 1966, Wilson even said he could accept the CAP. Three months later Wilson held a weekend meeting at Chequers, at which it was agreed to send him and Brown, who had recently become Foreign Secretary, on a tour of EEC capitals to explore the possibility of entry. The meeting was particularly significant for arguments, from the Foreign Office and DEA, that there was 'no alternative' to Community membership for Britain, if she wished to remain a major power. Once the Wilson-Brown tour was announced, in November, it led to rising public expectations about an eventual application. Brown told friends that 'the juggernaut had started to roll and nothing could now stop it' (King, 1972, pp.95–96). Yet anti-market ministers did not make a stand against the tour. There was a simple reason for this: people like Richard Crossman saw no point in upsetting Wilson because 'the General will save us from our own folly . . .' by vetoing the British application (Marsh, 1978, p.96). This prediction was to prove correct, and it leads to doubts about the seriousness of Wilson's bid to 'enter Europe'. But Wilson's interest in Europe *does* seem to have been serious at this point, since he devoted considerable government time, and committed both his own prestige and the stability of sterling, to a successful application. He also had great faith in his ability to win over de Gaulle.

The visit to Paris in January was the key meeting of the Wilson-Brown tour of early 1967, but de Gaulle did not seem impressed by Wilson's claim to be pro-European. The fact is that, like Macmillan before him, Wilson maintained faith in NATO, nuclear co-operation with America and the link between sterling and the dollar. In April, with their tour over, Wilson and Brown persuaded the Cabinet to make an EEC application, though (as with Macmillan) this was only in order to discover if appropriate terms were available. A substantial Labour revolt in the Commons could not prevent this being approved, but in mid-May de Gaulle publicly expressed doubts about the British step. Wilson made another vain bid to win the General over, at Versailles in June, and in July submitted the new British application. Increasingly however – rather than rely on de Gaulle – Wilson joined the Foreign Office in hoping that other EEC members would goad de Gaulle into agreement. Brown even pathetically complained to Germany's foreign minister, Willy Brandt at one point, 'Willy, you must get us in so we can take the lead in [the] EEC'.(!) (Brandt, 1978, pp. 162–63). In November however the uncertainty over the application helped to create another sterling crisis, which forced Wilson to accept a devaluation. Shortly afterwards, de Gaulle delivered a formal veto of Britain's second EEC application, attacking Wilson's 'extraordinary insistence and haste' in pressing it. Such was the logic of the British position however – with the Foreign Office insisting there was 'no alternative' to EEC membership – that the application was left 'on the table', ready to be taken up whenever the Six felt appropriate.

Labour's attempt to enter Europe thus ended in disaster for Wilson. The man who had earlier opposed devaluation but hoped for EEC membership was forced to agree to devaluation and had the door to the EEC closed in his face. Wilson had been able to win over the Cabinet to an application, but he could not manipulate de Gaulle into accepting British membership, and the General, to be fair to him, never gave Wilson reason to believe his application would succeed. Unlike Macmillan in 1961–63, however, Wilson was at least spared the frustration of two years' formal negotiations before the veto. If there was a fundamental reason why Wilson pressed for entry, it was probably an appreciation that business interests, most Whitehall officials and international observers could see nowhere else for Britain to go. But failure, especially when linked to the devaluation, proved very costly. The irony is that in 1968–70 the British economy strengthened, with trade being boosted by the devaluation. In February 1969, when de Gaulle approached the British Ambassador, Christopher Soames, about creating a possible, non-supranational alternative to the EEC, the Foreign Office had their revenge for the 1967 veto: the other members of the EEC were informed about de Gaulle's ideas, to the great embarrassment of the General. Shortly afterwards he resigned the Presidency, to be succeeded by the former premier, Georges Pompidou.

Pompidou was concerned about growing German power, and may have seen Britain as a possible counterweight to this. At any event, in December 1969, at a Community Summit in The Hague, he proved ready to accept a 'package' of agreements which included taking up the British application. Wilson was ready to begin talks about this but, with Britain's economy improving and public opinion ill-disposed to entry, he was more cautious than in 1967, and lost office before the formal negotiations began.[3]

Heath and EEC entry

There was never any doubt that, when he became premier in June 1970, Edward Heath, who had handled the first application, would press for EEC membership with greater vigour than Wilson. Heath believed entry would make British industry more competitive and, alongside a new industrial strategy and administrative reforms, would vastly improve the country's economic future. Unlike Wilson, Heath did not have to contend with a divided party, although Enoch Powell led a small group of Conservative anti-marketeers who opposed any loss of parliamentary sovereignty. To convince the continentals of his commitment to the EEC, Heath was even ready to distance himself from the US, avoiding use of the term 'special relationship'. With the position of sterling stronger than in 1967, and with the Commonwealth far less important than a decade earlier, Heath seemed in a better position to seek entry than Macmillan or Wilson. The key change which ensured Heath's success however, was the readiness of the French government, as seen at the Hague summit, to take up the British application. Some of those close to Pompidou were still doubtful about Britain's commitment to Europe, and this was to cause difficulties. Also Heath could not be seen to make too many concessions in the negotiations, especially at a time when public opinion was opposed to membership. Heath promised during the election that membership would only come with 'the full-hearted consent' of parliament and people – a pledge which opponents were soon to exploit. During the entry negotiations, which began immediately after the election, the government was ready to accept the existing EEC treaties but needed to secure adequate 'transitional' arrangements and some protection for Commonwealth trade, and it was concerned about its net financial contribution to the Community. (The difference between what Britain paid in, and what it received back, was always likely to be adverse because, in 1969, the Six had agreed to finance the CAP through VAT payments and the income from all external tariffs: Britain would receive little from the CAP but, as a major trading nation, would pay large amounts from tariffs) (Young, 1972; and Kitzinger, 1973).

Negotiations on the British side were first led by Anthony Barber. But he soon became Chancellor of the Exchequer, and was replaced as 'Mr Europe' by Geoffrey Rippon. Whitehall officials, now fully familiar with the workings of the EEC, handled the detailed talks on such issues as CAP, West Indies sugar and New Zealand dairy produce, but key decisions were taken in ministerial meetings between Rippon and the Six. By late October 1970 the initial, 'fact-finding' stage of the talks was over and Rippon was able to settle some of the easier entry terms. But in early 1971 the French negotiating stance became tougher, especially regarding Britain's financial contribution. In March the French also began to create problems over the future of sterling, and there was some fear that the talks would fail. At this point Heath, encouraged by Willy Brandt, decided on a personal meeting with Pompidou in Paris. Preparations for this meeting were handled in highly secret talks between Ambassador Soames and the Secretary-General of the Elysée Palace, Michel Jobert, which succeeded in ironing out some points of difference. Just before the summit, West Germany decided to 'float' its currency, a step which upset the French and may have drawn Pompidou closer to Heath. At their meeting on 20–21 May the two men got on well and Heath convinced the President that he was more committed to a European future than the special relationship. In contrast to Macmillan and Wilson, Heath succeeded in winning over a French leader and the terms for British entry were settled the following month. Then again, it could be argued that Pompidou had decided on British entry earlier, and was simply pressing for the best terms in early 1971. After all, France now had British money to help pay for the CAP: by 1977, it was estimated, Britain would be paying nearly a fifth of EEC income.

In a White Paper issued in July 1971 Heath tried to portray EEC entry as being in line with established British policies. Membership, the Paper declared, would improve Britain's economic performance, allow her to influence EEC policies (notably by encouraging an 'outward-looking' trade policy) and need not lead to 'any erosion of essential national sovereignty'. Thus traditional British aims – security, independence, economic strength, freer world trade – were simply to be achieved in a new forum. Yet opinion polls were firmly against membership at this time, Powell was increasing his attacks on the EEC and Labour opponents were growing in strength, arguing that the Common Market would increase food prices, bring greater unemployment (due to continental competition) and end Labour's ability to pursue socialist policies at home. Views on the EEC, of course, had long cut across party lines. In 1971 Harold Wilson refused to oppose membership outright, but he was ready to attack Heath's *terms* of entry – a position which was consistent with Wilson's approach since 1962. Thus the consensus on membership which had existed in 1967 had disappeared. Among Labour politicians, Tony Benn strongly advocated a referendum on the issue, while James Callaghan suggested Labour could re-negotiate Heath's terms. Faced with these difficulties, Heath delayed the key Commons vote, on the principle of membership, until 28 October. It proved a wise move because, over the summer, the opinion polls improved, the number of potential Conservative rebels dwindled and Labour pro-marketeers (led by Roy Jenkins) became committed to voting for Heath's terms, despite Wilson's position. There were more Labour pro-marketeers than Conservative anti-marketeers, and on the day Heath won a healthy majority of 356 to 244.

Problems over the EEC's common fisheries policy delayed completion of the Treaty of Accession for Britain, Eire, Denmark and Norway until December. It was signed on 22 January 1972 and then had to be voted into law. Although Labour pro-marketeers now towed the party line and voted against sections of the European Communities Bill, the government always managed a majority (sometimes as low as eight votes). Labour anti-marketeers complained that the pro-marketeers were probably colluding with Heath. They also bitterly complained when, in April, the government began to use 'guillotines' to push the Bill through. The myth soon grew that Heath pushed membership through a reluctant House of

Commons, without proper debate and without a popular mandate. In Norway, by contrast, a referendum was held which rejected community membership. In March Wilson agreed that a referendum might be held on the issue by a Labour government, leading Roy Jenkins to quit the Shadow Cabinet. The EC Bill finally passed into law in July and three months later Heath was able to attend his first Community summit in Paris. Here, future steps for greater cooperation were discussed, including a Regional Development Fund and the achievement of Economic and Monetary Union. British membership formally came into effect on 1 January 1973. Already however there were signs that Britain had joined the Common Market just as the years of high growth were coming to an end. Anthony Barber's 1972 budget, designed to stimulate the British economy ahead of Community membership, simply fuelled inflation. Currency instability, which brought the floating of sterling in July 1972, soon destroyed any hope of Economic and Monetary Union and 1973 was to see massive oil price issues and begin the years of 'stagnation'. 'May we not have signed the Treaty of Rome just before the collapse?' asked one press commentator (King, 1972, pp.143–44).

If Heath had been able to succeed where Macmillan and Wilson had failed, it was because of a change in French policy. Pompidou, perhaps because of his fear of Germany or a desire to spread the costs of the CAP, or maybe simply because he was not Charles de Gaulle, had decided to accept British membership after a decade of vain pressure from governments in London. Yet there can be no doubt too that British policy had changed over this period. In 1961 Britain was still one of the strongest European economies, the Commonwealth and Sterling Area were enormously significant to policy-makers and the EEC was a novel political issue. In 1971 France overtook Britain as the world's fourth largest trading power (West Germany and Japan were already larger), the Commonwealth and Sterling Areas seemed things of the past and the Common Market was a major political concern. In 1961 Macmillan believed he could take a firm line in negotiations, acted too slowly and could not convince de Gaulle of Britain's commitment to Europe. But in 1971, Heath was ready to accept the Treaty of Rome and even the protectionist CAP as they stood, he pursued negotiations with determination and he displayed little interest in the special relationship. Yet in 1971, as in 1961, Community membership continued to cause deep controversy. The high point of pro-market consensus had been in early 1967 when Wilson, the Conservatives, public opinion, the press and businessmen were all in favour. But farmers had always been opposed, food prices were always likely to rise thanks to the CAP and the threat to national sovereignty was the oldest British concern about European integration. The inflation and unemployment of the early 1970s re-fueled such concerns. It would require more than a decade of membership before the public and the two main political parties accepted that Britain was in the EEC to stay.

Notes

1. PRO CAB128/30, CM(57) 3, 8 January 1957.
2. PRO CAB128/35, CM(61) 42nd and 43rd.
3. The section on Wilson's government is based on my article, 'Harold Wilson's bid to "enter Europe" in 1967', in R. Bridge and H. Yasamee, eds, Festschrift for Roger Bullen (forthcoming).

References

Brandt, W. (1978), *People and Policies*, London, Collins.

Camps, M. (1964), *Britain and the European Community, 1955–63*, London, Oxford University Press.

Crossman, R. (1975), *Diaries of a Cabinet Minister, Vol.I, 1964–6*, London, Hamish Hamilton & Cape.

Dixon, P. (1968), *Double Diploma*, London, Hutchinson.

Gore-Booth, P. (1974), *With Great Truth and Respect*, London, Constable.

Jebb, Gladwyn (1972), *The Memoirs of Lord Gladwyn*, London, Weidenfeld & Nicolson.

Kitzinger, Uwe (1973), *Diplomacy and Persuasion*, London, Thames & Hudson.

King, Cecil (1972), *The Cecil King Diary, 1965–70*, London, Jonathan Cape.

Macmillan, Harold (1972), *Pointing the Way, 1959–61*, London, Macmillan.

Macmillan, Harold (1973), *At the End of the Day, 1961–3*, London, Macmillan.

Marsh, Richard (1978), *On the Rails*, London, Weidenfeld & Nicolson.

Maudling, Reginald (1978), *Memoirs*, London, Sidgwick & Jackson.

Roth, Andrew (1972), *Heath and the Heathmen*, London, Routledge Kegan Paul.

Williams, Philip (1979), *Hugh Gaitskell*, London, Jonathan Cape.

Young, S.Z. (1972), *Terms of Entry*, London, Heinemann.

9

Britain in search of a role, 1957–73; a role in Europe, European integration and Britain: a witness account

Reginald Hibbert

Dean Acheson's famous remark about Britain losing an Empire and not finding a role established a fashion in thinking from which it is difficult to break away. Nevertheless, I think it is important to make an effort to do so. My argument will be that Britain in the post-war years, including the 1960s, was not in fact seeking a role. It thought that it already had one, that the world-wide nature of this role was long-established and well-known and that, while there had been evolutionary changes, there had been no break in the continuity of its performance. It may be possible to claim, with historical hindsight, that Britain ought to have been seeking a role; but in fact it did not feel the need to do so.

To talk about a country wanting or seeking anything can always, of course, be a little misleading. Foreign policy is a very contingent and reactive process. It tends to come into existence retrospectively. At any moment in time it is easy to identify a country's foreign relations and foreign affairs, but much more difficult to identify with certainty its foreign policy or even to be sure that it has one. There is usually no lack of assertions by political leaders, officials and analysts confidently defining policy, but these are heavily tainted by image-building linked to domestic and personal politics. Pragmatism and compromise are bound to play a major role in foreign policy, but few leading figures care to admit to such flat and tedious qualities. They prefer to decry them as the characteristic vices of the Foreign Office.

The process of political image building is closely related to the existence in each country of popular feeling about the country's role in the world. This tends to be an inertial, largely inarticulate force, very slow to change. The politician's art is to tap it. The stateman's is to shape it. In Britain in the 1960s popular feeling was formed by generations which had grown up before the Second World War. I myself was one of the youngest of those generations. I was in my forties in the 1960s. We took it for granted that Britain was a world power, entitled to a seat at all the top tables. Europe was not then a top table. In so far as it might eventually be a candidate to become a top table, it would be natural for Britain to belong to it. But first it would have to qualify.

This feeling was nurtured to a large extent by Britain's experience of continuity, which was and is to this day unique in the Community and very nearly outside the Community. The unbroken functioning of Britain's innumerable undisturbed institutions ensured that memory of the past and procedures from the past were brought to bear continuously on the shaping of the present. As a result Britain's starting point in approaching any international problem was that of being a world power, of belonging to the exclusive small-number groupings, no longer perhaps the Big One or Big Two, but certainly the Big Three or Big Four. Bigness was not yet, and perhaps is still not, a quality ascribed to numbers above four, such for example as six.

There is one particular aspect of British continuity to which I would draw attention. That is the important weighting given to military factors in Britain's processes of policy formation. This was an inheritance from imperial days. The Committee of Imperial Defence was set up in 1923; and the views of the Chiefs of Staffs Committee and eventually the Joint Intelligence Committee (JIC) had a gradually increasing influence in British policy-making from then onwards. The Mountbatten reforms in 1960 and subsequent changes had the effect of reinforcing the growing authority of the intelligence community, and so of focusing attention at the top on world security issues rather than, for example, on Britain's more prosaic needs as a nation of traders. Britain has never had a higher diplomatic school; nor, until fairly recently, have Whitehall and Westminster cultivated think-tanks and academies. The Imperial Defence College (IDC), later the Royal College of Defence Studies (RCDS), served as an all-purpose high-school for administrators. Pre-occupation with world security was, and still is, deeply embedded in the British system.

It is impossible to end this series of opening general comments without mentioning the special relationship. It fitted British pre-dispositions perfectly. It was image building; it flattered popular feeling and imagery about Britain's world role; it was a direct continuation of Britain's wartime experience, so deeply engraved in the national psyche; it gave substance and sense to Britain's mission to serve world security. In the 1960s it was being carefully restored after the serious accident of Suez.

The drift of my approach to my subject will already be clear from these preliminary observations. I must add a few comments about the twelve years which preceded 1957.

First, there was the five-year period between 1945 and 1950 during which the wartime coalition against Germany collapsed (in the Middle East, in Germany, and finally in the Far East, in Korea), and a new coalition against the Soviet Union took shape. By the end of that five-year period the two main problems of the post-war era had emerged in definitive form – the problem of containing the Soviet Union and the problem of accommodating a divided Germany in a divided Europe. From this early date, the French and British approaches to these two problems differed. For the French, the second problem, Germany, consistently transcended the first. For Britain, the first, the Soviet Union, consistently transcended the second. Both Britain and France were addressing themselves to questions of security but, for all the reasons which I sketched earlier, Britain's view of security was loftier and scanned a more distant horizon than France could allow itself as it struggled to recover its identity.

The British attitude which was formed in those early post-war years can be easily summarised. It was to rebuild the countries of Western Europe with US help and under US protection; to secure reconciliation between France and Germany; to re-create something like the wartime alliance, but this time against the Soviet Union, on the familiar, conventional basis of inter-governmental co-operation; and to work for the restoration to Britain of its former primacy in the world, or as much of it as could be achieved. This attitude was common to Attlee and Bevin, Churchill and Eden. Its principal elements can be traced, persisting but gradually modified as necessary, through successive governments down to the present day. They can even be seen trying to survive the disappearance of the Soviet Union and the reunification of Germany.

By 1950 Britain had secured the pattern of relationships which suited it in Europe; the Brussels Treaty, the OEEC, the North Atlantic Treaty and the Council of Europe as a purely inter-governmental institution. To this was added in the early 1950s the pragmatic process by which Federal Germany was brought into existence and admitted to the circle of relationships which I have described, the WEU being added to the list of approved institutions in 1954. There, in the mid-1950s, Britain's creative diplomacy came to an end and began to be overtaken by the creative diplomacy of others.

The greater French concern about the German problem and the greater British concern about the Soviet problem produced their first major contradiction when the Federal Republic of Germany (FRG) was being created. The British reaction was empirical. Western Germany had to support itself, and German soldiers were needed to fill the defence line against the Soviet Union. It was a question of finding ways to do these things which were acceptable to the United States and to Germany's western neighbours. For France, faced with the prospect that western Germany was not going to be held down and fragmented, it was a more fundamental question – how to devise a framework within which the FRG could be made safe for France. The way to a solution was opened by the French Government's espousal of the Schuman Plan. The necessary ideology was ready to hand, prepared by the European Movement. The process, which was of the first importance for France but not a central issue from Britain's point of view, culminated in 1957 in the formation of the EEC, facing Britain with unexpected and unwanted choices.

Before Britain's experience in this predicament is examined, there are two other themes which deserve mention.

The first is the transition during the 1950s to a defence policy based on nuclear deterrence. The V-bomber force was built up, and work was set in train on the Blue Streak and Blue Steel weapons systems. The British H-bomb was tested in 1957. In 1958 the McMahon Act was amended in Washington. Britain's standing as a nuclear power reinforced British confidence in Britain's vocation as a world power and was to have far-reaching consequences in her relations with the US on the one hand and with France on the other in the course of the 1960s.

Finally, it is important to remember Britain's world-wide pre-occupations in the 1950s which made a single-minded European focus in her policy-making unimaginable. The list is impressive. The Baghdad Pact and SEATO took shape.

Anthony Eden played a distinguished role in the Geneva Conference ending the war in IndoChina. The Malayan Emergency was slowly overcome. Africa, south of the Sahara, remained an area of large British responsibilities. There was the Franco-British intervention at Suez, but this was not seen in Britain as a warning to concentrate on Europe but rather as a grave personal error by Anthony Eden requiring careful fence-mending with the United States. It had a baneful effect on Franco-British relations in that it deepened French mistrust of the Anglo-Saxons and indirectly sealed the fate of French Algeria.

After the Suez episode, there occurred one of the periodic changes in the top world leadership which affects the course of international relations. Harold Macmillan became Prime Minister; in mid-1958 General de Gaulle became President of France and in 1960 John F. Kennedy became President of the United States. One of de Gaulle's first acts set the tone for the following ten years. In September 1958 he sent letters to Eisenhower and Macmillan proposing in effect a tripartite directorate for world affairs, indicating that France wanted a radical change in the NATO system. This was parried, and it has been argued that de Gaulle could hardly have expected it to be accepted. But it is interesting that there was a reflection of the same sort of thinking on de Gaulle's part in the Soames affair in 1968 at the very end of his period of office. He then suggested that if Britain really wanted to enter the EEC it should first discuss and, by implication, agree with France the future shape of Europe. The Wilson Government in London leaked de Gaulle's approach to the Germans and others and Franco-British relations plummetted. The point to be made here is that the two episodes, separated by ten years, show an extraordinary singleness of purpose in de Gaulle. They show that what he was against was not Britain nor America: it was Anglo-Saxon hegemony. He was aiming to restore France's former primacy in world and European affairs. This was a part of the process of raising France from the trauma inflicted on it in the war and the aftermath of war. It was not very different from the aim of successive, post-war British governments to restore as much of Britain's primacy as possible. The difference was that Britain had started at the top while France had started at the bottom.

De Gaulle stood firm with France's allies on major issues, on Berlin in 1961 and during the Cuban missile crisis in 1962; but he did not budge from his desire to change NATO. When his aspiration for France to join the US and UK in a Big-3 directorate was disappointed, he whittled away piecemeal the French contribution to NATO and finally withdrew France from the Organisation in 1966.

De Gaulle was not, and by his nature could not be, a Euro-enthusiast. But he seems to have regarded the EEC, which was only a year old when he came to power, as a perhaps useful institution which could help France on its upward trajectory. The sort of use which could be made of it appeared in the Fouchet plan in 1960. The aim was clearly political – a grouping of states led by France.

It was in these circumstances that Britain had to decide what to do about the EEC, now that, contrary to expectations, it seemed to have come to stay. The economic arguments for trying to join it were equivocal, although the termination by France in 1958 of the negotiations for a Free Trade Area made it more uncomfortable for Britain to contemplate a future outside the Common Market. But it was the political arguments which became compelling. Politically, Britain could not accept being left out, while not being convinced that the organisation was really necessary. One of the difficulties in understanding the way in which the European Community has grown, and above all in understanding why it has been so hard to make it acceptable to British public opinion, has been and still is that the motivation among the participants for each major development has been political, while the means used to achieve each development have been economic. It has not been easy to make the immediate economic measures seem necessary and beneficial, or to demonstrate their connection with somewhat intangible and long-term political advantages.

Both the US and the UK were concerned about the loose French gun on the NATO deck and about the fact that a new shape was appearing in Europe from which Britain was excluded. The British application in 1961, along with Ireland and Denmark, to join the EEC was a serious attempt by Britain to catch up with a new reality.

Prime Minister Macmillan had been busy image-building and facing up in the traditional British style to world dangers. He played a key role in bringing about the first NATO Heads of Government meeting in 1958. In 1959 he made his well-publicised visit to Moscow; but the moment at which a deal might have been done with Stalin's successors, if it ever existed, was already past. A session of the Council of Foreign Ministers on Berlin was sterile, and the situation in and around Berlin became more critical, culminating in the building of the Berlin wall in 1961. This was followed by the fiasco of the Vienna summit between Kennedy and Khrushchev; and then in 1962 there was the Cuban missile crisis. Dealing with the Soviet Union, staying close to the United States and keeping NATO strong were clearly at the top of the agenda.

The evolution of Britain's nuclear deterrent at this time also put a very important premium on the trans-Atlantic tie. There was a turning point in British defence arrangements at the beginning of the 1960s. Blue Streak was cancelled and the future of the British airborne nuclear deterrent became dependent on the availability of the US Skybolt. When this was cancelled by McNamara in 1962, Britain's defence structure, based since the mid-1950s on the concept of nuclear deterrence, faced crisis. Rescue came in the form of President Kennedy's agreement with Mr Macmillan at Nassau to supply the submarine-launched Polaris missile. The change was momentous. The special relationship, while fading in many other respects, acquired a very special and very important content.

The Nassau agreement was very unwelcome to de Gaulle who recently had had somewhat indecisive talks with Macmillan at Rambouillet. De Gaulle had once again been extending his feelers to see if Anglo-Saxon hegemony could be prized open to make more room for France. The outcome of Nassau confirmed in him his go-it-alone attitude.

During this time the negotiations for British, Irish, Danish and eventually Norwegian entry to the EEC proceeded seriously. There were real difficulties on the economic side, more especially in relation to agriculture and Commonwealth interests, but Britain persisted. In the end it was not economics which brought the negotiations to a standstill. De Gaulle imposed his veto, a political act, in January 1963. This brought to an end what I would identify as the second post-war period. It had lasted since 1950. It was the period in which two separate European systems were developed, a security system, NATO, led by the US and Britain, and an economic system, the EEC, led by France, the newly formed FRG being accommodated in both. From 1963 onwards, until de Gaulle's fall in 1968, a period of stalemate ensued. France had not managed to change NATO, and Britain had not managed to change the EEC.

De Gaulle's rebuff to Britain was made the more disagreeable because it was followed by the visit of Chancellor Adenauer to Paris to sign the Treaty of Friendship between the FRG and France. It had been one of Britain's post-war aims to promote the reconciliation of France and Germany; and this was now achieved in somewhat rueful circumstances for Britain.

A digression about relations with Germany may be appropriate at this point. Britain has been a good helper of Germany since the war, second only to the United States. The British Army of the Rhine and RAF Germany have steadily occupied their forward positions in the defence line in the north German plain. Britain has stood firm in Berlin. Britain contributed constructively throughout the period during which the FRG was evolving, over the rearmament of Germany and in the absorption of the FRG as an equal in the western defence system. It is arguable that Britain has not managed to draw the political dividends from this helpful posture that might have been expected, and that France, while contributing less, has profited more. I have been very used over the years to hearing British Ministers and senior officials expressing mild frustration because Germany would not use its weight to counter-balance France. The cause may lie in the difference between British and French attitudes which I diagnosed at the beginning. Britain's first pre-occupation was always security against the Soviet Union, and relations with the FRG were subsumed under this wider heading, so that they could be seen to be serving as a means to an end rather than as an end in themselves. For France, by contrast, relations with Germany were always an end in themselves. Germany, having a need for rehabilitation in the world greater even than France's, responded to this. It may be that Britain has over the years underestimated Germany's needs as she has underestimated France's. An inter-governmental alliance against the Soviet Union was not enough for either.

No sooner was the Franco-German Treaty of Friendship signed, however, than Franco-German relations and most other relationships in Europe passed into the doldrums. Adenauer retired and Erhard took over in Germany. De Gaulle's patience was tried when the Bundestag, in ratifying the Treaty, added a rider asserting the primacy of NATO. This was the period when De Gaulle's spoiling tactics were in the ascendant. In the EEC itself there was the empty chair episode in 1965 and 1966, ending in the Luxembourg compromise. But there were also the French withdrawal from the Geneva disarmament talks, the refusal to partici-pate in the test-ban and non-proliferation treaties, the cultivation of Moscow, the withdrawal from the international gold pool, the demand for an end to dollar hegemony, and the arms ban on Israel in the 1967 Arab-Israeli War (so strikingly in contrast to the attitude at the time of Suez).

Britain was also in the doldrums in these years, but for reasons unconnected with membership or non-membership of the EEC. Britain was in the toils of political and economic difficulties of its own. Sir Alec Douglas Home became Prime Minister in 1963, only to be succeeded by Harold Wilson with a knife-edge Labour majority in 1964. The Labour Party conference had swung towards nuclear disarmament in 1960. A serious balance of payments crisis hemmed the Labour government in. Denis Healey's defence white papers between 1964 and

1966 announced force reductions, then the acceptance of limits on Britain's world-wide role; and finally the withdrawal from east of Suez began. Sterling had to be devalued in 1967.

Labour's majority was increased to 96 in 1966. Being more secure in Parliament, the government drifted towards a new application to join the EEC. The performance of EFTA and the Commonwealth had been disappointing. The Kennedy Round in the GATT did not meet all the hopes placed on it. The Johnson administration in the US, caught in the vicious spiral of the Vietnam war, seemed less attractive than the Kennedy administration had been. The political reasons for trying to join the EEC seemed increasingly strong. A fresh application to join was made in the spring of 1967 and was vetoed by France a few months later, in November. So the de Gaulle era ended. De Gaulle fell in 1968 and President Pompidou took over.

By now a new political force had appeared on the European stage – German Ostpolitik. Willy Brandt's first success with crossings of the Berlin Wall was at Christmas 1963. Thereafter, during Erhard's Chancellorship until 1966, and then under Chancellor Kiesinger until 1969, with Brandt as Foreign Minister, the Ostpolitik developed slowly but steadily, only briefly checked by the suppression of the Prague Spring in 1968. In 1969, the initiative was taken to propose to the Soviet Union Four-Power talks on Berlin and negotiations between FRG and GDR. In 1970 the FRG concluded treaties with the Soviet Union and Poland.

Brandt became Chancellor in 1969. In the same year Richard Nixon became President of the United States, with Henry Kissinger at his side. A year later Edward Heath became Prime Minister in the UK. Another of the periodic changes in the top team of world leaders had occurred, releasing policy currents in new directions,

The new directions were Ostpolitik, détente and the re-launch of the European Community. President Pompidou could no longer safely stick to the de Gaulle line. Germany was stirring and beginning to steal France's clothes. The United States was becoming engaged in the SALT talks with the Soviet Union. Kissinger's diplomacy of linkages was taking shape. Super-power diplomacy was beginning to make political cohesion in Western Europe seem more desirable. At the Hague Summit in 1969 agreement in principle was reached on enlargement of the European Community. The French extracted their price in the Common Agricultural Policy and the financial regulations; but the door was at last open for Britain. In the timely fashion which only historical chance can contrive, Edward Heath, committed to the European cause, became Prime Minister in 1970 and was able to push through the door, together with the Irish and Danes, the Norwegians falling by the wayside.

Just prior to Britain's entry, there were two important initiatives which formed part of the Community re-launch. One was the start of European Political Cooperation: the other was the Werner Report looking forward to economic and monetary union. The first was much more welcome to Britain than the second. The growth of European Political Cooperation has carried the members of the Community, but not of course the Community itself, in the political, inter-governmental direction which is congenial to Britain. The impulse towards economic and monetary union has carried it in the supra-governmental direction which Britain has resisted since the beginning in the 1950s.

In spite of the bright new dawn in 1972 and 1973, Mr Heath's signature of the Treaty of Accession turned out not to be so decisive a step as it appeared. Shortly after Britain's accession, Mr Heath himself had difficulty in being as 'European' as other members wanted over energy policy in the first oil crisis. Various strands of opinion in Britain were soon hankering back to free trade area ideas and inter-governmental structures, chafing against the Commission as 'the Brussels bureaucracy'. So it has continued to the present day. The political reasons for British membership continue to be as strong as ever and as under-appreciated as ever by the British public. If Britain has managed to acquire a new role, it has done so very hesitantly and appears not to have much idea what to do with it.

Conclusions

In talking about the European Community at any period of its existence it is hard to avoid taking sides. One tends to be quickly identified as being pro-European or anti-European. Membership of the Community has been and remains such a contentious issue that debate about it has taken on a life of its own and for much of the time bears little relationship to political and diplomatic reality. The discussion tends to be conducted with a high-flown vocabulary, focused on abstract concepts such as sovereignty, federalism and subsidiarity.

The advantage of examining the period 1956–73 is that, thanks largely to General de Gaulle, the motives and preoccupations of governments are somewhat easier to descry during that period than at other times. General de Gaulle was not inclined to use Euro-speak to sweeten his pronouncements. And in the latter part of the period it is possible to see fairly clearly how the balance between the different forces contributing to the European Community started to change as the cold war began gradually to be alleviated and Germany began to assert itself once more as a prime mover in Europe.

The EEC, now the EC, has become many things as it has evolved, and it serves different purposes for different countries. But the tap-root from which it originally grew is still there. Way back in the 1950s it started as a framework for accommo-dating a reviving but divided Germany in the western half of a divided and shattered Europe. The problem of accommodating Germany is to this day one of the prime concerns of those who try to shape Community politics at the highest level. But it so happens that in the last two years the Community's environment has changed completely. Germany has become united. Europe is no longer politically divided. The Soviet Union has been dissolved. NATO, which was formed to contain the Soviet Union, no longer has a Soviet Union to contain. The European Community, which was designed for a divided Europe and a divided Germany, has to redesign itself to cope with an open, whole Europe and a central, potentially dominant Germany.

The ideology of the European Movement is even less suitable as a guide in this topsy-turvy situation than it was in the settled days of the iron curtain. It has become more necessary than ever to look below the rhetoric and identify with care the true national objectives and interests of the Community's member states, particularly the larger ones, and adjust policy to allow scope for them.

It is possible to speculate that the EEC has never been the institution that Europe really needed. Theoretically, it might have been better to have a political nucleus of states combining the functions of European Political Cooperation and the WEU, with an outer circle of states joined in an economic community. But this was impossible when the presence of United States forces and the US nuclear umbrella were essential for the defence of Europe. Governments always have to start from where they are and not from some theoretical point. It is not impossible that something like the theoretical model I have suggested will eventually emerge. If it is to do so, France, Germany and Britain will have to show much more sensitivity to one another's political requirements than they have shown hitherto. The promise of 1972 and 1973 when Britain entered the Community has still to be realised.

10

The free trade alternative to the EC: a witness account

Douglas Jay

I am asked to speak on the 'Atlantic Alternative'. But this is not quite an accurate description of the alternative to strict EC membership which was open to this country in the 1960s and 1970s and may in part be available now. The real alternative would have been continued membership of EFTA, retention of free import of food from the Commonwealth and elsewhere, the achievement as an EFTA member of free trade in industrial goods with the whole EC, and co-operation with the US in successive GATT rounds of cuts in world tariffs including those of the EC. I would call this the Free Trade Alternative rather than the Atlantic Alternative. Since EFTA achieved complete industrial free trade with the EC group in the 1980s, the UK, if it had chosen this alternative, would have enjoyed complete industrial free trade with EFTA, zero industrial tariffs with the EC, free imports of food because of EFTA exemption from the CAP, and progressive cuts through GATT in tariffs with the US and rest of the world. This would have led to our participation in the now completed EFTA-EC agreement for a joint 'European Economic Area' and possibly later closer union between the two groups. This course has always been the real alternative.

In examining this alternative, one must, I think, consider first the choice as it existed in the 1960s and 1970s, and the results of the choice then made, and secondly the choice which faces us now; since the choice we made earlier has provided us with experience we did not have then.

The original choice depended naturally on both the political and economic consequences likely to follow one course or the other, since the economic must, evidently, greatly influence the political consequences. Economic strength gives political power. One must therefore understand the basic nature of the EC, as conceived and revealed by the purposes and motives of its founders. Here my thoughts return to a three-hour conversation with Jean Monnet – or rather private lecture from him – in 1952. For Monnet, the supreme objective of all political, economic and personal endeavours was to prevent another war between France and Germany. This in his view could only be done by political and constitutional union between the two; and that in turn could only be achieved by an apparatus of economic union designed to turn itself stealthily into political union before

Parliaments and electorates understood what was happening. Paul-Henri Spaak openly admitted that this was the strategy; and it has been faithfully and single-mindedly followed. The original Coal and Steel Community, Common Market and CAP were devised, not basically for their economic value, but as a pretext for setting up the Brussels Commission, as a centralising expert body, to manage them. The 1992 Single Market (which by spawning a wild rush for mergers, cartels and joint ventures by the great, multi-national firms may well diminish competition on balance) was designed to justify the Single European Act; and the Single Currency and Independent Central Bank are in turn supposed to require 'political union'.

Monnet, let us remember, as well as Robert Schuman, Adenauer and de Gaulle were all born and brought up in Eastern France or Western Germany, and had seen the area torn apart by fearful conflicts. This was their world view, and the wish to avoid further wars was a worthy and indeed noble aim. But it was based on two factual assumptions, which were and are highly questionable: first that another Franco-German war was the major threat; and secondly that the Brussels appar-atus would prevent it by tying down Germany. On a dispassionate and less localised view, the risk of a new Franco-German war was one of the most remote possibilities in the post-1945 world. History suggests that smaller powers do not usually fight one another when faced by greater powers; and in the post-1945 world the great powers were the US, the Soviet Union and later Japan. For a time after this the centralizing EC was defended not very convincingly as a further shield against the Soviet Union in addition to NATO. Now that that threat has evaporated, the argument has changed back to the fear of a resurgent Germany (the main motive said to be propelling M. Mitterand and M. Delors). Yet the second assumption, that the centralizing mechanism in Brussels would constrain an aggressive Germany, is equally questionable. I do not believe myself that the resurgence of a militarist Germany is even remotely probable. But if it were, would such a Germany really be restrained by a scrap of paper?

Indeed the very idea that you can keep the peace by creating another European superpower (and this is the real motive of Gaullist anti-Americanism) is surely grotesque. The conversion of Germany into a Great Power by Bismark led to three Great Wars. If a Greater Germany had not been created in Bismark's time, the Great Wars of 1870, 1914 and 1939 would in all human probability not have occurred. On political grounds, grounds of peace and war, we do not want more Great Powers, which are far from guarantees of peace. It follows from this that the basic motive and purpose of the whole design for centralizing power in Brussels was founded on two fundamentally questionable assumptions. Yet the process involved the UK, if it participated, in major sacrifices, both political and economic. In the 1960s the UK had shown its enthusiasm for genuine international co-operation fairly emphatically by becoming members of the UN and its agencies, NATO, the OECD, EFTA, the Council of Europe, and WEU, not to mention the IMF and the World Bank. It was pointed out in the early 1960s by William Pickles of the LSE with memorable clarity, which has not been notable in the debate since then, that if you go beyond this, and join supranational (as opposed to inter-national) institutions, you involve yourself in an inescapable dilemma. If the supranational authority responsible for decision and for legislation is not accoun-table to, and representative of, the people so governed, then you are in breach of the most fundamental of democratic principles: that people should not be coerced by laws or decisions made by a body which they had had no part, even indirect, in selecting. On the other hand, in so far as you make the legislative authority elected by, and responsible to, an electorate outside your own country, then you so far cease to be an independent sovereign state. With a supranational authority, that dilemma is inexorable. With an international body, it does not arise. That was, and is, the kernel of the political choice confronting the UK by the EC in its present form as designed by Monnet and his followers.

The basic political question therefore was this: should the UK gratuitously place its people in this dilemma on the questionable assumption that this was a necessary and effective means of preventing a future war with an aggressive Germany? And the kernel of the *economic* choice was as follows: should the UK abandon the policy of free trade in food imports which it had maintained since the 1840s with massive national support and apparently great economic success? That policy enabled the UK to provide a higher real wage for its working population at a lower sterling cost, and so gave us a marked advantage in labour costs over nearly all competitors. That this in turn gave us both higher living standards and a huge expansion of international trade over these hundred years was almost unanimously agreed by the whole British liberal and academic establishment from Richard Cobden and John Stuart Mill to Asquith, Churchill and Keynes. Yet this ortho-doxy was suddenly reversed in a few years in the 1960s, almost without serious argument. I find it hard to believe that the established view was all wrong for a century, or alternatively if right, that it was also right to reverse that view overnight. For even in the 1960s 30 per cent of UK imports in value consisted of food, and the average wage-earning family was still spending nearly 30 per cent of its income on food.[1]

The CAP is the most extreme form of protectionism ever invented. CAP import taxes on food from outside the EC are so devised that however low world prices fall, the taxes are so raised that none of the benefits can be passed on to the consumer. This applies to all the main temperate zone foodstuffs, notably grain, feeding stuffs, meat and dairy produce. In addition, special outright prohibitions on imports are imposed by the EC, for instance on meat and dairy produce from Australia and New Zealand. These food taxes, in themselves, are the most regressive and reactionary forms of taxation ever imposed since they fall with greatest weight on the poorest consumers, and are all the more insidious for being so devised that most people do not understand what is happening. It remains to be seen how far the CAP reforms agreed in May 1992 will actually mean lower retail prices. At the Munich G7 meeting in July 1992 the French Government was able to block all progress.

The CAP system is peculiarly damaging to the UK, because it deprives us of our one great advantage in international trade, lower labour costs at a given level of real wages and salaries. The resulting higher food prices were bound to provoke, as they did, irresistible pressure for higher pay rates. In so far as these pay claims were granted, higher labour costs would rise. So far as they were not granted, real living standards would fall below what they would have been. Those of us who believed in the 1960s that entry to the EEC on these terms would be damaging, then argued as follows. If the UK both raised its labour costs unilaterally and removed all tariffs on manufactured imports from the rest of the EC, there would be a growing visible trade deficit mainly with the EC, which together with the Budget transfer, would heavily burden our future balance of payments, and so handicap our internal economic policy and future output and employment. This would of course not be a once and for all burden, but one continuing as long as the food taxes were in force. It was likely that in the early stages of the proposed leap in the dark a sharp rise in the RPI and pay rates would occur, that over the next 15 or 20 years a persistent balance of payments deficit would emerge, and that this deficit would largely take the form of a visible deficit with the rest of the EC.

This is substantially what happened. My own estimate in 1968–70 of the extra burden on the balance of payments (then in surplus) was about £560m (Jay, 1968) a year in the money values of those years, which would be about £2½ or 3 bn today. The actual current payments deficit overall was in fact £15 bn in 1988, £20 bn in 1989, £13½ bn in 1990, and £4½ bn in 1991, even with 3 million unemployed.[2] With the EC alone, the visible deficit was £13½ bn in 1988, £15 bn in 1989, £9.864 bn in 1990 and £429m even in the depressed 1991. So I must apologise for under-estimating the damage. By the 1980s the UK had slid into the first deficit in manufactured trade for more than a century: £17 bn by 1989.

The effect of the CAP food taxes on the economy as a whole depends not just on the system but on the quantities. If the CAP target prices set were reasonable (as in the previous successful UK deficiency payments system) or the taxes were kept below 15 per cent as in the British pre-1846 Corn Laws, the effect might have been minor. But they have been, and are, not so kept. In the 1970s the CAP tax on grain was over 100 per cent, that on meat averaged about 100 per cent and on dairy produce 250 per cent.

According to figures given by the House of Lords Select Committee[3] on the EC Report on the CAP of July 1991, the excess of CAP prices over world prices still varied in the 1980s for grain (including wheat) from 10–100 per cent, and for dairy products from 100–200 per cent above. According to figures from the Australian Government,[4] endorsed by the British Treasury, EC meat prices in 1990 were between 100–150 per cent in excess; and the average UK household was at retail paying 32 per cent (on low incomes 52 per cent) above what it would pay for food if the UK was exempt from the CAP. In current money values this would cost about an extra £5 a week for every man, woman and child in the UK. That burden continues as long as the CAP price levels prevail.

The crucial question, therefore, is how far these higher food prices led to higher labour costs, and how far these higher costs affected the balance of payments and the economy generally. The years in which food prices rose were 1973–76; and in these years UK average earnings rose by higher amounts than in any years since the war, from 12.9 per cent in 1972 to 26.1 per cent in 1975; following a rise in the RPI from 7.1 per cent to 24 per cent. This suggests that wage-earning households generally defended themselves effectively against the higher food prices. Part of this rise in the RPI was certainly due to the oil price explosion in 1973. But food prices are more likely directly to affect pay claims than oil prices. And the fact that food prices rose faster in the UK than other prices [RPI without food by 77 per cent, and food by 105 per cent from 1972–76[5] and that UK prices generally rose faster in those years than those of other OECD countries, shows beyond reasonable doubt that the forcing up of food prices by the CAP in 1973 to 1976 was one major cause of the 1976 price-pay explosion. UK labour costs in sterling actually rose by 72 per cent between 1973 and 1980.

How far in turn did the rise in labour costs affect the UK trade balance, and how far does it affect it now? This depends on elasticities of demand which, though crucial, are not easy to estimate. Indeed neither the UK official statistical authorities, nor even the academic authorities, strangely enough, seem even to have made the attempt. An extra £5 a week per head in food costs would mean £10 a week for the average salary-earning or wage-earning household if you assume only one dependant on average per earner. With a disposable income of £250 a week, an extra £10 would represent an addition to labour costs of about 4 per cent, not a negligible figure. To impose this in the same 4 years (1973–76) as tariffs on manufactured imports from the Continental EEC fell to zero would lead one to expect a heavy worsening in the visible balance of trade with the rest of the EC. In fact it led to the huge trade deficits with the rest of the EC, and so to trade and payments deficits with the world as a whole which I have just recorded. This deterioration cannot seriously be blamed on other general defects in the British economy, because, even though such defects certainly existed, they did not for 25 years have this devastating effect. We sometimes now forget that from 1945–70 our balance of payments was in surplus or balance for two years out of three, unemployment hardly ever rose above 3 per cent, and the price level seldom rose more than 5 per cent a year. Since 1972 a balance of payments deficit has been persistent, the RPI annual rise has twice reached 20 per cent, and unemployment (at 2 per cent in 1974) has moved up to 10 per cent or nearly 3 million, UK real growth rate per year averaged 2.8 per cent from 1946–70, and only 1.9 per cent from 1972–91. Growth in output per head in manufacturing as a whole fell from 4.0 per cent a year in 1961–73 to 0.7 per cent in 1973–79.

It is not taking the problem seriously to say that the troubles of, for example, the car industry over the last 20 years were due to other causes such as restrictive practices, trade union obstruction and so forth. All these existed from 1945–72. Yet in those years output rose progressively from a negligible figure to a record of 1.9 million cars in 1972 from 1972 that figure suddenly fell by half to 0.8 million in 1982,[6] spreading acute depression throughout the engineering industry and the West Midlands generally, where it had not been known for 50 years. It can hardly have been a coincidence that in 1972–76 labour costs were increased and import tariffs removed simultaneously. You cannot blame the fall in home car output on falling demand. Demand for cars did not fall; but imports rose until in 1989 we imported £5 billion worth of cars – one quarter of our total trade deficit. The car industry was only one dramatic instance of what was happening in manufacturing industry generally. General engineering and textiles were also seriously affected. The evidence is that the abandonment of free food imports in the 1970s, as well as the oil crisis, was a decisive turning point in British economic history from which we have not yet recovered.

If instead we had remained members of EFTA throughout the period, where should we stand now? We should have entirely avoided the burden on our costs imposed by the CAP. Imports of food would have flowed in natural economic channels from the most efficient producers in North and South America, Australia, New Zealand and elsewhere. We should as an EFTA member have enjoyed free trade each way on industrial goods with the rest of EFTA and the EC, as the EFTA countries have done for 15 years. We should have retained some not negligible preferences for exports to the Commonwealth. And above all we would have operated effectively through the GATT freer trade rounds, as a partner with the US and our other natural suppliers and food exporters, in reducing tariffs on a world scale, including the Common External Tariff of the EC. Most important of all we should have become, politically, the effective leader of a free trade group including the EFTA, Commonwealth, and Cairns group of nations, instead of, as EC members, being perpetually pushed into either resisting something we did not want to do, or else into giving way to pressure to our own disadvantage. In the GATT Uruguay Round, as EC members we have been forced into the ludicrous predicament of having to defend a protectionist system, and resist a freeing of world trade which would be so wholly in our own interest.

So much for the mistakes of the past. We have allowed our whole economic position in the world to be grievously damaged on the strength of a highly questionable theory that a hypothetical aggressive Germany could be suppressed by the construction of a West European superpower. The Danish referendum has brought us back to realities, and fresh starts can be made. The question now is: how do we get out of this impasse? The tragedy is that de Gaulle offered us the way out in 1969 (after his two celebrated 'non's'). On 4 February of that year he invited the British Ambassador to a talk and made a remarkable confidential offer. He said he personally (I quote from Harold Wilson's account) 'foresaw the Common Market changing and would like to see it change into a looser form of free trade area with arrangements by each country to exchange agricultural products'. He would be quite prepared to discuss with us 'what should take the place of the Common Market as an enlarged European Economic Association' (Wilson, 1971). 'He suggested confidential talks between Britain and France'. There would be (according to Jean Lacouture's life of de Gaulle) 'a resulting political association in which France, Britain, Germany and Italy would play a major part'. (Lacoutre, 1991)

De Gaulle was indeed a rare character. He was not only an extreme French nationalist, harbouring an ill-fated feud with Roosevelt, but he also at times of wider vision grasped the value of future harmony between France and Britain and understood the basic economic needs and long-term interests of this country far better than anyone at that time in Whitehall. However, the Foreign Office, without the Cabinet ever being informed, misled the PM into turning the offer down, and infuriated the General for good by publicising what had been offered in strict confidence. Talks on these lines might not have succeeded – 'might-have beens' can never be proved. But not to pursue them in good faith was one of the mistakes of this century.

The state of the UK balance of payments and economy today says all that is necessary about the damage that was done by the mistakes of 1969 and the 1970s. But we have to start from here. In doing so, there are, I suggest, three major political questions about which we should clear our minds.

1. Do we want the UK to remain an independent self-governing nation?
2. Do we remain faithful to the ultimate democratic principle that people must not be coerced by laws they have had no share in enacting? and
3. Are our future liberties and security ultimately safer if dependent for their

preservation in the last resort on the countries of West Europe or those of North America?

First do we wish to remain an independent self-governing nation? If we do not, we contemplate a rather bizarre world in which Namibia, Estonia, Sri Lanka, Albania, Croatia, Taiwan – not to mention others – would be independent states, but the UK would not. Not merely would we then cease to be a permanent member of the Security Council of the UN, but presumably cease to be members of the UN at all. I would remind those who say that this is ridiculous and unthinkable that the extreme Continental Federalists, of whom M. Delors is one, do see themselves as moving toward such a Federal superstate with all real power at the centre, and that each of the centralising measures they devise, whether political or economic, are steps towards this.

Yet it would surely be very strange, when the popular call everywhere is for devolution and de-centralisation of power, notably throughout the former Soviet Union and Eastern Europe, and even in the UK, that we should engage in what would be the greatest exercise in centralisation since the consolidation of the Tsarist Empire. We must therefore give a clear answer 'Yes' or 'No' to the question: Do we wish to remain an independent nation? Those who answer 'No' should say so. And those who answer 'Yes', as I do, must make up their minds at what point they should take a stand and not surrender so much to the centre as will deprive us of the power to retain the rest.

Secondly, do we wish to preserve the basic democratic principle that people governed by a system of laws must have some part in influencing these laws – government by consent, and not dictation? If we do, and if we wish to remain a nation and not the province of a superstate, we cannot hand over to external authorities the basic powers of government. For we are then involved in the Pickles dilemma that if we surrender such powers to an elected central authority, we lose our independence; and if we surrender them to an unelected bureaucratic commission, we flout the basic principles of democracy. Transferring powers to an elected Parliament in Strasbourg or elsewhere simply got us off one horn of the dilemma and on to the other. If therefore we wish to remain an independent democratic state, it follows that we must (while remaining, of course, members of genuinely international authorities from the UN downwards) under our own parliament retain central decisions over peace and war, defence, internal law and order, the livelihood of our own people, and therefore the currency and the budget. And we must whenever possible bring decisions nearer, and not further away from, the people affected by them.

Thirdly, in the world in which we live, are our liberties and our security basically safer if they depend on partnership with the countries of Western Europe alone or of North America, also? In deciding who are our best friends when it comes to the test, experience is on the whole a better guide than ideology. We should accordingly not wholly ignore the hard facts that in the Second World War it was the US which gave this country the decisive economic and military help which enabled us to survive and eventually prevail; that it was Marshall Aid which made West European recovery possible, that it was NATO which held off the Soviet threat; that more recently US support was decisive in the Falklands exercise, and that in the Gulf War the British and US authorities worked effectively (almost automatically) together, while some of our Continental partners did not show much stomach for the fight. In matters of defence, experience argues that authority must remain with NATO.

In the light, then, of experience and present facts, what should be the policy and strategy of the UK? The basic goal, I believe, which I have called the Free Trade Alternative, should be politically not to create a centralising superstate structure intended to rival the US, with an economic identity based on barriers against the rest of the world, but rather a partnership of independent states, each practising government by consent through liberal institutions, devolving legislation and decisions whenever possible closer to those affected; open economically to the trade and economic life of the rest of the world, and open also to any nation to join who accepts these principles, whether or not that nation is located in the rather arbitrary boundaries of 'Europe'. In such a partnership only those decisions which had to be taken centrally would be so taken, and they would be taken by international and not supranational authorities.

How, in the world as it is, should we progress towards this goal? There are two broad routes which the UK might follow. The first would be a dash for freedom. The EFTA countries have now negotiated with the EC the formation of an European Economic Area including both groups, in which the EFTA countries would enjoy industrial freedom of trade with the EC, and would share the arrangements for the Single Market on services etc. but would be exempt from the CAP, the Common External Tariff and much of the Brussels centralised legislation. Meanwhile the US, Canada and Mexico are also now moving towards a North Atlantic Free Trade Area. If the UK opted for the dash for freedom, we would transfer from formal EC membership to membership of the wider EEA, which would give us in effect the position de Gaulle offered us in 1969. It would confer on us three major advantages compared with the present dead-end, while preserving industrial free trade with both EFTA and the EC. First we should be liberated from the CAP burden on our labour costs and living standards, and our inflationary problems would thus be eased. Secondly, we should escape the detailed, restrictive legislation emanating from Brussels. And thirdly, we should be free to join our natural allies in the US and Cairns Group of countries in working through GATT for freer trade on a far wider and indeed world scale, instead of being able only to mumble mutely as at present and be outvoted in the confines of the EC.

The wider alliance pressing for wider world free trade against the high protectionism of the EC would have a much greater chance of making real progress. It could also well be called the Atlantic Alternative.

Certainly, at the very least, if the UK chose the dash for freedom, our food import trade would revert to the world's most efficient low-cost producers in a few years. Our trade in general has been much less distorted than might have been expected by 20 years of the CAP and EC preferences. Even today, 60 per cent of UK exports go to countries other than the original EC Six, and almost 50 per cent to countries other than the present EC Twelve.[7] If the distortions caused by EC membership, particularly the CAP, were removed, trade would flow back before long to its natural channels. My guess would be – and it can only be a guess – that the dash for freedom would soon give the UK about double the annual growth, and hence greater political influence in the longer run, than any alternative.

Such a dash for freedom, however, will be said by some not to be practical politics, a phrase sometimes used by those who do not have the courage to act decisively. If, however, that pessimistic argument is accepted, the second, and second best, strategy would be broadly as follows. While remaining members of the EC, we would at least aim at converting it, step by step, into a looser but wider group, both politically and economically. Politically this would mean opposition to any more transfer of power over internal affairs to any of the EC authorities.

Economically, avoidance of any further centralisation of power would be particularly crucial to the UK. We have already lost, in the ways described above, more than any other EC member by the imposition of the CAP on our economy. In the past few years our economy has been even more seriously damaged by adopting, in disregard or ignorance of the last 70 years' experience, the fixed ERM exchange rate system, at a grossly over-valued rate, which has forced the UK into stagnation and chronic unemployment – higher than at any time since the Great Depression. We have suffered all this simply in the name of centralisation. To add to that the acceptance of a single currency and an unaccountable central bank would be not so much adding insult to injury as adding unconditional surrender to unilateral disarmament.

A single currency does not extinguish a balance of payments deficit, as some seem to imagine. It converts the deficit country into a depressed area, because the higher costs which gave rise to the deficit show themselves in industrial failure and high unemployment, as Northern Ireland has discovered in the last 70 years. Secondly, if you transfer the power over a modern economy away from democratically elected parliaments and hand it to an unaccountable committee of central bankers, the decline into heavier and persistent unemployment will be even steeper. For the professional philosophy of central bankers (and particularly German ones) is always to give priority to price levels and to 'fighting inflation', and to assume that unemployment does not much matter. This is revealed again with delightful naiveté by the text of the proposed rules for an EC central bank which harp solemnly on fighting inflation and nowhere mentions unemployment. Central banking, in short, is too important a matter to be left to central bankers. To surrender control over national economic policy to them would be as sensible as giving the Chiefs of Staff the power to declare war. And there would be a special irony if the EC, originally conceived as an instrument for tying down Germany, finished up as an instrument for handing over economic control of Western Europe to a committee of German bankers.

Meanwhile, in operating the negative strand of this strategy, the UK would be wise also to preserve one particular principle. We should not attempt to veto other EC members from further centralisation, if they wish to adopt it. To attempt a general veto on these issues would simply invite conflict and possible defeat. We should each adopt the alternative we prefer. The independents who opted out of centralisation would not form a 'second rank' as the propaganda would like us to believe, they would in fact be the gainers.

If Britain is to remain in the EC the overriding aim would be to widen membership as far as possible. By widening the group it would become less centralised; less illiberal and less authoritian. In a wider group there would be more scope for differences of circumstance, of history, of tradition, of inclination, of natural advantage and of climate, to be enjoyed. In a group stretching from

Portugal to the Ukraine the myth of economic convergence would be shown to be undesirable and impractical. Freedom for each member to choose what its own people want will thus naturally follow from a growth in numbers.

The existing EFTA countries, whether as full, or somehow associated, members, must in these circumstances be accepted on liberal terms, and doubly welcomed by the UK. Nor is there justification for excluding either the ex-Communist Eastern European countries or the newly independent Baltic republics if they wish to join. Already the EC has been compelled by the logic of events to accept association arrangements with Poland, Czechoslovakia and Hungary. To offer them economic aid by way of loans and grants, and then block their exports by CAP and other barriers was too manifestly absurd to be tolerated. And why stop short of the new independent republics in the ex-Soviet Union, if they are establishing genuinely democratic constitutions and free trade policies, and if they wish to join? And why indeed, under these conditions, stop short at the Ural Mountains? Trade does not stop nowadays at mountain ranges. Both M. Delors and Chancellor Kohl are now for obvious, if different, reasons opposing such widening. If they are successful in this, the EC will become an instrument for dividing, not uniting, Europe.

If the EC Group was widened, and if the North American Free Trade Area went ahead, the way would be open, the case would be strong, and the negotiations more manageable for further progress under GATT auspices and in the spirit of the Free Trade Area option, for liberalisation on a world scale. The UK would then be well placed to give leadership in promoting initiatives which it genuinely welcomes rather than perpetually turning down those it does not. That may be at present no more than a vision, or at least a goal. But if realised, it would also yield the supreme reward of widening dramatically the market for the products of the Third World, whose populations are so much larger, and poorer, than those of the two rich men's clubs, the EC and the US. In such a wider and more liberal world rather than in narrower groups dominated by central bankers, it would almost certainly be easier to resist deflationary pressures and so maintain high levels of employment, which from the point of view of the welfare of ordinary people everywhere, is just as important as liberal trade policies. That would be the greatest prize of all.

Notes

1. CSO Annual Abstract of Statistics, 1965 and CSO Series Family Spending 1991.
2. CSO Monthly Review of External Trade Statistics, March 1992.
3. House of Lords Select Committee on EC Report on Common Agricultural Policy, p.57.
4. Bureau of Agricultural Economics, Canberra, 1990.
5. Economic Trends, Annual Supplement, 1992.
6. Society of Motor Manufacturers and Traders, 1990.
7. Monthly Review of External Trade Statistics, Annual Supplement, 1992 and Direction of Trade Statistics, Yearbook, 1991, International Monetary Fund.

References

Douglas Jay (1968), *After the Common Market*, Harmondsworth, Penguin, p.62.
Harold Wilson (1971), *The Labour Government* 1964–1970, London, Weidenfeld & Nicolson.
Jean Lacouture (1991), *De Gaulle the Ruler*, London, Collins Harvill.

11

Missing the boat at Messina and other times?

Miriam Camps

At the end of the war in Europe, I was here, in London at the American Embassy, working with an organisation which very few people have heard of, but which, in a very real sense, was a remote ancestor of the European Community, namely the Emergency Economic Committee for Europe (EECE). This was one of three intergovernmental organisations set up just at the end of the war in Europe, the other two being the European Coal Organisation (ECO), and the European Central Inland Transport Organisation (ECITO). Later, I was involved in the formation of the UN Economic Commission for Europe, which took over the work of these three emergency organisations, and, later on, I was concerned with the formation of the Organisation for European Economic Co-operation (OEEC). I think I can claim to be the mother of the OEEC. There are many fathers, but I am the only mother; I wrote the first paper in the State Department on why there would be a need for a European organisation as a counterpart to the ECA, the US agency set up to administer Marshall aid. By this time, of course, I was in the State Department, in Washington, and I dealt not only with certain aspects of the Marshall Plan but later, tangentially, with aspects of the negotiations on the Schuman Plan. At that time, the UK, the US and France were still formally 'occupying' Germany and therefore the US High Commission in Germany was concerned with those parts of the negotiation having to do with certain reserved powers still exercised by the occupying powers. Later, after I came to live in Cambridge (England), I looked at things more from a British perspective, and less from that of a US Government official.

Here I shall be drawing very heavily on the volume of 'contemporary history' I wrote in the early 1960s: *Britain and the European Community, 1955–1963*. (Camps, 1964) I have looked at some but not, as yet, as many of the documents which have now become available at the PRO as I promised myself I would do when the files were open. What I have seen so far has contained few surprises, perhaps because I was in the fortunate position of having that book read in draft by three officials – Sir Frank Lee, Russell Bretherton and Sir Frank Figgures. Those of you who are now studying the history of the period will know all three were very much involved with these questions. The book was also read by Richard Mayne and one or two other people intimately connected with the European side of the negotiations.

At the end of the war, the leadership of Western Europe was Britain's for the asking. During the first decade after the war, the British Government, had it taken the lead and tried to create a strong European Community, could have written the script. By the time of Messina it had lost the initiative, and, for most of the time since then, the British Government has been reacting to situations created by others.

The British failure to give their relationship with Western Europe a higher priority in the early post-war period was one of the biggest of several missed opportunities to establish a satisfactory relationship with continental Western Europe. Also, many of the actions taken and the attitudes adopted in this early period created problems for the British later, particularly in the unsuccessful Maudling Committee negotiations on a free trade area, and, later on, in the first accession negotiations as well. When the OEEC was being formed, both the United States and France pushed for a stronger European organisation than the UK was prepared to contemplate. The Americans, in particular, urged that a commitment to the formation of a European customs union should be one aspect of the European response to Marshall's speech. The French argued for a stronger and more independent role for the secretary-general of the OEEC. And both the French and Americans argued that the OEEC should be set up as, what was called in the jargon of the day, a continuing organisation. The British wanted a purely intergovernmental organisation which would last only for the Marshall Plan period; they were not interested in a long-term future for the organisation. I think many people date Monnet's conviction that the OEEC was not a strong enough organisation to respond to Europe's needs and that something more ambitious would be required to these early decisions about the structure of the OEEC. Although the British played an active, and, for the most part, a constructive role in the OEEC, the British view of its role and purpose was always a strictly limited one.

There were understandable reasons why the British Government, in the post-war decade, missed the opportunity to create the kind of European Community which would have been more responsive to their own needs than the Community they eventually joined. It would have been almost unrealistically far-sighted for any British government in the immediate aftermath of the war to have realised fully the shifts in relative power that a decade later had become obvious. But although it is understandable that there was no overriding priority given to Europe in the immediate post-war period, it is also clear that the European relationship was given a lower priority in the famous three Churchillian circles – of the North Atlantic, the Commonwealth and Europe – than it should have been given. Mistakes and misjudgements made in this early period complicated later efforts to find an acceptable arrangement with the Six.

One of the factors to which more attention should have been paid was the discussions in the resistance groups about post-war economic plans. Last year I read a very moving book, *Letters to Freya* by Helmuth James von Moltke, who was involved with the German resistance (Von Moltke, 1991). I was struck by the extent to which even the German resistance, albeit small, was thinking in terms of post-war economic arrangements on a Europe-wide basis, as were the resistance movements elsewhere (Lipgens, 1982). In the early post-war period, people from the resistance in France, the Low Countries and elsewhere were playing a very active part in the European discussions. They did not know precisely what they wanted, but they wanted something. I suspect that the fact that the British Government had so few connections with those wartime discussions was probably important in making them underestimate the extent of the drive on the Continent for something more than a purely intergovernmental system on the OEEC pattern. But let me now move on to Messina.

No boats were missed at Messina, that is at the meeting held there in early June 1955. There was no reason for the British to have gone to Messina, and although I have heard it said that they were asked but did not bother to go, I doubt whether they were, for there was no reason why they should have been asked. A meeting of the foreign ministers of the Six had been planned for some time, they needed to decide upon a successor to Jean Monnet, who had recently resigned as the head of the High Authority in order to be freer to work for a renewal of the European drive for unity. The British knew there were memoranda containing new proposals being prepared by officials in the Benelux countries, by the Germans and by the Italians – copies of these papers had been given to British officials. It was no secret that things were stirring, but there was no feeling on the Continent that the Messina meeting itself was something that the British should have attended. The British errors and misjudgements came a little later.

Let me remind you what the situation was like early in 1955 when the Six first began discussing new plans. After a very heady period of rapid progress during 1952 and 1953, the integration effort of the Six suffered a severe setback when, in 1954 the French Assembly refused to ratify the treaty establishing a European Defence Community. Many people felt the process of integration on a six country basis was stalled, perhaps dead. Eden had then taken the lead in negotiating the Paris Agreements; these ended the occupation regime, opened the way for Germany to join NATO, and transformed the Brussels Treaty organisation into the WEU, which, of course, included the UK. Moreover, at the end of 1954, the British Government had signed an association agreement with the European Coal and Steel Community, an agreement very warmly welcomed by Monnet and the Six. There was an understandable feeling in the British Government that relationships with the Six had been satisfactorily settled: there was the association agreement with the Coal and Steel Community and the WEU for defence matters. Although the Six might be discussing new economic plans few thought anything much was likely to happen. However, contrary to British expectations, the Messina meeting proved to be an important turning point. This resulted less from what happened at the meeting itself, than from the fact that Spaak was appointed, soon after the meeting, to organise work to give effect to the resolutions adopted at Messina. In effect, the Spaak Committee did the preparatory work for two new treaties, a treaty for what subsequently became Euratom, and a treaty for a Common Market. I wonder whether had Spaak not been given that job at that time, Monnet, on his own, would have been able to generate the necessary momentum to launch the Common Market. At that time, Monnet was much more interested in Euratom. The Common Market was, at the start, much more a Benelux operation than a Monnet concern.

At the Messina meeting, it was clear that everyone wanted the British to play some part in the work of what came to be the Spaak Committee. There was no freezing out of the UK. On the contrary, the resolution adopted at Messina stated explicitly that 'the Government of the United Kingdom, as a power which is a member of the WEU and is also associated with the ECSC, will be invited to take part in this work' (Camps, 1964, p. 322). The British did participate in the work of the Spaak Committee during the summer and early autumn of 1955.

There are several things about this phase of British participation which should be noted. The UK participants were called representatives, not delegates, and they were not as committed as the delegates from the Six to the resolutions which had been adopted at Messina. These representatives were officials, mainly from the Board of Trade and the Treasury. Russell Bretherton, from the Board of Trade, was the senior official concerned with the Common Market. Nobody from the Foreign Office took part and I have been told that officials in the Foreign Office were told by the Permanent Under-Secretary (Harold Caccia) that these were purely economic matters and should be left to the Board of Trade and to the Treasury. If this is true, it was a misjudgement.

Throughout the discussions in the Spaak Committee during the summer of 1955, there was endless insistence by the British representatives that the work of the OEEC should not be prejudiced in any way, and that many of the objectives that were being sought should be pursued through the OEEC rather than in some new organisation. In the aftermath of the French rejection of the EDC the delegates from the Six were very careful to avoid concepts implying too much 'supranationalism' and were cautious and tentative about institutional arrangements. The whole tone of the discussions in the Spaak Committee was very different from that of the early days of the Coal and Steel Community. This was not out of deference to the British; no one wanted to stir the embers of the EDC debate in France. Had the British, at that stage, been more prepared to think new thoughts about their role in Europe, perhaps new arrangements which were not too uncongenial for the British could have been found. But none of the Six were willing to rely simply on the OEEC. They wanted to move beyond the OEEC; the British did not. And the constant British emphasis on the adequacy of the OEEC was unwelcome and counterproductive. Some of those present could remember all too well times when the British had not been so enamoured of the OEEC as they now claimed to be when something more was under consideration. In 1950, for example, the British would have liked to down-grade the OEEC and to transfer much of its work to NATO. Their preferred organisation was always NATO; the OEEC was considered to be a useful organisation for certain well-defined tasks, but they had never wanted to see the OEEC develop into something more far-reaching. The fact that the UK had been largely successful in keeping the OEEC under its control and confined to tasks directly related to the Marshall Plan, made the rest of the Six resent and distrust the constant British harping on the adequacy of the OEEC.

During these early discussions in the Spaak Committee, it also became clear that all the Six were thinking in terms of a customs union and not a free trade area. The Board of Trade representative (Russell Bretherton) did suggest that there might be advantages in a free trade area, but he found little interest in examining that possibility. In a free trade area countries eliminate tariffs with one another but keep their own tariffs vis-à-vis third countries and do not have a common commercial policy. Because of the system of Commonwealth preferences, a customs union presented problems for the British which a free trade area would not have done. At that time, it was simply an article of faith that the system of Commonwealth preferences, if nothing else, ruled out British participation in a European customs union. There were other objections as well, notably the loss of autonomy in tariff matters and the pressures toward further integration inherent in a common tariff regime.

Partly because of this well-known British objection to a customs union, there was, at first, hope that the British might participate in Euratom. The British were at that time ahead of the other European countries in the development of atomic energy, and certainly Monnet felt they had more to offer and were more important to Euratom.

Early in September 1955 the foreign ministers of the Six met at Nordwijk, a Dutch seaside resort, to review progress. A British minister was invited to that meeting, and I suppose you could say that then a boat was missed, for no British minister went and the Six rejected the suggestion that an official attend instead. Cyprus was contending for ministerial attention but I think it was a mistake not to have gone. Then, in November 1955, there came a more serious blunder. Spaak presided over a meeting which was to wind-up the work of the experts who had been meeting during the summer and early autumn; the next stage would be the drafting of the treaties. When the British representative (Bretherton) was asked for his views, he read out a statement which had been drafted in London, after discussions in the Trend committee, the inter-departmental committee concerned with these matters. There was nothing new in the statement. It reiterated the well-known British views on the need to avoid duplication with the OEEC and on the difficulties in a customs union. It expressed concern at even the rather modest amount of supranationality that was envisaged for Euratom. Finally, it said, the Government had reached no final conclusions and would like to study matters further when all the details were known. The tone of the statement was rather uncompromising, and the impression created was undoubtedly far more negative than those who had drafted the statement thought it would be. I was in Brussels at the time, and wrote a leader for *The Economist* on my return, called 'Britain and Europe's "Third Chance" ',[1] which commented on the impact which this rather unimaginative statement had made in Brussels. It seemed to me to reflect a lack of feeling for European attitudes: it was not that the statement said anything that had not been said before; it was not that it rejected anything outright; rather, it hit all the wrong notes, and it hit them very hard.

There are various accounts of what happened next. The British tend to say that Spaak threw them out. Others, the continental Europeans, usually say that the British walked out. I think that Spaak opened the door, the British walked through, and he then shut it behind them. It was clearly a parting of the ways. Again, had the British been more sensitive to European feelings, ways might have been found to enable them to continue to participate. But Spaak and others clearly wanted more of a commitment in principle than the British Government was then willing to give. Had the parting of the ways not come then, I think it would have come soon after. But this episode was a crucial turning point, and presumably, what people really mean when they refer to 'missing the boat at Messina'. It is worth noting that there was no Cabinet level discussion of the statement that was made in Brussels; it was based on discussions among officials. It was, of course, fully consistent with the views on the limits to co-operation in Europe which had characterised British policy since the war.

The disappointment and resentment among the Six which had been aroused by the tone of the November statement became even stronger a few weeks later when Sir Hugh Ellis-Rees, the chief British delegate to the OEEC, called a special meeting of the OEEC Council to which he spoke in the strongest terms, warning of the danger should the Six proceed with their customs union plans outside the OEEC. These warnings and threats of dividing Europe, trade wars and so forth, were also reiterated in bilateral representations in the capitals of the Six. This hostility shown by the British to the plans of the Six at the end of 1955 was an immense mistake. It showed a serious underestimation of the strength the *relance* had acquired, and it showed that the British were out of touch with the changes in the French attitude which had occurred during the summer. It was wrongly assumed that a strong and clear statement of British views might cause the Six to abandon their plans or to transfer them to the OEEC.

Today it seems odd that anyone could have thought seriously that this might have been the result of a strong, unvarnished statement of the British position. But it was not quite as ill-founded an assumption as it may seem. The desire for British participation had been made clear at Messina. There is an interesting document in the PRO written by Bretherton of a conversation he had with Clappier, the French delegate, in which Clappier said that the French would not go ahead with the Common Market unless the British joined.[2] Remember, too, how protectionist the French were at that time. Marjolin's memoirs give a graphic account of how widely the Common Market was disliked in France (Marjolin, 1989). It was terribly unpopular. Not only the British but the Germans and the Dutch found it difficult to believe that the French would, in the end, accept any trade arrangement that was not highly protectionist. So the feeling that the whole thing might go away if the British stated clearly just what their position was, was not as strange an assumption as it may now appear. But the way it was done, the character and tone of the statements made in the OEEC and in the bilateral representations made it seem like a malign attempt to wreck the plans of the Six. The result was to harden the position of the Six and to make them much more suspicious of British intentions later on in the free trade area negotiations and even in the first accession negotiations than they might otherwise have been. Spaak personally became convinced that time spent trying to bring the British along was time wasted.

It was against this background of, first, not really believing that the Six could be serious, and then of a misguided and inept attempt to dissuade them from going ahead by bluntly pointing out the difficulties and dangers that might follow, that the British Government then sought to regain the initiative by proposing, about a year later, an OEEC-wide free trade area. Negotiations were carried on for the better part of two years, mostly in the Maudling Committee. There were a lot of things wrong with the way the OEEC-wide free trade area negotiations were launched and carried on. And they are widely dismissed by continental writers as nothing more than a deliberate British attempt to undermine the Common Market. It may well be true that had the negotiations succeeded the Common Market might have been undermined. But the total dismissal of the proposal as simply an attempt to kill the Common Market is, in my view, a misreading of what the British were trying to do. I think the proposal was a genuine attempt to find a way to link the UK with the Six and that it was widely assumed that it would be seen in that light by the Six. There were, at the time, some who argued that it might even pave the way for the success of the Common Market, by reassuring the Germans, particularly, but also the Dutch and the Belgians that the external tariff of the Common Market would not be too high.

At the start of the negotiations, many of the technical difficulties of linking the Common Market of the Six with a wider free trade area were not appreciated, in part because the shape of the Common Market was not yet clear. And the fear that the free trade area would tend to supersede the Common Market – the famous accusation that the 'lump of sugar', i.e. the Common Market, would be dissolved in the 'cup of tea', a British-led free trade area, was not a widely-held concern until fairly late in the negotiations, although I suspect one or two people, Marjolin probably among them, had felt from the beginning that there was such a risk.

There is not enough scope here to say much about the long and, in the end, unsuccessful negotiations to establish an OEEC-wide free trade area. But since it was a crucial phase in the development of British thinking about their relationship with the Six and, also, an illustration of another time when British willingness to make concessions earlier might well have brought success, it is worth a little attention.

It was a mistake to have launched the negotiations within the framework of the OEEC, but it was difficult not to do so, given all the British had been saying about the OEEC and also because of the position the low-tariff countries had been taking in the OEEC on the link between further action on quotas and some action on tariffs (Campus, 1964, Chapter 4 and 5). It was also a mistake to have included in a single White Paper not only the British-inspired 'OEEC plan' but also a comprehensive summary of the essential points in the British negotiating position. Then, at the opening of the negotiations the British, as too often in this period, badly overestimated their bargaining power with the Six. They felt their big problems were likely to be internal ones, and that they would have great difficulty in persuading British industry that it would benefit. The kind of case they made to arouse domestic support was precisely the kind of case that was least likely to appeal on the continent, and such points were initially under stressed: the flat statement that agriculture must be excluded; the emphasis on the purely commer-cial aspects of the plan: the emphasis on the fact that Commonwealth preference must not be jeopardised; the rejection of many of the aspects of freeing trade, such as harmonisation of tariffs and institutional arrangements, that the Six in working out the Common Market had felt to be necessary. In the course of the negotiations concessions were made on agriculture, on tariff harmonisation, on institutional arrangements and on other key points, but the concessions were made grudgingly, too slowly, and too late.

It is easy to fault the British handling of the negotiations. But many continental Europeans fail to look at the other side of the picture. The British Government did feel it was making a real move toward the continent. There was much initial enthusiam for the plan in Germany and in the Benelux countries. And, from the PRO documents, one is struck by how often and how firmly British ministers were told, not just by those in the Six, like Erhard, who were, from the beginning, sympathetic to the free trade area proposals, but also by French ministers who were not very sympathetic towards it, and by Spaak, that if the British would simply go slow, if they would not push their ideas until after the Common Market had been safely ratified by the French Assembly, then negotiations would be pushed through to a satisfactory conclusions.[3] There is document after document which testifies to the fact that they were given very far-reaching commitments from ministers in the six governments. Had the British made the concessions they were prepared to make at the end of the negotiations earlier on, I think there is a good chance the negotiations would have succeeded; whether this would, or would not, have been desirable is another question. But, by the autumn of 1958, when the French in effect brought the negotiations to an end in an abrupt and unpleasant way, they had clearly run into the sands. The Commission was by then playing a key role in organising the position of the Six and de Gaulle was, once again, in power in France. By then the only kind of agreement that might have been found would have been exceedingly cumbersome, limited in scope and, very likely, unworkable.

Following the breakdown of the negotiations at the end of 1958, there was a period of bad blood between the Six and the UK, and there was a great deal of talk of the Six 'dividing Europe'. There was a particularly ill-tempered leader in *The Times* entitled 'France the Wrecker'.[4] However, although the negotiations and the manner of their termination generated much ill will and acrimony, they did make an important contribution, both to the evolution of British policy towards Europe and to giving the Six a strong sense of cohesion. Just as, later on, the first accession negotiations forced the Six to fill in many of the gaps in the Treaty of Rome, so the free trade area negotiations pushed them into putting flesh on the bare bones of the Common Market.

It is true, as the Europeans complained, that the free trade area proposal involved no 'choice', no real departure from past policies by the British Government. But it did, I think, represent a shift in the Government's attitude toward Europe, and it marked the beginning of a new process of questioning the assumptions and priorities which had been inherited from the early post-war period. Europe began to move slowly but perceptibly up the scale, and the Commonwealth to move down, and the relationship with the US to come into a truer perspective. As the Six maintained, the free trade area was essentially a plan for exchanging commercial advantages. But, as the Six were discovering, commercial advantage was cementing the foundations of the Common Market, and without the industrial interest in expanding trade with Europe, which was clearly awakened by the free trade area proposal, the first application to join the Community would not have been made as early as 1961.

The decision taken following the collapse of the Maudling Committee negotiations to go ahead with the little free trade area of the Seven, the EFTA, seemed to me at the time, and still seems to me, to have been a mistake. It represented no real movement in British policy; it was a step sideways, a holding action. Advocates of the plan argued that it would keep other countries from being drawn into the orbit of the Six, and that it would increase pressure on the Six to reach some kind of 'bridge-building' arrangement with the Seven. The Swedish and Swiss markets were of particular interest to Germany. It was also argued that it would demonstrate that a free trade area (as opposed to a customs union) could work and that it would open the way to an agreement between the two groups that would clearly respect the integrity of the Six. None of these arguments seemed to me persuasive and certainly none was good enough to outweigh the complications that the commitment to EFTA seemed likely to create for any later British negotiation with the Six. I am sure from conversations with officials. I had at the time, that the British Government would not have gone ahead with the EFTA had the Government reached the point of seriously considering joining the European Community.

It is ironic that by the time the EFTA Treaty came into force, the British Government was beginning to do just that and to re-examine the assumptions on which it had operated since the early post-war period. 1960 and 1961 were the years of a genuine evolution in government thinking. Early in 1960 there was a profound re-examination of British relations with the Six. On 1 January 1960, Sir Frank Lee, who had been the Permanent Secretary at the Board of Trade, moved to the Treasury and the Economic Steering Committee. An interdepartmental committee of senior civil servants under his chairmanship, examined in a totally new way the UK's relation with the Six. The whole spectrum of possibilities from abandoning the attempt to find an accommodation with the Six to joining the Community were examined in considerable depth. That committee reached the conclusion that joining the Community was likely to be the best course of action. The arguments for joining were essentially political; there were economic reasons as well, but the overriding reasons were political.

In conclusion it would be simplistic and rather misleading to point to any one time or event and to say that *then* was when the British missed the boat. What can be said is rather different: In the first post-war decade, for reasons which may today seem shortsighted but were understandable given the wartime experience and the character of the immediate post-war problems, the UK did miss the chance to create a European Community to fit its own specifications. Less understandable is the fact that for too long the British underestimated the strength of the movement towards a new form of unity on the Continent and consistently overestimated their own bargaining power.

The Government was slow to undertake a basic review of British policies and interests and clung for too long to assumptions formed in the early post-war period. This review finally began in January 1960, and led to the decision in the summer of 1961 to open negotiations with the Six looking towards membership. The decision marked a real change in British policy and the beginning of a long search (not yet over) for a relationship with the Six that was *qualitatively* different from anything that had gone before.

This last point suggests the fundamental reason why 'missing the boat at Messina' has always seemed to me to be a poor catchphrase: it contains the assumption that there was a boat the British wanted to catch. I do not think there was. There were various things that the British Government did not want to see happen, and there are some other things that they would have liked to have happened, but, until the summer of 1961, I think it is misleading to talk about 'missing the boat'.

Notes

1. *The Economist*, 19 November 1955. See also Camps, 1964, pp.44–45. Some of the Six had hoped and expected a far more positive British response and felt badly let down.

2. PRO CAB134/1044; cited in Burgess, 1988, p.402.
3. See, for example, PRO PREM11/2133, 8 May 1957.
4. *The Times*, 18 November 1958.

References

Burgess, S. and G. Edwards, (1988), 'The Six plus One: British policy-making and the question of European economic integration, 1955', *International Affairs*, vol.64, no.3.

Camps, Miriam (1964), *Britain and the European Community, 1955–1963*, London, Oxford University Press.

Lipgens, W. (1982), *A History of European Integration*, vol.1, Oxford, Clarendon Press.

Marjolin, R. (1989), *Architect of European Unity: Memoirs 1911–1986*, trans. by W. Hall, London, Weidenfeld & Nicolson.

Von Moltke, H.J. (1991) trans. and ed. by B.R. Oppen, *Lettes to Freya*, London, Collins Harvill.

12

To join, or not to join: the 'Appeasement' policy of Britain's first EEC application

Wolfram Kaiser

In his memoirs Harold Macmillan describes Britan's first application to join the European Economic Community (EEC) as 'a radical and almost revolutionary step' (Macmillan, 1973, p.24). Most of the Prime Minister's contemporaries agreed that this decision symbolized a significant break with the past. By joining the Community Britain seemed at last to have found a new role. More recently this view has been challenged. Stephen George now suggests that 'it is probably most accurate to view [the application of 1961] as a change of tactics in pursuit of the same strategic ends, in the light of changed circumstances' (George, 1991, p.44). In his analysis more emphasis is put on the amount of continuity in Britain's policy *vis-à-vis* European Integration. However, this interpretation clearly needs to be substantiated by checking against the historical records. So, what precisely were the motives behind the government's decision to open formal negotiations with the EEC and why was the application launched in 1961 despite the danger of a French veto?

The original decision in 1955 not to join a European common market had only confirmed the well-established post-war policy of participating in intergovernmental co-operation in Europe while strongly resisting moves towards integration. At the time the case against a British role in the Messina initiative was purely political. The Foreign Office argued that participation in a European common market would be incompatible with Britain's political relations with the Commonwealth and the United States and ultimately, detrimental to her position as a world power. The economic judgement of the Treasury and the Board of Trade was not so clearcut. They felt unable to say whether economically, joining a common market in Europe would be preferable to the status quo, but did warn strongly against the grave dangers involved in the possible exclusion from the Common Market which the European Coal and Steel Community (ECSC) powers might set up among themselves. Britain might then subsequently be forced to join on their terms.[1] However, the economic departments failed to impress this view on the ministers involved because of the bold prediction by the Foreign Office that under no circumstances would the Six manage to agree on a common market without British participation.[2]

By 1959, of course, the desperate attempt to find an economic arrangement with the newly founded EEC by means of the envisaged industrial Free Trade Area had completely failed. While the European Free Trade Association (EFTA) of the outer Seven was about to be set up as a means of putting economic pressure on the Six to come back to the negotiating table, the government started to rethink its European policy. For the first time since the war its underlying political assumptions were seriously called into question. Also, the initiative came right from the top. It was the Prime Minister, Harold Macmillan, who provided the political impetus. At a meeting with his Chancellor, Derek Heathcoat-Amory, and Foreign Secretary, Selwyn Lloyd, at Chequers in November 1959 the decision was made to set up a small committee of leading civil servants to analyse the various options.[3]

Initially the economic case for joining the EEC now seemed less clear than even in 1955. The most attractive features of the original plan for an industrial Free Trade Area were the combination of full access to the European market and the prolongation of most of the Commonwealth preferences while the government would have retained its autonomy in the area of foreign trade policy. The main departmental protagonist of that plan, namely the Board of Trade, and its President, Reginald Maudling, did not want to lose those advantages and were still hoping for a wider trade arrangement in Europe despite mounting American opposition. The Treasury, on the other hand, was now more relaxed about the export competitiveness of British industry than in 1955 and saw some economic advantage in the EFTA arrangements. Moreover, it was increasingly anxious that ministers should not choose accession to the EEC as an easy escape route to avoid implementing any unpopular but necessary domestic measures to cure what was increasingly seen as the British economic disease of perpetually recurring stagflationary periods.[4] But the Foreign Office believed that the Treasury view was also temporarily blurred by the election boom of 1959 which made the danger of getting no arrangement with the EEC seem less threatening.[5]

By May 1960, however, the economic ministries had come round to what was now the Foreign Office view. In the report by the Economic Steering (Europe) Committee on the long-term aspects of the split between the EEC and EFTA ('Sixes and Sevens') it was stated flatly that from a purely economic point of view, joining the EEC would 'almost certainly' be the best solution.[6] In any case, this argument was considered to be of subsidiary importance only and the economic debate became more and more marginalised during the next twelve months. Increasingly, those cabinet ministers who were already thinking in terms of ultimately joining the EEC saw this as a purely political problem. For example, Edward Heath, who had moved to the post of Lord Privy Seal in July 1960 and was responsible for European Affairs, was so utterly uninterested in the economics of Britain's relations with Europe that he only bothered to inquire about the positions of the Federation of British Industry (FBI) and various other industrial interest groups some three weeks before the final decision to apply was made.[7]

In the autumn of 1959 the political case for a close initial association with the EEC had been put forcefully for the first time in a discussion paper by the Planning Section of the Foreign Office.[8] Essentially, it argued that the EEC's economic, political and perhaps ultimately, military strength would increase dramatically while Britain's relative decline continued, as a result of which the United States would be attracted more and more to the continental European countries.

Britain was bound to lose her special position *vis-à-vis* Washington unless she quickly found a new political relationship with the EEC. This theme was developed further by a group of senior civil servants in July 1960 in answer to a number of written questions by Macmillan on the political and economic implications of association with or entry into the EEC.[9] They argued that only by deciding in favour of a close political relationship could Britain hope to influence the EEC members and prevent the emergence of a French-dominated 'Third Force' in Europe. In 1955 it was thought that joining a European common market would be detrimental to Britain's position as a world power. Now the opposite view was firmly held that it would actually enhance Britain's standing in the world considerably. The long report reflects the strong Foreign Office belief that retaining the 'special relationship' with Washington must be paramount to any other considerations. The conclusion seemed almost inescapable that 'foreign policy considerations therefore require us to be in the inner councils of the Six. . . . We must show ourselves prepared to join with the Six in their institutional arrangements and in any development towards closer political integration'.[10]

The French plan for more co-operation among the Six in political and ultimately, military matters made it even more urgent for the British government to determine its relationship with Europe. At the end of 1959 the EEC countries started regular political consultations among their foreign ministers but during 1960 it became increasingly clear that de Gaulle had set his mind firmly on much more far-reaching proposals. He ran into stiff opposition from The Netherlands government in particular, but in the other EEC countries, including Germany, the reaction was also mixed. In Bonn, Adenauer himself embarked upon a delicate balancing act domestically as well as externally. Although he was prepared to go a long way to please the French he could not afford to antagonize the United States by agreeing to anything that could have been interpreted as an intrusion into NATO competences. Nevertheless, until the final demise of the Fouchet Plan in 1962 it was always feared in London that the EEC might fast turn into a political animal under French leadership which would be detrimental to the interests of Britain and the Atlantic Alliance. In the meantime, the British government had bound itself to an economically inferior grouping which lacked any political cohesion. The EFTA connection became increasingly embarrassing as its members failed to keep in step with the EEC acceleration of tariff reductions and the Swedes and Swiss in particular followed an increasingly aggressive line *vis-à-vis* Washington in a last-ditch attempt to get US agreement to a wider economic arrangement in Europe without any political content.

In Whitehall the leading civil servants were already agreed that Britain had to be part of the EEC's emerging political structure. However, they were unclear as to how to reach an acceptable institutional settlement. The Economic Steering (Europe) Committee paper of May 1960 which had largely been inspired by the Joint Permanent Secretary to the Treasury, Frank Lee, proposed 'near-identification' as the only politically feasible solution. The memorandum said that Britain should seek 'an arrangement which would go as far as possible towards acceptance by the Seven of most of the essential features of the Common Market without formal participation in it'.[11] Full membership still seemed impossible because of the government's political commitment to the Commonwealth and EFTA and Britain's traditional aversion to any kind of supranational features.

Macmillan was anxious that Britain should lead Europe politically. 'Near-identification' without a full role for her in the institutions of the EEC was hardly going to do the trick. The Prime Minister was determined to tackle the problem head-on. When discussing the committee's conclusions he asked his colleagues whether '. . . we should not better go the whole way and secure the full advantages of membership of the Common Market. To "go into Europe fully" would at least be a positive and an imaginative approach which might assist the Government to overcome the manifest political and domestic difficulties. "Near-identification" [has] less attractions, and not appreciably less dangers'.[12]

With his detailed questionnaire about the implications of a close association with or entry into the EEC, Macmillan attempted to confront his colleagues in the cabinet with the ultimate necessity of applying for full membership of the Community.[13] At the same time, the Prime Minister wanted to sound out opinion when the cabinet met to discuss the resulting report. Significantly, in the cabinet meeting on 13 July Macmillan received most support from Lord Home who was then still Secretary of State for Commonwealth Relations and who had been very wary about the comparatively limited implications of Plan G for the Commonwealth only four years earlier. Now he thought that there were some strong arguments in favour of joining the EEC 'from the point of view of our future political influence in the Atlantic Community'.[14] However, other ministers, especially Maudling and Butler, argued strongly against British membership of the Community. Warning Macmillan against asking the cabinet too early to agree to the envisaged EEC application, Heath recalled several months later that the questionnaire had only provoked opposition on grounds of principle because the discussion was not streamlined to lead to the inevitable conclusion.[15] But at the time even those ministers who wanted to see Britain go into the EEC decided that the time was not yet ripe for a new approach after the prolonged row over the acceleration of tariff reductions and the future of the OEEC.

The way Macmillan's mind was moving was clearly illustrated by the fact that in the cabinet reshuffle shortly after the major discussion on Britain's European policy, all those ministers who had declared themselves in favour of joining the EEC were moved into key positions: Lord Home became Foreign Secretary, Heath Lord Privy Seal with special responsibility for European Affairs, Sandys moved to the Commonwealth Relations Office and Soames to the Ministry of Agriculture. When the bilateral discussions with the Germans, the French and the Italians started in the autumn of 1960 Macmillan's aim was two-fold: to improve the political climate in Europe but also to make clear to the sceptics in his own cabinet and in the Conservative Party that any solution short of full membership was no longer available. When Macmillan wrote his long memorandum on world politics at the end of December which he half-jokingly called 'The Grand Design' his main concern was not the nature of the arrangement Britain wanted but how best to handle the application to join the EEC both domestically and externally.[16] When Heath made his announcement at the WEU Council meeting on 27 February 1961 that Britain was now seriously prepared to consider harmonizing tariffs in an arrangement with the EEC, the internal debate had already moved on considerably. In March Macmillan requested a new report by civil servants. This time, however, they were asked to analyse not the problems arising out of EEC membership but how they might be overcome in negotiations. It was an entirely different exercise from the questionnaire which Macmillan had prepared in July 1960. It was now implied that solutions must be found to the three principal issues which formed the basis for the internal opposition against joining the EEC, namely the Commonwealth, agriculture and sovereignty.

When the issue of British participation in a European common market had first been discussed in 1955, the Foreign Office was by far the most ardent protagonist of the dogma that Britain must never join any institutions which were not entirely intergovernmental. However, the shock of the Suez War suddenly made the actual ability to exercise power seem rather more important in the field of foreign policy than any constitutional purity. By 1961 the Foreign Office argued forcefully that the considerable loss of sovereignty involved in joining the EEC would be offset by the additional influence Britain could exercise over the Community's development and that, in any case, the wider political reasons must be decisive.[17] As regards agriculture the main argument against taking part in a common market had always been Britain's commitment to a cheap food policy combining Treasury subsidies for home agriculture and Commonwealth Free Entry. Although the EEC countries had not agreed on the exact shape of their arrangements for agriculture by early 1961, it was already clear that Britain would need to participate in a system of managed markets and that Commonwealth Free Entry would have to go. However, the Ministry of Agriculture, Fisheries and Food was already convinced that the old subsidy system was too costly. Also, joining a common market in agriculture was increasingly seen as a way to curb imports from the Commonwealth and thereby strengthen home production.[8] Within the cabinet the new Minister for Agriculture, Soames, argued that the strong opposition by the National Farmers Union (NFU) was only directed against joining the EEC without derogations. As there would not necessarily be a decrease in their net-income the farmers who, of course, constituted an influential section of the Conservative Party, could surely be convinced of the necessity of a different system of subsidies.[19] Finally, fears about a further erosion of the Commonwealth connection loomed large among the Empire wing of the Conservative Party and some cabinet ministers like Butler were partially allayed only when the tour by several ministers to all Commonwealth countries in early summer 1961 showed that opposition to Britain's entry into the EEC seemed much less vocal than had been anticipated originally. Only this finally brought about the decision to initiate negotiations with the EEC about full membership when the cabinet met on 21 July 1961.[20]

Analysing Britain's European policy between 1955 and 1961 which was nearly entirely executive-led, it is clear that the fundamental decisions were based on political considerations only. When the government opted against membership of a common market in 1955 it was thought that it was incompatible with Britain's role as a world power. Subsequently, it was left to the Treasury and the Board of Trade to find an acceptable economic arrangement with the new European grouping. When even in the Foreign Office the perception of Britain's relative decline had at least partly caught up with reality by 1961, the same political logic which was applied in 1955 now made it imperative for her to join the EEC. It was a decision which again exemplified the primacy of politics over economics in Britain's post-war policy *vis-à-vis* European integration.

Although there remained a lot of emotional attachment to the Commonwealth, by 1961 this relationship had clearly rendered itself useless as a symbol of Britain's international power. Before Suez and the second wave of decolonisation after 1957, the Commonwealth had helped to compensate for Britain's quite dramatic economic and political decline. While the significance of its economic arrangements had long been questioned within Whitehall, by 1961 it was obvious that the Commonwealth also lacked any political cohesion. For Britain to retain what was still perceived as a world power status and a 'special relationship' with the United States, it now seemed inevitable to substitute the Commonwealth with the European Economic Community.

At the beginning of the 1960s only very few civil servants and even fewer politicians were in search of a new role for Britain. On the contrary, the decision to apply for EEC membership was a desperate attempt to retain the old role of the United States' principal ally by assuming the political leadership of Europe. Together with the 'winds of change' philosophy it marks the first stage in a long process of modernization of Britain's external relations but, as regards the underlying motives, it was certainly anything but a revolution. What might have seemed quite adventurous at the time, in reality reflects an inherently conservative approach to Britain's position in the world.

In 1961, apart from internal agreement on the EEC application, it was equally essential, of course, that Britain would actually be allowed to join. The government had previously over-estimated its influence and bargaining power on several occasions, not least during the Free Trade Area negotiations. Macmillan himself had played no small part in this, especially in 1955 when the Foreign Office took the view that the Messina initiative was destined for failure without British participation. As Young has rightly pointed out (Young, 1988, p.99) Macmillan, although critical of government policy towards Europe in the early 1950s, never had any clear idea of what precisely Britain's place in Europe should be. However, he instinctively feared the dangers inherent in Britain's exclusion from a European common market when in November 1955 the Foreign Office reversed its well-established policy of supporting any moves towards further integration on the continent within days and tried to redirect the Messina initiative into the orbit of the OEEC.[21] It can now safely be assumed that Macmillan, in the absence of any realistic alternative policy, was personally responsible for this and the resulting futile interventions in Bonn and Washington which produced much ill-feeling among the ECSC countries (Burgess and Edwards, 1988, p.406).[22]

Even before the failure of the Free Trade Area negotiations Macmillan and the Foreign Office had started to think in more depth about the best tactics to bring Britain closer to Europe. Increasingly, the importance of the new relationship between de Gaulle and Adenauer was understood. In October 1959 Macmillan wrote to Lloyd: 'The core of the Common Market is the Franco-German Alliance. In the last resort it is the governments of these two countries which we must influence'.[23] What was needed, the Prime Minister thought, was a 'carrot and stick' policy, with the carrots reserved for the French who were thought to be in a very strong position politically, and the stick applied to the Germans who appeared to be very weak because they were so dependent on others for the provision of their external security.[24] Macmillan developed this theme as early as June 1958 when, facing the prospect of a breakdown of the Free Trade Area negotiations, he sent a defiant note to his cabinet colleagues, saying 'we should not allow ourselves to be destroyed little by little. We would fight back with every weapon in our armoury. We would take our troops out of Europe. We would withdraw from NATO. We would adopt a policy of isolationism. We would surround ourselves with rockets and would say . . . "Look after yourselves with your own forces. Look after yourselves when the Russians overrun your countries". I would be inclined to make this position quite clear . . .'.[25]

Macmillan threatened Adenauer when they met in October 1958 that Britain would take her troops out of Germany and withdraw from NATO if the continental countries 'declared economic war upon her'.[26] He repeated this on other occasions and even as late as August 1960 when he tried to enlist the Chancellor's support for a settlement of the problem of Sixes and Sevens.[27] But Adenauer was not in the least impressed. For him it was imperative to preserve a good relationship with the United States, on whom Germany's security really depended, and to continue the Franco-German rapprochement which had long since become the second essential string of German foreign policy. Britain, on the other hand, came a very poor third. Macmillan's utterances only increased Adenauer's deep-seated suspicions of the British motives, in particular after the Prime Minister's journey to Moscow in early 1959. In a letter to Federal President Heuss, Adenauer wrote in April 1960 that he did not trust Macmillan and that he found his threats very embarrassing (Koerfer, 1987, p.399).[28] Later in the same year Adenauer told Macmillan bluntly that '. . . the British people [know] quite well that the troops in Germany [are] there for the defence of the United Kingdom and not for that of Germany.'[29] Significantly, the Foreign Office in London shared this view. They found their Prime Minister completely out of touch with reality and became increasingly irritated with his somehow pretentious threats which, if meant seriously, could risk the very basis of Britain's foreign policy. The simple fact was stated clearly by the Deputy Under-Secretary of State, Evelyn Shuckburgh, in a note on one of the Prime Minister's memoranda: 'No NATO, no American participation in our defence. . . . No American participation, no defence. . . . Consequently, the need to preserve NATO . . . , which alone guarantees us the American contribution, overrides any considerations of tactics *vis-à-vis* France and Germany'.[30] From this perspective, of course, in the bipolar post-war world Britain was in an equally weak position to Germany, only that with regard to European integration, the United States supported the EEC and not Britain on Sixes and Sevens; and that made Macmillan's threats look even more embarrassing.

Of course, however ill-conceived Macmillan's use of threats to enlist German support might have been, the key to Britain's entry into the EEC was really de Gaulle. As early as 1959 Macmillan began to think in terms of a strategic trade-off between Britain's European interests and France's ambitions in the field of defence and security. De Gaulle's 1958 memorandum on tripartism and the need to re-organize NATO had, it seemed, opened up this new tactical route towards a European settlement. At a meeting with cabinet colleagues at Chequers in November 1959 Macmillan, for the first time, hinted at the possibility of helping France develop her own nuclear capability and delivery systems.[31] During 1960 Macmillan set his mind ever more firmly on bribing the French leader into accepting Britain into the EEC. Increasingly, only one carrot seemed to be sufficiently attractive for de Gaulle to swallow. At the end of 1960 Macmillan stated flatly in his 'Grand Design' memorandum: 'De Gaulle's second – and to him vital – ambition is the nuclear weapon. Can we give him our techniques, or our bombs, or any share of our nuclear power on any terms which i) . . . are publicly defensible . . . and ii) the United States will agree to? At first this seems hopeless. But since I think it is the one thing which will persuade de Gaulle to accept a European settlement . . . – I think it is worth serious examination'.[32]

Arguably, what de Gaulle really wanted from Macmillan was a clear indication that Britain would give up her 'special relationship' with the United States and ultimately, accept French leadership of Western Europe. Although de Gaulle would usually talk to Macmillan in the most oracular style he told the Prime Minister plainly at their meeting at Rambouillet in March 1960 that Britain would have to choose between the United States and Europe.[33] The French President later suggested in his memoirs (De Gaulle, 1970, p.232) that the fact that Britain was obviously not prepared to make this choice was the ultimate reason for the veto which he applied in January 1963. However, at the beginning of 1961 Macmillan believed that giving de Gaulle something on tripartism and his nuclear ambitions might be sufficient. The stark fact, of course, had not escaped the Prime Minister's attention that this carrot did not grow in British but in American soil. Consequently, when the two leaders met in April 1961, Macmillan tried in vain to convince President Kennedy that a new approach to France would be necessary to find a way out of the European impasse. At Kennedy's request he wrote a long memorandum only a few days after his return from Washington explaining exactly what he thought was needed to bribe de Gaulle politically.[34]

Kennedy's prompt response, however, dealt Macmillan's efforts to find a way into the EEC a most severe blow. In his memorandum the President rejected outright any possiblity of helping the French with their nuclear programme.[35] It was added that the United States might do something as regards closer informal tripartite consultation and some form of minor technical assistance for the development of delivery systems, but clear conditions must be attached to any such offers and a quid pro quo extracted from de Gaulle in terms of more co-operative French policy *vis-à-vis* NATO. In Macmillan's mind this was clearly not enough. But although he continued to impress upon the American President the need for a more forthcoming attitude, Kennedy refused to go any further. The American counter-proposals of May 1961, although almost certainly insufficient as regards France, show clearly how far Macmillan himself was prepared to go and how traditional his approach really was.[36] Firstly, Kennedy suggested that the French might be given the post of Supreme Commander in Europe (SACEUR) if they remained in the integrated NATO command structure. Macmillan did not agree – superficially because that might be interpreted as a first step by the Americans out of Europe but really because he could not see Britain relegated, if only symbolically, to third place within the Atlantic Alliance.[37] Secondly, the Americans revived the Herter Plan of 1960 and advocated that all British and some American nuclear weapons alongside any future French capability should be put under NATO command. This proposal had some support within Whitehall.[38]

However, Macmillan strongly opposed any such plans on the grounds that Britain would lose what for domestic political reasons, he liked to portray as her 'independent' nuclear force when, of course, by 1961 Britain's bomber force was about to become obsolete and she was already totally dependent on the United

States for modern and credible means of delivery. Macmillan was probably right in assuming that to accept Kennedy's proposals was to waste a British asset without getting anything from the French in return. But it also illustrates the extent to which de Gaulle's vision of 'la grande nation' was the French equivalent of Macmillan's idea of Britain's special position as a world power alongside the United States.

The degree to which the economic, political and military aspects of Britain's policy *vis-à-vis* the EEC were inter-related is significant. As has been explained, Macmillan saw a clear link between Britain's European interests and France's ambitions in the field of defence and security. It is equally clear how limited the British government's capacity was to create the conditions which alone, from Macmillan's point of view, would have enabled Britain to join the EEC. In this respect Britain was totally dependent on the United States government which, partly for external, partly for domestic reasons failed to be forthcoming in any meaningful way. By May 1961, that is long before the government decided to apply for EEC membership, it must have been obvious to Macmillan that he had already lost what he sometimes handled almost like a diplomatic chess game. In his own reasoning the conclusion was inescapable that there was now not the slightest chance for the envisaged British EEC application to succeed.[39] Originally, the cabinet had agreed to make a new approach to the EEC only under the condition that Kennedy would get a 'favourable response' from de Gaulle when the two leaders met in Paris in the early summer of 1961.[40] But instead of reporting any encouraging new developments Kennedy only confirmed after the visit that de Gaulle 'had no particular wish to see the United Kingdom join the Six'.[41] The question must then be asked, of course, why the British proceeded with the application.

In an interview with his official biographer in 1979 (Horne, 1989, p.257) Macmillan suggested that he believed that de Gaulle did not want Britain in the EEC but that 'once he had let us start [to negotiate], he couldn't say no; . . . I felt we would leave him no excuse to exclude us'. This may, to some extent, reflect a certain amount of wishful thinking which had always played a considerable role in Britain's European policy. However, this alone does not sufficiently explain why the application was actually launched in 1961. A historical interpretation will have to take account of Macmillan's thinking and conduct as well as the general political setting. In fact, by June 1961 the government had arrived at an external and domestic impasse. Primarily in order to secure his vital short-term aims, Macmillan followed his strategy of dual 'Appeasement': To apply for EEC membership seemed necessary firstly to please the new United States government and secondly to calm down the internal divisions over Europe within the Conservative Party.

Since the Schuman Plan of 1950, US governments had always wished to see Britain within the evolving European organizations but had never tried to pressurize the governments in London into departing from their traditional policy. By the end of the 1950s, however, the United States' balance of payments position deteriorated sharply and the administration in Washington became increasingly impatient with what it regarded as Britain's attempt to secure the best of all worlds economically without making any politically significant commitments in Europe. When he visited London at the end of 1959, the American Under-Secretary of

State, Douglas Dillon, made it crystal-clear to Macmillan and Heathcoat-Amory that the US government would continue to support the EEC for political reasons whereas EFTA was regarded as a purely economic grouping which involved considerable discrimination against the United States. In addition, Dillon stated categorically that the US government did not share Macmillan's interpretation that the existence of EEC and EFTA implied the danger of a political split in Western Europe and that a purely economic arrangement between the two groups was now quite unacceptable.[42] The new Kennedy administration took an even stronger view. In a key meeting with Heath and Whitehall civil servants in March 1961, at which Britain's policy towards the EEC was discussed in detail, the Under-Secretary of State, George Ball, said that the US now wanted Britain to join the EEC.[43] When President Kennedy met Macmillan only one week later, he confirmed the views held by Ball who was, of course, a close confidant of Monnet.[44] From Kennedy's perspective it was now increasingly important to keep the EEC's development compatible with American political and security interests in Europe. In this reasoning, Britain had to join and lead the EEC primarily to put a break on de Gaulle's more ambitious plans to create a 'Third Force' in Europe under French leadership and quite separate from the United States and NATO.

Whether the United States administration meant to force the British government into the Community or not, is not important in this context. Kennedy himself stated unambiguously his belief that it was now inevitable for Britain to join the Community. For Macmillan, this was decisive. In making the EEC application Britain showed the goodwill which now seemed necessary to appease the new administration into confirming the 'special relationship' in the only field in which it had ever really existed, namely defence and security. At a time when the United States administration was involved in a fundamental re-think of their previous European policy, including their commitment to provide Britain with modern means of delivery for her nuclear weapons, it was imperative for the government in London to comply with Washington's wish in order to retain the previous relationship in general, and a credible nuclear deterrent in particular. It is clear, therefore, that the Atlantic partnership was the controlling element, not only in Macmillan's realization that Britain must now join the EEC, but also in the decision to apply for membership in 1961 even though a French veto was at least highly likely. Ironically, of course, the United States did not regard Britain's EEC membership as important enough to override other considerations *vis-à-vis* de Gaulle's ambitions in the field of defence and security. Overstretched and overstrung, Britain's attempt to square the circle was again destined for failure.

Moreover, the application of 1961 served the second purpose of appeasing the pro-European and anti-European factions within the Conservative Party. By the summer of 1961, pressure to apply for EEC membership had increased sharply. A large section of the cabinet and the Conservative parliamentary party were now in favour as well as most of the press and some influential interest groups, i.e. the 'City' and a majority of business and industry.[45] By applying for membership Macmillan could prove to them his determination to take Britain into Europe. At the same time, however, it was possible to avoid antagonizing the opponents of membership because by the summer of 1961 it seemed almost certain that the point would not be reached for years to come at which Britain had to face the fact that she did, indeed, have to choose between the Commonwealth and Europe. A failing EEC application was now bound to be less damaging for the Conservative Party than a prolonged row over Britain's European policy. In retrospect it seems a misjudgement, therefore, that the EEC application was a sign of Macmillan's 'great political courage' (Camps, 1964, p.334). The basic fact is that in July 1961 the cabinet only decided to initiate negotiations in order to find out whether EEC membership was compatible with Britain's other commitments. It is clear now that internally this was interpreted in various and conflicting ways. While Macmillan hoped that it meant accepting membership of the Community as inevitable rather than desirable in the long term, sceptics like Butler probably looked forward to a breaking-point in the negotiations or a French veto. In this sense, for the Conservatives the application of 1961 was really the beginning of the famous 'agreement to differ' policy of the 1975 referendum. It was seen as the only available escape route for the government from a grave economic and political crisis at home.

Because the government was still not prepared to face the basic facts of the new post-war world order, the realization that Britain had to join the EEC was entirely for the wrong reasons. Equally, the decision to launch the application in 1961 was made at the wrong time. It primarily served the government's short-term interests externally and domestically and if anything, took Britain further apart from Europe because of the antagonizing effect of de Gaulle's veto. The government should have blamed itself entirely for the devastating result which a frustrated Macmillan described in his diary at the end of January 1963 (Horne, 1989, p.427): '. . . de Gaulle is trying to dominate Europe . . . [The veto] is the end – or at least a temporary bar – to everything for which I have worked for many years. . . . All our policies at home and abroad are in ruins'.[46]

Notes

1. PRO CAB 134/1026/MAC(55) 35th mtg., 2 Aug. 1955.
2. PRO CAB 134/889/ES(55) mtg., 1 Nov. 1955.
3. PRO PREM 11/2679 29 Nov. 1959.
4. PRO CAB 129/102, I/C, (60) 107, 6 Jul. 1960.
5. PRO FO 371/150279/M 6114/278, 11 May 1960.
6. PRO CAB 134/1820/EQ, (60) 27, (27 May 1960; CAB 134/1819/EQ (60) 8. mtg., 27 May 1960.
7. PRO FO 371/158273/M 634/186, 28 June 1961.
8. PRO PREM 11/2985 (no exact date).
9. PRO CAB 129/102, I/C. (60) 107, 6 Jul. 1960.
10. Ibidem.
11. PRO CAB 134/1820/EQ. (60) 27, 27 May 1960.
12. PRO CAB 134/1819/EQ. (60) 8th mtg. 27 May 1960.
13. PRO CAB 129/102, I/C. (60) 107, 6 July 1960.
14. PRO CAB 128/34/CC. (60) 41st mtg. 13 July 1960.
15. PRO FO 371/158264/M 634/12, 7 Feb. 1961.
16. PRO PREM 11/3325 (29 Dec. 1960, 3 Jan. 1961.
17. PRO CAB 134/1821/EQ. (61) 5, 26 Apr. 1961.
18. PRO MAF 255/430, 6 Feb. 1961.
19. PRO CAB 128/35, I/CC. (61) 24th mtg. 26 Apr. 1961.
20. PRO CAB 128/35, II/CC. (61) 42nd mtg, 21 Jul. 1961.
21. PRO BT 11/5715/CRE. 3677/59/1, 22 Oct. 1955.

22. The source in Burgess/Edwards ('personal information') is very weak but it is the only logical conclusion. Unfortunately, written proof does not seem to exist as there is only a summary account of the important meeting of the Economic Policy Committee which does not reveal the source of the proposition to appeal to the governments in Bonn and Washington. See PRO CAB 134/1226/EP. (55) 11th mtg. 11 Nov. 1955.
23. PRO PREM 11/2679, 22 Oct. 1959.
24. Ibidem.
25. PRO PREM 11/2315, 24 Jun. 1958.
26. PRO PREM 11/2328, 8 Oct. 1958.
27. PRO PREM 11/2993, 10 Aug. 1960.
28. Quoted from Adenauer to Heuss, 20 Apr. 1960: BA Koblenz/Nachlaß Heuss.
29. PRO PREM 11/2993, 10 Aug. 1960.
30. PRO PREM 11/3334, 16 Sept. 1960.
31. PRO PREM 11/2679, 29 Nov. 1959.
32. PRO PREM 11/3325, 28 Dec. 1960, 3 Jan. 1961.
33. Cf. the discussion between Macmillan and de Gaulle ten months later: PRO PREM 11/3322 (end-January 1961 – no exact date).
34. PRO PREM 11/3319, 28 Apr. 1961.
35. PRO PREM 11/3319, 8 May 1961.
36. Ibidem.
37. See Caccia to Macmillan: PRO PREM 11/3319, 5 May 1961, and De Zulueta to Caccia: PRO PREM 11/3319, 9 May 1961.
38. Cf. Shuckburgh to Macmillan: PRO PREM 11/3325, 26 December 1960.
39. It seems that the Prime Minister was fully aware of this. See for example Macmillan's message to Caccia: '. . . (de Gaulle) may well make his general co-operation conditional on some satisfaction for his nuclear ambitions. I should be very glad if I were wrong about this, but I do not think that I am' cf. PRO PREM 11/3319, 9 May 1961.
40. PRO CAB 128/35, I/CC. (61) 24th mtg. 26 Apr. 1961.
41. PRO CAB 128/35, I/CC. (61) 30th mtg. 6 Jul. 1961.
42. PRO PREM 11/2870, 9 Dec. 1959. For Macmillan's reaction see T 234/717/HOP. 354/4/01/A, 10. Dec. 1959.
43. PRO FO 371/158161/M 614/45, 30 Mar. 1961. In a previous meeting with Ambassador Caccia, Ball had stated even more categorically that Britain must join the EEC within the next five years. Cf. PRO FO 371/158161/M 614/34, 16 Mar. 1961.
44. PRO PREM 11/3311, 6 Apr. 1961.
45. For the cabinet cf. PRO CAB 128/35, I/CC. (61) 35th mtg., 22 Jun. 1961; PRO CAB 128/35, II/CC. (61) 42th mtg. 21 Jul. 1961. Also the interpretation by Soames in retrospect (Charlton, 1983, p.244).
48. Quoted from Harold Macmillan Diaries, 28 Jan. 1963.

References

Burgess, S., Edwards, G. (1988), 'The six plus one: British policy-making and the question of European economic integration, 1955, *International Affairs*, 64 (3): pp.393–413.
Camps, M. (1964), *Britain and the European Community 1955–1963*, Princeton/London, Princeton University.
Charlton, M. (1983), *The Price of Victory*, London, BBC.
De Gaulle, C., 1970, *Mémoires d'espoir. Le renouveau 1958–1962*, Paris, Librairie Plon.
George, S., 1991, *Britain and European integration since 1945*, Oxford, Clarendon Press.
Horne, A. (1989), *Macmillan 1957–1986: Vol.II of the Official Biography*, London, Macmillan.
Koerfer, D. (1987), *Kampf ums Kanzleramt. Erhard und Adenauer*, Stuttgart, Deutsche

verlags-Anstalt.

Macmillan, H. (1973), *At the End of the Day 1961–1963*, London, Macmillan.

Young, J.W. (1988), 'German Rearmament and the European Defence Community', in Young, J.W. (ed.), *The Foreign Policy of Churchill's Peacetime Administration 1951–1955*, Leicester, Leicester University Press: 81–107.

13

Winds of change: Britain, Europe and the Commonwealth, 1959–61

Lawrence J. Butler

When Harold Macmillan announced, in July 1961, his government's intention of applying for membership of the EEC, he stressed that if closer relations with Europe 'were to disrupt the long-standing and historic ties between the United Kingdom and the other nations of the Commonwealth the loss would be greater than the gain'.[1] This neatly summarised the Cabinet's recent deliberations on entry to Europe, discussions which had concluded that Britain should embark on negotiations with the Six in order to determine whether the 'special needs' of Britain and the Commonwealth could be accommodated within an enlarged Community.[2] In the lead-up to this decision, the likely effects on the Commonwealth of British entry to Europe had been a prominent theme. Indeed, the probable effects on economic and political relationships within the Commonwealth were seen in London as being the thorniest of the problems which would have to be addressed.[3] The Cabinet generally agreed that nothing should be done which might damage the Commonwealth relationship. What value, then, did ministers ascribe to the Commonwealth? For convenience, the economic and political aspects of this question can be considered in turn.

At the outset, it is worth stressing that the exhaustive Whitehall analysis of Britain's policy options, completed in July 1960, drew the conclusion that political, and not economic, considerations were paramount. In this light, the general recommendation in favour of Europe stemmed from a desire to maintain Britain's influence in the world.[4] Entry to the Six would be, as the Cabinet later noted, essentially a political action with economic consequences.[5] A further point which ought to be stressed is that in the period under discussion, namely late 1959 to mid-1961, the Commonwealth was itself far from being a static entity. Discussions on the Commonwealth in these years took place in a framework of rapidly accelerating decolonisation, particularly affecting British Africa. The Commonwealth, then, was expanding and looked set to continue to expand in the foreseeable future. Its growth and changing character would inevitably affect relationships within the association, introducing a new element of unpredictability with which London's policy-makers would have to grapple.

Documents now available which relate to the British government's discussions on the economics of the Commonwealth link give little impression that London believed that the relationship had outlived its commercial usefulness to Britain, as some recent commentators seem to imply (Sanders, 1990, pp.100–20). From the secure vantage of virtually any point since the mid-1960s, the long-term, autonomous trends in world trade appear indisputable, in particular that British commerce was being drawn inexorably closer to Europe and away from traditional Commonwealth markets. In 1960–61, the evidence available to policy-makers in London was by no means so clear-cut. Successive Cabinet discussions demonstrate ministers' determination to safeguard as much as possible of the special economic relationship forged between Britain and the Commonwealth in the previous thirty years. The most potent testimony to this conviction lay in the Cabinet's decision to seek membership of the EEC on 'special terms',[6] designed to maintain the special Commonwealth links, and in the great lengths to which Macmillan's government was prepared to go, after October 1961, through the good offices of Edward Heath, to negotiate acceptable terms (Miller, 1974 pp.324–28).

In its assessment of Britain's policy options on Europe, Whitehall predicted that the major headaches in negotiating British entry were likely to emerge not in the political, but in the economic sphere. The central difficulty would be the existing arrangements whereby Commonwealth produce enjoyed free entry into Britain, that is, the system of 'preferences' dating from the Ottawa agreements of 1932. The Six could hardly be expected to accept the continuation of the system as it stood. However, Britain could not accept the EEC's Common Tariff and give the Six preferential treatment over the Commonwealth.[7] Specifically, Britain could not accept a Common Tariff on the so-called 'temperate foodstuffs' imported from the Commonwealth, not only because of the damage this would cause to Commonwealth producers, but also because it might raise food prices in Britain.[8]

On a more general level, it seemed to officials that patterns of world trade, and specifically of British trade with the Commonwealth, would in time change. It was recognised that the proportion of Britain's trade conducted with the Commonwealth had already begun to decline and that this trend would probably continue. However, even in 1960, they noted, about one fifth of Britain's exports still enjoyed preferences in Commonwealth markets. While the value of these exports was also gradually declining, officials believed that these markets would, as they rather coyly put it, 'still be worth having' for another ten years or more.[9] Given Britain's critical and continuing balance of payments problems in this period, and directives from the highest level to maximise exports across the board, this interpretation is understandable.[10] A further advantage of the Commonwealth identified in Whitehall was that the association enabled underdeveloped members to derive the maximum in economic aid from their 'older' fellow members. Though, as will be suggested, aid questions were not without their own potentially uncomfortable political dimension, officials concluded that aid through the Commonwealth was beneficial to Britain, which was in a position to tap into the consequent expansion in overseas commercial opportunities.[11]

Nevertheless, a fundamental question remained: would it be possible for Britain to join the EEC without 'substantially weakening' the Commonwealth connexion? If Britain joined, the other members of the Commonwealth were thought bound to view this as an implicit rejection of them. This would only be aggravated if a

European federal state, including Britain, were to emerge in the future. The economic consequences of British membership of the EEC would themselves have political effects, whose severity would depend largely on how far the precise terms of entry negotiated by Britain impinged on the interests of individual Common-wealth countries. It was generally agreed that if the Commonwealth lost the right of free entry into Britain, particularly for its food exports, the repercussions would be grave for cereals producers like Canada and Australia. Worst hit, however, would be the much less diversified New Zealand economy, heavily dependent on the British market. Injured Commonwealth members were likely to insist on the re-negotiation of their trade agreements with Britain, which would in turn lose its preferences in their markets. Ultimately, the very existence of the economic underpinnings of the Commonwealth relationship would be at risk.[12]

In addition to these cool, measured assessments by Whitehall of the Common-wealth's value, Macmillan had, of course, to contend with the vocal Common-wealth lobby within his own party (Kahler, 1984, pp.132–25). Concern to forestall internal party criticism may explain Macmillan's muted enthusiasm when announcing Britain's intention to seek EEC membership. This, combined with right-wing press defence of the Commonwealth link, created a delicate situation for Macmillan, and partly explains Britain's subsequent efforts to negotiate favour-able treatment for the Commonwealth.

However, political, and not economic considerations were dominant in London's deliberations on entry to Europe. In the political sphere, perhaps even more than in the economic, a continuing role was clearly envisaged for the Commonwealth, albeit one tailored to changing circumstances. Official and minis-terial discussions demonstrate that the three traditional spheres of interest in Britain's global policy, the Atlantic, the European and the Commonwealth, were still seen as being as interconnected and mutually reinforcing as they had been when delineated afresh in Churchill's post-war summing up (Sanders, 1990, p.1). It has become a commonplace that Britain was anxious in this period to recon-struct and reinforce its 'special relationship' with the United States, and that under Macmillan the strains so evident at the time of Suez were overcome. But as early as 1959, the Foreign Secretary, Selwyn Lloyd, was warning Macmillan that the unexpected success of the EEC raised the possibility, which Britain had to prevent, of the EEC supplanting Britain as the principal external influence on US policy. This would require a British posture which was both European *and* Atlanticist.[13] Moreover, whereas in 1956, and up to 1959, Britain's coolness towards the Six had been dictated by the need not to prejudice the Commonwealth link, by 1960 there appeared to be a real danger that the growth of the Six would 'seriously affect' Britain's position in the world, and that if Britain did not join the Six, this would in itself ultimately be harmful to the Commonwealth.[14] This underlying fear had already led the Foreign Office, late in 1959, to emphasise that the Commonwealth had to be made to see that the consequences for them of Britain's not joining Europe might well be much worse than if she joined.[15] London recognised that if the EEC did evolve into a powerful economic and political bloc, it would be the only geopolitical grouping nearly approaching the stature of the two superpowers, and that if Britain chose to remain aloof from the Six, its world influence would decline, partly because of the increasing political importance of the Six, and partly because of the likely decline in Britain's relative economic strength. In the short-term, Britain might possibly preserve its special relationship with the United States, but it seemed inevitable that the latter would come to attach growing significance to the views of the Six. Moreover, Britain's declining status would be likely, gradually, to reduce its influence in the Commonwealth and in the non-aligned countries generally. Conceivably, the EEC might itself come to have more influence with some Commonwealth countries than Britain.[16] The consolidation of Europe, coinciding with the dismantling of Britain's colonial interests, therefore threatened Britain's political influence and its pretensions to world power status.[17]

There was little comfort here for latter-day Imperialists, or rather for those who might seek a Commonwealth alternative to association with Europe. As Selwyn Lloyd put it in 1959, 'we ceased to be on an equal basis with the United States and [the] USSR when we gave up the Indian Empire. We have been in retreat since'.[18] Such views were reinforced by the strong Foreign Office conviction that 'going it alone' via the Commonwealth nexus was emphatically not an option open to Britain. This outlook permeated the discussions surrounding Whitehall's major policy study of Britain's global position in the coming decade, a study conducted between July 1959 and February 1960. During these discussions, in an effort to deter Commonwealth enthusiasts, Sir Patrick Dean, Deputy Under-Secretary of State at the Foreign Office, introduced a sobering note of realism: 'The truth is that the Commonwealth is not and will never be a source of power in absolute terms comparable with say the USA or possibly Western Europe'. Much was unpredictable, he added, depending as much on good fortune as upon policy decisions. While the Commonwealth might 'greatly increase the power and prestige of the UK', it might equally become 'more of a weakness than an asset'.[19]

Evidence of the potential weaknesses of the Commonwealth was, of course, abundant in 1960. Ironically, the greatest single threat to Commonwealth unity came from within its own ranks, specifically over the problem of South Africa's continued membership. The apartheid regime had already come under fire from existing and aspiring Commonwealth members. These tensions exploded following the Sharpeville massacre in March 1960. With London set squarely on its course of wooing Pretoria, and anxious to keep South Africa in the Commonwealth even after it became a republic, the embarrassing prospect loomed of concerted Afro-Asian attempts to secure vigorous United Nations sanctions against South Africa. Macmillan's government therefore sought the impossible: trying to avoid the isolation of South Africa by international opinion, while avoiding giving offence to the outraged countries of Africa and Asia. In order to pre-empt tougher measures, Britain was even prepared to suggest a United Nations investigation into the Sharpeville incident, a means of dissipating tensions, but one which would set an uncomfortable precedent for greater international scrutiny of conditions within Britain's own colonies, bearing in mind that a state of emergency had been declared in Nyasaland in 1959.[20]

Britain faced further embarrassment after Sharpeville in the form of calls from some colonies for a boycott on trade with South Africa. As South Africa was quick to point out, however, colonial governments had no power to impose such a boycott, because prior to independence, responsibility for their external relations remained the prerogative of London. Macmillan's government took this development seriously. In soon to be independent British Guiana, for example, feelings were running high and civil violence could not be ruled out if anti-South African measures were frustrated by Britain.[21] London accordingly decided not to use the coercive powers available to it, a sensible choice but one lacking heroic motives. Although the effective expulsion of South Africa from the Commonwealth in May 1961 was a defeat for Macmillan's preferred 'quiet diplomacy', based on the hope that Pretoria might be more susceptible to persuasion if it remained within the Commonwealth, it would surely be mistaken to infer that this reversal led London to review unfavourably the Commonwealth's value, and to reject it in favour of Europe. As Stephen George has recently argued, London's growing interest in Europe substantially predated the eruption of the South African issue, which was probably a consolidating, and not a determining factor in British policy (George, 1990, p.32).

Another reminder of the fragility of the Commonwealth arose in 1960 in relation to a proposal by Home, the Commonwealth Relations Secretary, for a Commonwealth aid plan for Africa, seen as an opportunity for British initiative in a non-political sphere, and a useful diversion from events in South Africa. The plan drew predictable objections from the Treasury, which was alarmed at the prospect of increased aid commitments at a time when Britain was itself hamstrung by balance of payments problems.[22] More germane to this discussion, however, was Selwyn Lloyd's response. Lloyd was concerned about possible African reactions to the scheme and feared that a Commonwealth aid plan might be interpreted in Africa as an instrument of 'neo-colonialism'. This would be unfortunate, especially since, in Lloyd's words:

The Commonwealth has so far remained remarkably free from accusations of this kind. Indeed the intangible nature of the Commonwealth relationship is probably essential to its survival in Africa: it would surely be dangerous to institutionalise it.[23]

It could be argued that a continuing absence of sharp definition of its nature has enabled the Commonwealth to survive into the 1990s.

Despite these and other complications too varied to be summarised here, the British government was committed to maintaining the Commonwealth. As Whitehall collectively concluded in July 1960, and as ministers subsequently agreed, Britain had to avoid a position in which it was forced to choose between the Six and the Commonwealth, because whichever were chosen, relations with the Commonwealth might be adversely affected. There was, in effect, no choice: Britain would have to convince the EEC that the Commonwealth was valuable, while convincing the Commonwealth of the benefits it might expect from Britain's association with Europe.[24]

How had this conclusion been reached? Although its precise value eluded policy-makers in London, the Commonwealth was seen as being an 'important buttress' of Britain's world position. This was because Britain was not only the founder, but also the 'central pivot' of the Commonwealth, and because the association was thought to depend so heavily on *British* 'care and initiative'. If it were weakened as a result of British action, officials reasoned, it might collapse entirely. To some degree the influence derived by Britain from the Commonwealth was thought to compensate for Britain's economic and military decline, apparent from her sluggish growth relative to Europe and from her undisguised dependence on the United States for her defence.[25] As recently as June 1960, after all, agreement had been reached with the United States on the supply to Britain, admittedly on highly preferential terms, of the ill-fated Skybolt missile (Dockrill, 1988, p.72). Furthermore, Britain was thought to derive indirect influence through the Commonwealth on non-Commonwealth countries. Thus India was judged to be an important influence in Asia generally, just as it was hoped post-independence Nigeria would become in Africa. Here, it may be worth adding another general observation. There is growing evidence that even as late as 1960–61, in relation to Africa, ministers in London did not envisage 'decolonisation' as embodying the abrupt termination of British interests and involvement: rather, they seem to have thought more in terms of the translation of the colonial relationship into something more palatable in an age of cold war and mass nationalism, a more flexible system of ties attuned to modern requirements. Thus, for example, London was careful that in negotiating political withdrawal from East Africa, it retained overall control of the East African Land Forces, a valuable manpower reserve at a time when heightened East-West tension threatened to spill over, militarily, into Africa.[26] Is it too fanciful to discern in Britain's colonial policies under Macmillan a desire to escape the century-long aberration of formal Imperial commitments in favour of the more agreeable, and much less costly, 'informal influence' of the mid-nineteenth century?

Officials acknowledged that if Britain joined Europe, there might be a short-term risk that she would be suspected by African countries of drawing close to what was termed the 'colonial rearguard', namely France and The Netherlands. How serious this factor might become would depend largely on the outcome of the bitter struggle then being waged in Algeria, and on France's highly contentious use of the Sahara as a nuclear weapons testing-ground.[27] On the other hand, it was predicted that by joining Europe, Britain would become economically stronger, and so enjoy greater scope for influence in the non-aligned world through trade and aid.[28] Nevertheless, there was general agreement that if the Commonwealth were to disappear, or to be significantly weakened, Britain's world status and prestige would suffer, along with its capacity to influence US policy.

Closely related to this concern, and evident throughout London's discussions, was the background of the cold war. This was of inescapable relevance in 1960 with a deteriorating situation in Indo-China and fears about possible Soviet intervention in the war-stricken Congo, the latter resembling, in Macmillan's eyes, the Balkan situation in 1914 (Macmillan, 1972, pp.265–66). In this context, the Commonwealth was portrayed as being vital to the West as a whole, offering a 'unique bridge' between the West and the newly-emerging countries, a vehicle through which Britain could retain the goodwill and friendship of former colonies and the non-aligned world, a forum where new members could meet older Commonwealth countries 'on equal terms', and an association beneficial to British trade.[29] In Cabinet, Macmillan stressed the need to maintain good relations with Africa and Asia, so that newly-independent countries in particular would join the Commonwealth and so remain orientated towards the West.[30] This was only one aspect of his more general belief that closer co-operation in the 'free world' was essential if Communism were to be contained.[31] Most famously, of course, in his 'Winds of Change' speech in Cape Town in February 1960, Macmillan had described the emergence of African nationalism in terms of the dissemination and up-take of European values, and had argued that resistance to nationalism, and impediments to decolonisation, might drive colonial populations into the arms of the Communist bloc (Horne, 1989, p.195; Macmillan, 1972, p.156). Officials in London emphasised that any loss of influence in the new countries would create opportunities for Communist expansion, because it was in Africa and Asia that the 'free world's' continuing struggle with Communism was expected to be fiercest, on both the ideological and economic fronts. Here, to use Whitehall's unenlightened language, the Commonwealth played 'an invaluable part in keeping out of Communist clutches a large part of the world's more backward populations'. To drive home their point, officials reminded ministers of American alarm in 1957 at suggestions that India might leave the Commonwealth in the aftermath of Suez, thereby undermining the association's credibility.[32]

The cold war dimension had already been explored by Britain's ambassador in Paris, Gladwyn Jebb, writing to Sir Patrick Dean at the Foreign Office in April 1960. Jebb predicted that the EEC was likely to become 'much more powerful' than Britain, even with the latter's 'tenuous' links with the Commonwealth. This might make the EEC more attractive to the United States than Britain:

. . . either as an ally in containing the Russians in the West and Africa, or as a friendly bloc which will itself take on the job and allow the Americans to concentrate on the Pacific and the Far East.[33]

In turn, if Britain were detached from Europe, the prospects for its special relationship with the United States were not good.

One final point which can be cited in defence of the view that the British government *did* value the Commonwealth is that London went to considerable lengths to 'sound out' Commonwealth opinion, to consult with Commonwealth countries and to reassure them that Britain would strive to defend their interests in the forthcoming negotiations with the Six. Thus, in spring 1961, Cabinet ministers visited each Commonwealth government, emphasising that Britain was merely applying for EEC membership in order to discover whether acceptable conditions were available.[34] Similar consultations were held with the colonial governments, a number of whom were preparing themselves for imminent independence.[35] These efforts could, of course, be dismissed as being a largely cosmetic attempt by Britain to soften the potential blow to the Commonwealth of British entry into Europe. Yet if Britain did not value the political relationship with the Commonwealth so highly, would it have deemed such close consultation to be necessary? Equally, are we to dismiss the months of arduous negotiation undertaken by Edward Heath and his team in Brussels as an elaborate charade designed to placate Commonwealth sensibilities? Even if they were, is it not significant in itself that London still judged this a course worth attempting?

To conclude, from the available evidence it does not appear that in 1961, Macmillan's government was, as is sometimes held, turning away from the Commonwealth in favour of a new Eurocentric orientation. On the contrary, the British government had come to believe that association with *both* Europe *and* the Commonwealth was essential if Britain's world status were to be defended, and above all, if the highly-prized 'special relationship' with the United States were to be maintained. It has been argued here that Britain's interest in Europe in this period was in keeping with traditional British policy goals, goals given a fresh relevance and currency by the unnerving and unfamiliar dynamics of world politics as the 1960s dawned, in a climate of pronounced East-West tension and headlong European retreat from formal empire.

The aim of Macmillan and his colleagues appears to have been to attempt to keep in equilibrium the three fundamental elements in Britain's global outlook – the Atlantic, the European and the Commonwealth – in the face of autonomous developments, especially within Europe, to which Britain was obliged to respond. The realignment of the 'three circles' attempted by Macmillan was not an abdication of the third, or Commonwealth circle. Rather, it reflected a pragmatic recognition that in order to maintain the vital Commonwealth relationship, adjustments were needed in Britain's links with the United States and Europe. Equally, however, the Commonwealth was itself seen as being a factor which could contribute to stronger ties between Britain, the United States and Europe. In this sense, then, developments in British policy in this period represented, as David Reynolds has argued, not a strategic, but a tactical shift (Reynolds, 1991: 221).

Notes

1. *Parliamentary Debates House of Commons*, vol.645:928–37, 31 July 1961.
2. Public Record Office, (hereafter PRO), CAB 128/35 Pt.2, CC(61)44, 27 July 1961. I am hereafter endebted to C.J. Morris, University of Leeds, for her guidance on relevant Cabinet sources.
3. PRO CAB 129/102 Pt.1, C.(60)107, 'The Six and the Seven: the long-term objective', 6 July 1960.
4. Ibid.
5. PRO CAB 128/34, CC(60)41, 13 July 1960.
6. Ibid.
7. PRO CAB 129/102 Pt.1, C.(60)107, 6 July 1960.
8. Ibid.
9. Ibid.
10. PRO CAB 129/102 Pt.2, C.(60)135, 'Exports. Directive by the Prime Minister', 27 September 1960.
11. PRO CAB 129/102 Pt.1, C.(60)107, 6 July 1960.
12. Ibid.
13. PRO PREM 11/2985, minute by Lloyd to Macmillan, 13 December 1959.
14. PRO CAB 129/102 Pt.1, C.(60)107, 6 July 1960.
15. PRO PREM 11/2985, SC(59)40, 'UK policy towards Western Europe: the Six and the Seven', 27 October 1959.
16. PRO CAB 128/35 Pt.1, CC(61)24, 26 April 1961.
17. PRO CAB 129/102 Pt.1, C.(60)107, 6 July 1960.
18. PRO PREM 11/2985, minute by Lloyd to Macmillan, 13 December 1959.
19. PRO FO 371/152133, minute, 15 March 1960.
20. PRO CAB 128/34, CC(60)21, 29 March 1960; ibid., CC(60)29, 6 May 1960; Holland (1985:223–5).
21. PRO CAB 129/101, C.(60)89, memorandum by Colonial Secretary, 'Requests from within the Empire Commonwealth to boycott South Africa', 31 May 1960; CAB 128/34, CC(60)34, 2 June 1960.
22. PRO PREM 11/2880, minutes by Home to Macmillan, 3 May 1960, and Macleod to Macmillan, 4 May 1960.
23. Ibid., minute by Lloyd to Macmillan, 5 May 1960.
24. PRO CAB 129/102 Pt.1, C.(60)107, 6 July 1960.

25. Ibid.
26. PRO CAB 128/34, CC(60)2, 18 January 1960; ibid., CC(60)11, 22 February 1960.
27. PRO CAB 128/33, CC(59)56, 5 November 1959; ibid., CC(59)57, 10 November 1959.
28. PRO CAB 129/102 Pt.1, C.(60)107, 6 July 1960.
29. Ibid.
30. PRO CAB 128/34, CC(60)51, 22 September 1960.
31. PRO CAB 128/35 Pt.1, CC(61)24, 26 April 1961.
32. PRO CAB 129/102 Pt.1, C.(60)107, 6 July 1960.
33. PRO FO 371/152132/ZP25/36/G, Jebb to Dean, 14 April 1960.
34. PRO PREM 11/3556, Cypher No.291 Prime Minister to Commonwealth Prime Ministers, 31 May 1961; CAB 129/105, C.(61)87, note by Prime Minister, 'The Commonwealth and Europe', 28 June 1961; CAB 129/106, C.(61)104, memorandum by Minister of Aviation, 'Visit to Commonwealth capitals in Asia', 18 July 1961; ibid., memorandum by Commonwealth Relations Secretary, 'Europe: talks with the New Zealand, Australian and Canadian governments', 21 July 1961; CAB 128/35 Pt.2, CC(61)42, 21 July 1961.
35. PRO CAB 129/106, C.(61)103, memorandum by Colonial Secretary, 'European Economic Questions: Colonial Reactions', 18 July 1961.

References

Dockrill, M. (1988), *British Defence Since 1945*, Oxford, Blackwell.
George, S. (1990), *An Awkward Partner: Britain in the European Community*, Oxford, Oxford University Press.
Holland, R.F. (1985), *European Decolonization 1918–1981, An Introductory Survey*, Basingstoke, Macmillan.
Horne, A. (1989), *Macmillan, 1957–1986*, London, Macmillan.
Kahler, M. (1984), *Decolonisation in Britain and France*, Princeton, Princeton University Press.
Macmillan, H. (1972), *Pointing the Way, 1959–61*, London, Macmillan.
Miller, J.D.B. (1974), *Survey of Commonwealth Affairs: Problems of Expansion and Attrition 1953–1969*, London, Oxford University Press.
Reynolds, D. (1991), *Britannia Overruled: British Policy and World Power in the Twentieth Century*, Harlow, Longman.
Sanders, D. (1990), *Losing an Empire, Finding a Role: British Foreign Policy Since 1945*, Basingstoke, Macmillan.

14

Teaching European history in English secondary schools, 1945–75

Athena Syriatou

The thirty years following the Second World War were the most crucial for the construction of European unity. The British at the time, however, displayed a political, cultural, and ideological ambivalence towards this movement; both a socialised aversion and a tempting attraction to the idea of belonging to Europe. Why was this so? One way to explore this question is to look at schools during the period in which Britain finally decided to link its history with the most economically developed part of Europe. This chapter will analyse the mechanisms by which the British State communicated ideas of 'Europe', and Britain's position in it, to its adolescent citizens between 1945 and 1975; by focusing on how the educational establishment intended to convey ideas of Europe, much can be learned about the convictions of British society as a whole. This will be done first by considering the idiosyncracies of the English educational system and the different levels of influence the various educational bodies and professional groups had on the planning of the history syllabus; by examining the syllabuses of the eight O- and A-level Examination Boards; and finally, by looking at a sample of popular textbooks from the period.

In order to understand the way popular beliefs are created, it is necessary to look at the institutions which cultivate and reproduce them. Primary and secondary schools, by being a citizen's right and an obligation of the state, play a major role in the formation of cultural identity. Their increasing importance in this century has competed with and sometimes replaced the importance of social class, family or the church in the task of cultural reproduction. As Pierre Bourdieu argues, 'the school is the fundamental factor in the cultural consensus in as far as it represents the sharing of a common sense which is the prerequisite for communication' (Harker, Mahar and Wilkes, 1990, p.96). Furthermore, 'the study of educational knowledge is a study in ideology, the investigation of what is considered legitimate knowledge by specific social groups and classes, in specific institutions in specific historical moments' (Apple, 1979, p.45). It is the legitimation of ideas that makes schools special as compared to other institutions which are responsible for the formation of ideology. Although mass media, including the press, or books with a general readership can impose ideas on people, it is mainly in schools that there is a normative dimension to these ideas. Pupils receive them as the 'right' answer as if they were the contents of the agreed repository of a society.

Secondary schools, by addressing themselves to adolescents, have the intrinsic aim of building character rather than simply transmitting knowledge, and this is especially true in the English educational system. Moreover, the study of history, more than any other subject, cultivates beliefs about one's own national identity and the identity of other nations. The teaching of European history, or rather of the most crucial epochs in the histories of other European nations, was intended to show pupils the diversity of European nations: to make them aware of cultural, religious and sociopolitical similarities and differences within Europe, and to examine the historical conflicts and continuities between them. It was in this way that an image of Europe was eventually built. Thus, the task of this chapter is to analyse the conventional attitudes of the educational establishment in England and Wales towards European history, wherever this establishment can be identified.

The English educational system is strikingly complex. Compared to the majority of the continental countries, it is a highly decentralised system, with various centres of decision making. The Butler Act of 1944, which introduced compulsory secondary education in a tripartite system, although it provided more schooling for more pupils for a greater time of their lives, did not provide equal standards of education for all students. Leaving aside the public schools, which had hardly ever been affected by any major state educational reforms, the grammar, secondary modern, and less popular technical schools, were not compelled to follow any set of educational norms by the Ministry of Education, despite their financial links to the Ministry through the local education authorities. Moreover, secondary school teachers were not uniformly qualified, either between or within the different types of school. Finally, there was no national teaching curriculum. Those decisions were left to the headmaster or headmistress of an individual school.

Thus, it is difficult to generalise how the subject of European history was handled in a typical English secondary school. An average, however, can be extrapolated by looking at examinations. The syllabuses of the eight Examination Boards did provide a common denominator, in the form of Ordinary and Advanced level certificates, with which all candidates nationally were confronted. With regard to teaching practices, a representative sample of the most commonly used textbooks can also provide information on general beliefs about European history. While it is not possible to reconstruct a representative sample lesson on European history over a thirty year period in such a wide variety of schools, it is possible to examine what the scholars were selling as European history.

In England, the Examination syllabuses are not written by civil servants attached to the Ministry of Education, but rather by professionals working for the Examinations Boards: educationalists, teachers or academics. Very often the committees which meet to write the syllabus seek independent advice from academics or other prominant educationalists. The work of these people, who form a substantial part of the educational establishment, has been of immense importance, not only because of the obvious role which the certificates play in selecting students for the universities (and therefore for mobility up the social ladder), but also because the lack of a national curriculum in this period meant that the examination syllabuses suggested, if not innovations, at least some basic standards for the teaching of history in secondary schools. Public control over the work of the Boards was exercised through the Schools Council. But the Schools Council, which was dominated by teachers, local educational authority advisors, and HM inspectors, was generally unwilling to exercise criticism. Because the same people very often sat on interlocking committees in the Council and the Examination Boards, there could be no conflict between one body of control and the projects proposed by the other.

Individual examining Boards prepared feasibility studies, the Schools Council assessed the results, made a judgement and put forward proposals to the Secretary of State. But the boards simply assumed that an appropriate curriculum would somehow emerge from within the system as a result of the changes in the examination structure – in effect, they worked on the principle that if the cart is placed in position the horse will sooner or later put itself between the shafts. (Bercher and Maclure, 1978, p.43.)

Thus, during the thirty years from 1945 the educational establishment responsible for vital decisions on the history curriculum in England did not come from above, as was the case in many continental countries. Nor did it come from below, since neither pupils, parents nor school teachers, other than the Head of School, had the final say in these decisions. It was rather a 'middle out' establishment of professional people who, by and large, in the words of Stuart Maclure, were using 'traditional methods of *a priori* reasoning, taking evidence, sounding opinion and seeking to mobilise agreement within the various educational bodies'. (Bercher and Maclure, 1978, p.42).

The history syllabuses of the eight Examination Boards which were produced by this establishment are not easily categorised. Not all Boards had a uniform attitude towards European history, and there were remarkable changes during the span of thirty years which are examined here. However, they can be divided into three groups and three chronological phases. The two London Boards, the University Entrance and School Examinations Council at Senate House, and the Associated Examining Board, formed the group which was the most radical and responsive to change. The Oxford and Cambridge Schools Examination Board, the identical Oxford Delegacy of Local Examinations, and the University of Cambridge, formed a second group, which had a more traditional approach to history, although Cambridge offered a wider and more elaborate selection of topics. The Joint Matriculation Board of the Northern Universities (JMB), the Southern Universities and the Welsh Board, roughly formed a group of their own. While the JMB was the most popular Board nationwide in the subject of history and was more rounded in terms of content than the others, all offered syllabuses which were modest in appearance and precise in their intentions.

During the late 1940s and early 1950s, most of the syllabuses focused on British history, and to a lesser extent on European history. The kind of European history offered was always *Western* European history. In a note preceding a syllabus chart in Cambridge, for example, it was stated that 'the history of Northern, Eastern, South-Eastern Europe, Russia, and extra European areas will be included only so far as it is of general European importance'; more precisely, the Board appears to have meant 'Northwestern European importance'.[1] The periods of British and European history covered at this time varied between the Boards and the different levels of examination.

During the 1950s, most of the Boards offered British and European history in equal proportions. However, the date at which British history began to be examined again varied between the Boards and the different examination levels. Most began to examine Britain in 55 BC, during the Roman invasion. Some started with William the Conqueror in 1066 AD. While these were the two most popular dates, others were given prominence. The conquest of the Anglo-Saxons in 450 AD, Arthur's ascension to the throne of Wessex in 871 AD, and the Treaty of Paris ending the Seven Years War in 1763 all appeared regularly in the syllabus details. Most syllabuses were ended ten to fifteen years before the year of the examination.

By contrast, the dates at which European history started to be examined were much more inconsistent and varied among the Boards. There were at least twelve different dates upon which examinations were based. To mention only a few, some Boards, such as the UESEC, started with the invasion of Europe by the Barbarians in 395 AD; some, such as the JMB, with Charlemagne's attempt to unite Europe under his influence in 800 AD; while the AEB began much later in 1789, with the French Revolution.

All the main boards had a syllabus on the history of the British empire, either as a separate section, or included under general British history. They all offered economic history, but only British economic history. Four of the Boards offered an American history syllabus. Almost all, however, provided for the special examination, which, in two thirds of cases concerned Britain, in one third European, and in a few instances American history. Ancient history was offered by the majority of the Boards, with a particular emphasis on the Classical years of ancient Greek civilization, and on the rise and peak of the Roman Empire. The only exception to this was the Cambridge Board, where both ancient Greek and Roman history were extensively examined. World history, which was still termed 'International Relations' for the post-1919 period, was offered by only two examination boards, Cambridge and the AEC, and was especially focused on the international organisations. Nevertheless, while there was a reasonably broad selection of topics, it should be stressed that where the syllabuses dealt with international or European subjects, they focused largely on the role of Britain within them.

During the 1960s, the basic structure of the syllabuses remained the same, with only a few changes worth mentioning. By that time, most of the Boards offered world history, preoccupied, as before, with the multitude of newly formed international organisations. Apart from Britain and Europe, areas which played a crucial role in the international history of the twentieth century were beginning to be examined with more frequency. The United States, the Middle East, Japan, China and Africa, were now covered. The AEB by that time presented the most globally oriented syllabus in the country, and yet its central preoccupation was still on Britain and its influence in the world. Histories of the Commonwealth countries, for example, were examined from the period from which they were colonised, until the date of independence. The three Oxford and Cambridge Boards also expanded the scope of the syllabus to include the Balkans, the Near and Middle East, Africa, and the Far East. International events, which played a major role in the development of world politics, such as the Hague and Geneva Conventions, or the disarmament conferences, were also covered. It is worth mentioning that their syllabuses were now followed by an extensive bibliography which was historiographically up-to-date, recommended for the teachers.

The beginning of the 1970s brought an even greater degree of change and general experimentation. The anti-establishment (especially educational establishment) movements manifested so abruptly during the previous years in the Continental universities, although never experienced intensely in Britain, had their effect here too. A spirit of reorganization of the cultural reproduction mechanisms, such as education, was at that time the top issue in most countries of the western world (Cohn-Bendit, 1968, pp.23–80; Touraine, 1968, pp.63–95). These efforts were reflected in the syllabuses of the Boards; the outlook became broader and large sections were added to explain the educational aims of historical inquiry as a whole, and to elaborate on the ideal expectations of the examiners. The candidate was now expected 'to analyse historical material, construct a historical argument, and display historical judgement',[2] rather than 'knowledge' as was previously the case.

Although European history was still one of the major topics on the syllabuses, now it had to compete with two other fashionable subjects: local history, and history of world powers and world events in the twentieth century. The former reflected a new paedagogical attitude in which the pupils were supposed to be motivated by looking for the visible evidence of history around them. The latter, which was the ascending subject of all boards, later to become the most popular in some of them, was supposed to examine the twentieth century as a special historical phenomenon.

It is felt that an understanding of the twentieth century world history is important because, in an increasingly inter-dependent world, it gives the background and perspective necessary for an understanding of current problems from a global rather than a national or continental view. It also lends itself particularly well to a study of an essentially interdisciplinary nature.[3]

The interdisciplinary nature of history was encouraged at this time, and was stressed for any history subject. In one note for candidates it was explained that they were expected to show knowledge of economic and social history, the history of ideas, developments in science, literature and the arts, and when necessary 'to treat European History in its world context, and English history in its European or World context'[4].

In 1976, a new syllabus appeared in the Associated Examining Board on 'European Studies', which seems to be the direct product of the country's first years as a member of the European Community, designed by pro-European educationalists. The description stated that

The syllabus is designed to enable teachers to bring out both the common threads in the experience of the Europeans and the diversity that exists and it is likely to continue. The syllabus should lead to an understanding both of the tendency towards integration and coordination and the desire to preserve national and regional identity.[5]

Two years later the same board added a new course as if to balance out the previous one, this time on 'American Studies' which had similar targets as the

European course, focusing on American life, culture, economy, the cities and so forth.

The syllabuses of the examination boards were well designed and adequately balanced. They were concerned with national as well as European and world history in more or less the proportions that a liberal system would demand. The kind of European history they offered was obviously focused on the north-western European outlook, which only occasionally touched matters in eastern or southern Europe. There were major gaps in the syllabuses: Mesopotamian and north African civilization, Hellenistic history and the history of the fall of the Roman Empire. Continuities were not built into the transition from the ancient to modern world. More regrettably the absence of Byzantine history which had been an old victim of the Papal educational legacy, deprived the pupils of the illumination of one of the most important phases of Eastern European civilization, and consequently obscured an important aspect of European identity.

The majority of schools chose subjects in British and European history of the late eighteenth, nineteenth and twentieth centuries for the two levels of examination. This happened mainly because they assumed that pupils would prefer to continue with the subject they were taught in their previous forms, than to go back and select one of the subjects from the previous years at school (schools usually taught history in chronological order). So, ancient history, medieval history and surprisingly enough the history of the British Empire, were amongst the least popular subjects. Economic history and world affairs were relatively unpopular as well, although they increased in popularity in the 1970s. As to sociopolitical subjects concerning the problems of the twentieth century, they did not even appear in the statistical charts at all during the first years of the 1970s. The dates where they stopped were not ten years from the time of the examination but around thirty or more, which shows that at that time the very recent historical subjects were not popular.

Textbooks play a substantially different role in British schools than is the case in other European countries. Textbooks were not prescribed by the Ministry of Education in England as was the case for many centralized educational systems on the Continent. They were not approved or officially recommended by any other educational authority either, as was the case in other more liberal educational systems which issued catalogues of a number of approved textbooks (Bercher and Maclure, 1978, pp.21–34). Like the syllabuses, they were recommended by the head of the school and the teaching staff, and they were usually the property of the school.

It seems that the three main categories of secondary schools in England and Wales were evolving a different role for the textbooks in these years. The modern schools of the 1940s and 1950s, and later the comprehensives, did not use textbooks extensively. Some textbooks were in the school's library for the pupils to consult when they were at school; but mainly, it was the notes of the teacher upon which they were supposed to base their homework. Textbooks were written in a rather simplistic manner even for the later forms. They were usually full of illustrations, in order not to discourage the pupil with long passages of text. This was especially usual during the later years of the 1960s and beginning of the 1970s, when all school publications became glossier.[6]

Textbooks in grammar schools had a more central place in the teaching procedure. They were usually given to the pupils at the beginning of the academic year, to be kept for the whole year. Although the most important unit still remained the work in the classroom, textbooks were more generally and widely used. They were supposed to be used in a critical manner, as the basis of an argument, and not as a 'bible'. Pupils were encouraged to read books from the library in order to have other sources of information to construct an argument. In public schools textbooks played an even less important role, as students could draw on well-stocked libraries for alternative sources. Easily obtainable books could be used as starting points for discussion, and essay writing, for example.[7] This is very characteristic of British education. The majority of continental countries, as mentioned above, exerted more central control over the curriculum by placing much more import-ance on the use of an officially recommended text.

The textbooks selected here have been chosen from those which were mainly used in grammar schools, where they were, after all, more important. There was enough shared use of these texts in both secondary modern, comprehensives and independent schools, to assume safely that they represented an 'average' of the picture of Europe being presented to British pupils in those years. The study of European history did not necessarily involve a separate book on European history. Very often, extracts of European history were found within surveys of British history, where they dealt with Britain in Europe and the world. Other books do not specify which country's history they are dealing with, implying that they are dealing with the most important events world-wide, nevertheless dealing mostly with European and British history. The former are mostly old fashioned textbooks written during the late 1930s and re-edited until the late 1950s. The latter being books which appeared during the first years of the 1960s.

In the first category, belongs *The New Groundwork of British History* which was widely used in public and grammar schools, during the 1940s and early 1950s (Warner, Marten and Muir, 1943). Although it deals basically with British history, European events appear either as subjects related directly to Britain, or as themes of European history in their own right. 'Europe and the Crusades' is one of them, while a whole unit of chapters devoted to the French Revolution, and its repercus-sions in Britain, occupies a number of pages. Obviously imperial history is considered part of British history, and number of chapters are devoted to the histories of the colonized countries, and the efforts of the British to save them from barbarism. The last chapters are devoted to the First World War and they give a world view rather than examining only the British factors in the course of the war. A special chapter was devoted to 'European Revolutions in the Twentieth Century', while social changes were dealt with in their world-wide context.

A second example from the 1950s is *Outlines of European History* (Grant, 1947). Starting from the classical world, with Greeks and Romans, and proceeding to the Middle Ages, whole chunks of British history can be found amongst a selection of other subjects of general European importance. So, among chapters on 'The Rise of the Medieval Empire', or 'The Crusades' there are chapters on 'British Isles to the Norman Conquest', as well as 'British History from 1066 to 1485'. The last section of the book covers the modern world. The Stuarts, the Tudors, and so on are spread among other chapters which cover European themes, creating the impression that British history is of European importance. Moreover, when it comes to the nineteenth century, it is conflict on the Continent which is emphasized. In the same section a special chapter is devoted to the history of 'Great Britain in the nineteenth century 1815–1875', focusing on consensual parliamentary reforms. This chapter is followed by 'Forty Years of Peace Between Two Wars' (1875–1914), where the author has very good intentions to describe a long period of peace for the European countries. Yet, we read, it was only in England that peace was really preserved. Even the parliamentary reforms which appeared in France during that period did not work as 'smoothly in France as with us' (Grant, 1947, p.444).

Denis Richards' *An Illustrated History of Modern Europe 1789–1945*, was written during the late 1930s but re-edited and re-published up until the mid-1960s. The illustrations, which come from *Punch* magazine, give the impression of a sarcastic British response to events in Europe. In the first six chapters the course of the French Revolution is extensively examined, reaching the years of the Second Republic and the Second Empire in 1871. Germany and the Austrian empire, the unification of Italy and Germany, and the Eastern question, are the main subjects examined from the nineteenth century. Russia and Poland are also surveyed from 1789–1914. The end of nineteenth century and the first half of the twentieth, is portrayed through the clash between the German Empire and the Third Republic from 1871–1907, the Balkan states fighting amongst themselves, and the two world wars. Europe in that context is an arena of conflict and war. Again we see in this book that all countries which enter the realm of European history from the eighteenth century do so through revolt, changes in borders, and through involvement in multinational alliances and wars. It is a rather confrontational approach to European history, which predominated, contributing to a rather dismal picture of European affairs.

The series of textbooks by C.F Strong, first published at the beginning of 1960s, proved popular and were widely used in grammar and comprehensive schools during the 1970s. They are written in the modern style of historical prose concentrating not on events, wars and great deeds, but on everyday life in the specific historical period examined. They are meant to deal with world history from the early ages until modern times, but nevertheless, there is little world history and much concentration on Britain and Europe. In the first book of the series the author deals with Ancient Man and Ancient People, where Egypt, Mesopotamia, China and India are examined. The other two thirds of the book are devoted to Greeks, Romans, the Goths and the Normans, again concentrating on familiar ground. The author in his next book focuses on the Middle Ages, almost wholly concentrated on Britain and Europe, apart from the voyage he has to take for the great discoveries. *Men and Machines* is also concentrated on Britain and Europe but other areas of the world manage to get a share too. America, India and the South Seas, are included, but the primary focus is on the role of Europeans on other continents. Finally, the twentieth century is again examined through the scope of the two world wars, followed by the cold war. Soviet Russia and the United States are given separate chapters, while some new chapters are devoted to the new nations in Asia and Africa.

In conclusion, in the examination syllabuses and the content of the textbooks, the representation of European history was a standard western European 'self indulgent' outlook. The product of middle class educationalists, rather than derived from the doctrines of ministerial civil servants, this body of work has some common characteristics, but varies considerably in practice. It is possible however to draw some general conclusions. The history of Europe presented in school textbooks was almost wholly concentrated on the northwest of the Continent. Other regions were only drawn in when in crisis or at war.

The images of Europe which result, although they are not wholly negative, were very distinct from that of a great British tradition of dealing with crises by mobilizing agreement and consensus rather than violence. British history, that is, patronizes the teaching of European history. Very often the European history included in surveys of British history stressed the aftermath of continental adventures on British life. This, of course, is not necessarily negative but it was often the case that all that was taught from a European episode was its resonance in England. This is true of Grant's textbook, in a reverse way, where British history can be constructed from diverse sections in a survey of European history – but the same cannot be done for the history of any other European country. Gradually during the late 1960s and early 1970s world history started to make its presence felt. In the decades to follow world history overtook both British and European history in students' preference.

European history in Britain was presented with a great degree of professional conscientiousness, but unable to escape completely the national tendency to see Britain as the centre of the world. This happened without indoctrination from a central authority; it was a product of the 'middle out' educational establishment. The greatest virtue of the British educational system was that individual efforts towards different directions were fostered.

The images of Europe which emerge from this evidence are not uniform. Ancient cultural origins, dramatic events, and institutional differences, emphasized in different proportions within the diversified teaching experience in Britain, all contribute to the idea that Europe and Britain are distinct. However, no matter the disparity of positive and negative impressions about Europe, as presented by school historiography and practice during the thirty post-war years, European history teaching in Britain emphasized that Britain's relationship with Europe had always been its most important relationship.

Notes

1. University of Cambridge Local Examination Syndicate, history examination syllabuses for ordinary level, 1962, p.3.
2. University Entrance and School Examination Council, history syllabus 1972, p.116.
3. Associated Examining Board, history syllabus 1976, p.139.
4. UESEC, history syllabus 1971 p.109.
5. AEB, history syllabus 1976 p.155.
6. This conclusion is based on both an analysis of a substantial number of textbooks, and oral evidence. Graham and Anne Morris, interview with the author, 6 February 1992. Graham and Anne Morris have been teachers of History and English for almost thirty years, in number of secondary modern, grammar, comprehensive and independent schools. The continuous advice of Mrs Joan Lewin was also taken in consideration. Mrs Joan Lewin has been teaching history in Teachers Training Colleges in London for more than thirty years.
7. Professor Conrad Russell, interview with the author, 24 March, 1992. Sir Russell was a pupil at Eton during the years 1949–54.

References

Apple, M. (1979), *Ideology and Curriculum*, London, Routledge & Kegan Paul.

Barker, E. (1971), *Britain in a Divided Europe*, London, Weidenfeld & Nicolson.

Bercher, T., Maclure, S. (1978), *The Politics of Curriculum Change*, London, Hutchinson.

Cohn-Bendit, D. (1968), *Obsolete Communism the Left-Wing Alterantive*, Hamburg, Andre Deutsch.

Grant, A.J. (1947), *Outlines of European History*, London, Longman, Green and Co.

Harker, R., Mahar C., Wilkes C. (1990), *An Introduction to the Work of Pierre Bourdieu*, London, Macmillan.

Richards, D. (1943), *An Illustrated History of Modern Europe*, London, Longmans Green and Co.

Strong, C.F. (1961), *Early Man and the First Nations*, London, University of London Press.

Strong, C.F. (1962), *The Old World and the New*, London, University of London Press.

Strong, C.F. (1964), *Men and Machines*, London, University of London Press.

Strong, C.F. (1966), *The Story of the Twentieth Century*, London, University of London Press.

Strong, C.F. (1968), *The World Today*, London, University of London Press.

Warner, G.T., Marten, K., Muir, E. (1943), *The New Groundwork of British History*, London and Glasgow, Blackie & Son Limited.

Touraine, A. (1968), *Le mouvement De Mai, Ou Le Communism Utopique*, Paris, Editions Du Seuil.

III
Britain in the Community, 1973–92

15

The awkward partner: an overview

Stephen George

In its first twenty years of membership of the European Community (EC), Britain acquired an unenviable reputation for being an awkward partner. This chapter reviews British policy towards the EC since membership in 1973, looks at the reasons for this record of awkwardness, and reviews the prospects in 1992 that Britain would continue to be seen as the awkward partner of the EC in the future.

The reputation and the record

Britain's reputation was not the result of the record of any single government: it resulted from a cumulation of episodes covering both Labour and Conservative governments.

After two abortive applications, Britain finally achieved membership of the EC under the one Prime Minister who is generally acknowledged to have been fully in favour of European integration, Edward Heath. Yet even in the brief period of British membership during which Heath was Prime Minister, there were complaints from the original six member states about the clumsy and insensitive manner in which the newcomers conducted themselves (George, 1990, pp.60–70).

This was nothing, though, compared with the renegotiation of the terms of entry under the Wilson Government. At least Heath had been prepared to handle Britain's grievances as part of normal Community business: Wilson, for domestic political reasons, elevated the discussion to the level of a formal renegotiation, and insisted on conducting it as though it were a confrontation between enemies rather than a discussion between friends. Even after the renegotiation, and the referendum in which the British people overwhelmingly accepted the renegotiated terms, there was no change of heart by the government. Disputes over proposed EC regulation of the pollutants that could be deposited in rivers, and over whether Britain, as the EC's only oil-producing state, should have a separate seat at the 1975 Conference on International Economic Co-operation (CIEC) combined with a persistently hectoring tone to consolidate the reputation for awkwardness (George, 1990, pp.71–106).

Callaghan, as Wilson's Foreign Secretary, was closely associated with the renegotiation, and he was the prime mover in the demand for a separate seat at the CIEC. He was not therefore seen in Brussels as the ideal replacement when

Wilson resigned in March 1976. In fact the Callaghan Government was more co-operative than the Wilson Governments had been, but there were still areas of disagreement. In particular, three areas demonstrated that Britain was still far from being in the mainstream of Community developments: the question of direct elections to the European Parliament, which had to be delayed a year because the British parliament did not pass the legislation in time for them to be held as scheduled in 1978; Britain's refusal to become a full member of the European Monetary System (EMS) when it was set up in 1978; and finally the issue of Britain's net contributions to the Community's budget, which had been one of the central elements of the renegotiation, and was raised again in 1978 (George, 1990, pp.107–36).

Although it is Mrs Thatcher who is remembered for her battle with the EC over the size of the British budgetary contributions, it was in the last year of Callaghan's Government that Britain came to the end of its transitional period of membership and the full extent of the contributions to the budget became apparent. Despite being fifth out of nine in its share of the EC's gross domestic product, Britain was set to become the largest net contributor to the budget, a situation that both Callaghan and his Foreign Secretary, David Owen, indicated was unacceptable. Even without the arrival in office of a monetarist Prime Minister dedicated to reducing public expenditure, there would have been a protracted renegotiation of the renegotiated terms on this issue.

Margaret Thatcher took up the argument with relish, and from 1979 to 1984 fought a hard and sometimes bitter battle for a system of rebates on the contributions, in the meantime blocking progress in other areas of Community activity. While the other member states were prepared to accept that Britain had a genuine grievance, and that something had to be done about it, the uncompromising and often nationalistic tone adopted by Mrs Thatcher was what really soured relations during this period (George, 1990, pp.137–65).

In 1984 the rebate issue was finally resolved at the Fontainebleau meeting of the European Council. In the following year agreement was reached on the 1992 programme to free the internal market of the EC from remaining barriers to free trade in goods and services, a cause close to the heart of Mrs Thatcher. For a time it looked as though the Community had turned in a direction that would allow Britain to become a less awkward member. However, the difficulties soon began again.

While Mrs Thatcher interpreted the 1992 programme as being just about the freeing of the market, both the European Commission and her partners considered that it needed a social dimension, and also that the single market would not be complete without monetary union. Both of these developments were roundly rejected by Mrs Thatcher, most notably in her speech at the College of Europe in Bruges in September 1988 (Thatcher, 1988).

Eventually her rejection of monetary union was the cause of Mrs Thatcher's downfall. As it became increasingly obvious that the other member states were prepared to push ahead to a single currency with or without British participation, concern began to grow in business and financial circles that Britain would become a second-class member of the single market; and in political circles the spectre was raised of repeating the mistake made in the 1950s, when Britain could have been a founder member of the new Communities, but missed the train and found itself scrambling to get on after it had left the station (George, 1991a).

With the arrival of John Major in office there were hopes that a new era was dawning in Britain's relations with the rest of the EC. However, this was largely based on a rather facile analysis of the cause of Britain's difficulties being simply the personality of the Prime Minister. As I hope to have shown above, the record went back to before Mrs Thatcher, and although a change of leader might have been a prerequisite for a new start, it was unlikely that it would be sufficient in itself to ensure such a change. Before addressing the prospects for Britain to become a less awkward partner under the new government, then, it is necessary to try to establish what were the underlying causes of the awkwardness.

The causes of Britain's awkwardness

The budget

First, it has to be stated that Britain did have genuine problems with the *acquis communautaire*. Heath adopted a deliberate strategy in negotiating for entry of overlooking many of the difficulties in the hope that they could be dealt with after membership had been obtained. The record of two failures made it vital in his view to seize the opportunity that presented itself in 1972 and not risk delay that might allow circumstances to turn less favourable (Young, 1973, p.211). As a result of this, the original terms of entry, although Labour's former chief negotiator said that they would have been acceptable to the previous government, really were far from ideal. In particular, the budgetary arrangements were designed for the Community of six, and were never going to suit Britain (George, 1992a, pp.42–45). Also, the Common Agricultural Policy (CAP), which dominated payments from the budget, was not designed in such a way that British farmers stood to gain much from it. This resulted from Britain not being involved in the negotiations that agreed the arrangements, a consequence of having missed the train.

Britain's natural differences from the Six

Other problems arose for Britain in adapting to Community rules because it is a very different country from the original Six in certain important respects. For example, Britain is an island, and so regulations that make sense for continental countries are not necessarily suitable for application in Britain. This was the issue in dispute over the pollution of rivers. As an island, Britain has rivers that flow faster than those in continental countries, and can take larger quantities of pollutants without becoming as polluted.

Similarly, the dispute over the separate seat at the CIEC was based on the genuine difference that Britain was an oil-producing state, whereas the other members of the EC were not, and this was bound to lead to a difference in perspective.

The attitudes of the administrative and political élites

There were problems for the British administrative and political élites in adapting to the Community's way of working.

First, there was a fundamental difficulty about accepting what was seen as the undertow of European regionalism in the EC. As a legacy of the period when Britain was the dominant power in the capitalist world there was a strong belief in globalism: that international problems should be tackled on a global not a regional basis. In the era of US hegemony, this translated itself into support for the Atlantic alliance. Whether justified or not, the British administrative and political élites persistently suspected the rest of the EC of a Gaullist tendency to pursue a line at odds with the United States, and to interpret problems in a narrow manner, looking only to see what was in it for them (George, 1991b, pp.33–5).

Linked with this suspicion of regionalist tendencies was a suspicion of what were seen as the centralising tendencies of the Commission, which some other member states seemed prepared to accept. It was always the view of British governments that the EC should not become too close an organisation which would drain authority away from member states. This was reflected in Callaghan's statement that 'The Government has never accepted that the Community should develop into a federation. It is our policy to continue to uphold the rights of national governments and parliaments'. Almost exactly the same sentiments were expressed by Margaret Thatcher in her Bruges speech when she asserted that 'willing and active co-operation between sovereign nation states is the best way to build a successful European Community . . . working together does *not* require power to be centralised in Brussels' (Thatcher, 1988, p.4).

Cultural differences were also reflected in the approach to institutional developments, indicative of a deep philosophical difference between the British and continental views, expressed eloquently by Malcolm Rifkind when he was a Foreign Office Minister in 1983: 'To us, institutions must be subservient to policies. Closer co-operation should not be forced but must grow out of practical ways in which as a Community we can work together for our common good. Substance and reality must come before form' (quoted in Judge, 1986, p.324). This contrasted with what often appeared to be a continental desire to set up institutions with grand objectives and see what they could achieve.

Perhaps cultural differences also partly explain the tone of British interventions in the Community debate. That tone has often been unhelpful to the British case. Rarely have British politicians managed to sound *communautaire* when defending the national interest, something at which the French are masterly. In addition, the constant round of negotiation and compromise that is the hallmark of the Community method has not come easily to British politicians, used not to the coalition systems of government that prevail in most other European states, where negotiation and compromise are necessarily the stuff of daily government, but to the adversarial structure which is thrown up by the British electoral system in which the winner takes all.

Pressure groups

While the trade unions in Britain took a long time to adapt to membership of the EC and were for some time hostile, the Confederation of British Industry (CBI), the main employers' association, was an early advocate of membership and has remained an enthusiastic supporter of integration, but integration defined in a particular way. Both the early hostility of the unions and the support of the CBI for a particular form of integration contributed to policies of British governments that enhanced the reputation for awkwardness.

Early hostility among trade unionists to membership of the EC led to a boycott of the various European institutions, such as the Economic and Social Committee and the joint committees of employers and trade unions that monitored particular sectors of EC activity (Butt Philip, 1992, p.160). Although the boycott was abandoned after the 1975 referendum, there was still little enthusiasm for the EC, and this was a factor that Labour Prime Ministers had to contend with particularly. During the 1980s, though, there was a steady change of attitude, fostered partly by the learning process of British trade union officials working alongside their European counterparts, and partly by a reaction to the policies of the Thatcher Governments in Britain.

In contrast with the refusal of the British government even to meet with the trade unions to discuss policy, British union officials found themselves involved in extensive discussions about EC policy. The arrival of the socialist Jacques Delors in office as President of the Commission in 1985, and the subsequent championing by the Commission of a social charter that embodied many of the objectives of British union leaders, helped to accelerate the process that had already begun of gradual conversion to a more pro-EC stance. This conversion certainly influenced the leadership of the Labour Party in its policy review exercise in the 1980s (Rosamond, 1990; George & Rosamond, 1992, pp.178–9; Rosamond, 1992, pp.97–8), but by that time it was too late for trade unionists to influence the government, so long as Mrs Thatcher remained Prime Minister.

In contrast, the CBI exercised a consistent pressure on the Conservative Government in favour of the EC, but with a strong de-regulatory bias (Butt Philip, 1992, pp.158–9). In particular the CBI was strongly opposed to the social charter, and to the idea of a social dimension to the 1992 project. This position must have strengthened the resolve of the Government to oppose the charter, although that position was also clearly in tune with its ideological position on intervention in the free market.

Public opinion

The language of negotiation, though, has also reflected the attitude to the EC of both the British public and the membership of whichever political party was in office.

Although 'opinion on European integration has not been as negative as is commonly supposed' (Nugent, 1992, p.176), nevertheless 'British opinion has been significantly out of line with the average Community opinion' (Nugent, 1992, p.179), with the proportion of the population supporting integration some 10 to 15 per cent lower than the Community average, and the proportion opposing it some 5 to 10 per cent higher. Of the twelve member states, only Denmark has consistently shown less public enthusiasm for integration.

On the more precise issue of British membership of the EC, with the single but obviously vital exception of the referendum in 1975, public opinion was for a long time consistently negative, with strong support for the defence of national sovereignty. However, views on British membership among the public seem never to have been particularly strongly held, which helps to explain why it was possible for the 1975 referendum to produce a large vote in favour of British membership when opinion polls before the immediate run-up to the referendum had shown a consistent majority against membership, and the polls soon returned to showing the same picture after the referendum.

The relative weakness of public views on membership of the EC meant that it had little discernible impact as an electoral issue. On the other hand, it 'tempted and encouraged politicians to use patriotic and nationalistic political rhetoric' (Nugent, 1992, p.196) when discussing the Community, and 'to tap nationalist sentiment and reap popular support' (Nugent, 1992, p.195) by defending British interests in an aggressive and confrontational manner. Mrs Thatcher was particularly prone to give way to this temptation. In its turn the negative rhetoric of politicians for long reinforced the public's negative perception of the EC.

Party management

In addition to the domestic public, party leaders also have to play to another audience, which is smaller but more strongly political: the memberships of their political parties. Without party members, leaders would be unable to win elections, so they are a particularly important audience. Although the leaders can mould the opinions of the party memberships to a certain extent, they cannot afford to get too far ahead of the opinions of the members.

Opinion within the political parties has evolved differently in the Labour and Conservative Parties. Labour activists were consistently anti-EC throughout the 1960s and 1970s, but in the course of the 1980s there appears to have been a remarkable sea-change, so that by the early 1990s the membership of the Party was apparently in advance of the leadership over the EC.

In the Conservative Party, however, there appeared to be solid support for entry in the 1970s: 'The 1971 Conference voted overwhelmingly for entry, by 2,474 votes to 324 against' (Ashford, 1992, p.123). But this was attributable largely to 'the consensus among the business, financial, agricultural, and press supporters of the party' (Ashford, 1992, p.123), the strong lead given by Edward Heath, and a reaction against the audacity of President de Gaulle of France in 1963 in rejecting the first application for membership, which was made by a Conservative government. The lack of any deep-seated commitment to the ideal of European integration amongst ordinary Conservative Party members became apparent after the change of leader in 1975: 'The election of Mrs Thatcher as leader in 1975 did not alter the party's commitment to membership, but led to less enthusiasm' (Ashford, 1992, p.148). There is no doubt that Mrs Thatcher's lukewarm attitude reflected that of a majority of members of her party, and that her nationalistic tone in negotiations with the rest of the EC was extremely popular within the party.

The consequence of these different evolutions of party opinion, with Labour members moving from scepticism to support and Conservative members moving from support to scepticism, was that throughout the period of British membership of the EC the party in office has contained a majority of ordinary members who were sceptical about the benefits of the EC. This was bound to have an influence on policy, or at least on the manner in which the policy was presented.

Britain as spokesman for doubters

The domestic political situation described and above has contrasted with that facing the leaders of many other European states, whose public audiences have strongly supported anything to do with European integration, and whose party memberships have been enthusiastic supporters of the EC. One result has been that the British have sometimes been prepared to voice publicly doubts about policy proposals that other governments may have felt, but not felt able to articulate given that their domestic audience would see such a statement as a retreat from support for integration. Some of Britain's reputation for awkwardness may have resulted from others hiding behind the British veto.

If these are the main reasons for the attitudes and policies that earned Britain the reputation of being an awkward partner, it should be possible now to assess the prospects for a change in British policy following the change of British Prime Minister in 1990.

Changing factors

The budget

Although the British budgetary problem appeared to be resolved at Fontainebleau, the agreement there was not stable in the long term. It was based not on a re-design of the system of budgetary contributions, but on an agreement to give annual rebates to Britain. That agreement had to be reaffirmed every time there was a change in the budget's basis. So, when an increase in the size of the budget was agreed in 1988, there was a certain amount of manoeuvring around the question. As more member states became net contributors to a budget that had to support the poorer members, so the special position negotiated for Britain became less defensible. In the long term a new basis for the budget, which would make the rebates unnecessary, had to come; but in the meantime there was the potential for Britain to find itself the odd one out in budgetary discussions again.

In the 1988 agreement on increasing the size of the budget, a new element was introduced into the formula which related contributions directly to the size of a member state's Gross Domestic Product (GDP), and if this element became a larger proportion of the total in future it would automatically redress the imbalance between Britain's relative economic strength and its relative contributions.

The taming of the CAP would also go some way to redress the British budgetary imbalance, which was always partly due to high gross contributions not being balanced by substantial payments from the European Agricultural Guidance and Guarantee Fund, which accounted for 60 per cent of the total budget. Whether the CAP would be tamed remained open to dispute at the time of writing. Reforms had been agreed, but they were facing hostile protests from European farmers. On the other hand, it could be argued that eventual reform was inevitable in the light of pressures from the United States and from the Cairns group of agricultural producers, and in the light of the need to open the EC market to agricultural products from the states of Central and Eastern Europe.

More generally too the budgetary debate seemed likely to go Britain's way. When the issue of the rebate arose it was in a Community of nine (ten after Greek accession in 1981), and Germany was the only other net contributor. In 1992, in the Community of twelve, France, The Netherlands, and Denmark were also net contributors, and the rejection of the Delors 2 proposals for increasing the size of the budget in June 1992 showed that there was no enthusiasm for raising contributions to high levels. On this issue the position of Britain was likely to become that of one member of a contributors' block which would often find itself in disagreement with the demands of the recipients' block, consisting of Greece, Ireland, Italy, Portugal, and Spain.

Britain's natural differences from the Six

On other issues Britain remained different from the heartland members of the EC. Its geographical status as an island, which was the basis of the dispute under Wilson over the emission of effluent into rivers, re-emerged as an argument for retaining border controls after 1992. The argument that it is sensible for an island to check for the movement of drugs and terrorists at its borders, and to operate quarantine regulations against animals to prevent the spread of rabies, had some force but was not accepted by the Commission. It gained added force when combined with a continuing cultural suspicion about the effectiveness of the regulatory authorities in other member states. Put bluntly, if border checks were only carried out at the point of entry into the Community, the British would be asked to trust Sicilian customs officials to prevent the import of illicit drugs. Other national customs and excise authorities may have had the same doubts, but the complexities of implementing border controls within the continental land mass are such that they may have felt they had to accept the risk and counter it by policing operations. Because it is an island, Britain did not have to accept the risk, and was resisting being made to do so.

The attitudes of the administrative and political élites

Problems arising from the attitude of the administrative and political élites had eased by the start of the 1990s. Partly this was a result of British officials and politicians undergoing a learning process; partly it was a result of differences being neutralised by events.

An example of the learning process is British officials learning the trick of speaking in the language of the Community, seen clearly in the adoption by the British of the term 'subsidiarity', part of the terminology of continental federalism, as a means of arguing against creeping centralisation and of writing into a legal document a principle that would protect states' rights and could not be ignored by the notoriously centralising European Court of Justice.

An example of problems being neutralised by events is the changed attitude of the British government, after the departure of Mrs Thatcher, to the emergence of an EC security and defence identity. This was attacked by Mrs Thatcher as a move that would weaken the Atlantic alliance. The problem with this position was that the United States, under the Bush Administration, was pressing the EC to do exactly that. Unable to afford to police the turbulent new Europe that had emerged from the collapse of communism, the United States wanted the EC to take on the task. That required a security and defence dimension (George, 1992b).

Suspicion of centralising tendencies remained, but the British were no longer alone in this, if they ever were. Ironically, given accusations by Mrs Thatcher that it was 'a treaty too far' in the direction of centralising powers in the EC, the terms of the Maastricht Treaty demonstrated the limits of the extent to which the other member states were prepared to go in increasing the powers of the central institutions.

The increase in the powers of the European Parliament (EP) was strictly limited, and disappointing to the Members of the EP themselves. The creation of the two intergovernmental pillars of a new European union, placing co-operation on foreign policy and external security, and on internal security, completely outside of the EC decision-making procedures, demonstrated the same reluctance to entrust too much to centralised procedures.

On these issues the British position may often have seemed out of line because others felt that they could play to a domestic political audience which favoured integration by espousing firm support for supranationalism, without any risk of having to live with the consequences, because they could shelter behind the British veto. The approach of the British government to the intergovernmental conference negotiations, which was low-key, forced the others to be more honest about the limits to which they were prepared to go, and the British representative had the tremendous satisfaction of being able simply to concur with French proposals that were precisely in line with what the British wished to see, and a long way from the more advanced federalist positions taken up by President Mitterrand in the recent past, when he had been sure that Mrs Thatcher would save him from himself.

Pressure groups

While the attitude of the CBI on the social dimension of 1992 fitted well with the ideology of Mrs Thatcher, her position on monetary union increasingly came into conflict not just with that of the CBI, but also of the City of London. Throughout the 1980s the government resisted pressure from these sources for British membership of the exchange rate mechanism of the European Monetary System. This was only agreed in October 1991, and by that time a considerable pressure had built up within the EC for further moves to full monetary union and a single currency as a means of completing the internal market. In the face of continuing British obstructionism, other member states of the EC were openly saying that they were prepared to proceed together even if some states were not prepared to take the steps necessary. It was Mrs Thatcher's defiant response to this situation that provoked the resignation of her Deputy Prime Minister, Sir Geoffrey Howe, and eventually brought about the fall from office of Mrs Thatcher herself (George, 1991a).

On the issue of monetary union, John Major came into office with the strong support of industrial and financial interests for a more accommodating attitude that would make Britain appear less of an awkward partner. But on the issues connected with the creation of a social dimension to the 1992 project he faced equally strong pressure not to accommodate the wishes of the Commission, the Germans, the French and other member states.

Also, the high level of non-EC foreign investment in Britain made it unlikely that the British Government would support those member states such as France which were concerned to develop large European firms to match Japanese and US

companies in world markets (Bulmer, 1992, p.13). 'Such has been the transformation of Britain's industrial base since the early 1970s that by 1990 the British
Radio and Electronic Equipment Manufacturers' Association (BREMA) com-
prised fifteen members, no less than eleven of whom were controlled by Japanese
or Korean parent companies' (Butt Philip, 1992, p.164).

Public opinion

Hostility among the British public to the EC began to modify in the 1980s, and
although 'the extent to which the British are becoming "good Europeans" must not
be exaggerated' (Nugent, 1992, p.189), by the end of the decade the Labour Party
was able to win a victory over the Conservatives in elections to the European
Parliament (EP) by posing as the more pro-European of the two main parties.

The gap between opinion in Britain and opinion in the other member states had
narrowed by 1992. British opinion had 'slowly adapted to, or at least became
reconciled to, the reality of Community membership' (Nugent, 1992, p.200).
Meanwhile the rejection of the Maastricht Treaty by the Danish people in a
referendum in June 1992 not only demonstrated concern in Denmark: it was the
key for an outbreak of popular discontent with the way in which the Community
appeared to be going among people in other parts of the EC, especially Germany
and France. The implication of the narrowing of the gap between British public
opinion and that in other member states was that the policy and rhetoric of the
governments might differ less in future.

Party management

However, the narrowing of the gap between British public opinion and opinion in
other member states did not necessarily mean that the Conservative government
could easily and quickly adapt itself to a pro-EC stance for domestic consumption,
because opinion amongst Conservative Party members was much more sceptical
about the Community, and even hostile towards it, and the problems of party
management may well be a more important determinant of government behaviour
than considerations of what will be acceptable to the general public. This
remained an important constraint on the pace of any change of direction that the
new Prime Minister might have wished to make.

Britain as spokesman for doubters

Retreat from the more advanced anti-Community positions sometimes taken up by
Mrs Thatcher had become necessary by 1990 because of the changes introduced
after 1987 by the Single European Act (SEA), which confirmed the use of majority
voting in the Council of Ministers for a range of measures connected with the
freeing of the internal market. In fact, the SEA simply codified and made legally
binding for a limited range of issues a practice that had become increasingly
common in the Council, of not using the veto. It was obvious to everybody that the
single European market measures could not be passed unless there were majority
voting. But it was equally obvious to everybody except Mrs Thatcher and a few of
her supporters that the principle would have to be extended to other areas of

Community competence. A Community of twelve states simply could not operate on the veto principle, and any expansion of membership would make it even more imperative that where there was a clear case for binding common rules, these should be agreed on the majority basis.

Once the veto had implicitly or explicitly disappeared from the decision-making process, the whole nature of the bargaining game changed. What had been a feasible if unpopular means of negotiating, that is confrontation to get concessions, backed by the threat of a veto, became unviable. It became that much more important for Britain to be able to win allies in negotiations so as to be able to construct either a qualified majority for measures it supported, or a blocking minority for measures that it opposed. For this reason it was also necessary to present a more accommodating face to the rest of the Community, since however much some governments may have hidden behind Mrs Thatcher's skirts, they could not afford to be seen publicly to be allies of the dreadful anti-Community British if they represented countries where integration was perceived as a good thing.

This need to win allies probably lay behind John Major's overtures to the German Christian Democratic Union during his visit to Germany in March 1991 (George, 1992c, p.69). Because of Mrs Thatcher's stance, the British Conservative Party had never been accepted into the Christian Democratic fold. This had resulted in the British group in the EP sitting separately; but more significantly, the Conservative government was excluded from the caucus meetings of Christian Democratic Prime Ministers that preceded European Council meetings. While in the new diplomatic context that was emerging in the EC, Britain would have no permanent allies, to be on the inside of such a powerful caucus would obviously be advantageous.

Conclusion

So in the middle of 1992 the signs were not all one way for the future of Britain in the EC. However, developments did seem to be moving in the British direction. While governments in other member states had faced embarrassing electoral reverses in the preceding year, John Major, courtesy of the perverse effects of the British electoral system, had secured his own mandate and a comfortable working majority in Parliament. The Danish referendum result was the catalyst for discontent in several member states about the federalist direction in which the Community seemed to be moving, and the loss of control by citizens over their own affairs. Cultural differences within Europe remained sufficiently obvious that the Danes at least were not convinced that their chosen way of life could be protected within a more centralised EC.

In this situation, it seemed quite possible that Britain would become not only a less awkward and more normal member of the EC, but a leading member, moving it towards the type of looser Community with better protection of national sensibilities and prerogatives that successive British governments had always advocated.

Note

1. *The Times*, 1 October 1977.

References

Ashford, N. (1992), 'The political parties', in S. George (ed.) *Britain and the European Community: the politics of semi-detachment*, Oxford, Clarendon Press, pp.119–48.

Bulmer, S. (1992), 'Britain and European integration: of sovereignty, slow adaptation, and semi-detachment', in S. George (ed.) *Britain and the European Community: The Politics of Semi-Detachment*, Oxford, Clarendon Press, pp.1–29.

Butt Philip, A. (1992), 'British pressure groups and the European Community', in S. George (ed.) *Britain and the European Community: The Politics of Semi-Detachment*, Oxford, Clarendon Press, pp.149–71.

George, S. (1990), *An Awkward Partner: Britain in the European Community*, Oxford, Oxford University Press.

George, S. (1991), 'Britain and the European Community', in Peter Catterall (ed.), *Contemporary Britain: An Annual Review, 1991*, Oxford, Basil Blackwell, pp.75–84.

George, S. (1991b), *Britain and European Integration Since 1945*, Oxford, Basil Blackwell.

George, S. (1992a), 'The policy of British governments within the European Community: The Politics of Semi-Detachement, Oxford, Clarendon Press, pp.30–63.

George, S. (1992b), 'The European Community in the new Europe', in C. Crouch and D. Marquand (eds), *Towards Greater Europe? A Continent Without an Iron Curtain*, Oxford, Basil Blackwell, pp.52–63.

George, S. (1992c), 'Britain and the European Community', in Peter Catterall (ed.), *Contemporary Britain: An Annual Review, 1992*, Oxford, Basil Blackwell, pp.68–75.

George, S. and Rosamond, B. (1992) 'The European Community', in M.J. Smith and J. Spear (eds) *The Changing Labour Party*, London, Routledge pp.171–84.

Judge, D. (1986), 'The British Government, European Union, and EC institutional reform', *Political Quarterly*, 57 (3), pp.321–8.

Nugent, N. (1992), 'British Public Opinion and the European Community', in S. George (ed.) *Britain and the European Community: The Politics of Semi-Detachment*, Oxford, Clarendon Press, pp.172–201.

Rosamond, B. (1990), 'Labour and the European Community: learning to be European?', *Politics*, 10 (2), pp.41–46.

Rosamond, B. (1992), 'The Labour Party, trade unions, and industrial relations,' in M.J. Smith and J. Spear (eds) *The Changing Labour Party*, London, Routledge, pp.89–101.

Thatcher, M. (1988), *Britain and Europe: Text of the speech delivered in Bruges by the Prime Minister on 20th September 1988*, London, Conservative Political Centre.

Young, S.Z. (1973), *Terms of Entry: Britain's Negotiations With the European Community, 1970–1972*, London, Heinemann.

16

Harold Wilson and the renegotiation of the EEC terms of membership, 1974–5: a witness account

Bernard Donoughue

Harold Wilson's handling of the question of Britain's entering and remaining in the European Community can, for the sake of clarity, be divided into four quite distinct periods. The first one was the period of Labour opposition between 1971 and 1974, during which the Labour Party under Wilson established its position in relation to Heath's successful negotiations for entry and adopted its manifesto position ahead of the two 1974 general elections. The second period, the six months from October 1974 to March 1975, was the phase of renegotiation, covering the EEC summits and the detailed ministerial and official negotiations. This culminated at Dublin on 11 March 1975, where the renegotiations were concluded. The third was after the Dublin summit, and covers a time of cabinet, parliamentary, and party discussion of the Dublin agreement. Finally, the fourth period encompasses the referendum campaign through to 6 June and the verdict then given by the nation.

During the first period Wilson operated with characteristic caution. The Heath-Pompidou agreement secured British entry on 1 January 1973. That presented a serious problem to the Labour Party, which was fundamentally divided on this issue, with a majority in parliament and among constituency activists certainly against entry. Therefore Wilson's task was twofold: on the European issue he had to keep the options open for a future Labour Government to stay in the EEC – and that meant preventing the party committing itself in principle against entry. Secondly, within the Labour Party, Wilson had to preserve unity, as is always a priority for any Labour – or indeed any party leader.

I believe that he achieved both objectives very skilfully. On the EEC he worked to prevent the party conferences of 1971–73 from passing any motion in principle against membership of the EEC. He led successful opposition to motions opposing membership in principle, and indeed successfully resisted motions which were firmly pro, which would have split the party. He moved the crucial motion in 1972 which actually accepted the principle of membership, shrewdly making it palatable to conference by attaching the conditions that a future Labour Government would renegotiate terms and would then hold a referendum or an election to legitimise the final decision. That motion was passed comfortably by 3.4 million votes to 1.8 million votes. It meant that any future Labour Government must renegotiate terms. It also, crucially, meant that a future Labour Government could, given the right terms, stay in Europe.

As for the Labour Party, Wilson faced a very difficult situation, with passions high and a fundamental divide on the EEC question. In the event his tolerance and flexibility prevented a fatal rupture, which had always seemed on the cards. In 1972, on the great Commons debate and vote, he allowed the pro marketeers to vote with Heath and the government without victimisation; 69 voted yes with the government and 20 abstained. Subsequently of course Roy Jenkins and Harold Lever resigned from the shadow cabinet – which was the main reason Jenkins did not resume as Chancellor in March 1974. As Wilson then explained to me, 'because of Roy's resignation, I have to stick with Healey'. Yet despite that, the party was not fatally split. It was able to fight the 1974 elections reasonably united.

Labour won the first (March) 1974 election, just, though it lacked a secure overall majority. Without that secure political base in London, it could not begin those promised renegotiations on Europe. Our European partners understandably made it clear that they had to negotiate with a firm majority government which could deliver what it negotiated and promised, otherwise it was a waste of their time – after all, they were not keen on holding the negotiations anyway, feeling they had already spent a lot of time on Britain's tardy entry. The first Labour Government in 1974 was not in that position. In fact it was defeated 29 times in its first five months between March and July. Not suprisingly, the question of Europe came up for discussion only rarely in cabinet or in Downing Street at that time.

However, on the 14 September 1974 during the recess, Wilson attended an EEC summit. There were no regular heads of government summits before that time; but Giscard D'Estaing had taken over as President of France and, having both an orderly mind and a grand view of his office, he introduced them. He organised this September summit and others followed effectively at quarterly intervals. Heads of government were invited to Paris but not foreign secretaries. At the meeting Britain's EEC membership was tentatively raised at lunchtime, though not during the formal proceedings. Wilson fired a couple of opening shots across the continental bows, making it clear that Britain objected to the present formulation of the EEC budget and that he rejected any moves toward political union. But there was little serious discussion of these major points, because he was not talking from a secure political base and because formal renegotiations had not begun.

Wilson returned to London committed to remedy the weakness in his political base. Six days later, on 20 September, he dissolved parliament. It had of course always been his intention to hold an early election, probably in the autumn, but the European situation crystalised the need for it to happen before the new political season began.

The opinion polls in early October promised Labour a big lead in the election. But, not for the first or last time, there was a slip towards the Conservatives in the final days which resulted in a disappointing overall majority of only three. But it was at least a majority, and it was won on a clear manifesto commitment on the EEC: Labour would renegotiate with its EEC partners and consult the British people by means of a referendum or an election. In fact it was pretty clear that it would not be by means of an election: there had already been two elections that year and nobody wanted, or could afford a third, so it would be a referendum. Renegotiations were now able to begin in earnest; and that leads into the second period of this story.

Harold Wilson was a great believer in the political utility of manifestos. His approach was to establish an acceptable manifesto, then to get official party support for it, then genuinely attempt to meet its commitments. That was one of his main ways of party management. Providing that he was trying to meet the manifesto commitments, he could not be officially opposed in the party and he had a firm political foundation from which to gather support against his (many) opponents.

Therefore the Labour election manifesto, and the party conference resolutions underlying it, were the foundation point of his approach to the EEC renegotiations. Half a dozen or so policy conditions relating to the EEC were contained in those party documents. Some were more major than others, and some were really sub-issues of the major issues, but all had to be considered and, to a greater or lesser degree, met in the renegotiations.

The first issue was the EEC budget, where under the existing arrangements Britain's contributions to the EEC were significantly in excess of what she received and relatively greater than her national income would indicate. For Harold Wilson, as for Mrs Thatcher later, this was an important issue and principle of fairness – especially as the Brussels forecasts were that in future years Britain's contribution situation would get worse rather than better.

The second major policy issue concerned agriculture: the absolute lunacy of the Common Agricultural Policy (CAP). Wilson wished (with no hope of success) to negotiate major general reforms of the community's agricultural policy. But within it were particular micro issues of concern to him, especially the access to Britain of Commonwealth agricultural products. He was very concerned about New Zealand: about maintaining the export markets for its high quality and cheap butter and lamb. He was concerned about protecting sugar exports from the Caribbean. He was above all concerned to preserve access of cheap foods into Britain – a perfectly respectable and non-partisan objective. He knew that the Common Agricultural Policy had become a ramp, and a high price ramp, to protect relatively small groups of farmers, especially in France and Germany. He wished to confront and reform that. The political reality, however, was that the Europeans, and especially the French, were willing to make concessions on his micro demands only on condition that the basic principles of the CAP were left undisturbed.

On the economic side, the British Government opposed monetary and economic union, and there were economic financial and industrial sub-issues within that broad approach. It wished to preserve freedom of action on exchange rates. It had the not wholly ridiculous belief that if Britain entered a fixed European exchange rate mechanism while its economy was very divergent from the main European economies, it might, for instance, lead to a long period of recession and would probably always be subservient to German policy priorities. Wilson was much criticized for his caution in this area by parts of the Conservative opposition and by most of the conservative press. But time has proved him more right than most of his critics.

Ministers were also concerned about VAT (they wanted some freedom on VAT, on levels and on the right to preserve zero rating for some basic food and household goods) and about regional policy, which agitated both Wilson and Benn. The trade and poverty of the developing world was a final major area where Labour was committed to argue for change – Wilson often expressed fears that the EEC would become a bastion and closed fortress of the world's rich, neglecting the developing countries.

On the whole, however, Wilson's personal position on these negotiating policy issues was one of agnosticism. He worked hard on them, devouring vast quantities of complex briefings from the Foreign Office, from the Cabinet Office, and from the Number Ten Policy Unit (from whom he often requested extra briefs sceptical of the official line). But, except on the developing world and on New Zealand food, he did not seem to care too much about the policies as policies, and might happily have argued a different position had the manifesto required it.

Wilson was primarily concerned to secure enough concessions to satisfy his manifesto and party conference commitments. As always, his was primarily a party and not a policy concern. As for myself as his Senior Policy Advisor, this could at times be frustrating and irritating. But it was not a dishonourable position for a party leader – especially the leader of a party which was really a coalition of so many disparate elements – to have as a prime priority, that of keeping his party together.

In terms of government management, Wilson established two cabinet committees to handle the renegotiations on these particular policy issues. He set up the European Strategy Committee as the senior committee, with himself as Prime Minister in the chair to ensure that the manifesto commitments were met – the classic Wilson party management role. A second and subsidiary, though very important committee (EQS), was established to monitor the details of the renegotiations, with the Foreign Secretary, James Callaghan in the chair. The latter committee also monitored individual ministers who were negotiating in Brussels on issues relating to their departments. A sharp eye and a firm hand were often required here since not all ministers were entirely devoted to pursuing the government's policies. James Callaghan was very good in that role.

In fact it was a brilliant combination: Wilson in the party leader role; Callaghan negotiating the policy issues. They worked superbly together. Given the extent to which they had clashed in the late 1960's, it was quite remarkable how they now worked so trustingly together and held the other ministers in line. But it was an enormous work load for two senior men of around sixty. Wilson was conducting the rest of the British government at the same time, with many trips abroad and visits from foreign heads of state. In fact at this time he began to suffer the first symptoms of heart 'racing' and flutters, reflecting the stress and tension he was feeling. The parliamentary situation added extra pressure; having barely a minority meant that they were unable to pair. Callaghan was constantly being flown back from Brussels for a late night vote and then having to return there in the early hours of the morning. These negotiations were conducted in various places: in the Brussels Commission, in foreign ministers meetings, in ministerial bilaterals and between officials. James Callaghan and the Foreign Office team – especially Michael Palliser in Brussels – carried a huge work burden.

All serious disagreements which could not be resolved at these detailed negotiations were carried forward to the two heads of government summits held in

December and March. The first renegotiation summit was in Paris on 9 December 1974, again with Giscard D'Estaing in the chair. A great deal of prudent and constructive prior consultation took place in order to prepare the way for this summit. The Labour party had held its own delayed annual conference on Thursday 28 November and this was used as part of the preparation. Callaghan had arranged for Helmut Schmidt, the German Chancellor to address the conference, which he did brilliantly. Wilson also made a strong and clear speech; it was received attentively though cooly and there was no standing ovation. His political difficulties in carrying the party were underlined when Tony Benn, the leading opponent of EEC membership, was voted top of the National Executive Committee elections.

Helmut Schmidt was a most impressive, if at times morose North German. His role in shepherding Labour through its European troubles at this time should never be underestimated. After the conference he went to stay the night with Wilson at Chequers. There they effectively struck a most important deal. Schmidt promised that Germany would support Britain on its claims on the EEC budget providing that Wilson, in return, would stop dithering, ducking and weaving, and would declare in public, clearly and firmly, his support for Britain's continuing membership of the European Community if the terms were right. When Wilson agreed, Schmidt said that the British Prime Minister must now go to Giscard in Paris and make his position clear there. Schmidt telephoned Giscard from Chequers and then flew to Paris on the Sunday to arrange this. On Monday 2 December he telephoned to Downing Street to confirm the arrangements with the British end. When Schmidt was fully in action it was not always easy to distinguish between his suggestions and his instructions. He never really liked Wilson.

Wilson went to Paris at midday on Tuesday 3 December and returned on the following morning. His meeting with Giscard was extremely helpful as a preparation for the following week's summit. The British Prime Minister was able to explain to Giscard D'Estaing his domestic political problems and constraints. The French leader in return stressed that Wilson must make a public declaration of his support for Britain's EEC membership. He promised to help Britain in the renegotiations, but only if Wilson committed himself publicly and unequivocally. (The latter was a stance which did not always come easily to Mr Wilson).

The Paris visit was not a total success for Wilson. He ate oysters at dinner with the French President that evening and was very sick afterwards. He looked very pale on his return to Number Ten next morning and was attacked by one of his close, anti-European staff for being so foolish as to go abroad and eat foreign food. But on the wider level it did launch Wilson into a much more positive phase of politics toward Europe. On the following Saturday he made a speech to a small and somewhat bewildered group of Labour mayors from London local government in which he spoke in some detail on the EEC issue. Most importantly, he announced quite clearly that he would recommend that Britain stay in the EEC providing that the terms were right.

Wilson had met his part of the deal with Schmidt and now began to focus seriously on the European question. I recall spending a long time with him – together with his press secretary, Joe Haines, and his Principal Private Secretary, Robert Armstrong – drafting the Labour mayor's speech. He stated that he was now fascinated by the renegotiations. He saw achieving success in them as a political challenge to him personally – to stay in the EEC, to get the terms right, and at the same time to hold the Labour Party together. He never then – nor later to my recollection – talked of the possibility of actually pulling out of Europe. He did not seem to contemplate emerging from the negotiations with terms other than would justify staying in. (He later told cabinet that he had been pessimistic, but this never showed in his private conversations). Admittedly he did wobble momentarily during the discussion of the drafting of the mayor's speech. After being strongly attacked that afternoon by his Political Secretary, Lady Falkender, who was anti-European, he briefly dropped the key sentence from his speech which committed him to support continuing membership if the terms were reasonable. But the other three of us persuaded him to restore it. The following week, before leaving for Paris, he was very buoyant and confident of success in the coming negotiations, talking of making a tour of the capitals of Europe to prepare the way for Britain's affirmative vote. I recall him sitting in his study going one by one through his list of manifesto commitments and claiming that concessions were already being lined up for all except two – access for cheap Commonwealth food and the preservation of British parliamentary sovereignty.

Given the careful preparations, Wilson's positive frame of mind, and Schmidt's promises, the Paris summit on 9–10 December was able to make significant progress, especially on the budget issue and the Regional Fund, which preoccupied the second day's discussions. However, Wilson's mood seemed volatile. On the Monday I recall, he returned from the conference dinner to the British embassy in a very aggressive mood. He attacked his civil sevants for writing briefs which he alleged were too blatantly pro EEC (explicitly excluding the Policy Unit from this sin). He accused them of not negotiating toughly enough on access for Commonwealth food. It was embarrassing and unfair. He told me afterwards that this was a calculated display to cover himself from criticisms that he was too much in the pockets of the 'Eurobureaucrats'. He authorised me to reveal his attacks to others – an unusual stance in the light of his usual obsession with secrecy. He told me that the criticisms of him which he wished to deflect were coming from within the party and especially from within his personal staff.

The second morning's session at the conference centre in the Avenue Kleiber at first made no progress. Giscard would not yield an inch on the budget and eventually Wilson, who had already been very rough on his opponents around the table, said he saw no point in going on and he proposed that they break till the afternoon, which they did. After lunch he deliberately stayed away from the first session's discussion of the Middle East in order to underline his alleged willingness to pull out of the renegotiations if necessary. In fact Wilson needed to see Dr Stone again about his racing heart problem. He also knew that there was no serious danger of a breakdown of the negotiations since he had been privately assured by Schmidt that the budget question, currently the stumbling block, would eventually be resolved by the Germans. Giscard D'Estaing was apparently being overtly difficult in order to rescue the dignity of his foreign minister, who had already gone too far out on a limb against the UK. Having made his necessary gesture, D'Estaing softened at dinner in the evening and they agreed to examine a formula for a 'correcting mechanism' in relation to the EEC budget.

The latter was an ingenious device invented by British civil servants whereby payments from EEC funds to member countries were linked to their GDP. This did not affect contributions, any alteration to which would have breached the EEC's sacred 'own resources' principle of Community funding. But it would make it possible to compensate for unfairly excessive contributions through repayments. The mechanism was also the more acceptable to our partners because it was an EEC formula, applicable to all members and not just a special exemption for the UK.

Schmidt played a key role in securing approval in principle for this potential solution to the budget problem – though the actual numbers in the formula still had to be agreed (and Germany would have to pay!). Schmidt had delivered his part of the Chequers deal and Wilson had delivered his in publically declaring that he would recommend a yes vote if the terms were right. A major step towards getting the terms right had now been made.

Back from Paris, Wilson continued to suffer from his racing heart and had to retire to Chequers for a few days' rest. But he was soon back in action and at a meeting with Callaghan, Jenkins and Short in the week before Christmas the timetable for the referendum was agreed. It was decided there that the negotiations must end, regardless, by Easter, that a Referendum Bill would then be taken through parliament, and that the referendum itself must be held by the end of June at the latest. This was also an important political meeting for Wilson, as he observed afterwards, because Roy Jenkins there for the first time formally, if tacitly, committed himself to support the government's approach to the renegotiations, and especially to the referendum which he had previously strongly opposed.

During the first two months of 1975 the detailed negotiations continued and occasionally surfaced in Downing Street: in cabinet, in cabinet committees, or in private meetings between the Prime Minister and his colleagues. The main ministerial difficulties arose with Tony Benn, who was very concerned about regional policy; from Peter Shore, who pursued economic and trading issues; from Michael Foot, who was worried about parliamentary sovereignty; from William Ross, who was permanently worried about Scotland; and from Barbara Castle, who was generally and vitriolicly anti-European.

By March 1975, after months of what James Callaghan described as very 'fraught' negotiations, Wilson was fairly confident in private that the coming Dublin summit would be able to dispose of all outstanding issues and so it would be possible to bring forward the referendum to the beginning of June (the other remaining problem was the apparent unreadiness of the new Scottish local authorities to organise the vote). In order to avoid a final hiccup in Dublin, Giscard D'Estaing had crucially made Wilson promise not to raise again anything as fundamental and insoluable as the European agricultural pricing system.

Before Dublin, in the first week of March 1975, Wilson and Callaghan were briefed several times by officials – usually including Michael Palliser and Michael Butler from the Foreign Office, John Hunt and Patrick Nairne from the Cabinet Office, Robert Armstrong, Patrick Wright, Robin Butler, Joe Haines and myself from Number Ten. The remaining issues not fully resolved were the budget and New Zealand food – on which Wilson was optimistic – and some matters relating to iron and steel which were proving tricky, with Wilson quite agitated and demanding extra Policy Unit briefing.

My recollection is that these pre-Dublin briefings were conducted wholly on the assumption that: 1) the terms already agreed were satisfactory; 2) Wilson and

Callaghan would recommend 'yes' and 3) a majority of the cabinet would recommend 'yes'.

There was great confidence around the table. This confidence was reinforced by the positive reports from Armstrong, who had visited Paris, from Michael Butler, who had been to Bonn (where Schmidt had pneumonia), and Nairne who had visited Garrett Fitzgerald (also sick) in Dublin. At one moment I recall that Callaghan, either cautious or teasing, mentioned the possibility of an inconclusive result. Wilson interrupted sharply to state that we must have a positive result and must be prepared to work all day and night to achieve it.

The Dublin summit on 10 and 11 March was held in the small and elegant Patrick's Chamber in Dublin Castle. This location had a touch of history to it, since I believe Wilson was the first British Prime Minister to enter Dublin Castle since 1914.

The first afternoon session on Monday 10 March made little progress, being bogged down in a complex and incomprehensible German proposal for implementing the budget correcting mechanism. Negotiations continued over dinner until the early hours, at the Irish premier's residence, Iveagh House. One memorable feature of the proceedings was Wilson being forced, for privacy, to hold his debriefings during breaks from the dinner table, in a large lavatory at Iveagh House – where the chain was ceremonially pulled on the German formula. Another more *communitaire* gesture was when at midnight the other members presented Wilson with a lovely birthday cake to mark his 59th birthday

On the Tuesday, when Wilson led strongly for the British, all issues were cleared except the final budget formula and the question of access to Britain of New Zealand food (especially cheese). But little progress was made on the latter issues until late afternoon. Then suddenly, as often at these conferences, the log jam broke and settlement was quickly reached. The Germans and the French combined to support a new formula, greatly assisted by Ortoli, the excellent Commission President, and all were happy. Schmidt, the main financier of Britain's increased rebates, looked sick and dismal, but had been of great assistance. The French, as always, were very difficult at the official level, very legalistic and uncompromising, very clever. But Giscard D'Estaing was very skilful and ultimately helpful.

Most of the compromises negotiated in Dublin were achieved by Callaghan and the Foreign Office team led by Michael Palliser. They carried the main burden of work and Callaghan demonstrated that he was a most impressive foreign minister (just as he was later a much more impressive Prime Minister than many people realised). However, Harold Wilson's role was crucial. He took the lead in the battles in Paris and Dublin. After the agreement was announced on that wet and windy Saturday in Dublin, Wilson made it clear to the world's press that he would now recommend to cabinet and to parliament that the terms be accepted, which was the crucial next political step.

After Dublin, with the negotiating stage over, Wilson resumed full control. Now it was political control, the management of politics, which was necessary to bring everything to a successful conclusion in the referendum. Wilson had to sell his recommendation to stay in the EEC. He had to sell it in turn to his cabinet, to parliament, to the Labour Party and then finally to sell it to the referendum electorate. That was the prime task of this third phase – and he did it successfully, though with varying degrees of enthusiasm. At the same time he had a political imperative – to hold his party together. It was not an easy task. The cabinet and party contained a number of powerful and individual politicians. He handled them with great skill and when history takes a more balanced view of Harold Wilson – his reputation has gone through a bad patch – and his career is seen in perspective, he should get full credit for his skill in both keeping Britain in Europe and in holding together his party and his cabinet.

The cabinet met to discuss the Dublin agreements over two days, 17–18 March 1975. It was potentially a very dangerous situation for the Prime Minister, not only because his cabinet was deeply divided, but because on this issue he had to chair some very dogmatic and uncompromising individuals. On the pro side, Roy Jenkins was believed to be committed to resign from the cabinet if it decided not to recommend the terms for continuing membership of the EEC. Shirley Williams had stated in the election campaign that she would leave politics altogether if the cabinet said no. Therefore on the pro side were cabinet ministers – and some junior ministers – who were prepared to put this issue above the survival of the government or their own ministerial careers. On the other side were Tony Benn, Michael Foot, Peter Shore and Barbara Castle who were equally passionately opposed to Europe. The cabinet was in danger of being torn apart. The tension within Number Ten at this time was tangible and unforgettable.

Wilson handled that long cabinet meeting on 17–18 March with consummate skill. Every member was given an opportunity to speak. Yet, in a classic Wilsonian way, he prevented it from developing into a confrontation. He hated confrontations of all kinds.

Some of the first morning was deliberately devoted to a long and balanced report by Callaghan on the development of the negotiations. That blunted the edge of the discussion and afterwards Wilson was openly pleased that there had been no fireworks. That evening the junior ministers were summoned to Downing Street, to the state dining room, to air their views on the EEC. Wilson had deliberately and cleverly arranged to hold the meeting in the middle of the cabinet so there could be no discussion of the cabinet's final decision. The speakers were roughly evenly divided. Those against included Frank Judd, Stanley Clinton Davies, and Margaret Jackson (Beckett). The pro speakers were mainly minor figures. Prominent pro campaigners, such as William Rodgers and Denis Howell, had decided not to perform at this meeting.

On the second day of cabinet, the early part of the morning was again defused by a long presentation, this time on the referendum arrangements by Edward Short, the deputy leader. After that the Prime Minister went around the table asking each minister in turn his view of the terms. To begin, both he and James Callaghan stated firmly that they were in favour of a positive recommendation – though Wilson seemed to indicate that he had been in doubt until recently. He also suggested this in speeches and interviews. Whether true or not, it was certainly a useful device to gather in doubters to his position: by implying that he had shared and understood their doubts, but then suggesting that a reasonable doubter would, like himself conclude in a pro position. At the count the majority in favour of recommending the terms was 16–7.

Wilson then suggested a rare cabinet innovation – coffee break. This hopefully would allow tensions to subside – and he wished especially to create a break after ministers had declared their position. It was then proposed that after coffee the dissenting ministers would be asked whether they wished to register formally as dissenters who would actually campaign against the cabinet's decision. This was at Callaghan's suggestion and the hope was that some dissenters who had satisfied their consciences and their constituencies ahead of the national executive elections by declaring against in the main vote, would be dislodged from the minority at the second count. It did not work. But the coffee break was a small example of a typical Wilson approach – to cushion and smooth the sharp edges of argument and always to try to leave people feeling that they had room for manoeuvre and were not up against a wall. (The opposite, for example of Mrs Thatcher's handling of Michael Heseltine over the Westland helicopter affair).

The majority of 16–7 was satisfactory to the Prime Minister and greater than many would have predicted at the opening of the negotiations. This certainly owed much to the skilfull handling by the Wilson-Callaghan team. In fact five of the 16 majority had been publically committed against staying in the Community when Labour took office in March 1974. Three of them – Merlyn Rees, John Morris and Fred Peart – were very close to Callaghan and his influence on their change of position was certainly very important, possibly decisive. Lord Shepherd, the Leader of the Lords, was basically a loyalist and unlikely to oppose the Prime Minister. The fifth switcher, Reg Prentice, was in the course of a profound evolution of political views which ended with him as a member of a later Conservative administration.

If these five had remained hostile then the vote would have been 12–11 against staying in the EEC. Wilson and Callaghan deserve the credit for swinging the cabinet vote to a comfortable majority.

The minority of seven dissenters were politically a mixed bunch. Castle and Foot were from the old left, long against Europe. Benn was a newer recruit, though, like many late converts, the passion with which he supported the new cause outrivalled the passion with which he once took the opposite view. John Silkin was of the moderate left, but he was seeking to use the left as a base for a future bid for the leadership of the party and had to share their position.

Both Peter Shore and William Ross were, by many yardsticks, very right wing. But each was his own man and theirs was a more nationalistic – and in Shore's case a very seriously thought out – opposition to the Community. The seventh dissenter was Eric Varley. He seemed to dither and later indicated that he regretted his negative vote, but he was under immediate pressure from his close friends Gerald Kaufman and Lady Falkender, both strongly opposed to the Prime Minister's position.

I recall that in his study one evening shortly after the cabinet of 17–18 March, Harold Wilson expressed his sadness and considerable resentment that so many of those who had worked personally close to him – and whose careers he had greatly assisted – had, as he saw it, 'abandoned' him on the EEC issue. He named several, including some of his former PPs – Barbara Castle, Gerald Kaufman, Charles Morris, Eric Varley, Peter Shore and Thomas Balogh. He contemplated dropping some, including Mrs Castle, from his government. Such were the tensions and divisions created by this issue. Wilson never fully understood why other people sometimes felt so deeply on such issues – which he usually described as 'theological'.

Although many pro politicians and commentators complained about Wilson's apparent lack of commitment on Europe, and his remarkable tolerance of dissent, in fact this was part of the process by which he secured the maximum possible majority in cabinet without splitting the party. By himself appearing agnostic, taking a middle way and always basing his position firmly on the foundations of the party manifesto, he made it possible to build a clear cabinet majority. His predecessor, Hugh Gaitskell, though more impressive in many ways, might have had great difficulty in holding the Labour party together on such an explosive issue.

Wilson added to these leadership characteristics an unusual constitutional device which greatly assisted him in minimising the damage to his party during the stresses of the referendum campaign which now loomed ahead. This was the cabinet decision to suspend the normal collective responsibilty of cabinet and to allow dissenting colleagues to campaign openly against the government's decision on Europe.

This so-called 'agreement to differ' originated with Foot and Benn, who had asked Wilson in the new year of 1975 if they could openly campaign against the EEC. Wilson at that time refused and stamped on such divisive activities until cabinet had actually taken its decision. But he adopted it for the referendum period. He saw it as a welcome instrument of truly Wilsonian flexibility. He believed that it was acceptable to suspend normal cabinet collectivity and allow ministers to campaign how they wished for four reasons: because of the uniqueness of the situation; because it was an issue of great constitutional importance; because it cut deeply across all normal party lines; and because the adoption of the referendum itself was unique in British history.

This agreement to differ was made subject to the condition that there should be no personal attacks on fellow ministers [not always obeyed]. The final license was looser than Wilson originally intended. Ministers were eventually allowed to vote no in the Parliamentary debate, and junior ministers were allowed the same license as their seniors, though neither had been his original intention. No minister was allowed to speak in parliament against the cabinet decision – and when Eric Heffer, a junior minister, did, Wilson promply sacked him.

After securing a majority in cabinet, Wilson turned to parliament, making his initial statement immediately after the cabinet on 18 March. This was a low key affair. The later great Commons debate was over three days on 7–9 April 1975, on a motion to approve Britain's continuing membership on the terms set out in the white paper.

Wilson himself opened with an impressive speech (though only Varley from his dissenting cabinet colleagues had the courtesy to sit on the front bench with their Prime Minister) and Callaghan closed on the third day. There was a large yes majority: 396–170. But within Labour members there was actually a majority against: 145 were against and 137 in favour, with 33 abstaining. Some of the abstainers were really against but did not want actually to vote against their own government. Wilson saw the negative majority as having arisen because of his error in having allowed junior ministers to vote against. This was never his intention but he foolishly went to Northern Ireland on the day that cabinet discussed it; once conceded, it could not be recovered. But in reality this Labour vote was merely a true reflection of opinion among party activists – and therefore of the difficult party situation which Wilson faced in reaching and advocating the 'yes' position. A majority of activists in parliament, at conference and in the constituencies were actually opposed to staying in Europe.

Wilson certainly experienced great difficulties with the national executive committee. The NEC was a body he grew to loathe and he sometimes deliberately fixed official visits abroad to coincide with its monthly meetings and so to excuse his absences. Immediately after the 18 March cabinet, the anti-marketeers put down a motion at the NEC attacking Wilson and calling on the Party organisation formally to campaign against its own government. Wilson was furious. He summoned Foot and Castle from their beds to a midnight meeting and savaged them to the point where – so it was reported to us afterwards – even the normally indestructable Mrs Castle offered to resign.

The following day's cabinet was devoted almost entirely to this issue, with officials banished from the room. The Prime Minister attacked the dissenters for their conduct at the NEC and then, in a calculated move arranged beforehand with his deputy, Edward Short, he withdrew angrily from cabinet. He retreated to his study, where he was periodically visited by colleagues bringing news of the discussion. His withdrawal was intended to convey his willingness to resign over this issue (though it was impossible to establish how serious he was, he was certainly genuinely angry and was anyway beginning privately to plan his retirement).

His various protests worked. Michael Foot persuaded the left to moderate their activities while Shirley Williams rallied additional pressure from the right. The final NEC motion did not commit the party organisation to campaign against the government, simply allowing workers the same freedom to support or dissent as ministers had.

The NEC organised a special party conference to discuss the EEC issue. It was held on Saturday 26 April in Islington. Producing the Prime Minister's speech for this conference led to considerable tension among his staff in Number Ten. Wilson's own original draft was very non-committal. I recall thinking that it was as if, now that he had successfully managed the issue through the negotiations, through cabinet and through parliament, he had lost interest. For him it had been a political challenge, not a commitment to Europe. Nowhere in the draft did he actually say that he was personally in favour of remaining in the EEC: as if he was still playing the role of the uncommitted broker between the theological pros and antis, even though after the decisive cabinet the time for the middle way role was over and he really needed to assert his cabinet's decision.

Joe Haines, Robert Armstrong and I successfully defeated Lady Falkender's skilful and persistent efforts to water down his commitment. But the end product was still very muted and typified his unenthusiastic approach in the remaining weeks ahead. At the conference Wilson was very edgy, as if under hidden pressures, and there were no cheers for his speech. Predictably and by a big majority 3.7 million to 1.98 million – the conference voted against staying in the EEC. However Wilson did at least tell his audience that it would not be them but the referendum electorate which would decide the outcome, which nullified much of the impact of their vote.

The referendum ballot was scheduled for 5 June and the result was declared on 6 June appropriately the anniversary of D Day, the allied invasion of the continent of Europe in 1944. The referendum device for the EEC had been proposed by Tony Benn in 1971 and ironically it was the mechanism which defeated him. It had been strongly opposed by Roy Jenkins, as leader of the pros, being the main reason why he resigned as deputy leader in 1972; ironically it was the constitutional device which secured overwhelming success for his position. (Benn soon refused to accept the verdict of his chosen instrument, whereas Jenkins did).

The actual mechanics of the referendum were placed under the ministerial control of Edward Short, who did an excellent job. The campaign was very extended, much longer than a normal general election campaign, although it did not gain serious momentum until the second half of May. During those weeks British government came to a virtual halt and there was only a trickle of papers through Whitehall to Downing Street.

Three organisations replaced the parties in conducting the campaign. There was an all-party umbrella organisation mobilising the pros of which Roy Jenkins was president. There was a separate Labour Campaign for Europe, enabling Labour supporters to campaign for the EEC without sharing a platform with Conservatives and Liberals. And the antis had their own operation. Wilson was very careful not to associate with the all party campaign in order not to smudge his party image.

The government's own activities and tactics to win the referendum campaign were advised and monitored by a secret committee which met daily from the middle of May. It assembled in the Ambassador's Waiting Room in the Foreign Office, with Callaghan in the chair when he was in the country, but otherwise sometimes chaired by Roy Hattersley or John Morris. Other ministers attending were Shirley Williams, Bob Mellish, William Price, David Ennals and John Grant. Michael Butler and John Weston came with juniors from the Foreign Office, together with Tom Macnally, Callaghan's able political adviser. I attended representing the Prime Minister.

Robert Worcester came frequently to give his always shrewd analysis of the latest opinion polls, including his own. Early in the campaign the polls showed a steady majority of around 70–30 per cent for staying in the EEC. This slipped a little during the campaign to 67–33 per cent with the main doubters being among the working class categories, especially among women and in Scotland and the north of England.

Wilson seemed at first very reluctant to join in the referendum campaign. In the middle of May he had still not made a speech – and had not yet arranged a single speaking arrangement (his political speaking arrangements were under the control of his political secretary, Lady Falkender). Knowledge of this diary vacuum proved embarrassing at the steering committee and we successfully persuaded him to arrange a proper speaking programme. He spoke nearly every day in the final ten days. In these speeches he did declare himself firmly for a 'pro' vote, though his speeches seemed to me sadly flat, long and often rambling. They received little media coverage. Curiously he did not use his normal speech writer, Joe Haines, but usually dictated them himself. However the fact that, speaking as the Prime Minister of Great Britain, he presented himself to the electorate as a sometime doubter who was now in favour of staying in the EEC, undoubtedly had a beneficial effect on the 'pro' vote.

In the ballot on 5 June, 17,378,581, or 67.2 per cent, voted 'yes'. 8,470,073, or

32.8 per cent, voted 'no'. On a turnout of 64.5 per cent – nearly general election proportions – the yes majority of nearly 9 million was greater than the total vote against. The national approval for EEC membership was overwhelming. It should have been accepted as final and closed that chapter. But those on the left who had long argued for a referendum as the final and definitive voice of the people soon forgot about that and began to campaign again to overturn it.

The referendum result was a great success for the team of Wilson and Callaghan. Their approach to Europe was in some ways similar – and not dissimilar to that of Denis Healey and the late Anthony Crosland. Their approach was positive but not enthusiastic or ideological. They supported the Community of Europe but did not have a very wide vision of the EEC, seeing it as a trading, diplomatic and defence community, not a political or economic union in the closest sense. They were certainly not federalists. Both were sceptical of any great economic benefits to come to Britain from a more integrated Europe, and it could be argued that history has so far proved them right in that respect. Both genuinely supported their party's manifesto position – 'renegotiate, referendum, stay in if the terms are right'. That was a solid political basis and it enabled half the party and two thirds of the electorate to unite around that position, which, given the history of division on this issue, was a satisfactory outcome.

There were clear differences of emphasis, as their were differences of character (and of physical shape) between Wilson and Callaghan. Callaghan was certainly more internationalist, and he was reinforced in that by his Foreign Office advisers. He was also an Atlanticist. Wilson was more what might be called an Old Commonwealth Sentimentalist, especially about New Zealand lamb. He was at root a Little Englander and he did not very much like abroad.

Wilson was always mildly anti-European, in the sense that he seemed not to like continental Europeans, their style of life or their politics. He was basically a north of England, non-conformist puritan, with all the virtues and the inhibitions of that background. The continental Europeans, especially from France and southern Europe, were to him alien. He disliked their rich food, genuinely preferring meat and two veg with HP sauce. For holidays the furthest he could usually be tempted was the Scilly Isles, which enabled him to go overseas and yet remain in Britain. He had no distinctive personal style himself and did not appreciate that of the Europeans. Abroad he felt strong sentiments for the old White Commonwealth, especially Australia and New Zealand, but he never displayed or appeared to feel any racial prejudice. He was a genuine democrat in every sense, in his personal behaviour as in his political, never behaving grandly because of the high office he held. Politically he believed that British democracy and the British Parliament were the most wonderful political systems ever invented. His observation of continental politics in the 1930s, during the war, and after, did not convince him that many Europeans were fundamentally democratic or had much to bring to the British political system. I observed the delight with which he cancelled the then channel tunnel project in 1974. His chosen personal staff throughout much of his career as Prime Minister – Falkender, Kaufman and, for most of his time, Haines – together with such close political allies as Castle, Shore, Varley and Charles Morris – were anti-European. I was a solitary (and in March 1974 on this issue a very lonely) exception among his personal staff as a known pro-European.

Despite this background, Harold Wilson decided from October 1974 that a 'yes' position was the most practical choice. As a statesman – which part, but only part of his complex personality always was – he knew that Britain must be centrally placed in Europe's future. As a party leader, he saw it as the best way to hold Labour together – because the antis would not leave the party over Europe, but the pros would. As a shrewd politician, he saw the pro position as the most likely winning one. So he suppressed those of his personal instincts and prejudices which disliked and resented continental Europe and worked to keep Britain in the European Community. However those personal antipathies did periodically re-emerge, as has been shown in the above narrative: in his reluctance to come out firmly and publically state his personal preference for voting yes; in his reluctance to arrange his speaking arrangements for the referendum campaign; in the flabbiness and lack of conviction of his final speeches – the writing of which he was unwilling to leave to those of his staff now fully committed to achieving the maximum success for the 'yes' campaign. This reluctance was reinforced by the strongly expressed views of his political secretary, who periodically had great influence on him.

It could be argued that the whole conduct of the British referendum campaign in 1975 was very 'Wilsonian'. It was consultative. It was consensus seeking, always being managed from the top to avoid confrontation. It was flexible. It was non-theological. It even had characteristic elements of Wilsonian fudge – so that for instance it was never quite clear whether the referendum result was actually meant to be constitutionally binding. These were all recognisable Wilsonian qualities. They helped to achieve success in both negotiating terms on which Britain could stay in the EEC and in holding together the Labour Government while a majority of Labour activists opposed him. That was Wilson's contribution and achievement.

In conclusion, I will quote what he said on the 6 June from the steps of Number Ten when the result was known. In a statement he composed at Chequers (having predictably declined my telegraphed suggestion that he should include a sentence stating that he personally welcomed the result) he said:

The verdict has been given by a bigger vote, by a bigger majority, than has been received by any government in any general election. Nobody in Britain or the wider world should have any doubt about its meaning. It was a free vote without constraint, following a free democratic campaign, conducted constructively and without rancour. It means that fourteen years of national argument are over. It means that all those who have had reservations about Britain's commitment should now join wholeheartedly with our partners in Europe and our friends every where to meet the challenge confronting the whole nation.

The Daily Telegraph, never a friend of Labour, the next day concluded that 'the result of the referendum is quite frankly a triumph for Wilson'. I believe that to be true, Mr Heath had taken the British Establishment into Europe. Harold Wilson took in the British people.

References

The main sources for this chapter are the author's recollections, themselves sharpened by conversations with other participants in the events described.

The main published sources are:

Lord Callaghan (1987), *Time and Chance*, London, William Collins & Son.
Tony Benn (1989), *Against the Tide: Diaries 1973–1976*, London, Hutchinson.
Lord Healey (1989), *The Time of My Life*, London, Michael Joseph.
Lord Jenkins (1989), *European Diary*, London, Collins.
Lord Jenkins (1991), *A Life at the Centre*, London, Macmillan.
Lord Wilson (1976), *Final Term: The Labour Government 1974–1976*, London, Weidenfeld & Nicolson/Michael Joseph.
Lord Wilson 1976, *The Governance of Britain*, London, Weidenfeld & Nicolson/Michael Joseph.

17

Much ado about nothing: the Conservative Party and the social dimension of Europe

Daniel Wincott

The social dimension of the European Community has been misunderstood by most UK politicians. This chapter seeks to make a contribution to clarifying the nature of the social dimension, and its part in European integration in the 1990s. It will focus on the attitudes of members of the Conservative Party. The analysis suggests that Conservative scepticism about the social dimension is largely misplaced. Indeed, the argument here will be that opposition to the social dimension of Europe, so far from being a matter of principle for Tories, has been used by the Conservative leadership to promote internal party cohesion. Statecraft has been subordinated to party management.

To pursue the argument an analysis of Conservative approaches to European integration is required. Partly on the basis of this analysis three groups of Tory MPs will be identified. Conservative's attitudes to the EC can be defined in relation two broad issues: the nation and the economy (Wincott, 1992a). Some Conservatives believe that the EC threatens to undermine the nation, especially as embodied in Westminster, the mother of Parliaments. Others see the EC as a means of consolidating British power in the world, albeit at a more modest level than our imperial past once might have led us to anticipate. A similar analytic division exists over the economic issue. Again some Tories regard the EC as undermining the British economy, and destroying the dearly won free market here, while others see the EC as a means of furthering UK interests, by means of creating a very large free market in Europe. The first group of Conservatives seem to regard the single market programme as a Trojan horse for 'Euro-socialism'.

Partly on the basis of these underlying attitudes towards European integration the Conservative Party divides effectively into three groups on the issue. (Wincott, 1991, pp.7–12) There is a small group of enthusiasts on both sides. Neither convinced Euro-sceptics, nor convinced Euro-philes (whether federalists or not) make up a very large percentage of the total number of Tory MPs. The vast majority of MPs are agnostic over Europe, despite the fact that some of them have strong views on some European questions. Most are sceptical about some aspects of the EC, while believing that there is no viable alternative to membership of the Community, however it evolves. These MPs have a strong presumption that they will follow the line set by the leadership of the Party, following the 'famous Conservative tradition'. Nevertheless they need to be led. John Major's refusal to sign the Social Chapter of the Treaty of Maastricht can be fully understood only as a sop to the far right and therefore as a means of bringing the 'silent' majority of the Party into line on the European issue.

The new right and the social dimension

To develop the present analysis the free market argument against the social dimension of Europe must be analysed. It is often assumed that many Conservatives support the creation of the single internal market in Europe, but baulk at tagging a social dimension to it. The social dimension does not, however, provide a valid reason for Conservatives who would otherwise endorse further European integration to oppose it. In order to understand this point the debate concerning the impact of the EC on the character and power of the UK 'nation' must be put on one side. Traditional Conservative opposition to foreign interference in UK politics is a logical reason to oppose further European integration. Indeed, when developed fully the present analysis suggests that it may be the only valid reason for Conservative Euro-scepticism. (Mount, 1992, p.243) Here we focus on the economic, and particularly the 'free market', reasons for supporting or opposing European integration.

It is worth noting how rarely the case against the social dimension, and European integration in general is set out purely in free market terms. For example, although many commentators have argued that Mrs Thatcher's opposition to further European integration was catalysed by the promulgation of the Social Charter by Jacques Delors, her famous (or notorious) response to Delors at the College of Europe in Bruges makes little explicit comment on the social dimension. In a well-known passage in that speech she did say 'We have not successfully rolled back the frontiers of the state in Britain, only to see them reimposed at a European level, with a European super-state exercising a new dominance from Brussels.' (Thatcher, 1988, p.4)

However, all she said specifically on the social dimension was:

And before I leave the subject of the Single Market, may I say that we certainly do not need new regulations which raise the cost of *employment* and make Europe's labour market less flexible and less competitive with overseas suppliers.

If we are to have a European Company Statute, it should contain the minimum regulations. And certainly we in Britain would fight attempts to introduce collectivism and corporatism at the European level – although what people wish to do in their own countries is a matter for them. (Thatcher, 1988, p.7)

Some Euro-sceptics have, however, chosen to take their stand unequivocally on the economic, free market issue. Those that do often end up adopting illegitimate forms of argument. David Marsland is one of the leading 'new right' commentators in Britain on social policy. He has clearly chosen to base his scepticism about the social dimension of Europe on economic liberal grounds. 'In my view *Little Englanders* and *federalist Eurofanatics* are both fundamentally wrong' (Marsland, 1990, p.11). Rather than providing a detailed argument about the content of the social dimension, he rests a good deal of his argument on the character of its supporters. 'When the Soviet President and union leaders as far to the left as Mr Gill – who abandoned the CPGB because it was too right wing – are joining hands to bless the European union and the Charter, we should be cautious indeed' (Marsland, 1991, p.1).[1] To be fair, Professor Marsland's views were published by a political society and a popular or professional journal. However similar *ad hominium* arguments have been published in leading academic journals. For example, Christopher Lingle has suggested that the character of the Social Charter can be identified by the fact that the President of the European Commission who was the drafter and chief proponent of the Charter '. . . is by no coincidence a leading member of the Socialist Party of France' (Lingle, 1991, p.130).

Lingle's intellectual failure is compounded by the fact that his argument adopts the style of Public Choice theory. Authors in the Public Choice tradition pride themselves on the rigorous deductive method they adopt, beginning from clearly stated premises, logically deducing conclusions, which should be then tested against empirical evidence. To hide behind such a shield of rigour, while making unsubstantiated, prejudicial statements is the worst kind of intellectual deceit (Wincott, 1992b).

Given how rarely the purely free market case against the social dimension is put, and that when this case is developed it is often unconvincing, a critical analysis of the substance of the case will be developed here. The scepticism of British Conservatives towards the Social Charter and Social Chapter is based on two related, but distinct, misunderstandings, if the 'national' question is put to one side. First, they are mistaken in their interpretation of the process of integration in Europe since the early 1980s. The logic of the freeing of the single internal market in the EC is powerfully neo-liberal. Even when the internal market is seen in the context of the broader process signified by the expression 1992, it is still, over-whelmingly about the creation of a Big Market (Grahl & Teague, 1990). This misunderstanding can be traced in the Labour Party as well (Short, 1991, Col. 338).[2] Thus neither the conversion of some elements of the Conservative Party to opposition to Britain's membership of the EC, nor the conversion in the opposite direction of the vast bulk of the Labour Party, can be justified on the basis of the development of the Community's social dimension.[3]

Secondly, ironically, 'free market' Conservatives have misunderstood the character of markets. So far from being completely spontaneous and mechanical means of organising a mass of atomistic individuals, markets are social institutions, which require rules to organise them, as serious analysts and advocates of the market since Adam Smith have recognised. The slogans of the free market have been spoken in rousing voice over the last 15 years. However, advocacy of the market has largely concentrated on the processes required to 'free' markets from existing government control. The less tantalising task of setting out exactly what governments do have to do – 'the weights and measures stuff' (Mount, 1992, p.240) – has had less energy devoted to it, perhaps understandably.

Most of the policies developed under the social dimension cannot be regarded as traditional welfare state or social policies (Majone, 1992, pp.4–8). Many of them are justified as necessary for the successful completion of the single market, '. . . but even if they no longer have to be justified in functional terms, measures proposed by the Commission in the social field must be compatible with the "economic constitution" of the Community, that is, with the principles of a liberal economic order' (Majone, 1992, pp.4–5).

Even when the creation of the single market appeared to be at its most neo-liberal, purely a barrier-removing exercise in 'negative' economic integration, it still relied on the 'positive' support of government agencies. Recent economic analysis has suggested that the rhetoric of the new opportunities was successfully hyped by the Commission and subsequently by business as well, and, in a self-fulfilling process, actually created the opportunities. Preliminary results of the economic analysis suggest that indeed

'. . . a general shift from Euro-pessimism to Euro-optimism could have an independent effect on the shape of the European economy.' (Baldwin & Lyons, 1991, p.56)

The Commission was not the only government organisation to generate this hype. In the UK the Department of Trade and Industry (renamed the Department for Enterprise) ran campaigns to 'publicise' the opportunities available under the internal market. It provides information to businesses on how they can take advantage of 1992. Thus the most 'free market' member state in Europe expended vast effort to 'encourage' British business to participate in it (Wallace, 1990, p.163).

Despite all these paradoxical 'positive' government efforts to engineer 'negative' economic integration, the limits to the neo-liberal 'barrier removing' project of European integration soon became obvious. The effort to sustain the economic momentum of 1992 required a move from the logic of removing barriers to that of building common institutions to integrate and regulate the European economy.

While some of the policies which have been proposed under the social dimension of the single market may be genuinely repugnant to the Conservatives, many more of them are part of this effort to sustain the momentum of 1992. This conclusion may be uncongenial to neo-liberals. Nevertheless an efficient labour market is as necessary as a free capital market for the creation of the European single market. The creation of a 'level playing field' in social policy, and the development of policies which will help the European labour market to clear effectively despite the cultural, geographic, and especially linguistic diversity of Europe are crucial objectives of the social dimension.

We shall see below that despite vocal opposition to the principle of the Social Charter, and later the Social Chapter, in practice British Conservative governments seem to agree that the social dimension at least does no harm to the single market, and may even help to bring it into being. Certainly they have been able to agree to almost all the directives promulgated under the auspices of the social dimension.

Three features of the free market argument against further European integration in general, and the social dimension in particular have been exposed here. First, it is not made very often in a pure form. Usually free market, and nationalistic arguments mingle in the mouths of Euro-sceptics. Secondly, when the attempt is made to present a pure form of the economic liberal case, illegitimate and unliberal forms of argument are often deployed. Finally these characteristics of the neo-liberal case against the social dimension may be a result of the fact that the pure free market case against the social dimension is not very convincing. We shall now turn to the stance of the Conservative administrations led by John Major to see how these issues have been played out in practical politics.

The Social Chapter

Under John Major, Britain's abstention from a formal commitment of principle to the symbols of the social dimension of the EC has continued through his refusal to sign the Social Chapter of the Treaty of Maastricht. However, Major's root and branch rejection of the Social Charter has partly disguised his repeated attempts to argue that he has fully supported the social dimension of the Community. It will be argued that John Major has begun to change the orientation of the Conservative Party in government towards the social dimension from principled (but ill-founded) opposition into qualified and tactical support. Thus John Major has argued that the United Kingdom has

> . . . long accepted that there should be a social dimension to the activities of the Community [and has] . . . played a full part in the social dimensions of the Community, and no one has gone further. [Moreover he has argued that] With Germany, we are the only member state that has implemented all the 18 directives so far adopted by the Community. We have made it clear that we will adopt and implement the majority of the Community's existing social action programme. Nineteen of the 33 measures so far published have been agreed by the Council of Ministers, and the United Kingdom has not blocked a single one of them.[4]

On the face of it this is an odd statement from Major in the immediate aftermath of his repudiation of the Social Chapter of the Treaty of Maastricht. It has, however, been restated by the new Secretary of State for Employment, Gillian Shephard, in her speech to the CBI, the first major speech on EC social policy after the 1992 general election. She followed John Major's line in emphasising the government's commitment to the social dimension of Europe. '[T]hanks to John Major's great achievement at Maastricht the Community's powers in the social affairs field will remain as they were. And I want to emphasise that we have *not* opted out of this. There *is* a substantial social dimension to the Community, to which we are fully committed' (Shephard, 1992, p.8).

Some of the arguments Major uses in order to justify his position seem to be convincing, *prima facie*. But taken together his arguments are contradictory. Their combination can only be understood as an attempt to hold the Tory Party together on the divisive European issue. Clearly Major's attempt to identify the social dimension as distinct from, and less than, the Social Charter and Social Chapter is an attempt to square the circle of principled opposition, to pick up the votes of right wingers, while seeming more *communitaire* to the representatives of other member states, and the 'Euro-enthusiasts' within his own Party. Many of the reluctant members of the European Community in the mainstream of the Party, not to mention those on its Thatcherite wing, find it easier to support a government which baulks at some, at least, of the Community's proposals.

Major uses two main arguments to justify his attitudes to the social dimension and the Social Chapter. Both relate to the potential for the Social Chapter to undermine economic competitiveness, and deter inward investment in Britain and/or the EC. It is unclear, however, whether the Government believes that the Social Chapter would undermine competitiveness in Europe in general, or only in the UK.

John Major often seemed to suggest that the industrial relations systems of other states embody different practices from those in the UK. In answer to a question from Dale Campbell-Savours 'Why is it that German competitiveness can stand the social chapter and British competitiveness cannot? What is the distinction?' the Prime Minister argued that 'The Germans have had a different structure of labour laws for many years'.[5]

Later this point was made forcefully by Douglas Hurd when he argued against the Social Chapter for the UK.

We find unacceptable . . . that there should be special status of some kind for discussion and agreements reached in a corporatist way between organised labour and organised management but purporting to cover the whole area of employment. It is said that we are in some way behind the times because we do not find that acceptable. Our difficulty is that the British people have visited and lived with that philosophy in the recent past – 25, 20, 15 years ago. *It may suit others – we are not saying that it does not* – but it does not work here, and we do not like it.[6]

However the other ground chosen by John Major for defence of his government's attitude to the Social Chapter, before the Maastricht European Council meeting was broader. 'Our arguments', John Major claimed, '. . . are based not only on our national interest but on the risks we perceive to the competitive position of the Community as a whole . . . [E]ven among . . . [other] member states there are many who fear the the effect of Community measures on their jobs and their ability to compete'.[7]

Gillian Shephard failed to follow John Major on his reasoning, outlined above, over why the UK could not afford to sign the Social Chapter at Maastricht while other (economically more successful) countries could. She did emphasise the unique character of UK industrial relations, especially over the previous few years. However, unlike John Major she did not argue that this uniqueness could explain the inability of the UK to sign the Social Chapter of the Maastricht Treaty. Instead she argued, in a slightly Thatcheresque manner, that the rest of Europe was starting to turn to the British model.

The call is now beginning to be heard across Europe. In Sweden, after a generation of tight restriction in the labour market and a corporatist strangle hold on decision making, there is an exciting urgency for change. In Eastern Europe the fledgling democracies are throwing off the burdens on their economies in a drive for growth. And among the EC Member States, it is not just the smaller and weaker economies which are having to face these realities.

Even in prosperous and economically powerful Germany, with its proud record on economic growth and low inflation, employers and economic experts alike are seeking to bring long needed flexibilities to their labour market. What is more, many are looking to Britain – once the sick man of Europe – for ideal conditions for investment.

A recent report from the German Chamber of Industry and Commerce revealed that Britain is the most favoured location for German investment in Europe – and second only to the United States world-wide. Almost all German firms in that report with production facilities in Britain were looking to expand their capacity. They know that our average *non-wage* labour costs are 40% lower than in Germany. And one can imagine how they would react in the current situation to my Department's figures this month showing that strikes are at the lowest level since records began over 100 years ago. (Shephard, 1992, p.4)

The first point to make is that the argument in favour of de-centralised rather than centralised wage bargaining is far from conclusive. The literature does seem to suggest that *both* centralised and de-centralised wage bargaining systems are more effective[8] than an intermediate system. It is not clear that de-centralised systems are more desirable than centralised ones, although the institutional framework and negotiating skills required to make a centralised system work are considerable.

Be that as it may, Gillian Shephard's argument seems directly to challenge the excuses Major had provided for Britain's unique failure to sign the Social Chapter of the Treaty. But at least Gillian Shephard is consistent on this point. Major and Hurd's own arguments are contradictory. Are we protecting ourselves from damaging provisions from Europe, and possibly even pointing out the errors of their own ways to them, getting them off the hook, or will it work for some of them but not for us?

There is evidence that some other member states were worried about the impact of the Social Chapter. Catherine Barnard (Barnard, 1992, p.29) has pointed out that the Iberian Countries refused to allow the French to strengthen the Social Chapter again once it had become clear that the British would not sign even a watered down version of the proposals. Paddy Ashdown has shown some support for the Conservative's argument about industrial relations.

I believe that some elements of the social chapter will lead us towards the recreation of the old corporate structure in Europe that we in Britain have got rid of during the past 12 to 15 years. I do not believe that it would be sensible for this country or for Europe. However, I greatly regret that, by opting out of the social chapter, the Government are opting out of the capacity to shape the social institutions. They have many friends in this context – the Portuguese, Irish and others would also wish to ensure that the application of the social chapter should be changed to make it more amenable to the views of their Governments. I do not understand why the British Government have deliberately denied themselves that opportunity.[9]

Equally, however, by refusing to sign the Social Chapter Major's government may not have lost as much influence as some of its critics claim. It is a matter of judgement whether the other states will use the Social Chapter machinery to develop new measures of EC social policy at the risk of excluding the UK, while at the same time placing the UK under pressure to sign up for the measures one by one (assuming Maastricht is eventually ratified). Alternatively the other eleven states may decide to use the Social Chapter relatively little, prefering to develop the social dimension using the pre-Maastricht legislative powers, which include the UK directly. Gillian Shephard clearly wants to believe that the latter scenario is more likely. She has suggested that the other members of the Community would be much more likely to attempt to develop the social dimension through the pre-Maastricht social policy machinery of the Community, in order to include the UK, rather than through the new machinery set up by the 11 at Maastricht. 'We shall have to wait and see to what extent our partners use their Agreement [over the Social Chapter]. I should not be surprised if many wished to continue to seek the maximum possible degree of consensus among the 12, on proposals made under the Treaty of Rome' (Shephard, 1992, p.8).

In the aftermath of the referendum vote against ratification of the Treaty of Maastricht, the prospects for the social dimension to continue primarily to be developed through the existing terms of the Treaty of Rome must seem good. Moreover after the Danish vote Britain's credit to influence the development of social policy seems to have been augmented rather more than it was diminished by Major's attitude in Maastricht. Gillian Shephard's 'success' over the Working Time Directive at the Labour and Social Affair's Council at Lisbon in June 1992 illustrates this influence.

It would be a mistake completely to discount Paddy Ashdown's argument that directives might be effectively imposed on Britain, without British Ministers having had a chance to influence their content. Even before the processes of ratification had seriously been begun some major companies started to implement the policies that they anticipated would be developed under the Social Chapter. For example, Unilever have already indicated their intention to ignore Britain's opt-out on the Social Chapter (Barnard, 1992, p.28). It seems unlikely that they would not press for a relatively 'level playing field' in terms of social and labour market regulation in the EC. The historical evidence, given the crucial role that such companies have played in the development of the EC since the early 1980s (Sandholtz & Zysman, 1989), suggests that such pressure might be successful.

Furthermore, the British opt out on the Social Chapter raises issues of unfair competitive practices. This is the true significance of Jacques Delors' claim after the Maastricht summit that Britain would become a paradise for Japanese invest-ment, a statement gleefully seized by Conservatives in subsequent debates in Parliament. By retaining membership of the EC, and so gaining access to the big market of Europe, but possibly avoiding some of its social and labour regulations, Britain might become a favoured location for inwards investment. However the British posture might be interpreted by the European Court of Justice as an attempt to distort competition, in contravention of Articles 2, 3 and 5 of the Treaty of Rome. Article 5, which has been of particular importance in recent rulings on competition states:

Member States shall take all appropriate measures, whether general or particular, to ensure fulfilment of the obligations arising out of this Treaty or resulting from action taken by the institutions of the Community. They shall facilitate the achievement of the Community's tasks. They shall abstain from any measure which could jeopardise the attainment of the objectives of this Treaty. (Barnard, 1992, p.22)

Some skill and considerable good fortune for John Major in developing a sustainable Tory position on the social dimension, on Europe more generally, and in holding the Tory Party together while gently moving to a more co-operative attitude towards the EC. His position does, however, remain problematic. Firstly, in order to sustain the position, the Treaty of Maastricht needs to be ratified. As the Danish vote has illustrated, this ratification lies beyond Major's control. More difficult still is the problem that even if the Treaty of Maastricht is implemented it will probably serve further to confuse the constitutional character of the EC (which was deeply confused in the early 1980s before EMU and a common security and foreign policy 'pillar' were serious possibilities). Certainly Maastricht did not turn the opaque structures of the EC transparent and accountable. Indeed Major's efforts since the Danish vote represent a more convincing attempt to clarify, decentralise (and, I believe make federal) the structure of the EC than do his achievements at Maastricht, despite his claims that:

The Maastricht treaty marks the point at which, for the first time, we have begun to reverse . . . [the] . . . centralising trend. We have moved decision taking back towards the member states in areas where the Community law need not and should not apply.

Let me inform those who are unaware of that fact that we . . . have secured a legally binding text on subsidiarity. That text provides that any action by the Community shall not go beyond what is necessary to achieve the objectives of the treaty.[10]

Conclusion

It is often thought that the tension between the creation of a large free market in Europe, and the attempts to regulate that market, particularly in order to achieve social ends explains both the acceptance of further European integration by John Major's Conservative Government, and the caution of that acceptance. This chapter has sought to demonstrate that this is not the most fruitful way of understanding the Government's attitude to the social dimension. Both the analysis of the free market critique of the social dimension itself, especially when the social dimension is placed in the context of the overall process of European integration which has been taking place since the mid 1980s, and the discussion of the Parliamentary and policy statements of the Conservative Government concerning the Social Chapter of the Maastricht Treaty demonstrate that neither logical principles nor calculations of the balance of advantage for the UK as a whole determine the Government's attitude to the social dimension. Instead the issue should be understood in terms of Conservative Party management. John Major has used opposition to the Social Chapter as a means of seeming tough on the European issue to his backbenchers, in order to allow him to negotiate a deeper European Union in other areas.

Notes

1. See also his 'Freedom and Progress in Europe', *Modern Management*, 1990 vol.4, no.3, p.11, which contains exactly the same paragraph, but with the phrase between the dashes cut, and reference only to the European union, not to the Charter.

2. Claire Short, *Hansard*, vol.201, no.35, 18 December 1991 col. 338. Short argues that both she and Norman Tebbit have legitimately changed their attitudes towards the EC because of the imposition of a social dimension on the previously free market capitalist system.
3. This point has been recognised recently by a former adviser of Mrs Thatcher. In his recent book *The British Constitution Now*, London: Heinemann, 1992 Ferdinand Mount, the head of Mrs Thatcher's Policy Unit from 1982 until 1984, recognises the failure of the new right to engage in the crucially important activity of setting out the 'legitimate tasks of government' in a free market. The key section of his text is subtitled *The Wealth of Nations Revisited* pp.238–48.
4. John Major, Hansard, vol.201, no.35, 18 December 1991, col. 279.
5. Hansard, vol. 200, no. 30, 11 December 1991, col. 861 and col 874.
6. Hansard vol. 201, no. 36, 19 December 1991, col. 480, emphasis added.
7. Hansard vol. 200, no. 30, 11 December 1991, col. 861.
8. In terms of lowering the unemployment-inflation trade-off, at least in the short run.
9. Hansard, vol.208, no.16, 20 May 1992, col.297.
10. Hansard, vol.208, no.16, 20 May 1992, col.266.

References

Baldwin, R.E. & R. Lyons (1991), 'External economies and European integration: the potential for self-fulfilling expectations' *European Economy*, Special Edition (1), pp.1–26.
Barnard, C. (1992), 'A Social Policy for Europe: Politicians 1:0 Lawyers *Int J Comp LLIR* 8 (1), pp.15–31.
Grahl, J., & P. Teague (1990), *1992: The Big Market*, London, Lawrence & Wishart.
Lingle, C. (1991), 'The EC Social Charter, Social Democracy and Post-1992 Europe', *West European Politics*, 14 (1), pp.129–38.
Majone, G. (1992), 'The European Community between social policy and social regulation', paper delivered at the Annual Meeting of the American Political Science Association, September 3–6.
Marsland, D. (1991), 'Community Charter: rights and wrongs', *Radical Society Discussion Paper*.
Marsland, D. (1991), 'Freedom and progress in Europe', *Modern Management* 4 (3), pp.11–2
Mount, F. (1992), *The British Constitution Now*, London, Heinemann.
Newman, M. (1991), 'Britain and the European Community: the impact of membership', in Lintner, V., and S. Mazey, *The European Community: Economic and Political Aspects*, Maidenhead, McGraw-Hill.
Sandholtz, W., and J. Zysman (1989) '1992: Recasting the European Bargain', *World Politics*, pp.42 vol., no.95–128.
Shephard, G. (1992), Speech to the CBI Conference After Maastricht – Prospects for EC Social Policy, Monday 18 May.
Thatcher, M. (1988), *Britain and Europe*, Conservative Political Centre, London.
Wallace, H. (1990), 'Britain and Europe', in Patrick Dunleavy et al. (eds) *Developments in British Politics 3*, London, Macmillan.
Wincott, D. (1991), 'After Maastricht: British party politics and European Union', *Leicester University Discussion Papers in Politics*, 91/2.
Wincott, D. (1992a), 'The Conservatives and Europe', *Politics Review*, 1 (4): 12–6.
Wincott, D. (1992b), 'The EC Social Charter, Social Democracy and Post-1992 Europe: an alternative prospectus', mimeo, University of Leicester.

18

The whole of Europe: a problem of boundaries, the division of Labour and overlapping forums

Brigid Laffan

The European Community emerged at the end of the 1980s as the core regional organisation for Europe as a whole. The economic and political fortunes of its members and of its neighbours are bound up with developments in European integration. European integration is characterised at present by an intense period of constitution building and the Community is faced with the prospect of a sizeable increase in its membership. This represents a remarkable transformation in the fortunes of the EC if we recall its weak institutional and political capacity for much of the late 1970s and early 1980s.

It is not wise to talk of alternatives to the EC as if Europe-wide forums can replace the European Community. The Monnet method of economic and political integration has proved robust, considerably more so than forms of co-operation based on traditional diplomacy. That said, the European Community is one of many institutions dotting the European landscape; such institutions are evidence of the intensity of institution building in Europe since the Second World War.

Following the collapse of communism and the consequent revolution in world politics, the international system is in a state of flux. The Soviet retreat from empire led to the re-emergence of the countries of East/Central Europe onto the European stage, to a rediscovery of Mitteleuropa, to the reunification of Germany, and ultimately to the disintegration of the Soviet state itself. The cold war which rested on bloc to bloc confrontation and a bipolar world is no more. The transformation of world politics is felt most keenly in Europe as states and regional organisations grapple with the scope and pace of change. A new European order is being fashioned not in a once off manner but is evolving from the existing medley of regional organisations. Almost three years after the events of 1989, there is still considerable uncertainty about the shape and stability of the new Europe: nationalist and ethnic conflict are on the ascent; the future US role in Europe is far from clear; the break-up of the USSR has destabilised arms control; and the geographical extent of the EC is as yet unclear.

A review of institutional arrangements governing relations between states in

Europe point to a density and diversity of ties (see Table 1). There is not as yet a Common European Home, rather a Europe of concentric circles or a series of villages (D'Estaing, 1989, p.654). For the European Community a major question for the 1990s is where its boundaries should lie. Western Europe is no longer protected by the clearly defined limits of the iron curtain.

Table 1 Europe's institutional landscape

European Community	12 member states
NATO	16 member states
North Atlantic Co-operation Council	35 member states
Western European Union	9 member states
EFTA	7 member states
European Economic Area	Europe 12 + EFTA
Council of Europe	27 member states
Sub-Regional Groups	Nordic Co-operation
	Baltic Co-operation
	BENELUX
	Central European Initiative

This chapter examines the Council of Europe, the Conference on Security and Co-operation in Europe and the North Atlantic Co-operation Council as arenas with a remit wider than Western Europe. They are not, however, alternatives to the European Community or European integration.

The Council of Europe – a window of opportunity

The Council of Europe, established in 1949 as a result of the Hague Congress, was regarded as the cradle of European unity. Its membership has gradually expanded from an initial ten member states to the present 27 representing all of the countries of Western Europe and four former communist states: Poland, Hungary, Czechoslovakia and Bulgaria. The latter joined in May 1992.

Notwithstanding the grandiose expectations of its founding fathers, the Council never became the catalyst for European unity for a number of reasons. First, although its policy scope as defined by Article One of its statute envisages agreement and common action in economic, social, cultural, scientific, legal and administrative matters, its capacity to act is limited by weak policy instruments. It negotiates conventions in an intergovernmental forum which must then be ratified by the member states. Second, its institutional apparatus is limited. The Committee of Ministers representing the interests of the member governments is the dominant institution and works on the basis of consensus. The Common Assembly is a delegated parliamentary tier with purely consultative powers. The Secretariat General has approximately 900 full-time officials in contrast to some 14,000 in the EC Commission. From the outset there was tension in the Council of Europe between the pro-integrationist continental European states and those countries, notably Britain and the Scandinavian bloc, that favoured co-operation within an intergovernmental framework.

The Council of Europe settled down to unspectacular co-operation in the social sphere, environmental matters, health and so on. The Council fulfils its most decisive role in the area of human rights. The Convention of Human Rights, and the institutional machinery that it has spawned has created a body of human rights law and given individual citizens an international means of redress; this is of immense value in protecting individual citizens from arbitrary state power. Article 3 of the Statute places human rights at the centre of the Council's activities. It states that: 'Every Member of the Council of Europe must accept the principles of the rule of law and the enjoyment of all persons within its jurisdiction of human rights and fundamental freedoms' (Vaughan, 1976, p. 42).

During the 1960s the Council of Europe also acted a a bridge-builder between the inner six and the 'outer seven' and continues to exercise a role as the manifestation of pan-West European issues with the exception of defence. Article 1 (d) of the Statute excludes national defence from the competence of the Council.

The Council of Europe responded to the renewed dynamism in the European Community by searching for a new role for itself in Europe. The Council commissioned a report from a group of Eminent European Personalities chaired by the former Italian Prime Minister, Emillio Colombo; this group was given the task of outlining the role of the Council in view of developments within the European Community. There were fears that closer integration in the EC might widen the gap between the soon to become Twelve and the outer fringes of Europe. The profound changes in Eastern Europe have provided the Council with a 'window of opportunity' to play an important role in healing the divisions in Europe and in reintegrating the former communist states in the family of pluralist democratic states.

At a meeting of the Committee of Ministers in May 1989, a declaration was adopted on the 'Future Role of the Council of Europe in European Construction' to mark the 40th anniversary of the organisation. A section of the declaration was devoted to relations with East European countries which:

- welcomed the reform policies in Eastern Europe;
- stated that the Council was willing to participate in the CSCE, particularly in its human dimension and in the fields of culture and education;
- stated that the Council would monitor developments in the East European countries with a view to developing contacts and extending co-operation;
- stated that co-operation should lead to the promotion of human rights, the rapprochement of individuals and groups across frontiers (Committee of Ministers, Declaration, 5 May 1989).

The Council adapted its traditional role as bridge-builder to the new Europe. So-called special guest status (observer status) was given to Hungary, Poland, Yugoslavia and the Soviet Union in 1989 and a contact group was set up to develop relations with each country. Special guest status allows the representatives of a country to speak in the Assembly but not to vote. Hungary requested full membership in November 1989 followed by Poland in January 1990 and Czechoslavakia and Yugoslavia in February 1990. Hungary was the first post-communist state to join the Council in November 1990. Poland and Czechoslovakia both acceded in 1991 and Bulgaria in 1992. There is a long line of states that have applied for full membership including the three Baltic states, Romania, Armenia, and Russia. A number of other former Soviet states have applied to special observer status. The timing of membership depends very much on political developments within these countries.

The Council will become a pan-European organisation during the 1990s. Accession to the Council offers the former communist states a stamp of approval for their reform processes from the organisation that prides itself as a promoter and protector of human rights and democratic freedoms. The reform process may be protected by international contacts and commitments. Accession to the Council enables these countries to make contacts with Western Europe in a multilateral forum and enables them to participate in a broad range of functional co-operation. One writer has drawn attention to the role of the Council as a possible stepping stone to membership of the European Community; countries would pass the democratic entrance exam at the Council of Europe first (Kohler, May 1989). Accession to the Convention for the Protection of Human Rights offers citizens additional protection and means of redress as these systems begin to observe the rule of law. It is important that individual citizens are given the right to institute proceedings at the Commission and Court of Human Rights. Membership of the Council of Europe is not regarded as a substitute for EC membership by any state wishing to join the core regional organisation.

The Conference on Security and Co-operation in Europe

Considerable attention is being paid to the Conference on Security and Co-operation in Europe (CSCE) as politicians seek to assemble the components of Europe's new political and security order. It has the advantage of being a multilateral forum with a Euro-Atlantic character. It endured as a forum for East-West contact during the so-called second cold war. The CSCE was part of the era of negotiations that characterised the *détente* of the 1970s. The holding of a pan-European conference on security was an aim of Soviet foreign policy for the entire post-war period. In 1954, Vyacheslav Molotov, the Soviet Foreign Minister suggested a conference of all European states in an attempt to interfere with the ratification of the Treaty of Paris designed to integrate the Federal Republic of Germany in NATO. The Western allies were slow to take up this and subsequent invitations because it was felt that the Soviet Union wanted to use such a conference to drive a wedge between the European allies and the United States and to get recognition for the post-war order. By the early 1970s, superpower *détente* and Chancellor Brandt's Ostpolitik created conditions in which a conference could take place. Preparatory talks were held in autumn 1972 and the Helsinki Final Act was signed in July 1975; initially the Soviet Union anticipated that the conference would last a few weeks.

Thirty-five countries signed the Final Act in 1975. The work of the Helsinki conference was divided into four baskets:

Basket 1: Principles guiding relations between participating states

Basket 2: Economic Co-operation
Basket 3: Co-operation in humanitarian fields
Basket 4: Follow-up

The CSCE negotiations were characterised by hard bargaining; the neutrals and non-aligned group formed a distinct caucus as did the European Community. Negotiations at the CSCE gave the EC its first experience at collective diplomacy.

A number of critical issues dominated the discussions on the four baskets. Two main issues surfaced in Basket One, namely, the applicability of the principles governing relations between states and the question of frontiers. The Soviet Union wanted to draw a distinction between states with different social systems whereas the West European states and Romania insisted that the principles should apply to all states. The Final Act states that the principles apply to relations with all other participating states irrespective of their political, economic or social systems as well as their size, geographical location or level of economic development (Preamble to Final Act, Questions relating to Security in Europe). This was a disavowal of the Brezhnev Doctrine at least at a declaratory level. The Soviet Union wanted the Final Act to recognise the permanence of the post-war borders in Europe. However, the Federal Republic of Germany, Ireland and Spain wanted to allow for the peaceful change of borders; the Final Act states that 'frontiers can be changed in accordance with international law, by peaceful means and by agreement' (Principle 1, Helsinki Final Act).

The basket on economics, science, trade and the environment was the least controversial of all. It was the third basket on humanitarian co-operation that proved to be the most contentious. The Soviet Union did not want any reference to co-operation in this field other than a short passage on educational and cultural exchanges. A *Pravda* editorial regarded this basket as an attempt at 'disarming the socialist countries of their ideology in the face of an offensive by the ideology of the bourgeoisie. Such a demand spells gross interference in the internal affairs of the socialist countries' (Quoted in Heneghan, 1977). On the other hand, the West European countries felt that they had to get concessions in this area. Western governments felt vunerable to domestic criticism if they accepted Soviet domination in Eastern Europe without doing anything for the conditions of the citizens of those countries. Moreover, attention to human rights might undermine Soviet control in the longer term and discontent in Eastern Europe was a threat to the security of the continent. Extensive concessions were gained by the Western powers in this area.

Initially the Warsaw Pact countries wanted to institutionalise the Helsinki process as they saw it as the embryo of a security system. As the negotiations continued they became less enthusiastic but agreed to a review meeting in Belgrade in 1977 which was the main item in basket four.

Follow-up

The CSCE process continued at Belgrade in 1977, Madrid in 1979, and Vienna in 1986–9. A number of expert meetings were held in Athens (1984), Ottawa (1985), Berne (1986), a Cultural Forum in Budapest (1985) and the Stockholm Conference on Confidence-and Security-Building Measures and Disarmanent

(1984–86). The Helsinki process survived the deterioration of superpower relations following the invasion of Afghanistan and the imposition of martial law in Poland in 1981. The West European countries, both neutrals and members of NATO, placed a high priority on maintaining dialogue and *détente* in East-West relations because the East-West divide was more acutely felt in Europe than in the United States.

The cooling of East-West relations in the late 1970s and early 1980s did however place clear limits on the effectiveness of the CSCE process. The follow-up meetings in Belgrade and Madrid gave rise to many procedural wrangles and disputes about the human rights record of the East European countries and the Soviet Union. The Vienna meeting (1986–89) benefited from improved super-power relations and the reform process in the Soviet Union. The 52 page document produced at the end of the meeting was the most ambitious ever in East-West relations. The Soviet Foreign Minister, Eduard Shevardnadze, described the document as a watershed which would speed up the corrosion of the curtain (Keesings Archives, January 1989, p.36413). The collapse of communism was to achieve this within a year of the meeting.

Basket 3 of the Final Document, which was regarded as a side-payment for the recognition of the post-war status quo in Eastern Europe, played a critical role in allowing a small but important protest movement to evolve in Eastern Europe. In the years after Helsinki, the Polish Committee for the Defence of Workers, Charter 77 in Czechoslovakia, and more than 100,000 people looking for exit visas from East Germany all cited the provisions of the Helsinki Final Act in their demands for the observance of human rights (Heneghan 1977, p.90). A recent assessment of the collapse of communism concluded that:

. . . the insistence on the introduction of human rights into the Helsinki process resulted in the slow but inexorable diffusion of the principle into Soviet type politics and contributed qualitatively to weakening the legitimating force of Marxism–Leninism. In effect, human rights transcended the universalist claims of Marxism–Leninism and provided the Central and East European Opposition with an intellectual basis from which to attack and thus erode the official systems. Its significance should not be underestimated (Schopflin, 1990, p.16).

It is fitting that the Helsinki process which contributed to reform and change in Eastern Europe should become one of the core features of the emerging order in Europe.

Helsinki since 1989

With the collapse of communism, the CSCE became an obvious arena for the construction of new relationships in Europe. It was the only pan-European and pan-Atlantic forum available. The German Government placed the Helsinki process at the centre of its strategy for German unification. The CSCE became an important arena for legitimising German unification and for embedding the new Germany in a pan-European framework. Hans Dietrich Genscher, the former Foreign Minister, regarded the CSCE as the 'Magna Carta' of the new Europe.

Before discussing the development of the process since 1989, it is worth considering its main characteristics. First, the Helsinki process established political norms rather than legal requirements for relations between states. Second, the Final Act recognised the formal equality of the participating states, large and small, and made provision for decisions by consensus. Third, the process involved discussions between different groups of states, NATO, EC, Neutral and Non-aligned Group, and the Warsaw Pact states. Fourth, the range of issues included in the remit of the Final Act was very wide, covering most areas of inter-state relations (Laffan, 1992).

A number of major developments have characterised the CSCE since 1989. First, a CSCE summit in November 1990 led to the signing of the Paris Charter for a New Europe which formally ended the cold war and signalled the beginning of new relationships in Europe. The CSCE process was to become a key political organisation in Europe's search for political and economic stability. The Paris Charter consisted of three parts covering the following themes:

1. Democracy, peace and unity
2. Future directions of the CSCE
3. CSCE structures (Laffan, 1992, pp.172–3)

The first part of the document continued the work of the CSCE in establishing norms and principles that should govern the political, economic and legal systems of the participating states. Particular emphasis was placed on human rights, economic freedom, the freedom to choose security arrangements, friendly relations between states and confidence-building measures (Paris Charter, Agence Europe, 22 November 1990).

Second, the Paris Charter heralded the establishment of a regular process of political co-operation in the CSCE. Provision was made for meetings at the level of Heads of Government, Foreign Minister level and at senior official level. The Heads of Government meet at least once every two years. The Foreign Ministers meet at least once every year. A Committee of Senior Officials prepares the work of the Council. Experts meet between sessions. Political dialogue has been greatly strengthened; the CSCE has the appearance of a standing conference.

Third, the Paris Charter provided the CSCE with an embryonic institutional structure. There is a small Secretariat in Prague, a Conflict Prevention Centre (CPC) in Vienna, and an Office of Democratic Institutions and Human Rights in Warsaw. This was formerly known as the Office of Free Elections. The institutionalization of the CSCE continued at the Prague Meeting of Foreign Ministers (January 1992). Provision was made for an intensification of meetings at Senior Official Level, the creation of a Consultative Committee attached to the Conflict Prevention Centre and the setting up of an Economic Forum. Institutions provide the CSCE with a sense of permanence and a capacity for action.

Fourth, the membership of the CSCE has expanded greatly with the disintegration of the Soviet Union and the extension of its geographical remit. The membership of the CSCE has risen from 35 in 1975 to 52 in 1992. In January 1992, ten Republics of the CIS including a number of Asiatic states were admitted as members. Fifth, the CSCE has developed a series of mechanisms to monitor human rights (Moscow mechanism), unusual military activities, and to provide a means for the peaceful settlement of disputes (Valetta mechanism). Sixth, the tasks of the CSCE have expanded to meeting the new security and political challenges in Europe.

In the period following the signing of the Paris Charter, the CSCE has had to respond to considerable and sustained political change, notably, the break-up of the Soviet Union and the war in Yugoslavia. Moreover, the transition from communism to democracy and economic reform is proving difficult for all post-communist societies. Despite the disappearance of the Berlin Wall, Europe is still divided between the stable west and the disintegrating east.

Any assessment of the CSCE must take account of the enormous challenges facing Europe as a whole. The CSCE is looked to as an important component of an evolving security order. It is attempting to preserve stability where it exists, to resolve conflicts, to engage in peace-keeping and to manage the transition from bloc-confrontation to co-operative security arrangements. Since 1989 the scope of what is meant by security in Europe has expanded to include political, military, economic, environmental and human rights concerns. In some ways the reach of the CSCE extends well beyond its grasp.

The experience of the CSCE in dealing with the Yugoslavian crisis, Nagorno-Karobakh and Moldova show that the CSCE was strong on the norms and principles that should govern relations in Europe but short on the means to enforce them. Ethnic/religious conflicts of the kind that are now breaking out in Europe do not lend themselves to easy resolution. Neither the CSCE nor other European organisations that engaged in conlict management could stop the use of force. The consensus rule militates against decisive action.

The Summit meeting heralded as Helsinki 11 in July 1992 has the task of adapting the CSCE to the new realities and to its experience since 1989. Suggestions for development include the establishment of a Troika system to manage CSCE business, the creation of a Security Forum (a mini UN), the development of a blue helmet force for conflict resolution, peace-keeping and peace enforcement, the adoption of the 'consensus-minus-one' principle to security matters and the creation of a High Commissioner for Minorities. There is general recognition that the CSCE is but one part of an extensive system of interlocking institutions and that an important part of the CSCE's work is to legitimise and to provide mandates for other organisations (Gartner 1992, Lucas 1992).

NATO has survived the disappearance of its *raison d'être* for the time being. Since 1989, NATO has been in search of a wider role for itself in the new Europe. NATO declarations now speak of risks and uncertainty rather than threats. NATO is in the process of broadening its concept of security beyond its defence aspects. At its Rome Summit (November 1991), the NATO states recognised the importance of the CSCE in Europe's evolving security architecture. In addition, NATO decided to establish the North Atlantic Co-operation Council (NACC) which would include not only the 16 NATO states but also the countries of East/Central Europe and the CIS. The purpose of the NACC is to respond to the security fears of the countries of East/Central Europe and to deal with post-cold war issues such as the implementation of the Treaty on Conventional Arms Forces in Europe, reforming the armed forces, and the conversion of the defence industries.

Conclusions

Europe is clearly in a period of transition as institutions respond to the challenges of post-communism and the disintegration of the Soviet empire. There are a medley of institutions with over-lapping membership and functions. A division of labour of sorts is being worked out. First, it is clear that the core of economic integration and co-operation in Europe rests on the activities of the European Community. The resurgence of formal integration arising from the 1992 project is driving economic integration. The EFTA states are no longer content with an EEA agreement and want full-membership. The three countries of East/Central Europe see their Association Agreements as precursors to full-membership.

The Community is also an important component of Europe's security environment as economic well-being is such an important part of security. Increasingly, the Community is concerned with the wider aspects of security and is committed in the Maastricht Treaty to a common foreign and security policy. This Treaty establishes an organic link between the Community and the Western European Union. The WEU is in turn linked to NATO.

The CSCE provides a Euro-Atlantic roof for European co-operation in a wide range of issue areas. Its most significant work is in the field of security where it is attempting to build a system of common security based on agreed principles and norms of behaviour. Since 1989 the CSCE has been provided with a set of institutions to translate the principles into reality. It is constrained by the intractability of the ethnic/nationalist conflicts it is confronted with and its weak capacity for action. The CSCE will be developed and strengthened as the 1990s progress.

The Council of Europe, once a distinctly Western European organisation, is rapidly becoming a Europe wide forum as more states join and are given observer status. The Council's role in promoting democratic values and in protecting human rights is very necessary in post-communist Europe. For the countries of East/Central Europe, rejoining Europe means ultimately joining the European Community.

References

d'Estaing, V., (1989), 'The Soviet Union and Europe', *International Affairs*, 4, Autumn, pp.653–58.

Gartner, H. (1992), 'The Future of the Institutionalization of the CSCE Process', paper presented to a conference on 'Redefining the CSCE: Challenges and Opportunities in the New Europe', Helsinki.

Heneghan, T.E. (1977), 'Human Rights Protests in Eastern Europe', *World Today*, pp.90–100.

Kohler, B. (1989), *Frankfurter Allegemeine Zeitung*, 5 May.

Laffan, B. (1992), *Integration and Cooperation in Europe*, London, Routledge.

Lucas, M. (1992), 'The Challenge of Helsinki 11', paper presented to a conference on 'Redefining the CSCE: Challenges and Opportunities in the New Europe', Helsinki.

Schopflin, G. (1990), 'The end of Communism in Eastern Europe, *International Affairs*, 66, January, pp.3–16.

Vaughan, R. (1976), *Post-War Integration in Europe*, London, Edward Arnold.

Reports

Conference on Security and Cooperation in Europe, 1975, *Helsinki Final Act*, June.
Conference on Security and Cooperation in Europe, 1990, *Paris Charter*, November.
Declaration on the Future Role of the Council of Europe in European Construction, Committee of Ministers, 5 May 1989.
Declaration by the Twelve on CSCE, 77th EPC Ministerial Meeting, 20 February 1990, Dublin Castle.
Keesings Archives 1989–1992.
Report of the Colombo Commission to the Council of Europe, June 1986.
Third Medium Term Plan 1987–1991, Council of Europe, December 1986.

19

The UK and the Exchange Rate Mechanism 1978–90

Helen Thompson

The UK and the birth of the Exchange Rate Mechanism

From the first murmurings from politicians on the desire for a zone of monetary stability across the EC, the UK was isolated. What was to become the Exchange Rate Mechanism (ERM) had its roots in the economic difficulties caused by floating exchange rates to France and, particularly, West Germany, rather than to the UK. The fundamental problem that Helmut Schmidt and Giscard d'Estaing saw as afflicting their respective economies in 1978 was a weak dollar and the failure of that currency to perform as a credible international reserve asset. In the words of one Treasury official, the system was born out of Schmidt's 'despair at the misbehaviour of the dollar' and represented a 'poking out of tongue at the raped international currency'.[1]

Schmidt's despair was threefold. First, with the Deutschmark bearing the brunt of the dollar's weakness, German goods were becoming increasingly uncompetitive and markets were being lost to the United States. Second, the floating dollar was producing an inflationary environment which was difficult for any state to insulate itself from. Third, he believed that the weak dollar represented an abdication of economic leadership from the United States to match what he considered its ineptitude on the diplomatic and security front. He found an ally in Giscard d'Estaing who believed that some monetary stability would inject a measure of discipline into the French economy. He was further anxious that the wild downward float of the dollar was making the Common Agricultural Policy (CAP) difficult to operate and that as a result French farmers were suffering. In sum, the prime interest of West Germany and France in calling for a system of exchange rate management in the EC was to protect their interests from those of the United States.[2]

While the Labour Government was offered a seat at a triangular negotiating table to discuss the practicalities of a system, before long it was clear that the UK would not be entering the proposed ERM. At one level this represented a political decision: the Prime Minister, James Callaghan, was not uninterested in participating but he did not believe that he could take either the Cabinet or the Labour Party with him. (George, 1990, p.127) At the same time, the Treasury developed an intellectual case that the proposed system was not compatible with the UK's economic interests. First, they argued that sterling alone among the EC states was a petro-currency which meant that it tended to move in the opposite direction to the other currencies as the price of oil fluctuated. Second, the UK's trading position had benefited rather than suffered from floating sterling. Third, it was unwise for the UK with its strong Atlantic trading links to be part of a system which could be construed as anti-dollar. Fourth, the proposed system would benefit strong currency states such as West Germany: the burden of adjustment would be on weak currencies and so the UK would be left having to use a deflationary policy to maintain sterling at an artificially high rate against the Deutschmark. The UK economy had suffered previously from the deflationary consequences of fixed exchange rates under the Gold Standard and Bretton Woods and was forced to leave the European snake after only six weeks of membership in 1972. The only support for participation in the system came from the Foreign Office who believed that it would strengthen the UK's position in the EC and that, contrary to the Treasury's arguments, it made sense on economic grounds.[3]

However, what is clear is that there was some divergence in how the UK government and Treasury officials saw what was being proposed and how the other EC states viewed the development. While the UK policy-making establishment debated the wisdom of sterling returning to a fixed exchange rate system to provide counter-inflationary discipline, what France and West Germany envisaged was more akin to a 'dirty float' to protect competitiveness against the United States.[4]

As such, when the system came into operation in March 1979, it represented an attempt to combine some of the advantages of a fixed exchange rate system with flexibility for the currencies of the EC minus sterling. Each member agreed a central rate for its currency in terms of a weighted composite basket currency known as the ECU. A collective set of central rates in a parity grid was created and it was these rates which had to be defended by all participants within 2.25 per cent of the parity or a 6 per cent band for the Italian lira. Pressure on the parities was recognised through a divergent indicator. If a single currency diverged by more than 75 per cent of its permitted divergence from its ECU rate, then some form of corrective action had to be taken, most likely intervention from central banks or through a change in interest rates. In the event of sustained pressure, the parity rates could be realigned relatively easily by collective agreement.[5]

Indeed, during its first four years, the ERM was characterised by realignments. The first realignment came only six months after the system began. By March 1983, there were seven realignments involving at one time or another all seven currencies and the Italian lira had been devalued four times. What the system achieved in these years was not inflation convergence as should occur in a fixed rate system and what the UK policy-making establishment appeared to debate the benefits of in 1978, but a measure of exchange rate stability.[6]

The Conservative Government and ERM 1979–83

When the Conservative government came into office in May 1979, it announced that it was reviewing the Labour government's policy of non-membership. In opposition, it had condemned the Labour government's policy: for example, when Callaghan finally announced in the House of Commons that the UK would not join the ERM, Thatcher declared, 'This is a sad day for Europe.' In office, the government was determined to show goodwill as an EC member on the issue. Thus, it agreed to contribute 20 per cent of its gold and dollar reserves to the European Monetary Co-operation Fund of the system and then dropped the Labour government's claim for an automatic interest rate subsidy if the UK were to join the ERM.[7]

However, at the same time, the new government was committed to a money supply target policy as the fundamental tool of economic management. This was incompatible with ERM membership in two ways. First, while the government wanted to direct monetary policy at monetary targets, ERM membership would have meant directing monetary policy at the exchange rate. Second, the central bank intervention required to keep a currency stable means that money will enter and depart circulation according to the requirements of that objective whatever the consequences for monetary growth. This discongruence in monetary objectives with the ERM states was compounded by the fact that rather than exhibiting any stability, sterling was now dramatically appreciating in the exchange markets with interest rates high and oil prices rising. As a result, the ERM states themselves were now not particularly keen for UK membership of the system believing that sterling's strength would be disruptive. All in all, this meant that the government's review of membership did little more than go through the motions.[8]

The issue briefly resurfaced in March 1980 when the West German government came to the view that UK membership would be beneficial to the ERM system. Chancellor Schmidt came to London and suggested to Thatcher that ERM membership could increase the UK's chances of securing a satisfactory deal on its budgetary contributions. However, the government showed little interest. With the Medium Term Financial Strategy with its commitment to £M3 as the be all and end all of policy only a few days away from completion and sterling continuing its meteoric rise, ERM membership at this point would have required a complete U-Turn in policy. As such, Schmidt's offer was not seriously explored.[9]

Nevertheless, eighteen months later, the government was without public notice completing that U-Turn of it own accord and the ERM issue resurfaced. By the autumn of 1981, the pound had been allowed to fall from its heights of 1980 and monetary policy was being used to stabilise sterling at its new level rather than to control £M3. Now, the government was demonstrating that it was prepared to order interest rate changes both to bring sterling down and to hold sterling up even if it was not prepared to admit that that is what it was doing (Smith, 1987, pp.98–104). With the battle against inflation now moved from the monetary to the fiscal front, the government was in effect operating a macro-economic policy, not particularly distinguished from most of the ERM states.

It was against this background that a relatively serious review of policy took place (Lawson, 1992, 112–13). The Foreign Office was now joined by the Bank of England in arguing for membership. The Bank believed that the system was now demonstrating its effectiveness in securing exchange rate stability and was anyway never convinced by the money supply policy. However, neither the Foreign Office nor the Bank of England was viewed favourably by Thatcher. Moreover, the Foreign Office's position was weakened by the fact that the Foreign Secretary, Lord Carrington, was not particularly interested in economic issues and, thus, was ill-equipped to press the department's case.[10]

At the same time, fundamental opposition remained in the Treasury and Number 10 (Lawson, 1992, p.113). While the exchange rate was now central to economic policy, no one particularly wanted to admit this and a lot of lip service was still being paid to the importance of monetary targets. There was neither a conceptual shift to thinking in terms of the operational guide to policy, whatever the actual policy being pursued, nor a willingness to engage in the rhetorical U-turn which would have been required. As a result, the government decided to remain outside ERM. Thus, the government finished its first term of office committed to a policy which was reasonably compatible with ERM membership but operating outside the system.[11]

A government divided 1985–1988:

By the time ERM membership became a salient issue again in 1985, the ERM itself had undergone a profound change. From operating as a 'dirty float' to protect competitiveness in which essentially monetary policy was the only macro-economic tool assigned to exchange rate management and realignments were frequent, the ERM was now akin to a relatively fixed-rate system. As a result, it now contained a distinct counter-inflationary bias both in monetary and fiscal terms. In regard to the former, the bias operated through West German leadership with the Deutschmark rather than the divergent indicator being the benchmark of the system. The Bundesbank set its monetary policy to fit its counter-inflationary objectives and others adjusted their monetary policy accordingly. A rise in West German interest rates meant that the other states would usually raise their rates so as to maintain the premium between their rates and those of the Bundesbank. As such, these states achieved counter-inflationary credibility in the financial markets through importing West German stability. In fiscal terms, the aim was now to use fiscal policy to defend parities rather than resorting to devaluation when those parities were under pressure. Thus, the weak currency states now looked to exercise tight fiscal control through public expenditure cuts and tax increases. In sum, from 1983 onwards, the ERM operated with less realignments and with a new economic and political credibility attached to maintaining parities.[12]

This change in the operation of the ERM is important in understanding the development of UK policy. It meant that by the time the government got around to giving very serious thought to the possibility of membership, they were talking about entry to a system in which the ERM states were already embarked on a common journey of convergence towards West German standards of inflation and restraint. The catalyst for the renewed debate in the UK was the sterling crisis of January and February 1985 when the pound fell as low as $1.03. Since the 1983 general election, the government had generally allowed sterling to float downwards to try and boost competitiveness. However, it was not now prepared to countenance the inflationary consequences of parity against the dollar or for the belief to take hold in the markets that it did not have an exchange rate policy. Consequently, interest rates were raised during January from 9.5 to 14 per cent in an eighteen month period to protect the pound (Smith, 1987, pp.119–23).

The costs of the crisis were clear. On the one hand, it left the UK with both exceptionally high nominal interest rates and even higher real rates. At the same time, it ruled out the income tax cuts which the government was previously proudly promising for the forthcoming budget since the markets were now looking for fiscal restraint from the government. Moreover, there were clear lessons to be learnt from the crisis which directly related to the issues that the ERM sought to address. First, the crisis rammed home the fact that no UK government could afford for the markets to believe that it did not have an opinion on the exchange rate without very damaging consequences. Second, while the ERM currencies also fell sharply against the dollar in January and February 1985, none of them were forced to raise rates 4.5 per cent in eighteen months. Indeed, in January, France and Italy were able to cut their rates. For the ERM currencies, their value against the perennially volatile dollar was evidently not the ultimate arbiter of their credibility. Third, as a result of the crisis, the government re-adopted an economic policy quite compatible with ERM membership: the government was recommitted to exchange rate stability, monetary policy was being used to achieve that end and restraint was being shown in fiscal policy.[13]

Certainly, the crisis was enough to convince both the Chancellor, Nigel Lawson, and his Treasury officials that the time was now right to enter ERM. From the spring of 1985, a new policy debate was initiated with support for membership now coming from most of the Cabinet, the Treasury, the Foreign Office and the Bank of England. (Smith, 1992, p.48). In addition, 1985 saw a succession of financial commentators and economic bodies, ranging from the clearing banks to the CBI making calls for the UK to enter the ERM. However, Thatcher, provided with intellectual ammunition from her former economic adviser Sir Alan Walters, remained unconvinced and vetoed Lawson's proposal to enter in November 1985 (Lawson, 1992, pp.497–499). All Lawson was able to secure from Thatcher was a public commitment that the UK would enter the ERM 'when the time is right.'[14]

The underlying reason for Thatcher's opposition to ERM membership is difficult to assess. Some have understood her as being very conscious that ERM membership would have put an undesirable onus on interest rate rises in the run-up to an election if there was a run on sterling. However, such an argument for non-membership would only make sense if Thatcher was prepared to adopt an attitude of benign neglect towards the exchange rate which she manifestly was not after 1985. Indeed, as Sam Brittan, commented in dismissing the argument, a much smaller rise in rates might be necessary inside ERM than outside where doubts existed about the government's exchange rate objectives. Thatcher's own explanations of her opposition were somewhat contradictory. On successive occasions, she declared that membership would be too 'deflationary' and too 'inflationary' (Brittan, 1989, p.33). Later, she said that she did not want to use up 'precious reserves' but was quite prepared to countenance using reserves to defend sterling outside the system. Offering a different explanation in 1986, she told *The Financial Times* that her concern was to avoid a repetition of the abortive entry to the snake in 1972. On the other hand, the significance of Sir Alan Walters is somewhat debatable: Treasury officials, for example, have commented that he was the least of their problems in trying to persuade her of the merits of entry (Smith, 1992, p.60).[15]

Nevertheless, whatever the incoherencies in Thatcher's public position, there was a certain logic to her opposition in terms of the interests of the Conservative governments in the run-up to the next election. If Lawson had won the argument in November 1985, sterling would have almost certainly have entered the ERM with a central rate of around DM3.70. While realignments would have been possible, there would have been a definite onus to maintain the parity at least in the short to medium term. Yet what non-membership allowed the government to do was to use a substantial fall in the price of oil to secure export led growth through a depreciation in sterling through the first nine months of 1986: the inflationary consequences of the devaluation were offset by a fall in the price of oil. While Lawson is now claiming that the 1986 devaluation was an accident to which he mistakenly acquiesced by failing to take sufficient action early enough to stop it, this view is hard to reconcile with the fact that the government cut interest rates four times on a falling pound (Lawson, 1992, pp 647–57). Rather, the devaluation was crucial to the UK enjoying an expanding growth rate in the run-up to the 1987 general election (Keegan, 1989, pp.182–86). By contrast, the ERM states led by West Germany allowed the full benefit of the oil price to feed through into a lower inflation rate. From now on the UK and the ERM states were on increasingly divergent economic paths.[16]

By October 1986, the government's position on ERM membership was ever more ambivalent. It considered that the pound was now low enough against the European currencies and that the aim should be to stabilize the pound but Thatcher was still not prepared to countenance ERM membership (Keegan, 1989, pp.190–92). This left a policy vacuum in which Thatcher was vetoing what Lawson and the Treasury wanted to do but not offering an alternative framework for monetary policy. At the same time, Lawson was committing himself to a policy of fiscal expansion in terms of both increases in public expenditure and income tax cuts which was out of step with the ERM states which he wished to join (Smith, 1987, p.128). Rather than seeking convergence of inflation, Lawson was adding fuel to an inflationary fire already kindled by financial deregulation and the easy accessibility of credit. What was perhaps striking was Lawson's repudiation of the fact that his fiscal expansion would make any difference in terms of inflation when the ERM states which he wished to join practised such demand management most assiduously.

However, Lawson appeared unaware of the contradiction. Rather, faced with the vacuum in monetary policy and seizing the opportunity offered by the international Louvre Accord on exchange rate stability, he embarked on a new policy from February 1987 of covertly shadowing the Deutschmark from a rate of about DM2.80 to DM3.00 (Smith, 1992, pp.98–106). Although it is implausible to suggest as some have done that Thatcher herself was unaware of the policy, there is no doubt that some at the Bank of England were deeply dissatisfied with what was happening and considered resignation.[17]

Lawson's hope appeared to be that successful experiment would demonstrate to Thatcher the case for ERM membership. However, shadowing certainly did not represent a *de facto* form of ERM membership as some later claimed. First, it did not guarantee any intervention from other EC central banks to defend the target.

Second, it did not provide a framework of stability for industry because it was not an announced policy. Third, without a formal cap on sterling's upper limit and collective intervention to support that cap, the speculators were given a likely option on the upward movement of sterling. Fourth, and most fundamentally, shadowing was distinguished from ERM membership by the absence of any fiscal dimension to the policy. As sterling came under upward pressure through 1987 and 1988, shadowing meant that monetary policy gradually became looser. Inside ERM, there would have been a certain obligation to tighten fiscal policy to offset lower interest rates but in fact the government's commitment to fiscal expansion reached its zenith in 1988 with Lawson's tax cutting budget.[18]

Shadowing came to an end in the spring of 1988. By the first week of March, the pound reached DM2.98 despite the Bank of England spending more than £4 billion to keep it down. As a result, Thatcher told Lawson that there would be no more intervention and with the DM3.00 cap broken, sterling surged. Lawson tried to keep a cap on that appreciation by ordering three further cuts in interest rates. However, by June, monetary policy was detached from the exchange rate again and was being used to restrict the inflationary pressure in the economy without an intermediate target (Smith, 1992, pp.136–42).

The end of shadowing and the subsequent change in policy had two important consequences in terms of the ERM debate. First, from this point onwards, the public feud between Thatcher and Lawson over exchange rate management generally and ERM membership in particular intensified. While Lawson continued to make known his preference for ERM entry, Thatcher told the House of Commons that 'there is no way in which one can buck the market' (Smith, 1992, p.137). Second, in allowing the pound to rise and resorting to a tight monetary policy to try and reduce the growing inflationary pressure, the government reacted in the one way in which ERM membership would not have allowed. The standard action of the ERM states to the situation which the UK faced in the summer of 1988 – namely inflation and a deterioration in the balance of payments – was to act to control credit, encourage wage restraint or to increase taxes. All of these actions, if they had been undertaken by the UK government would have addressed the underlying source of inflationary pressure in the economy. Yet the reality was that control of credit, some form of an incomes policy and an increase in taxes were a complete anathema to the government, Lawson and the Treasury as well as Thatcher. While Thatcher alone did not want to enter the ERM, it was the economic-policy making establishment as a whole which repudiated the particular counter-inflationary management of the economy practised by the ERM states. Without that counter-inflationary framework, successful participation by the UK in the ERM at this time would have been very difficult.[19]

A new challenge to the UK: the monetary union debate

By the summer of 1988, the government was drifting even further away from the ERM states in terms of economic performance: most notably, while inflation continued to fall in the ERM states, it was now rising in the UK. Nevertheless, in terms of its position in the EC, a new imperative for ERM membership was appearing in the form of a new interest among the ERM states, led by the French, in a monetary union within the EC. Despite changes made to the operation of the

ERM in September 1987, known as the Basle-Nybourg reforms, the French government believed that the system was no longer delivering satisfactory economic outcomes for states other than West Germany. It considered that the Bundesbank was not forced to intervene enough to limit the strength of the Deutschmark. Most fundamentally, it was concerned that German monetary policy was too tight and aiming to secure levels of inflation below that which was desirable in view of rising unemployment. As such, the French government believed that if a European central bank were to replace the Bundesbank as the dominant monetary force in Europe, then the interest of all the EC states would be represented when monetary policy was being decided rather than just West German interests.[20]

In June 1988, the Delors committee was set up to examine the means necessary to achieve a monetary union. Although the idea of monetary union was dismissed by most in the UK government including Lawson, it did not seek to block the establishment of the committee. In part, the government was caught by the fact that the Single European Act set out the 'progressive realisation of monetary union' as an objective of the EC and this was used as the terms of reference of the committee. At the same time, Thatcher at least appeared to be convinced that the committee was not a serious enterprise. This misunderstanding was buttressed by a tendency both on her part and the Treasury's to see the debate as the product of Delors's alleged federalist ambitions rather than dissatisfaction with the ERM. As the committee deliberated, it became clear that the UK representative, Robin Leigh-Pemberton's influence on the proceedings was being weakened by the UK's non-participation in the ERM. As such, those in favour of entry believed that the their case was strengthened by the momentum towards monetary union. They argued that if the UK wanted to put the brakes on monetary union, then it needed credibility which could only come from ERM entry.[21]

Certainly, the other EC states were now anxious for the UK to join the system as soon as possible and the issue was becoming a touchstone of the UK's credibility in the EC. The UK's own commissioners started to make regular appeals for the UK to join. Indeed, on one occasion, the French and German governments threatened to withhold their agreement to the liberalisation of financial services unless UK membership of ERM was forthcoming.[22]

At the same time, the City became increasingly anxious that London's position as a financial centre would be threatened by the UK standing aside from EC monetary developments. The possibility now existed that Frankfurt could host a European central bank and in the process dislocate London as the operation centre of exchange and money markets in the EC. At the very least, City interests declared, the UK needed to be in the ERM as soon as possible. These anxieties in the financial service sector were understood by many in the government. Moreover, they were hard to ignore since the sector was central to the prosperity of the south-east of England which was the Conservative party's electoral basis and was increasingly the engine of growth in the UK economy (Moran, 1991, p.5).[23]

It was not surprising then that after the Delors Report was published in April 1989 and was enthusiastically received by all member states except the UK, Lawson and Howe put renewed pressure on Thatcher to move forward on the issue. After being threatened with a joint resignation from the pair if she did not replace 'when the time is right' with an actual timetable for membership, Thatcher finally agreed to what became known as the Madrid conditions for entry (Smith, 1992, p.164). These conditions were that the UK would enter when its rate of inflation fell towards those of the ERM states, the single market was completed and capital and financial markets were fully liberated.[24]

The most important criterion was seen to be that of inflation convergence because it served as a means of reconciling what was politically necessary in terms of the EC with what was economically very difficult in view of the particular counter-inflationary policy to which the government was committed. The problem for the government was that ERM membership at this time would have probably resulted in lower interest rates but with the government unwilling to countenance fiscal demand management or controls on credit or income, high interest rates were the only available means left to reduce inflation. The government was determined to reduce inflation and inflation could only be reduced outside the ERM within its own terms of reference.

Nevertheless, whatever hopes Lawson and Howe placed on the Madrid conditions as the way forward were soon dashed. In July 1989, Howe was sacked from his position as Foreign Secretary. Then, Thatcher allowed a situation to develop where her anti-membership economic adviser Alan Walters was perceived to be challenging the authority of Lawson on exchange rate management and ERM membership and Lawson resigned in protest.

By the end of October 1989, the pursuit of the Madrid conditions and the prospect of actual ERM entry before the general election appeared to be of little relevance. After Lawson's resignation, John Major took up the Chancellorship without giving any indication that he shared Lawson's conviction in the issue (Smith, 1992, p.165). At the same time, Thatcher declared that the whole system operated under a 'higgledy-piggledy set of rules'. Most fundamentally, the government made little effort to act against the fall in sterling precipitated by Lawson's resignation (Smith, 1992, pp.157–58). As such, it demonstrated both that it was not fully committed to exchange rate management and that it was prepared to see inflation rise rather than seeking the convergence prescribed in the Madrid conditions.[25]

The macro-economic reason for the disbandment of the conditions was that the government was simply not prepared to raise interest rates again whether the position of sterling demanded it or not (Goodhart, 1991, p.69). It was now not only necessary to get inflation down but to both avoid the growing risk of recession and protect mortgage holders from further interest rate increases. The government now seemed to believe that with 15 per cent interest rates, sterling could not come under indefinite downward pressure. However, it was that this belief was mistaken which was the eventual source of Thatcher's acceptance of membership.

The road to entry

As 1990 began, the new Foreign Secretary, Douglas Hurd was worried that non-membership was exacting an ever greater cost for the UK in its EC affairs. At the Strasbourg summit, at the end of December 1989, the UK was isolated and forced to agree to setting up two inter-governmental conferences (IGC's) to secure the necessary amendments to the Treaty of Rome in order to facilitate monetary and political union respectively. These conferences were scheduled to begin in December 1990. Hurd was alarmed at the prospect of the IGC starting without the UK having a credible position from which to argue its case and believed that ERM entry was essential to that credibility. As such, Hurd set to work to convince Major that ERM membership was now an overriding necessity.[26]

By budget day in March, Major was converted enough to re-instate the Madrid conditions into the public forum by noting that encouraging progress was being made towards the fulfilment of the conditions (Smith, 1992, p.168). He, thus, began a process in which what was meant by inflation convergence was redefined to suit the government's inability to actually achieve that convergence.

However, the key factor remained Thatcher's position and here the crucial events by which Thatcher came to accept the necessity of membership took place in March-April 1990. What the government faced was a dual crisis in terms of the UK's position in the EC and the economy. In terms of the EC, the crisis appeared in the form of a joint Franco-German initiative to hasten union. It was now absolutely fruitless for Thatcher to hope, as she had previously shown signs of doing, that the threat of monetary union would disappear under German procrastination. The imperative to be inside ERM before December 1990 was now further increased.[27]

In terms of the economy, sterling came under intense downward pressure through March 1990. Market attention zoomed in on the fact that the government was both operating without a monetary framework and was unwilling to defend the currency. With inflation rising again, the government could ill afford a further significant depreciation in sterling (Smith, 1992, pp.166–68). If sustained high interest rates could not succeed in achieving an appreciation in sterling, then the government was left with a bare counter-inflationary cupboard. Unwilling as it was to countenance a U-Turn in terms of wage control, credit control and fiscal policy, the government was left with the sole option of using a credible commitment to ERM membership to strengthen sterling to reduce inflation. If the markets were convinced that the government was committed to ERM entry and, thus, a floor for sterling, then it was highly probable that they would buy sterling to take advantage of the UK's high interest rates. With an appreciating pound, in addition to a tight monetary policy, the government could hope that inflation would finally come down.

In the same month, a rise in unemployment indicated that the government's aim of avoiding a recession was in some jeopardy (McKie, 1992, p.58). Combined with the fact that mortgage holders were continuing to suffer, this meant that the ability to reduce rates in the foreseeable future assumed a renewed importance for the government. However, such a course of action again required that sterling be credible in the financial markets and such credibility required a commitment to ERM membership. Once that credibility was achieved, interest rates could come down. To all intents and purposes, the government now possessed no means of achieving its macro-economic ends outside ERM. Thus, by the end of April, Major was able to secure Thatcher's acquiescence to the principle of membership and they looked to autumn of that year as the date of entry.

The problem for the government was that by the time September came, its economic strategy based on impending membership was seriously compromised. Yet within its own terms of reference, it had little option but to stick to its timetable for membership not least because of the forthcoming IGC. First, while the commitment to ERM had produced the desired appreciation in sterling, inflationary pressure continued to mount elsewhere in the economy (Smith, 1992, p.169). By whatever yardstick inflation was measured, the government faced going into a fixed exchange rate system with rising inflation. The situation was then compounded by the fact that as September came to an end, sterling began to fall again and the government was unable to stop that. Second, rather than being able to use ERM membership to avert a recession, the economy was already fast moving into recession by September (Smith, 1992, p.178). The government was in an ambivalent position. At one level, it was now a particularly inopportune time to enter the ERM: while the ability to cut interest rates would now be dependent on sterling's relationship to the Deutschmark, the recession would produce demands for just such action. However, with sterling falling and the government unwilling to sacrifice its counter-inflationary commitment, neither could the government begin to cut interest rates outside ERM. ERM membership alone could provide a counter-inflationary control against a reduction in interest rates.

Thus, Thatcher and Major agreed that entry should go ahead as planned. On 5 October 1990, it was announced that sterling would enter the system with 6 per cent margins and a central rate of DM2.95. Moreover, with the onset of recession and the Conservative Party conference due to begin the next week, Thatcher insisted that entry be accompanied with an immediate cut in interest rates to 14 per cent.

The consequences of entry

The government's embrace of membership, however, could not detract from the fact that entering the ERM in a recession involved quite different implications than those envisaged when the initial commitment to membership was made. Most fundamentally, entry at the rate of DM2.95 now represented a relatively high rate for sterling. It was clear that in the months preceding membership, sterling's appreciation contributed to the fall in orders and output of manufacturing industry. Now those companies would face the combination of falling domestic demand with competing abroad at a permanently difficult exchange rate and with unit costs still rising faster than elsewhere in the EC. Thus, while ERM membership could provide interest rate cuts which would hopefully stimulate economic activity, it would also tighten the squeeze for firms in the international sector.[28]

As a result of the manner in which ERM entry was finally achieved, the seeds were sewn of the policy disaster culminating in the exit from the ERM two years later in September 1992. First the fact that in both March 1990 and October 1990 the government was faced with no alternative to ERM membership within its own terms of reference meant that no thorough analysis of the nature and the likely consequences of the action was undertaken by the Treasury. Furthermore, the essentially short term partisan nature of the decision meant that there was a lack of consensus within the economic policy-making establishment as to what it was designed to achieve. For instance, the Bank of England with far greater awareness than either the government or the Treasury of the likely depth of the recession, believed that the inevitable deflationary bias of the ERM was just what was needed to deal with the long term consequences of Lawson's boom. Yet, there is no evidence that this is how the Prime Minister and the Chancellor or the Treasury understood membership.[29]

Second, with the government having delayed membership for so long after 1985 and in the process secured the benefits of first and independent fiscal policy and then a tight monetary policy, the UK entered the system with a fundamentally different economic position to the other ERM states. Most notably, the UK was in a unilateral recession and faced a distinct problem of corporate and personal indebtedness. While the cost of German reunification would be a problem for all the ERM states, the existing ERM states were not in such a fundamentally dissimilar economic position to Germany as the UK.

Third, the timing of the entry before the Conservative Party conference and the accompaniment of an interest rate cut with the announcement meant that the impression was given to the UK's ERM partners that the government was clutching at straws. This was compounded by the fact that the ERM states were not consulted on the details of entry including the choice of a central parity nor fully forewarned of the announcement itself. Certainly, it was clear in the preceding months that the Bundesbank was not enthusiastic about the UK's entry to the system in 1990 in view of rising inflation and the depth of the balance of payments deficit. In essence, the government achieved little credibility or goodwill from the manner in which entry was secured.[30]

In conclusion, the Labour government's isolation outside the ERM was not fully overturned by the Conservative government's entry into the system in October 1990. Despite the fact that the government, supported by the Treasury, the Foreign Office and the Bank of England, came to think that ERM membership was the way forward, the manner in which that conclusion was reached meant the government did not come to think of membership in quite the same terms as the ERM states did. As such, the UK government entered the ERM without having a clear conceptual idea of what ERM membership meant, not as an expedient action for itself but as a participant in a system which had evolved without it.

Notes

1. Non-attributable interview with a former Treasury official in 1992.
2. *The Economist*, 28 October 1978, p.23; *The Guardian*, 15 April 1991, p.13; Non-attributable interview with Treasury official.
3. HM Government, 1978, *The European Monetary System*, HMSO, London, pp.1–13; *The Economist*, 21 October 1978, p.58 and p.69; *The Economist*, 28 October 1978, p.23; Non-attributable interviews with former Treasury and Foreign Office officials in 1992.
4. *The Guardian*, 15 April 1991, p.13.
5. Treasury and Civil Service Select Committee, 1985, *The Thirteenth Report: The European Monetary System*, HMSO, London, pp.viii-xi; *The Guardian*, April 15 1991, p.13.
6. The Treasury and Civil Service Select Committee, 1985, *The Thirteenth Report: The European Monetary System*, HMSO, London, p.xi.
7. *The Times*, 7 December 1992, 8; *The Financial Times*, 12 May 1979, p.30; *The Financial Times*, 14 May 1979, p.1; *The Financial Times*, 22 June 1979, p.1; *The Financial Times*, 17 July 1979, p.32.
8. *The Financial Times*, 23 July 1979, p.20; Non-attributable interviews with former Treasury officials in 1992.

9. *The Economist*, 8 March 1980, pp.54–55; *The Financial Times*, 6 March 1980, p.1; *The Financial Times*, 28 March 1980, p.3; Non-attributable interview with former Treasury official in 1992.
10. Non-attributable interviews with former Treasury and Foreign Office officials in 1992.
11. Conclusions drawn from non-attributable interviews with former Treasury officials in 1992.
12. Ungerer, H. et al, 1989, *The EMS developments and perspectives*, IMF, Washington DC, p.2; *The Economist*, 19 September 1987, p.86; *The Guardian*, 15 April 1991, p.13.
13. *The Economist*, 15 January 1985, p.86; *The Economist*, 2 February 1985, p.97; *The Financial Times*, 2 February 1985, p.3.
14. *The Economist*, 23 November 1985, p.35; The Treasury and Civil Service Select Committee, 1985, *Minutes of evidence taken before the treasury and civil service select sub-committee*, HMSO, London, pp.2–14.
15. *The Financial Times*, 11 June 1986, p.12; *The Financial Times*, 19 November 1986, p.1.
16. *OECD Economic Outlook*, June 1987, p.128.
17. Non-attributable interview with former Bank of England official in 1992.
18. *The Economist*, March 12 1988, p.26; The Treasury and Civil Service Select Committee, 1987, *The Sixth Report: The 1987 Budget*, HMSO, London, p.60.
19. *OECD Economic Outlook*, December 1988, p.111; *The Financial Times*, 24 September 1988, p.48; *The Financial Times*, 26 September 1988, p.1.
20. Ungerer H. et al, 1989, *The EMS Developments and Perspectives*, IMF, Washington DC, p.73; *The Financial Times*, 8 January 1988, p.2; *The Financial Times*, 27 June 1988, p.16.
21. The Treasury and Civil Service Select Committee, 1989, *The fourth report: the Delors report*, HMSO, London, p.vi; *The Financial Times*, 27 June 1988, p.1; *The Financial Times*, 28 June 1988, p.44; *The Financial Times*, 25 June 1988, p.2; Conclusions drawn from a non-attributable interview with a former Treasury official in 1992; Non-attributable interviews with former Bank of England and Foreign Office officials in 1992.
22. *The Financial Times*, 8 June 1988, p.1; *The Financial Times*, 11 February 1989, p.4; *The Financial Times*, 25 February 1989, p.19.
23. The House of Lords Select Committee on the European Communities, 1990, *Economic and monetary and political union*, HMSO, London, p.252; Non-attributable interview with a banker in 1992.
24. *The Financial Times*, 27 June 1989, p.1.
25. *The Financial Times*, 30 October 1989, pp.1 and 6.
26. *The Financial Times*, 9 December 1989, p.1; *The Guardian*, 1 June 1992, p.21.
27. *The Economist*, 25 April 1990, p.57; *The Financial Times*, 23 April 1990, p.6
28. *The Financial Times*, 6 October 1990, p.61.
29. Non-attributable interview with a former Bank of England official.
30. *The Financial Times*, 6 October 1990, p.6; *The Financial Times*, 8 October 1990, p.1.

References

Brittan S. (1989), 'The Thatcher government's economic policy', in Kavanagh D. and Seldon A. (eds), *The Thatcher Effect*, Oxford University Press, Oxford.

George, S. (1990), *An Awkward Partner: Britain in the EC*, Oxford, Oxford University Press.

Goodhart, C. (1991), 'The conduct of monetary policy', in Wood G. et al., *The State of the Economy*, London, The Institute of Economic Affairs.

Keegan, W. (1989), *Mr Lawson's Economic Gamble*, London, Hodder & Stoughton.

Lawson, N. (1992), *The View from Number 11; Memoirs of a Tory radical*, London Bantam Press.

McKie, D. (ed.), (1992), *The election: a voters guide*, London, Fourth Estate.

Moran, M. (1991), *The Politics of the Financial Services Revolution; the USA, UK and Japan*, London, MacMillan.

Smith, D. (1987), *The Rise and Fall of Monetarism*, Harmondsworth, Penguin.

Smith D. (1992), *From Boom to Bust: Trial and Error in British Economic Policy*, Harmondsworth, Penguin.

20

Britain and European science policy

Ros S. Herman

Modern science, for better or worse, is very largely a European gift to human civilisation. Britons have contributed many of the increments in our understanding of the natural world that have transformed human existence and society. However, of the major scientific nations of Europe, Britain in particular is now significantly failing to reap commensurate economic rewards. Europe as a whole is outshone as an exploiter of technology by the US and South East Asia. As a result, states and companies alike are now having to keep close control over the level of resources they can afford to invest in scientific research and development for future innovation. At the same time, exploiting technological advances to probe ever more deeply into the mysteries of nature is an increasingly expensive business. To stay at the forefront of knowledge, and compete in the race to be first with significant results, researchers must have access to the latest and most sophisticated equipment. These factors explain the accelerating trend towards collaboration in research and development (R&D) across groups of states and companies that have developed since the end of the Second World War. This chapter will document Britain's increasing involvement in and dependence on such collaborations.

The earliest post-war collaborations emerged out of the scientific community's already well-entrenched habit of working closely with colleagues of similar interests, whatever their nationality. An example was the twelve countries which pooled their efforts to found the European Organisation for Nuclear Physics (CERN) in 1954. The warm political acceptance of CERN's high aspirations and costs owed much to the extremely high status enjoyed by science and scientists because of their contribution to waging, winning and ending the Second World War, and also to the ideal of continuing international collaboration but this time with peaceful objectives. The original stimulus to collaboration, was, however, the huge cost of the project to build what was at that time 'the single biggest machine in the world' (Goldsmith and Shaw, 1977, p. ix), which no one nation could hope to tackle alone. As science has advanced, the need to share costs has pervaded many disciplines, including astronomy, materials science and molecular biology, and CERN has formed a model for the dozen or so major international facilities for basic science that have been established in Europe over the past three decades (Herman, 1986, pp. 139–42).

While the applicability of results plays only a small part in defining the objectives of such projects in basic science, another group of technical collaborations have had as their major aim to develop sophisticated world-class equipment within the defence, aerospace and later space industries. Since these began in the 1960s, it has become increasingly clear that companies confined to expertise and markets within a single national boundary cannot afford to make state-of-the-art products. A notable example is in civil aircraft: 'the Airbus Industrie family of aircraft, for which Britain builds the wings, have latterly come to represent a serious challenge to American dominance' (Williams, 1991, p.8). Britain's biggest current governmental commitment, to take another example, is to the European Fighter Aircraft, whose future is now uncertain due to German reluctance to proceed as planned.

Between the basic research and large-scale governmental collaborations lies the increasingly economically important area of supplying consumer demand for domestic and business machines from computers to fridges. As the 1970s progressed, products made by American and latterly Japanese companies, rather than European, supplied the demand. The EEC, as it then was, at last seized the initiative at the end of the 1970s, seeing the promise of the information technologies as one that Europe could not allow to dissipate through wasteful duplication and internal competition. The then Commissioner for Industry, Vicomte Etienne Davignon, saw the need to promote collaboration in such industries, attempting to adapt to European conditions the very effective centralisation of planning of industrial development undertaken with great determination and to spectacular effect by Japan. Working within the framework of the Community, Davignon convinced the heads of Europe's largest information technology companies to sit down together and define a workplan for joint research and development. The carrot was that the Commission would provide half funding of approved collaborative projects. Davignon's initiative, which led to the European Strategic Programme for R&D in Information Technology (ESPRIT), has been hailed as a great success, not only promoting sharing of pre-competitive knowledge, but also helping to prepare the ground for the mergers and rationalisations that have characterised the late 1980s (Sharp, M., 1991, pp.72–74, PREST 1991, Appendix 1, p.3).

The EC has followed up the success of ESPRIT by embarking on similar programmes relevant to other industries and technologies, notably biotechnology, which are collectively known as the 'Framework' programme. The Second Framework programme has just finished: it cost 5.4b ECU over the four years between 1987 and 1991. The Third Framework programme was adopted in April 1990, to run from 1990 to 1994 (to some extent overlapping with the Second): 5.7b ECU will be available over the period. At this level it amounts to 3.8 per cent of the Community's budget (CEC, 1990, pp.9–14).

A key point about programmes within the Framework is that they are driven by the need to promote economic competitiveness within the Community, and they work by providing funds primarily to companies but also, where relevant, to academic departments. The research involved is not therefore basic in the sense that it is connected with advancement of knowledge for its own sake. However, the borderlines in many areas are blurred and industrial scientists often wish to work with academics who have pursued particular ideas further than companies could have justified to do. Thus the EC's involvement has had the effect of blurring the borderline between basic and applied research, a trend that has also grown at the national level throughout Europe.

Britain's involvement with the EC Framework programme is cautiously enthusiastic: of contracts won during 1991, British companies and academic departments won 19 per cent of funds, slightly below her level of contribution of 20 per cent. Such funding can make a significant impact on individual institutions: at Imperial College, for example, EC funds from the Framework programme now constitute 10 per cent of all the College's external research income: the figure has grown steadily from 2 per cent in 1984.[1]

A recent report endorsed by Britain's minister for science, William Waldegrave, expresses general satisfaction with the Framework programme, though it recommends that it should grow more slowly than proposed by the Commission, and wants to see better evaluation and review procedures (Cabinet Office, 1992 pp.1–5). The document also opposes the trend to widen the scope of its work outside pre-competitive research.

What impact have the EC's Framework programmes had on the UK? Researchers at the at the Policy Research in Engineering, Science and Technology Group (PREST) at Manchester University, working with others at the Science Policy Research Group at Sussex University, recently conducted a survey of participants on behalf of the EC. They found that such policies had re-oriented the research community to the point where it regards itself as a part of 'an emergent European scientific community' (Georghiu 1993, p.vii). Most companies are pleased with the outcome of sponsored projects and keen to compete for further funds. They do not, however, regard the resulting projects as critical in the short term. ICI, for example, reported that projects are undertaken only 'if they are regarded as a strategic fit' (Georghiu 1993, p.47). Access to EC funds as the chief motivation for taking part, while gaining access to complementary expertise/results and developing longer European links also rate highly (Georghiu 1993, p.52). Nevertheless the report notes that 'availability of investment was a significant barrier to exploitation' (Georghiu 1993, p.v), emphasising the impression that projects were marginal rather than central, long-term and speculative rather than immediate and product-oriented. This would be in line with the EC's policy of sponsoring 'pre-competitive' research, but if pre-competitive comes to mean never-competitive, the value of the Framework programme as a whole would come into question.

The report's authors reported that academics were overall even more enthusiastic about the Framework programmes than their industrial counterparts. The report's conclusions made clear that participants were well aware that the EC was not engaged on research for its own sake, and that its wider agenda was reflected in the selection and shaping of programmes. It found, for example, that participants and others were concerned about the adequacy of peer review – but they were willing to acknowledge that 'taking into account other goals connected with relevance or cohesion will normally produced a different rank ordering of projects than one based purely on scientific quality'. Nevertheless, 'the reported results, the quality of the institutions taking part, and the high level of competition for funding all suggest that quality is at least adequate and sometimes very good'. But it pointed out that 'the benefits of EC R&D for academic institutions will not be durable as few research groups are institutionalised, most staff employed on projects are junior, and equipment funding procedures have inhibited benefits to the capital infrastructure for science' (Georghiu 1993, p.vi).

However, it is not at all clear how the research activity undertaken as part of the EC Framework programmes fits in to any British government strategy for R&D. The basic point is that current government policy lays down that the state should not support industrial R&D at all. The rationale for such a view has recently been argued on the basis that the public funding of R&D mops up economic surpluses rather than generating them (Kealey 1992, p.3). Whatever the rationale, the government has drastically cut the funds available to industry from the state for R&D. The withdrawal of such funds may well have encouraged companies to turn to the EC as a source of funding (PREST, 1988, Appendix 1, p.2). To put matters in perspective, though, it should be pointed out that EC funding amounts to only two per cent of national funding for R&D from public and private sources.

Nevertheless, the question of the relevance of the EC approach need to be re-examined in the light of recent developments such as the takeover of Britain's main computer manufacturer, ICL, by Fujitsu, and the recent announcement by Siemens of its intention to collaborate with IBM and Toshiba on a 256Mb memory (New Scientist, 1992, p.9). It is appropriate to invest European tax-payers' money in development work that may ultimately benefit non-European producers?

The government has also drastically cut its support for laboratories that operate under the auspices of ministries, many of which maintained expertise and research facilities that industry could draw on for help with R&D. The laboratories are effectively being privatised – they can offer their services to industry on a strictly commercial basis (Cabinet Office, 1991, p.3). In some ways the streamlining effected has forced some useful reconsideration of needs and priorities, but the sheer scale of the reductions in manpower lead to the suspicion that irreplaceable expertise and skills are being lost.

The government has been slightly more supportive of academic science, which is held to underlie technological development through both research and the provision of trained manpower. Funding for academic research has held up better than overall funding for universities, however, and therefore academic depart-ments have been keen to encourage industry to fund both teaching and research in relevant areas. Direct funding from industry is playing an increasingly important part in the funding of higher education, alongside other external sources such as charities and indeed the EC (Webster and Etzkowitz, 1991, p.6, Cabinet Office, 1991, pp.38–39). One important effect has been to squeeze the amount of money and effort available for basic research. Since the early 1980s the British scientific community has acknowledged its inability to do research of high quality across all scientific disciplines, let alone provide world class equipment. The implication is an increased reliance on international collaboration (ABRC, 1987, pp.23–24, Phillips, 1989, p.5). In this area too, Britain has led attempts to cut costs, notably in the case of CERN. However sometimes her efforts and actions have led to the accusation of being a 'bad partner' (Save British Science, 1989, p.6).

The British academic community in general has been slow to 'think European' except when actually forced to do so. For example, a recent decision to close a national laboratory for nuclear physics, the Nuclear Structure Facility at Daresbury, was considered in purely national terms rather than in the context of the pattern of European provision. Again, involvement with the EC by academic departments has grown slowly.

One potential problem is the government's attribution policy. Government can effectively claw back money won from EC funds by institutions which it supports by cutting back on core or other funding. The effect is to reduce or even eliminate the value of the money obtained from the EC. Such a policy brings into question the principle that EC support is meant to be genuinely additional in that it is allocated to enhance EC objectives rather than national ones (Williams, et al., 1991, p.9). Up to now Britain has been alone among the member states in taking this view, but in the current financial climate for public spending, the trend is for other countries, such as Germany and The Netherlands, to take a similar view. Another is the different criteria used in the selection of projects to fund: UK organisations have taken issue with the scientific merit of some of the projects funded, which they say fall below the standard that would be funded in the UK (House of Lords, 1990, p.94–95). On the other hand, there are now academics who would rather work with Brussels than with national funding agencies.

Thirty years ago it would have been acceptable to address an issue such as 'status as a scientific nation' impressionistically. For Britain the answer would have been unequivocal: although hardly any longer a major industrial or imperial power, it still enjoyed a dominant position in the world of international science. A by-product of subsequent attempts to document, explain and develop the relationship between science and national wealth has been the establishment of objective measures of outputs from and inputs to the R&D system. Some of these can be used to compare Britain's 'status as a scientific nation' to that of her European counterparts over the last decade.

The natural tendency of the policy analyst is to reach for governmental statistics, which are dominated almost completely by finance. However, Britain's status as a scientific nation depends largely on the results her scientists produce. Britain's scientific output in terms of the numbers of papers produced and published in international journals is increasing – it grew by 35 per cent between 1981 and 1991. However, as other countries, both inside and outside Europe, have stepped up their contributions, her share of world scientific output has declined, from 9.1 per cent in 1981 to 8.6 per cent in 1991 (ISI, 1992, pp. 1–2). Only the US publishes a higher proportion of the world's papers, with Germany coming very close indeed, perhaps just outstripping Britain's output by now. Britain's output constitutes 32.1 per cent of papers from EC countries (Martin, 1992, p.18). (It should be noted though, here and in the subsequent discussion, that there is a bias towards English language journals in the database used to produce these data). A more subtle indicator of the quality of a paper in terms of the impact it makes on future science is the number of citations it receives from subsequent papers. In terms of citations British papers are still better than the world average (1.03 on a relative scale in 1988), but have slightly fallen behind Germany's (1.05) and ahead of France (0.95) (Martin, 1992, p.9). The average impact of papers from countries less well developed scientifically, such as Portugal, Greece, Ireland is well below the world average. The overall figure for Britain conceals significant differences in citation rates between disciplines. Britain's papers in engineering and applied science are improving in number and quality, but her earlier excellent record for clinical medicine papers is now in decline. The lines crossed at 1.2 times the average citation rate per paper in the period 1987–91 (ISI, 1992, p.1). In making sense of these and subsequent figures, it is important to remember that modern academic science is an enterprise that the state and industry have deliberately developed and expanded way beyond the scope of a very few excellent practitioners. When assessing a nation's science, therefore, there is always a tension between the outstanding achievements of a very select group, and the mass outpourings of the entire community. Britain has a tradition of scientific excellence, for example as attested by her record in winning Nobel prizes. There is evidence that here once again Britain has slipped. Over the last 12 years Britain's 'score' has fallen behind the US, Germany, Switzerland, Sweden and Denmark in terms of prizes per head of population (Martin, 1992, p.9).

One important reason why the scale of national R&D systems have grown in modern times is the need to increase the supply of trained manpower. In spite of systematic efforts in the 1950s and 1960s, Britain (4.6 qualified researchers per 1000 labour force in 1987) now compares badly in numerical terms with Germany (5.6), Sweden (5.1) and most notably Japan (8.4) (OECD, 1992, p. 21). Greece (1.4), Portugal (1.1), Spain (2.1) and Italy (3.1) are clearly well behind. The situation is exacerbated by the now well-documented brain drain of highly qualified people to the US and other places where better equipment and support, not to mention better salaries, are on offer (Wilson, 1991). The trend applies both to industry and the academic world (Save British Science, 1989, p.5).

Producing trained people who can use their skills outside the academic world is one mechanism by which the academic scientist interacts with the outside world, and indeed justifies his or her support by the state. Such people – or indeed academics themselves – often wish to turn new scientific ideas into commercial products. A major indicator of the number of possible product ideas generated is the record of patents registered. Britain's share of patents registered in the US has been in very serious decline, especially compared with Germany's (Patel and Pavitt, 1988, p.39).

Once we come away from the purely academic system, of course, many other factors come into play. We have to consider the way that industry and the state formulate and address their needs for R&D and innovation. In fact as I hinted above, even the size and shape of the academic system is partly a response to pressures of this nature. It is beyond the scope of this chapter to address these issues in detail, but there is much evidence that Britain's policy responses to the challenges of making state-of-the-art and competitively priced products as well as maintaining the necessary national infrastructure to support a modern economy have fallen behind the efforts of her competitors. For example, Rothwell and Zegveld (1981, p.79) have reported that: 'In [West Germany] the federal government is continually adding to an existing and comprehensive set of innovation measures . . . To a great extent, government innovation policy has focused on the development and successful use of the infrastructure essential for providing the conditions under which innovation can flourish, particularly in small firms'.

In a more recent comparative study Irvine and Martin (1984, p.64) applaud the German system and compare it with that of the US in its effectiveness in identifying directions for the medium-term. However, in their view the Japanese system of macro-level strategic research forecasting for the long-term, centrally co-ordinated by government, is a model that Britain would do well to emulate (pp.151–53).

Another important lesson that can be learnt from the Japanese is that a country does not need to do R&D to benefit from it. By actively looking out for exploitable results a country can fairly easily take advantage of other's ideas. Countries like Britain that are good at generating ideas but not exploiting them may be investing their scarce national resources in efforts that will result in prosperity for others. A notable case in point is the development of monoclonal antibodies, a British invention patented and mainly exploited overseas. A more recent development is inward investment in research: foreign companies providing long-term funding for British laboratories with a view to acquiring control of commercial applications (Webster and Etzkowitz, 1991, p.8).

To arrive at an overall picture of the productivity of British science, though, it is important to assess performance against the objectives the state sets for science. One of these must be to underpin Britain's performance as a manufacturer, which has been has been abysmal over the last decade. For example, our export/import ratio in the manufacturing sector was 0.83 in 1987, compared with 1.48 for Germany and 2.73 for Japan. Italy managed 1.15, and France was still well ahead of the UK at 0.95 (OECD, 1992, p.62). Such contrasts feed through of course into indicators of national prosperity such as GDP per capita: 14.5 k$ for Britain in 1989, compared to 20.7 k$ in Germany, 17.8 k$ in France and 21.7k$ in Sweden. And it is of course on the basis of economic fortunes that the inputs to R&D, from government on the one hand and industry on the other, have to be assessed alongside other demands on resources. As Kealey (1991, p.1) has shown, it is too naive to argue that economic success is guaranteed by investment in R&D: the question of how much science we can afford must be asked. On the other hand, it is wrong to blame science and scientists for industry's failures. We must also remember that economic success is not the only objective of R&D. Public health and safety are important outputs too, as are government plans and policies in areas such as transport and the environment. So is the cultural heritage of science and awareness of it within the community. We also have to be aware of the way that science and scientists are placed within our cultural maps. Pride in our scientific achievements cannot be an excuse for failing to evaluate the investment we make in it in the context of other aspirations in education, training and enterprise. We should, for example, carefully consider the possibility that in order to get better returns on our investments in science we actually need to make greater investments not in research but in the training of other groups such managers and production workers. Another useful objective might be to increase the general level of education in scientific and technical issues so that all citizens would be more active participants as producers and consumers of technically sophisticated products and services. Scientists might have to accept as a concomitant of such changes a reduction in their status as a small élite group, the workings of which are immune from public scrutiny and criticism.

The most often-quoted indicator of a nation's seriousness about R&D is the proportion of Gross Domestic Product (GDP) that goes into Gross Domestic Expenditure on R&D (GERD). On this measure Britain (2.3 per cent in 1989) has lagged behind West Germany (2.9 per cent), Sweden (2.8 per cent), Japan (3.0 per cent) and the US (2.82 per cent) and is on a par with France (2.3 per cent).

Countries such as Italy (1.29 per cent) and Spain (0.72 per cent), though, spend less, and Greece trails miserably (0.45 per cent) (OECD, 1992, p.18). It is also important to look inside this figure. For example, as mentioned previously, the current British government view is that industry should take the lead in funding the research it deems necessary without government interference. However, British industry spends a lot less on R&D relative to GDP, than in Germany, Sweden, Japan and the US, where industry's contribution dominates the R&D scene. In Britain, industry pays for about half of GERD. The investment is concentrated in only a few sectors, most notably pharmaceuticals. Its investment has increased slightly in the last year, but on average, the British are more inclined than their German counterparts to distribute profit as dividends to shareholders than to re-invest it in R&D (Dobie, 1992). Industry actually performs about two-thirds of GERD. In other words, the government does pay industry to do research, even though it does not believe in such intervention. The disparity arises because of two sectors where government, in spite of its general philosophy, has found it hard to shed its responsibilities: the defence sector, and nuclear power. Indeed, the proportion of GERD spent in the defence sector is higher in Britain than for any other West European country. This has led to world-class expertise, but with questionable applicability to large civil markets. The direct involvement of government through its own network of laboratories has rapidly decreased over the last five years. Many have been closed, and those that are left are effectively being privatised, both in the defence and civil sectors. The decline can be charted both in terms of investment and numbers of personnel (Cabinet Office, 1991, pp.16, 48–9, OECD 1992, pp.25, 45). The academic sector, known in Britain as the Science Base, consists of the research effort in institutions of higher education plus the laboratories and experimental facilities maintained by the research councils. The vast majority of support comes from government, though significant funds come from other sources such as charitable foundations, industry, and indeed the EC. Government policy regarding higher education has inevitably affected the institutions involved, with severe financial cuts in the early 1980s, followed by strict control on funds combined with growing pressure to increase student numbers. The result has been to squeeze both the number of posts available for young academics and also the funds available for equipment and other forms of support such as technical staff. Meanwhile 'soft' money allocated by the research councils on the basis of peer review has actually held up quite well in real terms, but has not been able to compensate for deficiencies in overall support, especially in the context of ever-expanding demand for funds to purchase equipment whose sophistication and cost increases far more quickly than inflation. Another recent innovation has been the centralised comparative assessment of quality and quantity of the research in every single university department, with an element of funding being determined by the outcome. Individual institutions too are keeping far stricter control on finances. Such activities are resented not so much for their principles as for the amount of bureaucracy they generate for people who are paid to teach and develop new ideas rather than pore endlessly over departmental balance sheets. The result of all these changes has been increasing frustration and lack of morale within the system, which has frequently been voiced in public, as academics are far freer than their civil service counterparts to make such comments.[2,3] In spite of the relative health of the academic sector compared with government laboratories, Britain's investment in academic and related reseach is far less than that of Germany, whether considered on a GDP or per capita basis, as Irvine, Martin and Isard (1990) have shown. An interesting set of figures shows that the amount of money spent per researcher is far lower in Britain (£52.5k in 1987) than either in France (£59.2k) or Germany (£92.7k), thus indicating that the resources that are available are being spread too thinly (Atkinson et al., 1990, p. 16).

During the Thatcher era Britain's involvement with European collaborations in science followed the tone of engagement with the EC: grudging acknowledgement of the need to be there, but continuous review of the costs and purposes involved. The effects of such investigations have been useful, to other countries as well as ourselves. However such posturing does lay Britain open to accusations of 'bad partnership'. Politicians can afford to hunch their shoulders and enjoy the charismatic appeal of such a position, but for members of the scientific community, who need to collaborate on friendly and equal terms with foreign colleagues on a daily basis, the prospect that Britain may be on the point of withdrawing support can be harrowing and depressing. In addition to feeling vulnerable and exposed, British scientists also feel that their government's view results from the lack of any long-term strategy for science and technology. This seems almost like a personal insult, a philistinism with respect to scientists' chosen professionalism and loyalties. That Britain should be making a clearer commitment internationally is for example a central plank of the agenda of Save British Science, an organisation formed to lobby for increased government support for science.

For organisations like CERN, the concerns are mainly academic, but much broader issues are at stake for example, with Britain's participation in organisations with primarily technical objectives such as the European Space Agency (ESA). British policy analysts wrote in 1987 that 'Britain cannot expect to retain an effective capability in space at the current level of engagement. It is of course possible to opt out and rely on developed technology from elsewhere. But it must be recognised that this is not simply a choice about just another area of R&D. Space has far-reaching implications for British economic modernisation as well as for Britain's foreign and security policies' (Eberle and Wallace, 1987, p. 64). With the ESA, as to some extent with the EC, the government's contribution to space technology is dominated by collaboration – the subscription to the ESA (which amounts to 70 per cent of the total spent in 1986–87). But the contribution amounts to only 13.1 per cent of the total ESA budget, hardly enough to determine and shape policy (RIIA, 1988, p. 204). France's contribution is more than twice as great at 27.7 per cent, even greater than West Germany at 24.4 per cent. France has taken a dominant role in leadership as well as finance of scientific collaboration in general, with Francois Mitterand and Jacques Delors pushing forward ventures such as the ESA and the Framework programmes. Their strong political rhetoric for the importance of science and technology, as well as in the field of international collaboration in general has won France the opportunity to guide policy in such a way as to maximise returns from investments in such collaborations. For example, French companies have contracts to do more than half the work on the Ariane 4 satellite launcher programme. German involvement with international collaborations is not quite so ideological, but is solid and consistent. While in a better position to support such projects financially, Germany needs them far less than either France or Britain. This is indicated especially by Germany's lower involvement with the EC's Framework programmes: in 1991 German organisations numbered only 14 per cent of the partners involved in DGXII projects, in general research areas including biotechnology, materials and basic science, compared with a financial contribution of something over 18 per cent. Britain contributed 19 per cent of participants compared with 20 per cent of contributions, while France provided 20 per cent of partners for 19 per cent of contributions. The big three participated more or less equally in the DGXIII projects in information technology and telecommunications. For smaller countries, notably The Netherlands, keeping an eye on what is happening elsewhere is a well-established part of science policy, and opportunities for collaboration are welcomed. In fact in 1989 The Netherlands seriously considered inviting other countries to buy shares in national facilities it was planning to build. For the southern countries of Europe, with their much smaller R&D efforts, collaboration is a key to expanding their horizons, though it would be an unjustified insult to say that the gain was all one-way.

Countries outside the EC such as Sweden, Switzerland and Austria are members of collaborations such as CERN, ESA, and the European Molecular Biology Laboratory. They can and do also buy their way into EC programmes (CEC, 1990, pp.20–21). As a final note it is important not to become so Eurocentric as to forget that Britain, for internal and other reasons, has interests in collaborating in groupings involving countries other than European ones. Astronomy for example is a subject where colonial links, particularly with countries with clear skies and reliable climates are still apparent. Such enterprises include the Anglo-Australian telescope and telescopes at Mauna Kea, Hawaii. A new initiative to build telescopes with mirrors 8 metres across (the world's biggest) is now under discussion as a joint venture between Britain, the US and Canada.

In sectors with state involvement such as aerospace and academic research, Britain's participation in international collaboration has grown steadily since the Second World War. Before the 1980s, international collaboration between companies making consumer products was almost unknown. The advent of the EC's Framework programmes has filled the gap to some extent, particularly in the area of information technology.

The EC identified the need for industries in its member states to collaborate to avoid wasteful duplication and develop and open up markets for its products. Such development, its Commissioners have forcibly argued, requires international collaboration in inventing and disseminating new technologies through R&D. During the 1980s, the Framework programme has brought about such collaboration through partial subsidy for industry and other research organisations to work on selected 'pre-competitive' projects. More recently the EC has sought to address areas such as near-market developments and manpower resources. Such moves have inspired a certain amount of opposition, firstly about how to tackle commercially sensitive areas, and secondly, particularly in Britain, in terms of the overall rationales for outside interference with industry.

At the same time, basic scientists have continued to work within an international framework, and the growing expense of state of the art equipment has led to joint planning and sharing of large facilities. Except when forced in this way, British scientists have been slow to see Europe as an entity of special significance within the international scientific community. But the provision of funds in certain areas of basic science, by the EC and to some extent the European Science Foundation has changed attitudes. A question that will soon have to be addressed is whether national policies of selectivity and concentration should be co-ordinated across Europe, with countries hosting centres in disciplines where they have demonstrated particular strength. In existing facilities not under EC auspices, Britain pays a smaller proportion than either France or Germany. As a participant in EC programmes, however, Britain is on a par with France and Germany, both in terms of contribution and execution of work. Nevertheless, on almost any measure, the strength of scientific research and the provision of trained manpower is far greater in Germany than Britain. In terms of inputs, France is on a par with Britain, while her outputs lag behind to some extent.

The scientific community in Britain is going through a period of very low morale. The community needs to take the initiative in sorting out its internal problems, for example by proposing and implementing a career structure for academic science. But it also needs government, its major sponsor, to take the lead in setting out, in general terms, the philosophical framework within which it should work. In doing this the government should not aim to direct activities at a detailed level, but should show a clear understanding of the contribution that scientists make, both as researchers, innovators and teachers within the wider social and economic framework, and offer leadership in applauding, rewarding and enhancing that contribution in the context of national objectives. The government should also consider how debates over such issues can be brought out into a wider arena, involving more interest groups and the general public. These topics should be near the top of the agenda of the Cabinet minister for science, William Waldegrave, as he formulates promised government legislation on the framework for British science. Such a game plan should lay out explicitly the government's views on the relationship between industry, higher education and the government sector. It should also, of course, put its cards on the table with regard to the role of European collaborations and participation, and how such activities relate to government involvement with pre-competitive and near market research. Clearly the government should eschew a naive, unquestioning and ever-expanding support for science. However, it should not use the naivety of some of the scientist's demands as an excuse for dodging some difficult issues. German economic success, for example, is based on a very effective system where industry and government co-ordinate and reinforce each others' efforts through close contacts in funding, planning and execution at every level. Germany's networks of laboratories play a crucial part, for example, in disseminating new ideas and approaches. It is important not to rule out such mechanisms on ideological or narrow financial grounds. The Japanese model is instructive too. It shows that even without making an enormous investment in resources, Government can exercise a very strong influence through providing the context for information-gathering, discussion and debate about central issues such as quality of products and consumer requirements.

Another important issue, for Britain and Europe alike, is the future relevance of Europe as a unit. Increasingly, collaborations that arise spontaneously may wish, for whatever reason, to break away from the formulas currently on offer within Europe. Freedom and flexibility in this regard is to be encouraged, but there will always be a tension between letting the high-flyers rush ahead while the underdeveloped partners – such as the southern and now eastern groups of countries – are left behind. As Europeans in this sense, Britain and the British still have quite a long way to go, being preoccupied with their own problems.

Britain is right to question Euro-rhetoric, in science and other areas. But the questionings are thin fare intellectually, and reek of lack of serious engagement with the issues and challenges involved. Britain should concentrate in the first instance on harnessing in a constructive synthesis the views, knowledge and experience of the many partners and players in the scientific enterprise. Progress in this direction could lay the foundation for Britain to make a serious contribution to the future of science in Europe as well as improving the national effort in science.

Notes

1. Ron Irwin, interview with the author, 20 August 1992. Ron Irwin is the 'Europe Officer' at Imperial College, University of London.
2. Michael Berry said in a talk given at the Wolfson Debate at Wolfson College, Cambridge, on 16 June 1992 that 'there is, unfortunately a trend in our universities . . . towards greater bureacracy . . . I don't want to exaggerate, but for many of my colleagues bureaucracy is growing into a pervasive harassment. This could be fatal. To do successful basic research requires intense concentration, undistracted, over long periods'. Professor Michael Berry, FRS, is at the Department of Physics of Bristol University.
3. Roger Deakins, said at the Wolfson Debate at Wolfson College, 16 June 1992 that 'the intellectual edge of young scientists is being chilled by bureaucracy . . . it has gone too far'. Roger Deakins is senior administrator at the Cavendish Laboratory, Cambridge University.

References

Advisory Board for the Research Councils (ABRC), (1987) 'A Strategy for the Science Base', London, HMSO.

Atkinson, H., P. Rogers and R. Bond (1990), *Research in the United Kingdom, France and West Germany: a comparison*, Vol.1, Swindon, Science and Engineering Research Council.

Cabinet Office (1991), *Annual Report on Government R&D*, HMSO, London.

Cabinet Office (1992), *UK Paper on the 4th Framework Programme*, London.

Commission of the European Communities (CEC), (1990), Research Funding, 2nd edition, Brussels.

Dobie, C. (1992), 'British firms lag behind overseas rivals', *The Independent,*' 9 June 1992. p.18, London.

Eberle, J., and H. Wallace (1987), *British Space Policy and International Collaboration*, London, Royal Institute of International Affairs/Routledge & Kegan Paul.

Georguiu, L., J. A. Stein, M. Janes, J. Senker, M. Pifer, H. Cameron, M. Nedeva, J. Yates, M. Boden, (1993), *The Impact of European Community Policies for Research and Technological Development upon Science and Technology in the United Kingdom*, London, HMSO.

Goldsmith, M., and E. Shaw (1977), *Europe's Giant Accelerator*, London, Taylor & Francis.

Herman, R. (1986), *The European Scientific Community*, Harlow, Longman.

House of Lords (1990), *A Community Framework for R&D, 17th Report*, London.

Irvine, J., and B.R. Martin, (1984), *Foresight in Science: Picking the Winners*, London, Frances Pinter.

Irvine, J., Martin, B.R. and Isard, P.A. (1990), *Investing in the Future: An International Comparison of Government Funding of Academic and Related Research*, London, Edward Elgar.

Institute of Scientific Information (ISI) (1992), 'Critical condition: clinical research in UK fading fast', *Science Watch*, vol.3, no.6, pp.1–2.

Kealey, T. (1992), 'Government should not financially support R&D', British Association meeting at Southampton, 25 August.

Martin, B.R. (1992), 'What the bibliometric evidence reveals', British Association meeting at Southampton, 25 August.

New Scientist (1992), 'Chip makers of the world unite', 25 July, p.9.

Organisation for Economic Cooperation and Development (OECD) (1992), Science and Technology Indicators 1991 (Part 1), Paris.

Patel, P., and K. Pavitt (1988), 'Measuring Europe's Technological Performance: results and prospects', Paper no.36, Centre for European Policy Studies, Brussels, Belgium.

Phillips, D. (1989), 'Impact on Science Policy', talk to Science Technology and 1992 conference at Royal Society, 14 November 1989.

Policy Research in Engineering, Science and Technology (PREST) (1988), *Evaluation of UK Involvement in Industrial R&D Programmes of the European Community: exploratory study*, Manchester.

Rothwell, R., and W. Zegveld (1981), *Industrial Innovation and Public Policy*, London, Pinter Publishers.

Royal Institute of International Affairs (RIIA) (1988), *Europe's Future in Space: a joint policy report*, Routledge & Kegan Paul, London

Save British Science (1989), *Science Strategy for the 1990s: policy report*, January, London.

Science and Engineering Research Council (SERC) (1992), *Opportunities in Particle Physics: a report by the SERC Particle Committee*, Swindon.

Sharp, M. (1991), 'The Single Market and European Technology Policies', in Freeman, C.M., and Walker, W., (eds), *Technology and the Future of Europe: Global Competition and the Environment in the 1990s*, London, Pinter Publishers.

Webster, A., and H. Etzkowitz (1991), 'Academic-Industrial Relations: the second academic revolution?', SPSG Concept Paper no.12, Science Policy Support Group, London.

Williams, R. (1991), 'Overview of UK Economy, Society and Politics and the Role of Science and Technology', in Nicholson, R., Cunningham, C.M. and Gummett, P. (eds), *Science and Technology in the United Kingdom*, Harlow, Longman.

Wilson, T. (1991), 'Academic Pay: an international perspective', *AUT Bulletin*, February, pp.4–5

Index